de Gruyter Studies in Organization 28

Caiden: Administrative Reform Comes of Age

de Gruyter Studies in Organization

International Management, Organization and Policy Analysis

A new international and interdisciplinary book series from de Gruyter presenting comprehensive research on aspects of international management, organization studies and comparative public policy.
It will cover cross-cultural and cross-national studies of topics such as:

- management; organizations; public policy, and/or their inter-relation
- industry and regulatory policies
- business-government relations
- international organizations
- comparative institutional frameworks.

While each book in the series ideally will have a comparative empirical focus, specific national studies of a general theoretical, substantive or regional interest which relate to the development of cross-cultural and comparative theory will also be encouraged. The series is designed to stimulate and encourage the exchange of ideas across linguistic, national and cultural traditions of analysis, between academic researchers, practioners and policy makers, and between disciplinary specialisms.
The volumes will present theoretical work, empirical studies, translations and 'state-of-the art' surveys. The *international* aspects of the series will be uppermost: there will be a strong commitment to work which crosses and opens boundaries.

Gerald E. Caiden

Administrative Reform Comes of Age

Walter de Gruyter · Berlin · New York 1991

Gerald E. Caiden
Professor of Public Administration, School of Public Administration,
University of Southern California, Los Angeles, U.S.A.

⊗ Printed on acid-free paper which falls within the guidelines of the ANSI to ensure permanence and durability.

Library of Congress Cataloging-in-Publication Data

Caiden, Gerald E.
Administrative reform comes of age / Gerald E. Caiden.
p. cm. — (De Gruyter studies in organization ; 28)
Includes bibliographical references and index.
ISBN 0-89925-833-6 (U.S.) (alk. paper)
ISBN 0-89925-743-7 (U.S.) (pbk.)
1. Administrative agencies — Reorganization. 2. Executive departments — Reorganization. 3. Public administration. 4. Organizational change. I. Title. II. Series.
JF1525.073C35 1991
350.007'3—dc20 90-23490
CIP

Deutsche Bibliothek Cataloging-in-Publication Data

Caiden, Gerald E.:
Administrative reform comes of age / Gerald E. Caiden. — Berlin ; New York : de Gruyter, 1991
(De Gruyter studies in organization ; 28 : International management, organization and policy analysis)
ISBN 3-11-012645-1 Pb.
ISBN 3-11-012895-0 Gewebe
NE: GT

Typesetting: Knipp Textverarbeitungen, Wetter — Printing: Ratzlow-Druck, Berlin. — Binding: D. Mikolai, Berlin. — Cover Design: Johannes Rother, Berlin. — Printed in Germany.

This book is dedicated to the
memory of Keith, David, Charles,
Gordon, Dan, Tom, Moshe, S. K.,
and so many others who did not toil
in vain. Countless millions have
benefitted and continue to benefit
from their sacrifice.
They remain an inspiration.

Preface

In a new branch of a discipline, it is possible to point to its academic pioneers and their individual contributions. This is the case with administrative reform which was in the 1960s still staking out its claim on the fringes of public administration and organization theory. Twenty years later, administrative reform has come of age and is truly part of the discipline. Many pioneers are mentioned by name in this book which is dedicated to some of those who alas fell too early or were felled before their time, that is, before they could harvest the fruit of their toils. I was privileged to know them. Together they shared a vision of a better world brought about by improved public sector organization, administration and management. They knew first hand the realities of incompetence, waste, corruption, fraud, arrogant misuse of power and unprofessional conduct. They were aware of the skeptics who dismissed their moral stance, who accused them of being insufficiently objective, impartial, and scientific and who did not believe in the idea of administrative reform or that anything needed reforming. They were tempted many times to give up in despair and join the rest of the crowd pigging at the public trough and reaffirming that all was well, beneficial and progressive. Fortunately, they had the inner fortitude to resist and the conviction that ultimately right would be done.

And so it has proven to be. The malpractices of yesteryear, the norms of their day, are now seen for what they were, and in their place, other norms have been established, which no doubt will in time be superseded as progress continues to be made toward higher levels of achievement and accomplishment. This is the only reward they sought as they labored away in reform campaigns, pushing proposals, writing memoranda, lecturing, lobbying, organizing, propagandizing, corresponding, telephoning, and networking. When they were down, as often they were, they consoled one another and restored weary spirits. When they were up after scoring a small victory, they warned one another not to rejoice prematurely but to keep hacking away. They were still sufficiently few to know whose hand had done what and to learn from each other's experiences in promoting reform. Often, they pondered why, after the many defeats, insults and retributions they suffered they still persisted.

Perhaps, the answer can be found in Elie Wiesel's *Jewish Legends* where he tells this story.

> One day the evil spirit came to God and said, "Master of the Universe, what is the difference between this group of people who are pure, and these who are impure?" And God answered, "They, the pure ones, protested. The others did not protest." "So," said the

evil spirit, "had they protested, would You have listened to them?" And God said, "No." "Did they know that?" asked the evil spirit. And God said, "No, they didn't know it; therefore, they should have protested. Protest against Me, against Man, against everything wrong. Because protest in itself contains a spark of truth, a spark of holiness, a spark of God."

And Wiesel commented:

Therefore, little does it matter whether our protest is heard or not. Protest we must, because by the mere fact of protesting we show that we care, that we listen, that we feel.

Administrative reformers care, listen and feel.

Los Angeles
June, 1990

G.E.C.

Acknowledgements

This book would not have been possible without the assistance of Dr. Judith Truelson, School of Business, University of Southern California.

Permission to quote extensively from previously published work has been granted by the International Institute of Administrative Sciences, Brussels, for "The Vitality of Administrative Reform," *International Review of Administrative Sciences*, Vol 54, No. 3, September 1988, pp. 331-359 in Chapter 4, and by the Institute of Social Studies for "Implementation – The Achilles Heel of Administrative Reform," in A.F. Leemans (ed.), *The Management of Change in Government*, Martinus Nijhoff, The Hague, 1976, in Chapter 8.

Contents

1. Introduction

Administrative reform – the induced systemic improvement of public sector operational performance – came of age in the 1980s, twenty or so years after the winds of change had belatedly been recognized as demanding radical alterations in the way public business was being conducted. At that time, the world had seemingly settled down to an uninterrupted period of accelerating prosperity, decolonization and scientific and technological achievement. But inherited administrative systems were proving to be sluggish, inflexible and insensitive to changing human needs and novel circumstances. The East Bloc had embraced statism, bureaucratic centralism, central planning and scientific management; it was already troubled by elitism, administrative arrogance and ineffectiveness, and the excesses of the Cultural Revolution in China. The West had assimilated the welfare state, representative bureaucracy, public regulation and state enterprise; it was already worried about the runaway costs of the burgeoning public sector, administrative imperialism and inefficiency, and the excesses of the newly emerged counter culture. The Third World, taking charge at last of its own affairs of state, had dreams of rapid national development; it was saddled with law and order administrations which lacked the experience, resources and trained personnel to switch directions suddenly. All expected in time to solve their administrative difficulties not by overturning what they had but by overhauling and generally revising as they went along. They were all fairly confident that they would modernize in tandem with any new requirements. In this, they were to be proved wrong.

Delayed Recognition

With the revolution of rising expectations, the marvels of modern science, mass communications, the internationalization of human affairs and the globalization of economic transactions, the winds of change blew more fiercely. Wars and threats of war, invasions and threats of invasion, conquests and the threats of conquest contributed to world wide destabilization and an arms race that absorbed resources that might otherwise have been used for administrative modernization. Then the global economy went into an unanticipated tail spin accompanied by inflation, large scale public borrowing and shrinking markets which meant that promised resources were unavailable when expected. Alterations in administrative systems had not gotten to the essence but had merely tampered with formalities. They had not gone far enough or deep enough. In some countries, they had actually made things worse not better. Insufficient attention had been paid to administrative reform. Governments had been lulled into a false sense of security, believing that systems which had performed well in the past would continue to perform well and that alterations being made by managerial experts would enable them to perform better in the future.

By the time it was realized that defective administrative systems were a serious obstacle to progress, that what was wrong with them was fundamental, and that higher priority should be given to putting them right, the prevailing gales were fast blowing into hurricanes. Radical measures earlier recommended when they would have counted were belatedly accepted as were fads of the time (e.g. Planning Programming Budgeting Systems (PPBS), Management by Objectives (MBO), Organization Development (OD)) and untested nostrums. Given the wide array of suggested medicines, some were bound to work. Administrative systems seemed to revive but untouched were serious diseases (bureaupathologies) whose cure was actually being delayed by such temporizing. In the East Bloc, the declining performance of administrative systems reached crisis proportions. In the end, people protested and public leaders came to realize that nothing short of immediate, speedy transformation would suffice. The only trouble was that few knew what should replace them. Certain parts of the Third World had been in similar crisis for years but they still balked at taking medicines presented by outsiders such as the International Monetary Fund. The rest had just about managed to cope, relying more on native remedies to curtail the worst excesses of defective administrative systems resistent to change.

In comparison the West seemed fortunate. Its administrative systems had been built on more solid foundations and its wealth had enabled it to prop up poorly performing systems. Managerial improvements and inventive gimmicks had diverted attention from institutional defects – the lack of budgeting incentives to save public money, the lack of incentives to attract and retain talent, administrative inertia, tunnel vision, the persistence of public misconduct, a certain disregard for truth and justice, and a seeming lack of care and concern – that were growing more irksome. As elsewhere, administrative systems in the West were judged not so much by what they did well but what they did badly, and their clients tended to be much more openly critical of their performance. As public criticism mounted, administrative reform was all the more compelling.

Given the relentless population pressures and a continuing degeneration of the environment, there would be no respite from a permanent condition of turbulence and uncertainty, of future shock and other terms used to convey the message that tomorrow's world would be different from today's. Certain trends could be taken for granted. Public affairs would become more complex and complicated. Governments would learn only pragmatically when to intervene or not. The administrative state might shed some activities but would assume others, some still unimagined. Yet there would be persistent demands for better performance from public institutions. Better performance would require higher quality administrative systems, achieved in part through technological advances, managerial improvements, and administrative innovations, and in part through the correction of public wrongdoing and the continual enhancement of administrative capabilities, i.e. a systematic ongoing administrative reform program. Too much in the contemporary world depended on the performance of public organization, administration and management for administrative reform not to be given a higher priority on political agendas.

Shaken Confidence

Recent history has been somewhat unkind to administrative reformers for not only were they politically neglected by public leaders, they were also given short shrift by the practitioners too. Public leaders were careful to give much lip service to administrative reform (after all, who could be against it?) but they were careful to select only those reforms which did not threaten their power, standing and popularity and therefore served to reinforce existing institutions and arrangements and preclude viable alternatives. The practitioners were even more defensive and self-protective because reforms constituted so they believed an indictment of their own professionalism. If things were not as good as they ought to be, clearly the practitioners were at fault. They did not take kindly to such implied criticism, least of all sheltered public service careerists protective of their vested interests in the status quo. Actually, their caution turned out to be better founded than pure self-interest. The models on which the reformers based their reforms often as not turned out to be seriously defective.

Administrative theorists had warned the reformers that they might be on the wrong track. But the reformers for the most part could not understand the theorists, so they claimed because the theorists wrote too obscurely and rarely mixed with people outside the halls of academe. Left to their own devices, the reformers rarely conducted adequate research on their models or questioned the assumptions on which they worked. As it happened, some key models although quite promising at the outset turned out to be quite faulty when continued despite obvious evidence that they were ill-constructed for changing circumstances. In contrast, managerialism clearly worked and worked well in the private sector. Why not apply the successful practices of the private sector to the public sector and make public organizations more businesslike? This approach ran headlong into the political nature of administrative reform – whether or not public organizations should be made more businesslike; if so, where and how, with what sacrifice of nonbusinesslike considerations which made government fundamentally different from business, an unresolved debate that is likely to preoccupy administrative reformers in the 1990s.

But few in the 1960s anticipated or would have anticipated the stormy days ahead for administrative reform that were to prove so disillusioning and result in valiant efforts to fend off the reduction of the subject to narrow managerialism. In those pioneering days, reformers had wide vistas in mind, no less than the institutionalization of development administration in newly independent states to replace outmoded bureaucratic law and order systems of public administration. This involved not just introducing new organizations to speed national development but a reconstruction of the economy, government and society and a transformation of the administrative culture. Ill-defined as administrative reform was, there was reason enough to be optimistic. The social sciences in general, and administrative theory in particular, were looking anew at social dynamics, the transformation of social systems and the possibilities of accelerated modernization. Social scientists were more sympathetic than once they had been to the idea of progress through incremental, piecemeal reform which was distinguished from wholesale revolution and unresisted change. Case studies of reforms gave valuable pointers what to do, how to proceed, and which models to copy. The state of the art was not particularly well advanced but at least it was identifiable enough to be taken seriously. Great things were expected from a vigorous push to upgrade and improve administrative systems around the globe.

Even greater things might result if administrative reformers could construct a science out of what was still very much trial and error pragmatism, an unskilled amateur craft practiced by well intentioned missionaries. Reformers working in the Third World for international agencies early recognized this, convinced that administrative reform was more than the application of Western managerial concepts, whether the managerial ethos of the private sector or the organization and methods ethos of the public sector. In their efforts at the transnational inducement of administrative reform, they were embarked on institution building and the enhancement of administrative capabilities generally, i.e. systems engineering on a country specific basis directed at strengthening government performance, including administrative behavior as well as organizational structures. Several attempts by individuals and at international gatherings sponsored by the United Nations, the United States Agency for International Development and the International Institute of Administrative Sciences were made to sketch out comprehensive frameworks and inclusive definitions but reformers in the field went their own ways regardless. The attempt at communality failed and eventually petered out in the 1980s by which time most countries had adopted their own idiosyncratic programs borrowing where they could from their neighbor's experiences.

Many new items in the reform programs of the 1980s stemmed from the economic and financial tribulations confronting governments unable to pay for public sector expenditures without increasing taxation, borrowing and inflation, none of which were politically acceptable. Instead, governments squeezed public organizations by imposing budgetary limitations, restricting public sector employment and conditions, reducing public goods and services, downsizing government organizations, resorting to cutback management, and seeking greater value for money. This slimming down of the public sector was buttressed if not justified by an ideological campaign to reverse growing reliance on the administrative state and to get government off people's backs. Privatization involved the selling off of public assets, the transfer of government activities to the private sector, the end to public monopolies, and the direct delivery of public goods and services by non-governmental bodies. Debureaucratization was instituted to improve government-client relations by reducing red-tape and other bureaupathologies in government administration, streamlining public service delivery, eliminating unnecessary regulations and restrictions, and generally demystifying public laws and processes. Instead of imposing reforms, governments sought the active cooperation of career public servants in finding better and cheaper ways of conducting public business and went outside the public bureaucracy to inject managerial leadership. While all these measures reshaped and reinvigorated public administration, they still failed to get to the heart of why governments were not performing adequately and the underlying causes of increasing public disillusionment with public institutions. And they shed little more light on why reforms so often raised hopes but fell well below expectations.

Exploring the Reform Process

Despite experiencing many setbacks in attempting to improve the performance of public institutions, administrative reformers have always been committed people who really believed that they could made a difference. They recognized the imperfectability of human arrangements and the need to search continuously for better even when others were satisfied with the status quo. They maintained that as long as large public organizations were particularly prone to sluggishness, conservatism and entropy, administrative reform had a permanent place in public administration and an increasingly higher priority in government, not merely for the sake of improved administrative performance but for what better government could achieve in realizing mankind's dreams and ambitions. They believed that better means made for more attainable ends and they could identify in detail which means could be improved and which areas could be improved regardless of current performance. But reform was also the art of the possible; compromises had to be made; success in terms of original goals cold only be partial, incomplete and temporary. No matter how successful reform might be, there could never be any relaxation because the incubus of maladministration was ever present and active.

The imperfectability of public administration was obvious to everyone who ever did business with public organizations. But just criticisms were often taken out of context and exaggerated to make public administration look worse than it was. Nonetheless, the occasional administrative disasters that did occur revealed too much complacency about routine public maladministration that eventually resulted in administrative self-destruction. Was such complacency inherent in public administration? Were there other inherent administrative defects? Several researchers maintained that there were endemic diseases that persisted in all large scale organizations, particularly in public organizations, attributable variously to excessive bureaucratization, bureausis, bureaupathologic behavior, bureaucracy itself, and even to the very nature of administration in a government setting. If left untreated, these diseases would eventually handicap performance and finally cripple administration altogether. Public administrators should recognize that the battle against bureaupathologies was unending and they should take steps to protect themselves at all times. Hence, administrative reform should become a continuous ongoing activity than merely a periodic or episodic event.

Recognizing wrong did not mean that anything would be done to correct it. Administrators lived with some defects all the time and most people got used to faults in administrative systems and were not inclined to make waves to change what otherwise worked reasonably well. But wrongs festered and their harm mounted until it surpassed the threshold of tolerance at which point action was called for. Reform had its chance, providing reformers did not provoke needless opposition by failing to gain the cooperation of those most likely to be affected by radical departures in existing arrangements. Astute judgment was required as regards timing, scope, priorities, involvement and situational imperatives. A choice had to be made between either reforming from the outside or revitalizing from the inside; arguments pro and con seemed to point to a judicious combination of both approaches. Governments had available to them a widening range of instruments for mobilizing external and internal support for reform, assigning ongoing responsibility for reforms and generally monitoring the progress of reform, and the public had also found that it could even force reform on reluctant authorities. Although all the instruments had their good and bad points, their availability did mean that there could no longer be any excuses for failing to diagnose or at least set up a diagnostic apparatus to detect poor administrative performance.

Even when diagnosis was correct, a common mistake was to ignore the fact that many public organizations were institutional not instrumental bureaucracies and they had to be tackled accordingly. Reforming them was a political process spoilt by twelve common pitfalls – starting off badly, failing to adjust to situational imperatives, diagnosing incorrectly, following hidden agendas, being indecisive about key issues, planning poorly, thinking too conservatively, commanding insufficient resources, omitting feedback, neglecting monitoring, ignoring evaluation and displacing goals. Occasionally, there might be the danger of reforming too much, too quickly, leaving the recipients shell-shocked. These difficulties in implementing reform could be reduced by studying reform attempts elsewhere, particularly major reform programs recently launched in nine key countries which have become fashion leaders in administrative reform emulated by their disciples around the world.

Comparing Reform Experiences

The boldest reforms in recent years have been instigated in the East Bloc where the Soviet Union and the People's Republic of China have been retreating from bureaucratic centralism toward new as yet undeveloped forms of what they describe as market socialism. The economies of the East Bloc have not been performing well for at least a decade. The blame was put on the rigidity and systemic corruption of central planning and direction. The Soviet Union had prevented other Eastern European countries from experimenting with alternative economic systems until it became quite apparent that piecemeal reforms to strengthen the performance of bureaucratic centralism were not working. More radical reforms were required. They were instituted under Gorbachev's *perestroika* program for the Soviet economy and involved modifying and reducing central planning, introducing quasi-market systems, giving state enterprises more autonomy and competition, encouraging nongovernmental enterprise and entrepreneurship, and linking more with the global economy. New economic freedom required or needed to be accompanied by a greater measure of political freedom, a more distinct separation of state from party, and an end to the monopoly of the Communist Party. When economic reforms failed to reverse economic fortunes and actually increased economic uncertainty and instability, the political reforms released pent-up frustration and hostility to the systems in place and threatened to unravel them altogether. Diehards in the Communist Party and state bureaucracy were for reimposing authoritarian Communism while radical reformers wanted to persist in their experiments to replace bureaucratic centralism with more liberal forms of market socialism without embracing capitalist democracy. Meanwhile, China, whose economic reforms on these lines had preceded the rest of the East Bloc with the possible exception of Hungary, had been rather more successful until the turmoil of transition had brought it to the verge of crisis, whereupon it pulled back. Its bureaucracy was proving highly resistent to change; administrative reform was proving to be more difficult to achieve than economic or even political reforms.

No country in the West has been attempting a transformation of its basic institutions on such a scale. Some, like British Prime Minister Thatcher, have been attempting a transformation in national spirit but not by overturning so many basic institutions. Instead, they have been reforming significantly at the margins, also reducing the role of the administrative state, scaling back the public sector but much less drastically, deregulating private enterprise, dethroning bureaucratic power and influence in public policymaking, slimming public employment, and strengthening public management systems. Besides an ideological debate over the scope of government activities, at issue has been changing the administrative ethos that has governed public bureaucracies by replacing cautious bureaucrats with enterprising managers. Consequently, the rhetoric of administrative reform has been higher than it has been for several decades and the pace of reform has likewise quickened.

As usual, the fashion leaders have been the United States and the United Kingdom, this time, joined by Japan and Australasia, although Canada has often been the pioneer in the latest round of administrative reforms. The greatest attention has probably been focused on Prime Minister Thatcher's bold confrontation with the Whitehall Establishment and her privatization policy along with her government's intriguing experiments with alteration of public service delivery systems and managerial controls that have pushed public sector administration in new directions. In contrast, President Reagan shied away from grandiose reform schemes and concentrated instead on working from within to improve federal government managerial performance. He introduced several novel instruments to change the official mindset toward a more businesslike approach to American public administration. Both Australia and New Zealand went much further in this direction, particularly New Zealand's corporatization of public agencies, in quite an upset and challenge to traditional public service ideas and practices. Japan was much more conservative and conventional but it too achieved impressive results in improving public sector performance along more traditional lines. Throughout the West, administrative reform came to be seen more as a continuous activity than a periodic event. While basics may have been kept intact, much else was overhauled. What still remained was the riddle whether greater managerial freedom was compatible with political control and public accountability and how much traditional public service values would be compromised by the new mangerialism's emphasis on the bottom line.

The countries of the so-called Third World administratively shared little in common other than that almost without exception their administrative capabilities were limited and the deficient performance of their public sectors handicapped national development. The poorest among them had actually been going backward and the aid that had been extended to them had largely been dissipated without much to show for it. They could not afford reform which consequently remained almost out of their reach, almost but not quite because reforms were being tried all the time even if unpromising conditions aborted many of them.

Among notable exceptions which have come to serve as global models have been Hong Kong's successful anti-corruption campaign, the spread of the institution of ombudsman as citizen's protector, and the notion of people-centered development through self-management. Otherwise, obstacles to administrative reform have seemed crippling, as illustrated by experiences in Sub-Saharan Africa, the English-speaking Caribbean and Latin America. Nonetheless, Third World countries have kept trying and the international community has continued to encourage their efforts for something is better than nothing at all and every little helps.

Current Prospects

For the foreseeable future administrative reform will continue around the globe as well it might given the growing contrast between administrative potentialities and current realities. But there are still several glaring gaps in the administrative reform agenda. Some of the selfsame international bodies which urge member states to reform are themselves in need of administrative reform; their own administrative arrangements and performance leave much to be desired. So do military and other non-civil arrangements and performance in the public sector along with the ambiguous position within government of the large (and increasing) number of para-statal organizations and private contracting organizations. This enlarging gray area poses the question of public accountability and freedom to operate beyond public supervision. Another question that has yet to be squarely faced is that of bureaucracy and democratizing public administration. A third which has begun to receive some consideration is that of a demoralized public sector workforce. Assaults on the public sector have lowered its image, status and attractiveness. Unless this situation is soon reversed, current public service difficulties will only escalate with dire longterm implications. These and other gaps in the administrative reform agenda point to the dearth of research generally in public sector problems and specifically on administrative reform evaluation making advances in theory building scarce. What research has been done indicates how badly administrative reforms have sometimes been calculated and how poorly the craft of administrative reform has itself performed.

A craft is not a science and by no stretch of the imagination is the craft of administrative reform a medical or even organizational science. It does have some resemblance to the state of preventive medicine perhaps a century ago when although much was known about the human body and its afflictions, medical practitioners could not cure much and their many failures made sick people wary of them. Administrative reformers know much about public organization, administration and management and what afflicts them, but they do not as yet cure much and their many failures in the past have made public leaders wary of them. Yet just as the medical sciences progressed with institutionalization, so should administrative reform. The need for its institutionalization has been recognized around the globe. Each country has to decide what form of institutionalization best suits its particular circumstances. At the top of the administrative reform agenda for some time yet are likely to be financial considerations, probably with less emphasis on economy and efficiency and more on effectiveness and overall performance, particularly value for money, performance measures and productivity enhancement going well beyond the World Bank's gross national product (G.N.P.) per capita indexes and the United Nations Development Program's human development index (H.D.I.). All governments will be seeking healthier public organizations, if not healthy organizations that perform well and reliably and improve their performance in changing conditions. If anything has been learnt from reform experiences, it is not to expect instant miracles; progress in administrative reform is gradual, selective and piecemeal; attempts to hasten the pace or cover everything rarely succeed. Administrative reform is only a part, admittedly an increasingly crucial part, of the much greater enterprise of institutional reform which could well learn much from what is already known about administrative reform.

The kind of challenges involved in administrative reform can be illustrated by Italy, the world's fifth largest economy and one of the most successful countries in recent decades. According to *The Economist* (May 26, 1990), a highly efficient private sector contrasts with an inefficient public sector which labors under an elaborate system of political patronage and spoils (*lottizzazione*) and suffers from financial profligacy. The Italian government has not been able to live within its means and runs proportionately one of the largest budget deficits in the world equivalent in size to the annual national product. Tax evasion is common and attempts to improve tax collection have had little success. Generous social legislation has inflated costs. The National Health Service (about 80 percent of health services) is provided by local governments (through Local Health Authorities) but the costs are met by the central government through compulsory insurance contributions (which cover about 60 percent) and general revenues in a Byzantine administrative system that obscures public accountability and allows few performance incentives and little effective cost containment. One third of the population receives indexed pensions, mostly disability pensions sanctioned by politicians to keep local voters faithful. Some unprofitable public enterprises like Alfa-Romeo and Mediobanca have been privatized and turned around, but others are still suffocated by *lottizzazione* and most politicians oppose further privatization as the public sector provides their political bases. A bloated public bureaucracy is dominated by excessive legalism, lax law enforcement, politicization and high political executive turnover as well as a culture of corruption and mañana. As a result, reforms are always being proposed but political *immobilism* often prevents action and implementation.

The problem in Italy, as elsewhere, is not just institutional but also cultural. As the family is the enduring unit, little emphasis is put on public spirit or the concept of the public good. It explains the *parentela* or kinship system in dealing with the public bureaucracy – find a crony or relative to fix things. Given that "there is no alternation of power; government is one-party-dominated, consensus-hungry and decision-shy; ministers, even the prime minister, are weak; factions are often built around politicians who are short on political principle and sometimes long on corruption" (*The Economist*, 1990, 29), the prospects for reform are poor. What reforms will occur are likely to be marginal rather than radical. The country copes but it is misgoverned. It achieves much less than it could and should, and would if it were to study and take to heart lessons derived from the reform experiences of other countries which had similar if not worse administrative difficulties and yet succeeded in transforming their public sector performance for the better. In this, Italy is typical not exceptional. No country can fail to gain something to its advantage. Administrative reform has matured sufficiently in the past twenty or so years to present a more realistic and objective picture of what can be done. It has cast off much of the initially naive baggage that it carried for too long. It has since lost its innocence and found better guides to improving the conduct of public business in the contemporary administrative state.

In any consideration of administrative reform, two things above all else need to be kept in mind. Administrative reform deals with the administrative side of government, of the public sector, of public administration, organization and management, that is, with getting things done that have been politically determined. While it can improve political decision making, it cannot reverse political decisions, and it is political decisions which are largely responsible for poor government performance, many public sector deficiencies and much public maladministration. Political leaders make dumb decisions which are administratively disastrous. No amount of administrative reform can remedy such political errors, although innocent public administrators will be blamed and will be expected miraculously to produce good out of bad and success out of unavoidable failure. Administrative reform cannot substitute for political or economic or institutional reform.

On the other hand, political, economic and institutional reforms can rarely succeed without administrative reform. Administration is not neutral or merely instrumental. It has a life of its own, a rather elaborate and complicated life that cannot be taken for granted for it is in a perpetual state of incalculable flux. Often administration will go its own way regardless. Within reformers will be battling the prevailing systems, scoring a few victories here and there, for none is entirely blind to remedial defects and the self respect of professionals impels them to improve practices where there seem no compelling reasons not to. But for greater success and for systems as a whole to be reformed, external pressure for reform has to be present; the whole system has to be under outside threat, no mere idle threat either but effective sanction that will undoubtedly be exercised if improved performance does not occur. Political leaders have to demand better administrative performance, constantly monitor that honest attempts are being made to meet their wishes, and exercise effective sanctions when it is not forthcoming. They really do have to care and they have to be knowledgeable. They have to have vigilant guardians over and within administrative systems. They have to support and reward performers and maintain an administrative culture that fosters innovation, creativity and reform. If administrative reform has not performed well in the past, it is either because it has been attempting to do things that it could not do or it has not had the political encouragement and backing that it needed. Over the past two decades or so, these two lessons have been driven home. Administrative reform has matured in the meantime from its earlier naivete.

Reference

The Economist, Vol. 315, No. 7656, May 26, 1990, "A Survey of Italy: Awaiting an alternative," 30 pp.

2. Lost Innocence

This book is about worldwide efforts over the past two decades to improve public sector performance, that is, the economy, productivity, efficiency and effectiveness of public organizations and governmental administration. As global economic prospects declined and governments struggled to halt stagflation and stimulate their economies, they looked hard at galloping public expenditures, aggrandizing public bureaucracies and poorly performing public enterprises and did not like what they saw. They turned to administrative reform in hope of salvation partly because they were reluctant to embark on much deeper political reforms or more politically contentious policy changes, partly because they did not know what else to do, and partly because they really felt that a more businesslike public sector would provide solutions for economic ills. Either administrative solutions would substitute for political solutions (Brodkin, 1986) or administrative reforms were an imperative accompaniment, if not precursor, to far-reaching societal changes.

But whereas administrative reform of the 1960s was then well-grounded in social science theory in general and administrative theory in particular, was enthusiastically backed by international aid agencies as a cornerstone of development administration, and was being carried out confidently and assertively by its can-do practitioners, twenty years later this was no longer the case. Administrative reform had largely divorced itself from theoretical concerns. International aid agencies had all but disowned it or at least what they used to call administrative reform, i.e. the strengthening of public bureaucracies as engines of development. And administrative reformers had been chastened by the practical limitations and restraints encountered in making reforms a reality.

The new generation of administrative reformers is much less assertive and more tentative in its approach, trying to build in many cases on the ruins of its predecessors whose efforts were poorly rewarded. Administrative reform has gone through a sobering if not disillusioning period in which political realities overshadowed administrative niceties, the models it embraced collapsed altogether or did not meet the new political realities, and its practitioners groped and improvised as best they could with crisis management virtually without any help from the world of scholarship. There has been a decided loss of innocence, not just because of bitter experiences in trying to improve public sector performance, but because the world has moved on and the reforms of yesteryear no longer suffice. A different world requires different kinds of reform, different reform strategies, and different reform outcomes.

Disregard of Theorists

Since the 1960s administrative reformers – officials and others actually carrying out improvements in public sector organization and management – do not appear to have paid much attention to advances in the social sciences, organization theory and administrative science. They have drifted away from academic concerns and are largely ignorant of new theories and new theorists. They have stuck with the theories they learnt when young, that is, the world of theory as it was in the early 1960s. Much of what has happened since has largely passed them by. They have made no special effort to keep up with advances in theory. They have not retooled themselves in the latest research methods to comprehend contemporary research, let alone more sophisticated theory building. They do not understand the latest social science vocabulary and they have given up making sense out of the leading academic journals in organization and management, except those, like the *Harvard Business Review*, written for a wider lay audience. They are largely out of touch with the theorists, much of whose work is unintelligible to them.

Administrative reformers claim that the theorists are other-worldly, unrealistic, far-fetched, irrelevant, in any event, to be kept at arm's length. In this, they have received some academic backing.

> ...the theory of bureaucratic organization [has] provided few definitive answers to the specific problems that administrators and politicians face. Somewhat like modern medicine, it seldom prescribed direct treatment for specific diseases. Rather it tended to promote general purpose drugs that frequently produced side effects as dangerous as the diseases being treated. (Campbell and Peters, 1988, 55-6)

> Students of organizations have often put a damper on the enthusiasm of administrative reformers. They have argued that traditional democratic theory has provided a flawed model of administrative management of the public sector, that hopes for a firm theoretical basis for organizational design have been mostly unfulfilled, that prescriptions of organizational design tend to be contradictory, and that advice is often given without making explicit the assumptions and the methods used...(Ibid, 235)

A survey of research in public management in the United States in the early 1980s found "that beneath a mountain of often sage observations and impressions, there lies a very small database" (Garson and Overman, 1983, 3), that there was precious little research and what existed was "often not readily available to end users and other researchers" (Ibid, 4), was exceptional rather than typical (and therefore could not be generalized) and was "highly fragmented in terms of discipline, geographical location, intended incidence, and other dimensions" (Ibid, 11), and that researchers lacked any network that provided awareness of what others were doing in the same field let alone any information system that disseminated findings to practitioners.

Ten years before that research on public managerial innovations such as management by objectives (M.B.O.), planning-programming-budgeting systems (P.P.B.S.), program evaluation and performance budgeting, had been similarly faulted (Kimmel et al., 1974). Not surprisingly, when they had been implemented, their rate of success had been disappointing.

> One suspects that eminently rational men and women, sitting in their offices, spin their eminently rational plans for the edification of other eminently rational men and women until…no one would dare to suggest that the emperor had no clothes…what we have is more ideology than science… The reform movement has to reestablish communication with the universe it is trying to change. (Calista, 1986, 262-3)

The fault in this instance had been that American reformers had promoted the ideology of managerial omnipotence and bureaucracy. They had been "agents of bureaucratization with a false vision of the functions of organizations and of the political process" at a time when their whole approach was questionable. They had sided too much with bureaucracy, managerialism, Hegelian administrative principles, the administrative state, scientism, and rationality. Their snake oil had been willingly bought by self-interested or blinded public managers who failed to see the mischief caused thereby. So even when provided with the opportunity of mixing with administrative theorists and their managerial disciples, it was beneficial that theorists and practitioners rarely conversed or had much to do with one another. Consequently, since so few cross the few bridges between them, most administrative reformers are locked into a theoretical time-capsule and refuse to emerge from it. Those who do bother wonder why as the world of theory seems so unrelated and so unrewarding.

While it may be true that much contemporary theory or theorizing may be out of touch, barely comprehensible except to the learned few who seemingly write with themselves only in mind, and devoid of any practical application or guidelines, it has been largely theorists who have warned the practitioners in administrative reform not to fall too much in love with their models to forget what was wrong with them where they were culture-bound (and not universal) and how they had to be reshaped to meet specific circumstances. These theorists, virtually all academics, were dubbed the doubters, the spoilers, the trouble-makers, who always could find fault and cast gloom on any party. Given the tremendous strides that had been made in organization, administration and management since the beginning of the century and the great successes of post-war reconstruction, there was cause for optimism that the well-tried models of the past and the new models of the (then) present would work. If they were not working out as expected – and already in the 1960s there was mounting evidence to suggest that this was the case – it was not the models so much at fault as the people employing the models. They had not been properly prepared or they lacked the proper skills or they held the wrong attitudes. In time, given sufficient education, training, and experience, they would come around. Changing administrative systems needed patience and understanding but change they would; managerial engineering worked.

So it took time before it was realized that people were not failing the models so much as the models were failing people, that in the post-war turbulent world the models themselves were faulty. Though they worked or could be made to work, they fell short, often seriously short, of what was required. Given the benefit of the doubt, their dysfunctions were often ignored or discounted until they could hardly be denied. One by one the models were questioned and found guilty of grave shortcomings. There being no ready alternatives, they were patched up as best administrative reformers could manage. But, often as not, the reforms were dismissed by traditionalists as being unnecessary and by radicals as being inadequate, until overwhelming evidence suggested that minor patchwork was merely temporizing and delaying the inevitable replacement of the models themselves. While some popularized futurists had sketched out what the replacement models might be, no one had taken them seriously and by the end of the 1980s little had been done to anticipate their predictions. The world was saddled with outdated models with no practical substitutes. So the search, particularly in the East (Communist) Bloc, was on for something different. Meantime, the old patchworked models worked, albeit faultily, at least sufficiently to keep until something better might materialize, whenever that might be.

The Faulty Models

The disillusionment with prevailing administrative models (the prescriptions of administrative reformers) took place between the early 1960s and the late 1980s, after the post-war economic boom enjoyed by most countries ended with the energy crisis of the 1970s, the world trade recession of the early 1980s and the world environmental concerns of the late 1980s. Optimism gave way to pessimism, especially in countries that found themselves going backwards or stagnating, a situation they blamed on poor public sector performance, swollen public bureaucracies, incompetent public management, and ineffective administrative reforms.

(a) State intervention. At the head of the list was the 1960s reformer belief in state intervention, in the administrative state as an instrument of social betterment, an indispensable weapon against evil. Government was expected to provide answers to every problem thrust on it. Ominous signs soon appeared to suggest that too much faith had been invested in the administrative state. Society was increasingly dependent on its performance. Politicians promised things nobody was sure could be delivered. The overloaded government system could not cope indefinitely with extra responsibilities without being overstretched.

Public business suffered when public agencies could not handle their workloads or settled for lower quality performance. Politically, raised expectations were punctured, potential beneficiaries angered and taxpayers resentful. Administratively, bureaucrats unjustifyingly kept reassuring the public and asked for more resources to complete unfinished tasks. Intellectually, it was realized that complex social issues were not susceptible to easy solution and that bureaucratic answers were inadequate and even regressive. For too long legitimate complaints from the victims of the administrative state had been ignored as had a rising groundswell against further public initiatives, governmental interference, bureaucratization, arrogant officialdom and rising taxes. The message was clear: no further state interference in people's lives.

In recent years, assumptions about the administrative state have been revised. First, it was not inevitable or necessarily beneficial. It might actually compound social problems. It had allegedly sapped private initiatives, weakened individual enterprise, softened self-will, undermined individualism and made everyone too dependent on officialdom. Second, public agencies had been expected to do things beyond their capacity and the results had been disappointing. The experts had few workable solutions but identified many more problems for government to tackle. Public resources were too often spent on heavy administrative overheads and self-justificatory bureaucratic exercises. Third, strong executives tended to abuse their wide powers and use them to evade public accountability. They turned their agencies into private preserves. Fourth, bureaucratism "rewards conspiracy, sycophancy, ideological conformity, caution and class solidarity. It punishes innovation, originality and the work ethic" (Campbell, 1978). Fifth, more and more people felt that they could do better for themselves with less government and lower taxes. They could make better decisions and be more careful with their money. They wanted more control over their own lives and a greater say in what personally affected them. They did not trust officialdom or believe in Big Brother any more.

(b) Bureaucracy. Long before the post-war growth of the administrative state, its critics had warned of the dead hand of bureaucracy. Such warnings in the heady days of post-war reconstruction had been little heeded. It was expected that administrative science would be able to handle the dysfunctions of bureaucracy. Misgivings about bureaucracy did not prevent the bureaucratization of most organized activity and the dominance of the bureaucratic paradigm in organization theory. In administrative reform, virtually no other form of organization was considered. Indeed, reformers were surprised by the upsurge of the anti-bureaucratic counter culture of the 1960s and it took almost a decade before they heeded its message. By this time common bureaupathologies had become identifiable and the poor ability of bureaucracy to adapt to turbulence was increasingly obvious.

While the reform mainstream stood by bureaucracy, the radical fringe was prepared to abandon bureaucracy altogether. Suddenly, small was beautiful. Direct democracy had to replace the exercise of power by elites. Government organizations had to be bypassed by self-help organizations, voluntary associations, non-governmental organizations. People had to organize themselves, not wait for the slow trickle down of wealth. Predictions were made about the demise of bureaucracy (Bennis, 1966) and a serious search for alternatives to bureaucracy was started (Jun & Storm, 1973). Bureaucracy had been taken too far. Specialization had been overdone, making most work unattractive and transforming creative individuals into mindless robots. Elongated hierarchies had divorced elites from operating realities and made them overdependent on self-serving middle management engaged on too much unproductive busy work. Overreliance on rules and regulations had promoted inertia and rigidity, often defying plain common sense. Entrenched career systems had replaced the pursuit of excellence with the enthronement of mediocrity. Bureaucracy was incompatible with democracy. Bureaucracy itself was a blight on humanity. All of this was far too strong for the reform mainstream but it converted, at least temporarily, many influential reformers and raised sufficient doubt among many others to cause them to hesitate, rethink, and, more importantly, challenge the bureaucratic model which they had taken too much for granted.

(c) Westminster-Whitehall. Another pillar of orthodoxy to fall was the Westminster-Whitehall model that had been predicated on a strict dichotomy between politics and administration or a complete separation between political and administrative careers in government. The British had institutionalized the politics-administration dichotomy at home and abroad and the reputation of British public administration had been such as to influence countries even outside the British Commonwealth to adopt British ideas and practices, including the notion of the gifted amateur, the wise intellectual, the gentleman ruler-administrator. If the policies were correct, the administrative arrangements were appropriate and the staff were sufficiently public spirited to serve impartially, disinterestedly, honorably and follow correct channels, then administration would look after itself. What was important was getting the right people, the right decisions and the right rules. Important yes, but with the growth of the administrative state, the extension of government activities, and the elaboration of bureaucracy, the right people, decisions and rules were insufficient to ensure economic, productive, efficient and effective public sector performance. This late nineteenth-century model of public administration was increasingly inappropriate for late twentieth century conditions. Yet, the British were reluctant to abandon it and when they finally got around to changing it, the systems were too in-grained to allow much modification or indeed any in countries where government was more British than the British (as in the West Indies), although inappropriate and detrimental.

The countries which had not wanted to be British at all or which had tried to distance themselves from the mother country had challenged the Westminster-Whitehall model before the 1960s and increasingly so thereafter. A number of newly independent states abandoned it as soon as they could, sometimes with disastrous administrative consequences. Others shaped it more in accordance with local circumstances and improved on it, albeit on a demographically smaller scale. But it was the British themselves who admitted that their model was seriously flawed. It had been strongly criticized and resisted when put in place in the late nineteenth century. Rumblings of discontent had erupted every so often whenever the British government fared poorly. The Labour Party promised to change the system when it could but never got around to doing so until convinced in the early 1960s that without civil service reform, it would not be able to govern properly as long as public administration was led by largely untrained narrowly recruited, protected generalists who "remained a world apart, a closed, secretive society with little direct experience of the economy and society with which it was concerned" (Hennessy, 1989, 174). Its chance came and went with the Fulton Committee (1966-1968) which pretty much diagnosed what was wrong with Whitehall without tackling the bigger issues of the role of the state and the machinery of government and the place of Whitehall within them.

While a start was made on the Fulton Committee proposals, the economic and political position of Great Britain deteriorated so badly in the 1970s that the International Monetary Fund intervened to insist on its own financial reforms. Much of the blame for Britain's poor performance was attributed to the unreformed Whitehall. It was left to the incoming Thatcher Conservative Government in 1979 to tackle Whitehall, the Westminster-Whitehall model and the whole question of the administrative state in action and to attempt to change British administrative culture away from the cult of the generalist and more in the direction of professional management. During the 1980s, the Thatcher Government challenged other prevailing myths of government, cast aside traditional doctrines, put forward a different version of a streamlined, managerial state, cut and pruned officialdom, trampled over cherished conventions of the Westminster-Whitehall model, and relied on shock therapy to revitalize Whitehall. In the process, even the model that the Fulton Committee assumed was overturned in such a way that it was unlikely things would ever go back again. The Westminster-Whitehall model may not have been abandoned or shattered but it had taken quite a beating.

(d) Maoism. The same can be said about most of the other models beloved of the reformers of the late 1960s. In the most populous country in the world, the Cultural Revolution (intended to reinvigorate the revamping of Chinese society) was destroying, so it was claimed, the remaining strongholds of tradition, bourgeois mentality, bureaucracy and reaction and furthering the objectives of

Maoism. The Cultural Revolution was certainly destructive; it crippled Chinese enterprise for at least a decade and perpetuated totalitarian conformity and intolerance that almost broke the people's spirit. As it was, forced collectivization nearly ruined the economy; certainly it ruined rural life and productivity. At the time, it fooled many people not just within China, but as the truth emerged, even its instigators and converts began to disown it until in 1978 it could be openly criticized and a decade after that just memories of it made people shudder. Like pre-war Nazism, it was destined to the slagheaps of history.

(e) Centrally managed economies. In the largest country of the world, Stalinism had also by the 1980s been so discredited that it too was destined to abandonment. Although the Communist Party of the Soviet Union had denounced Stalinism in the mid 1950s, Soviet reformers had been unable to discard the key tenets of a centralized planned economy directed by party cadres toward the realization of an egalitarian society, the Marxist alternative to capitalism. Despite failures in agriculture, the system seemed to be working. There was full employment, massive post-war rebuilding of destroyed infrastructure, impressive scientific achievements, improvements in the standard of living across the board without apparent pockets of extreme hardship, accessible public amenities, and a wide measure of equal opportunity. Furthermore, the Soviet system had not been subject to unpredictable upheavals and dislocations. To the have-nots of the world, the Soviet model appealed and was a real alternative to American and post-colonialist prescriptions for them.

Central planning became an article of faith for many countries and also for international financial agencies. To get a substantial loan from the World Bank, one had to show how it would be used and how it would fit into a national economic plan. So countries produced plans, some based on sophisticated economic forecasting, cyclical budgets and controlled economies, others based on flimsy information, wish lists and sheer guesswork. Most were not worth the paper on which they were written; they never worked (and were never intended to work). Poor countries blamed themselves. They were too poor even to undertake meaningful planning. But even rich countries could not make economic planning work; they blamed the concept of centralized economic planning itself. It could not be done and those countries which claimed they could do it were either lying or deceiving themselves. Even if the technical problems could be overcome, the blueprint approach of planning was incapable of overcoming the complexity of the real world, the inherent bias toward inefficient public sector projects, and institutional corruption. In 1983 the World Bank outlined the disillusionment of Third World countries that occurred during the 1970s. By then cracks had appeared in several Eastern European countries and China. Once Gorbachev revealed the magnitude of failure in the Soviet Union, even the remaining true believers had to admit defeat. The World Bank proposed in its place macroeconomic management, economic regulation, and a coherent and consistent framework of fiscal, monetary, exchange rate, wage and trade policies, without however stipulating policies or institutions (World Bank, 1983, 64). Unfortunately for countries that had been wedded to central economic planning, the switch could not be made suddenly and the long process of readjustment unless carefully controlled could be accompanied by economic chaos. In any event by the end of the 1980s, the central planning model was being abandoned save in a handful of dogmatic hold-outs.

(f) Public enterprises. State-owned enterprises (S.O.E.s) were another model whose days seemed to be numbered. In the 1960s, they had been heralded as the driving force behind national development, taking advantage of the best of both public and private administration. As public entrepreneurs, they would be freed of the restrictions of civil service and work in the public interest with the advantage of special rights. In the East Bloc, they had largely replaced private enterprise. In the West, they had a prominent place in the supply of public utility services, postal and telecommunications, local government services, river valley development, and housing and they had taken charge of the post-war nationalized industries. In the Third World, they were a realistic alternative to hyperthetical local private enterprise and unwelcome foreign multinational corporations. The Italian Institute for Industrial Reconstruction (I.R.I.) had shown in the immediate post-war period and the 1950s "state enterprise as efficient and dynamic as leading private enterprise groups, yet still directly serving the ends of government economic policy and the interests of society as a whole" (Holland, 1972, 1). I.R.I. had embarked on the industrialization of southern Italy, modernized communications, built up a new steel industry, and ensured Italian control of electronics and nuclear power, and hopes were equally high in other Western European countries, particularly Great Britain and France, that state-owned enterprises would be as successful as they had been in Scandinavia. They were a natural vehicle for newly independent countries which nationalized foreign-owned companies, especially in agriculture, mining and oil industries. Many were created between 1960 and 1980, and over half the African S.O.E.s were created between 1967 and 1980 (Nellis and Kikeri, 1989, 660).

What was never anticipated was that in many cases, instead of getting the best of public and private enterprise, S.O.E.s seemed to get the worst, weighed down by civil service restrictions, unable to act entrepreneurially and exploiting their natural and legal monopoly as private fiefdoms. They often lacked incentives to perform in the absence of market pressures, government controls, and external threats. They incurred excessive costs, operated with low productivity, and borrowed hugely to cover their high operating losses. They invariably suffered from poor management, political intervention, insufficient reinvestment to cover depreciation and modernization, low motivation, and high opportunity costs, so that had they been closed down and their resources invested elsewhere, everybody would have been better off (Henriques, 1980). Instead of advancing national development, they had been a major contributor to heavy public debts, corruption, price distortions, wasted investments, and parasitism. In Africa, for example, they "present a depressing picture of inefficiency, losses, budgeting burdens, poor products and services, and minimum accomplishment of the non-commercial objectives so frequently used to excuse their poor economic performance…[they] are not fulfilling the goals set for them by African planners and leaders" (Nellis, 1986, ii). In short "many…should simply never have been created" (Ibid). In general, "too many…cost rather than make money; and too many operate at low levels of efficiency" (Nellis and Kikeri, 1989, 660). Their structural failure was in the separation of ownership and control. Only some form of privatization would overcome that. Even so, there was no guarantee that private ownership and management would fare better, although there might be less political interference, higher incentives to perform and greater commercial discipline. Nonetheless, by the end of the 1980s, privatization had become the new article of faith, especially in World Bank circles and among Western conservative governments, although globally more resources have been devoted to reforming S.O.E.s than to transferring them to private ownership.

(g) Workers' self-management. Just as high hopes had been held for the S.O.E.s, so they were held for worker-owned enterprises. The three major models much prized by reformers were workers' management in Yugoslavia and the collective (*kibbutz*) and cooperative (*moshav*) settlements in Israel, examples of non-bureaucratic industrial democracy. After World War II, Yugoslavia adopted highly centralized management and planning of the economy traditional to administrative socialism until its break in 1949 with the Cominform. Thereafter the direction of S.O.E.s was taken over by elected workers' councils which appointed a board of management but still subject to a general manager responsible for implementing government plans, policies and regulations. Gradually, between 1953 and 1963, workers' management was extended to other public goods and services, decision-making within each self-managing organization was decentralized and democratized, each undertaking became more autonomous and independent, and local government activities were transferred to local communities. In the following decade, the government withdrew from economic direction and control and workers' management became a legal reality, vesting social power in the workers themselves. The scale on which this all took place attracted considerable international attention and even though things were not going as smoothly or well as hoped, foreign enthusiasts of participatory democracy were sufficiently convinced to advocate workers' management as a universal model (Pateman, 1970). The successes of the Israeli *kibbutzim* and *moshavim* not only economically but also in providing alternative life styles before the 1973 Yom Kippur War similarly attracted foreign attention and enthusiasm. Yugoslav and Israeli experts were invited to share their know-how.

Whether the models were exportable became moot when both countries were hit by the economic blizzard of the 1970s. Workers' management was protected and favored for another decade before the naked truth was revealed. In Israel, the *moshavim* (small, self-supporting rural communities based on cooperativism) fell on particularly hard times and became an economic liability. So did the *kibbutzim* (small collectivized communities) after they had been encouraged by the government to overextend themselves. Their prospects depended more on government policies than self-initiatives. That too was the case in Yugoslavia where the government had never relinquished its control of the economy and its hold over social institutions. Workers' participation had taken place within a much wider context of public investment, political federalism, regionalism, underdevelopment, Titoism, social ownership, associated labor, and market competition, none of which sat too well with it, irrespective how well workers' participation operated. Throughout, it did not operate well; it was far too complicated for the average person to grasp and actual participation or workers' contribution was low with managerial and specialized staff retaining predominant influence. While Tito was alive, people did their best to make it work but after his death, conflicts of interest which had been hitherto contained threatened the whole fragile framework, enough to cause foreigners to back away.

These illustrations of faulty models show how administrative reformers were so anxious to remedy defective public sector performance that they seized on anything that hinted at improvement. But they were also convinced that they could make any promising idea work. So they fell prey to all kinds of fads and fancies which they took up without proper investigation and evaluation. Just as quickly they would drop them when they recognized them for what they really were – half baked ideas, wishful thinking, inoperable schemes, unrealizable ideals. At least, the reformers were receptive to new ideas, innovations, fresh beginnings and reconceptualizations. Further they were not too proud to admit mistakes. On the contrary, they were always aware that they were embarking on risky ventures, that they faced overwhelming odds, that Murphy's Law seemed to govern reform efforts (anything that could go wrong would), and that implementation was quite difficult. They could never completely overcome self-doubts and nagging questions. When something really did work, like the ombudsman, program budgeting, cutback management, non-prejudicial selection, productivity measurement, and policy evaluation, they tended to go overboard and exaggerate the benefits. Theirs was a chastening and often frustrating experience, especially when they would work so hard to bring about much needed improvements and dramatic changes in unacceptable practices only to see their efforts "dragged to a halt by the relentless, grinding power of settled arrangements to defy change of any kind, at every turn, and to the last hour" (Yackle, 1989, vii) and sometimes outcomes – the perpetration and intensification of wrongdoing – opposite to their intentions. No wonder they envied the freedom of action of managers in the private sector. No wonder that they advocated the same freedom for managers in the public sector.

The Challenge of Managerialism

While administrative reformers struggled for relatively small gains in the public sector between 1960 and 1990, private sector management apparently went from strength to strength. Despite continually high bankruptcy rates among private businesses, especially small scale and owner self-managed undertakings, low evaluation of business methods and behavior and generally low standing in public opinion of private corporations, regular scandals, occasional astonishing poor judgment, frequent reorganizations, shake-ups and shuffles, private management was held in higher and higher repute. Business management had been an amazing growth industry, spawning prestigious graduate schools around the globe and far out distancing anything catering for the public sector. Business management publications swamped the market. Business management research dwarfed government management research. Business entrepreneurs invested more heavily in business management education and training than their public sector counterparts. In many countries public sector studies were drowned in a sea of business management studies. As in business, nothing succeeded like success, so business management had to be considered as highly successful. One measure of the success of business management was that administrative reform or the term administrative reform was rarely heard in the private sector. The idea of administrative reform – the continual improvement of performance and the correction of wrongdoing – existed but it was not considered separate or distinct from business management itself. Business management was about the continual improvement of business performance and the correction of business wrong-doing. It was incorporated into business management practices in a way that it had not been incorporated into public sector management practices. Business undertakings might do much the same things as governments did to improve their performance – they might appoint external committees of inquiry, they might set up institutionalized management improvement schemes, they might reorganize, centralize, decentralize, recentralize, and do all those things identifiable as administrative reform – but they did not call it "administrative reform", a term almost exclusively reserved for the public sector. They did not even call it "managerial reform" though when talking about the private sector in general they might use the term "business reform". This contrast was not accidental; it reflected differences in mental attitude.

Business shortcomings so it was believed had or would have their own immediate penalties. If businesses did not offer what the public wanted, they lost their customers. No one was compelled to buy their products and services and if superior products and services were available, customers switched and defied product loyalty. If they did not pay their way then their creditors could legally seize their remaining assets and shut them down. They had either to raise prices or cut costs. If their bottom line did not satisfy their investors and their rates of return were inferior to generally prevailing rates, then their backers would switch if they could get out, or they became target of raiders who believed they could do better and get better returns. In a competitive situation, they had to meet prevailing expectations outside their control. They had to keep on their toes. They could not afford to relax; otherwise somebody else might steal a march on them. They could never feel completely secure. They had to keep running just to stay in the same place. To advance, they had to be better and do better. They had to keep up with improvements and, more importantly, they had to try to be first with improvements. They had every incentive to police themselves, improve their own functioning and adjust to changing conditions.

In theory, public undertakings should have been no different. They should also have offered what the public wanted. They should also have paid their way or at least showed worthwhile investment returns. They should have been on their toes, kept up with improvements and tried to advance the state-of-the-art. They claimed they did. But in most cases there was reasonable doubt. They often did not know what the public wanted and made no attempt to find out. Theirs' was a "take it or leave it" attitude. They were compulsory; their customers had no choice, no alternative. They were not likely to be replaced or disappear if they did not perform to expectations, whatever these might be. Whereas private undertakings had definite objectives, which were known, clear, straightforward, public undertakings often had unknown, unclear, complex, contradictory, muddled (or fuzzy or fudged) objectives, politically determined and manipulated. Their organization, administration and management was similarly politically determined and manipulated. They were not masters of their own house. They were *public* organizations which were publicly owned and directed and the public did not want them to act as private undertakings. As public organizations they were protected, given exceptional privileges but also placed under exceptional obligations. Usually, they were over protected and made too secure, irrespective of performance. So they were not constantly under pressure to improve or advance the state-of-the-art, if anyone knew what it was let alone should have been. They stuck to routines, played safe, and, because of their larger size, complexity and multiple masters, they had difficulty in changing directions (or indeed anything) quickly. Because of the lack of proprietary interest, the divorce between inputs and outcomes, the peculiarities of public budgeting, and the neglect of managerial concerns, there were not the same incentives for self-improvement and error correction as in the business world and among voluntary associations. On the contrary, they were prone to organizational arteriosclerosis.

Whatever the reasons, private managers had more freedom to act and to be their own reformers. They were encouraged to advance the state-of-the-art. They were expected to keep up with improvements. And they were rewarded and punished according to their performance in furthering organizational objectives. They did not get ahead unless they proved their competence on the job and they met organizational expectations, which increasingly included formal education and training in management in their own time and at their own expense. They conformed because exceptional rewards went to those who rose up the management ladder (so their personal investment usually paid off) and they could transfer their skills and knowledge to other organizations always eager to snatch talent away from others. Wherever they went they operated in a managerial environment where they spoke the same language and their contributions to improved management were appreciated. Perhaps this was a somewhat overdrawn, romantic picture of private management, but business management had been so able to project such an image of doing better that while business accepted public management qualifications without enthusiasm (except at the highest levels of government administration and in certain professional and specialist fields), public organizations snapped up people with private management qualifications when permitted, although they had difficulty retaining them.

Again, in theory, public management should have been no different. Public managers should have been encouraged to be their own reformers and judged on their managerial performance. They should have been formally qualified in public management and the potential high-flyers should have been eagerly sought out. They should have operated in an environment that appreciated managerial concerns and in organizations that strove for managerial excellence. Again the reality was often so different. Political concerns dominated managerial considerations. Public organizations were often seen as political party appendages and staffed with job seekers. In them, rewards went to the loyal, not to the competent. Little attention was paid to formal qualifications or experience or managerial trackrecord. The lower ranks were not supposed to exercise any initiative and were resented if they did. The higher ranks were political advisors, policymakers, trouble shooters and bureaucrats; they were not expected to be managers or know anything about management not derived from inherited bureaucratic ritual. Potential high-flyers were buried in unchallenging routine low level work and if they complained, they were branded troublemakers and encouraged to move elsewhere. Anyone who did show managerial abilities was swamped with so many activities that none of them could be done really well. Good managers were taken too much for granted so that, invariably overworked and underpaid, they longed to get out at the first opportunity if they did not start operating their own businesses first on the side. Meanwhile at the top, the organizational politicians, where they were not just time-servers, played their games without heed to the managerial consequences. Perhaps this picture was again overdrawn, too far-fetched, too exaggerated, but public management conveyed the image of incompetence, ignorance and poor performance, which prompted demands for administrative reforms based on managerialism, a managerialism derived largely from the private sector.

No doubt both images were distorted. If the truth was known, private management was not all that it was made out to be and public management was much better than generally credited. Nonetheless, managerialism had built up an aura of success. Administrative reformers had been conscious of this and also somewhat jealous. They had treated it with suspicion and avoided its whole-hearted embrace. They doubted whether self-interested management was wholly compatible with public-interested management. They wanted to protect public service ethics from business ethics, and public practices from business malpractices. While they probably would have accorded managerialism a higher place in public sector priorities, they still valued other administrative values – law abidingness, public accountability, reliability, equity, social justice and environmental protection – higher. Nonetheless, they have grown more supportive of managerialism and more warming toward privatization wherever administrative reforms have failed to influence the bureaucratic mind. After all, management applied to all human organizations wherever managers or executives had to define the right strategy and goals, develop people, measure performance, market the organization's services, raise productivity, invest resources, satisfy clients, exemplify organizational values, and provide public leadership (Drucker, 1988).

It was an easy step to advocate managerialism in the public sector and to propose administrative reforms based on successful managerial improvements in the private sector, particularly when business managers had turned around poorly performing public organizations, as for instance, in the case of the Human Resources Administration of New York City (Spiegel, 1975) and later the successful financial rescue of New York City's municipal government itself. The major objective was to get away from a *rules bound* administration in which senior staff spent their time advising on the making and revising of rules and the junior staff rigidly implemented them to a *performance bound* administration in which senior staff spent their time establishing and reviewing long term and shorter term objectives in consultation with junior staff who had autonomy to determine their working practices within the agreed framework and according to evaluated performance measures. Greater emphasis was to be placed on performance, accountability, planning and control, and the latest managerial technology (Ukeles, 1982) in order to do more with less (see Table 1). With the weight of the business community behind it, this manageralistic approach to administrative reform began to eclipse alternative traditional approaches despite great misgivings among theorists and practitioners of public administration and management who doubted its basic assumptions that public organizations could or should be managed like private organizations, that successful business

Table 1: Doing More With Less
The Managerial Approach to Administrative Reform

Managing with people

post civil service reforms
- active not passive recruitment of senior personnel
- hiring by line managers not staff examiners
- individual position descriptions replace classifications
- flexibility replaces rigidity in assignments
- performance appraisal and merit incentives
- decentralized personnel management

collective bargaining reforms
- excluding managers
- strengthening management side and weakening labor side
- conciliation and cooperation on specific projects (such as productivity)

enhancing employee effectivenes
- managing time better
- streamlining organization structure
- increasing span of control and reducing levels of management
- improving morale and motivation

Conserving public money

financial planning and budgeting
- setting financial priorities
- multiyear financial planning
- analysis of risk and uncertainty
- capital budgeting

financial reporting and control
- controlling the budget
- financial reporting and public accountability
- integrated financial management systems

fiscal strategies for cost reduction and revenue enhancement
- improving tax collection
- user charges
- cutback management
- debt management
- cash management

Streamlining operations

operational strategies for cost reduction and service improvement
- improving performance and productivity
- improving work processes, work measurement and work incentives and sanctions
- new technology such as computers and office automation
- customer service orientation and responding to complaints

Table 1 (continued): Doing More With Less
The Managerial Approach to Administrative Reform

improving basic services and development programs
- schools management
- human services (health and welfare)
- public safety (police and fire services)
- managing community service programs

managing support services
- decentralization
- information services and data processing
- buildings management
- vehicles fleet management

Public performance management

measuring public performance
- management by objectives without objectives
- principles of public performance measurement

using performance information
- reduction of constraints
- incentive systems
- improvement projects
- issue analysis and resolution
- management review meetings and an operations cabinet

Implementing public management improvement

creating an agenda and a constituency for effective public management
- diagnostic analysis
- operations analysis
- building a constituency through involvement and accountability

building the capacity for management improvement
- management development
- management education and training
- organizing and staffing operations improvement

Source: Jacob B. Ukeles, *Doing More with Less: Turning Public Management Around*, AMACOM, A Division of American Management Association, New York, 1982.

practices could or should be adopted by public organizations, and that manageri-alistic values should predominate in governmental administration.

The Political Reality

Throughout recent history, it has always been maintained that administrative reform goes beyond managerialism because it is concerned not just with improving organizational performance per se but with improving the performance of the whole public sector in accordance with public objectives. Administrative reform is concerned not just with the organization, administration and management of individual public organizations but the whole operation of government and the overall conduct of the public's business. It is concerned not just with the implementation of public policy but the nature of public leadership and the future shape of the international society. Its scope is far wider than narrow managerialism. Administrative reform is not just how public organizations operate but how governments at all levels function and perform, what they should do and who they should benefit.

In the public sector, political values have always overriden managerial values. Politicians have always intervened in the management of public organizations, sometimes paying attention to the smallest details and they have used administrative reform for purely political purposes, unrelated to managerial considerations. Governments shuffle and reshuffle ministries, for instance, without too much (if any) concern for their organizational, administrative and managerial effects. Indeed, reorganizations like many other administrative reforms are often motivated more by political considerations than by concerns with efficiency and are pursued to disorient public organizations by altering the distribution of power and influence in the governmental system (Preston, 1984). Reorganizations are responses to problems in government and they are political struggles among contending interests. "Fundamental political interests, within the bureaucracy and outside, seek access, representation, control, and policy benefits" (March and Olsen, 1989, 76). They reflect the shifting political influence of interest groups and how people think about government. They are rarely simple technical managerial exercises. Rather, they should be viewed more as political theater, exercises or games in the use or organization of political power, for they rarely result in the outcomes desired by managerialists (Hood and Dunsire, 1981) except perhaps better policy coherence (Lane, 1987, 123). "Changes in administrative structures or procedures can be seen as challenging elements of the core system of meaning, belief, interpretation, status, power, and alliances in politics" (March and Olsen, 1989, 111-112).

Thus, given their essentially political nature, simply because they are introduced in the political arena, administrative reforms to succeed have to conform to the prevailing political culture and gain at least tacit support from prevailing power brokers. Somewhere within every political system there are people who can be described as professional reformers. They also include professional *administrative* reformers often in academia and the public professions. These dedicated administrative reformers develop new proposals on their own and then legitimize them when they can by serving on task forces and study commissions that puzzled governments often find handy when they seek fresh ideas. They serve government as "in and outers" or the trusted "great and good" to advise, recommend and implement reforms. They staff think tanks, policy research institutes, training centers, advisory councils and generally make themselves useful to politicians and power brokers. Such reformers

> often seem uncomfortable with questions of power, preferring to deal with matters such as efficiency, rationality, representation and accountability. It is clear that reformers must consider how their reforms will affect the power of office holders to govern, and to govern effectively. (Pious, 1981, 3)

After all, administrative reform deals with the living constitution and inevitably will impact relations between the government and the governed.

Administrative reform, like other reforms of governance, "attempts to merge the real with the ideal" (Wingo, 1974, 2). At the one end, it deals with very practical matters of everyday public business, even petty details such as the design of forms and the recalculation of salaries. At the other, it deals with assessing government performance and predicting people's expectations of government and the search for the ideal in the affairs of men.

> It is the latter that bestows spiritual vitality, defines practicality, and puts forward images of what is possible, all in a way that distinguishes the step upward – reform – from sideways movements and downward slips. For the true problem of reform is recognizing it. (Ibid, 7)

Reform is not just pointing out the flaws of government practices but "showing how practices subvert, offend, or misrepresent governance principles" (Calista, 1986, 4). Reforms have to conform to the prevailing principles of governance and claim to rescue them from misuse or abuse. They are evolutionary not revolutionary, deliberate not chance happenings, partisan not neutral. Politics limits how far reforms can be taken and because politics cannot be stretched too far, reforms are compromises and invariably incremental and tentative and therefor incomplete.

Today administrative reform is all the things it has always been – visionary, radical, political, risky, contrived, planned, artificial, opposed, time-consuming, problematical, elusive – and more. But unlike the past, it can no longer be viewed as cyclical or episodic. Contemporary government is just too big to be tackled comprehensively at one time. Public organizations are too important to be left to their own devices and they mesh too much with non-public organizations to be treated alone. All organizations – public and non-public – suffer from too many bureaupathologies to be healthy all the time and not needing frequent remedial treatment. Administrative reform is or should now be seen as a continuous activity, institutionalized somewhere within government, professionally staffed, given adequate resources, allowed sufficient time, and politically supported so that reformers do not just spin their wheels but make a real impact on the conduct of public business. To overcome the costs of change and inertia, administrative reform cannot be isolated; it has to involve everyone interested in public affairs and provision has to be made for public contributions. The past thirty years' experience clearly points in this direction. Yesterday's innocence has to give way to tomorrow's sophistication.

References

Bennis, W., *Changing Organizations*, McGraw-Hill, New York, 1966.

Brodkin, E., *The False Promise of Administrative Reform: Implementing Quality Control in Welfare*, Temple University Press, Philadelphia, 1986.

Calista, D. (ed.), *Bureaucratic and Governmental Reform*, JAI Press, Greenwich, CT., 1986.

Campbell, A., "Running Out of Steam?" *Civil Service Journal*, Vol. 18, No. 3, Jan/Mar 1978, p. 5.

Campbell, C., and Peters, G. (eds.), *Organizing Governance, Governing Organizations*, University of Pittsburgh Press, Pittsburgh, 1988.

Drucker, P., "Management and the World's Work', *Harvard Business Review*, Sept-Oct 1988, pp. 65-76.

Garson, D., and Overman, S., *Public Management Research in the United States*, Praeger Publishers, New York, 1983.

Hennessy, P., *Whitehall*, Secker & Warburg, London, 1989.

Henriques, D., *The Machinery of Greed: Public Authority Abuse and What to Do about It*, D.C. Heath & Co., Lexington, MA., 1980.

Holland, S, (ed.), *The State as Entrepreneur*, International Arts and Sciences Press, Inc., White Plains, New York, 1973.

Hood, C., and Dunsire, A., *Bureaumetrics*, Gower, Farnborough, 1981.

Jun, J., and Storm, B. (eds.), *Tomorrow's Organizations*, Scott, Foresman & Co., Glenview, IL., 1973.

Kimmel, W., Dougan, W., and Hall, J., *Municipal Management and Budget Methods: An Evaluation of Policy Related Research*, Urban Institute, Washington, D.C., 1974.

Lane, P. (ed.), *Bureaucracy and Public Choice*, Sage Modern Politics Series, Volume 15, Sage Publications, London, 1987.

March, J.G. and Olsen, J.P. *Rediscovering Institutions: The Organizational Basis of Politics*, Free Press, New York, 1989.

Nellis, J., *Public Enterprises in Sub-Saharan Africa*, The World Bank, Washington, D.C., Discussion Paper 1, 1986.

Nellis, J. and Kikeri, S., "Public Enterprise Reform: Privatization and the World Bank", *World Development*, Vol. 17. No. 5, 1989, pp. 659-672.

Pateman, C., *Participation and Democratic Theory*, Cambridge University Press, Cambridge, 1970.

Pious, R., "Prospects for Reform," in R. M. Pious (ed.), *The Power to Govern: Assessing Reform in the United States*, Proceedings of the Academy of Political Science, Vol. 34, No. 2, The Academy of Political Science, 1981, pp. 1-4.

Preston, M., *The Politics of Bureaucratic Reform: The Case of the California State Employment Service*, University of Illinois Press, Urbana, 1984.

Spiegel, A., "How Outsiders Overhauled a Public Agency," *Harvard Business Review*, Vol. 53, No. 1, Jan-Feb 1975, pp. 116-124.

Ukeles, J., *Doing More With Less; Turning Public Management Around*, AMACOM, New York, 1982.

Wingo, L., "Introduction: The Ideal and the Real in the Reform of Metropolitan Governance," in *Reform as Reorganization*, Resources for the Future, Inc., Washington, D.C., 1974.

World Bank. *World Development Report 1983*, Oxford University Press, New York, 1983.

Yackle, L., *Reform and Regret*, Oxford University Press, New York, 1989.

3. The Way Things Were

In the 1960s, the field of administrative reform was fresh and open. It still appeared relatively new although it could be said to have existed ever since the dim recesses of human history when better ways of organizing social activities had first been conceived. No comprehensive study of the phenomenon had yet been made and there was no agreement on such basics as definition, core, scope and boundaries. Nonetheless, administrative reformers were convinced that their models worked. After all, they had done well during post-war reconstruction and they were invigorated by their successes in the West in democratizing the defeated Axis powers and in the East in imposing Communist Party rule over the administrative state. Cold War rivalry had intensified competition to win over the so-called Third World countries with offers of technical assistance to modernize their administrative systems. Many newly independent states were being helped by the super powers and international agencies to refurbish and overhaul the colonial administrative systems they had inherited and wanted in large part to abandon for something more in keeping with their ambitious national development schemes. On the whole, global conditions were quite favorable to administrative reformers who promised to make government more effective, state administration more efficient, and public management more dynamic, productive and honest.

Administrative reform could be fashioned in many different ways to assist practitioners dabbling along conventional lines in rather hit or miss fashion in their efforts to improve administrative performance. Despite the increasing popularity of the field, not much of lasting value had been preserved on record and many references in the standard literature going as far back as the Code of Hammurabi and the ancient pre-Confucian Chinese empire were being found largely irrelevant and unhelpful in the modern context (Caiden, 1969). Yet the need for reliable guidelines was clear. With the emergence of the organizational society and the increased bureaucratization of human activity, the growing importance of organization, administration and management had been recognized. Systematic research since the beginning of the century had raised expectations that through better means the elusive goals of humanity could be attained quicker or at least much preventable suffering could be alleviated. In complex societies, increased socialization, diversification and fragmentation needed more and more complicated mechanisms of integration and coordination managed by professional administrators, mechanisms that were quite delicate and often subject to breakdown. As almost everyone was on the end of somebody else's administration, no one was immune from administrative deficiencies and shortcomings. Thus nobody could fail to benefit from administrative improvements, particularly in the public sector which had been greatly enlarged and on which so many hopes had been pinned for a better future.

Past experience had already shown that administrative reform was no mere technical exercise of applying simple managerial principles or devising one best way that would suit all organizations, public and private, irrespective of circumstances, purposes, size, resources and operational norms. As far as the public sector was concerned, administrative reform involved tinkering with the machinery of government, it required both political and bureaucratic backing, and success was no mean political feat. Given the scale, it was experimenting in human engineering. To improve public sector performance (indeed, to improve the human condition altogether) change alone was insufficient; it was too slow and unreliable. The pace would have to be accelerated, objectives and priorities determined in advance, favored instruments chosen and empowered, vested interests defeated, resistance overcome, and reforms institutionalized. Administrative reform had to be seen as part of wider social transformation and administrative reform movements had to exhibit the same general characteristics as other social reform movements. Administrative reform would have to be publicly convincing and win general political support. It would have to command resources and respect. It would have to be allowed sufficient time to take effect and continuously monitored and evaluated to ensure that it was achieving intended results. All this was known by the 1960s to administrative reformers who confidently believed that they could meet these preconditions for success.

What administrative reformers in the early 1960s did not anticipate was that they would not be able to proceed at their own pace in their own good time. The world was entering what later was to be recognized as virtually a permanent state of turbulence. The natural pace of change would so accelerate that soon everybody would be suffering from "future shock" as their abilities to accommodate to change would be overtaxed. The reformers had expected some modicum of stability that would allow them to carry out their schemes in comfort. But the world was in too much of a hurry. It would not wait. Nor could the practitioners. Public officials had to deal with the issues of the moment, to get through daily burdens as best they could, and incorporate reforms as they went along. If the proposed reforms did not seem to fit or caused too many problems for them they were likely to be ignored or paid only lip service: rarely would they be implemented.

Administrative reformers tended to overlook the fact that societies were always in flux, being pushed by different forces in different directions; there was always movement that strained prevailing social arrangements. Response always lagged behind social needs and aspirations and was further exaggerated by deliberate resistance to change and stubborn support for the customary, compounded in turn by fear of the unknown and sheer inability to devise appropriate new arrangements in time. Reformers were too often caught in the middle. They were too radical for conservatives but not radical enough for turbulent times, seemingly always a step or two behind. Neither would give reform a fair chance. Conservatives would try to abort reform altogether while turbulence would quickly outdate it. Reform was too much for one, and too little for the other. Reformers were placed in a dilemma. If they were too bold, they would offend conservatives and scare people off. If they were not bold enough they would be overtaken by events and seen as irrelevant. They had to steer a careful path between, something that took judgment, skill and luck. Timing was important too. So was compromise; theirs was the art of achieving the possible without losing sight of ultimate objectives. Reform was a tricky business not lightly undertaken, and reformers needed whatever help they could get, both intellectual and practical.

At the time, social science research had begun to reveal more about how societies, organizations, groups and individuals adjusted to and assimilated change. Closed and open system models had been particularly suggestive, showing how systems preserved themselves, coped with threats, responded to turbulence, transformed themselves, and broke down under excessive strain. Systems seemed extraordinarily versatile and flexible, and to understand why and how systems analysis had benefited much from studies of physical matter, everything from galaxies to cells, from the largest to the smallest systems in the universe. Yet comparatively little research had thrown any light on reform defined as the artificial inducement of change against resistance in human systems. The notable exceptions had been studies of political revolutions, economic crises and development models, particularly induced modernization that sought to speed the development of traditional societies by removing obstacles to their modernization. Here intervention was welcome and reform necessary if societies were to increase their capacity to generate and absorb continuous change and broaden self-sustainable growth. Not surprisingly, the lead in administrative reform was taken by those desirous of speeding the development of underdeveloped or undeveloped or poor countries through reforming elites, the administrative state, public enterprise, developmental bureaucracies and innovative public management. These development administrators and researchers seemed most fired up about the prospects of administrative reform, most keen to experiment, and most respectful of administrative theory.

Administrative Reform and Administrative Theory

Unfortunately the development administrators and researchers eager to transform the public sectors of modernizing states could find little help in administrative theory. Despite a century of impressive progress social science could provide few answers to key questions about the relationship between social and societal reform and administrative reform although they were clearly linked. In contemporary society most societal reforms had administrative implications; they would impinge on government and require adjustments to be made in public administration. Most administrative reforms had societal repercussions too; they changed the nature of the public's business and the way in which it was conducted. Administrative systems, particularly public administration systems, were autonomous or at least semi-autonomous power centers and affected the fate of people even outside their immediate reach and jurisdiction. They were strategically placed to assist or prevent societal reforms. They institutionalized social changes. Their performance and the resources they absorbed profoundly affected the level of goods and services available, their distribution, the quality of life and access to opportunities. In poor countries in particular the administrative state very much performed the role of institutional and social reformer; it was not only expected to remedy social ills but also anticipate social needs. All administrators, but particularly public administrators, were social entrepreneurs and reformers if they took their social responsibilities seriously.

True, for at least a century administrative reform pioneers had left many diagnoses and remedies behind but there was no telling how accurate they had been, what follow up had occurred and whether the resulting reforms had been judged successful. Their own personal recollections of the reform process had largely been fragmentary, selective and doctored for the record. Few had left behind any identifiable trail for researchers to follow and analyze, and related records had since been lost, discarded and scattered. The same successes had been referred to over and over again. But the more abundant failures had been passed over with scarce a comment; embarrassed governments had even tried to suppress any mention. The record was distorted, making it appear that reform had been an inevitable process whereas its path had been uneven at best, strewn with failures and setbacks. At least, the record proved that homo sapiens was a born reformer ever desirous of improving the human condition, alleviating preventable ills and realizing dreams however inept at reform in practice. Mankind could be improved and every improvement could be bettered, providing human resistance to novelty was not underestimated. While such demonstrable assertions were reassuring, they hardly provided any practical guidelines to a new generation of aspiring administrative reformers

Much exaggeration about the potential benefits of administrative reform had arisen from the failure to distinguish administrative change from administrative reform and to attribute improvements in public administration to both under the rubric of reform. Thus, theorists who sought to identify the essence of administration, that is its unchanging elements taken from one state to another by the changing elements, saw change taking place in well-organized steps, in a mechanical, formal, planned fashion. They made administration appear at least on the surface more smooth working than it really was. Other theorists did see administration as ever-changing but often appearing stable because of a balance among variables although the system was in ferment all the time. In administrative systems, administrators coped as best they could with constantly changing forces. More important, administrators were change agents who incessantly strove to overcome the forces of resistance and inertia to achieve improved performance. Change could be distinguished from reform by discerning deliberately induced or contrived transformations of administrative systems which successfully overcame inertia and resistance. To reveal the nature of administrative reform, there had to be a switch from the static analysis of abstract principles and formulas to a study of the dynamics of whole administrative systems and how they adapted to their changing environment, particularly who or what was responsible for overcoming the forces that made for entropy. When the switch occurred in the 1950s and 1960s, the rewards for administrative reformers were immediate.

Meantime, with the general acceptance of the idea of progress, reform had become respectable and desirable, particularly after manmade disasters. Especially sought had been reforms, including strictly *administrative* reforms, that altered collective purposes and goals, changed the mix of resources, transformed attitudes and methods, improved standards and relationships, sped decisions, and achieved higher levels of economy, productivity, efficiency and effectiveness. As long as human arrangements were imperfect, so administrative reform would be in universal demand. Much depended on whether people settled for the ideal or the optimal or the satisfying. Administrative theory had opted for the highest attainable practice or the optimal rather than the unattainable ideal or complacent norms. Indeed, administrative theory and practice urged all administrators to be proactive and generate their own improvements and reforms. They should not wait to implement reforms only after failures had occurred as the satisficers did. Rather, they should seek to emulate the idealists who advocated reforms until their vision of administrative perfection came within reach. Administrators had an obligation to improve the state-of-the-art not just to keep out of trouble.

Accordingly, administrative sciences have had a decided reformist if not utopian bent ever since. Administrative theory could hardly deny that administrative reform was subjective in nature. Reformers assumed that their reforms would be improvements on the status quo and that the anticipated outcomes would be worth the struggle. Their assumptions could not be proved beforehand nor precisely calculated. Accepting that reform could never be an exact science, administrators and theorists alike were encouraged to seek ways and means to improve administrative performance and to provide the intellectual and organizational leadership needed to bring about accelerated progress. In fact, much administrative theory has been developed by reformers seeking an intellectual base for their practical remedies for governmental deficiencies and administrative defects. For instance, Woodrow Wilson, considered one of the pioneers of the discipline of American public administration, had believed that the whole purpose of studying administration was to improve administrative arrangements and practices. Social scientists, he thought, could analyze human phenomena with detachment and still have reform at heart. Many other administrative theorists had thought the same. Indeed, the reform tradition in administrative study has been so strong that its progressive values have been unconsciously imbibed. For this reason it has never been accorded the same academic status as other studies deemed to be truly scientific, objective, impartial, impersonal and detached.

This subjectivity of administrative reform unfortunately did make it prey to fashions, fads, and fancies. Inexplicably, certain reforms would suddenly catch on as universal panaceas only to fall just as quickly from grace to be replaced by others. The history of administrative reform has been littered with such episodes. Furthermore, whenever the situation was desperate enough, even cranks got a hearing, though rarely anything further. Irrespective of their origins, all reforms seemed to go through a similar cycle. They began with a radical reputation, then gained respectability and ended up either institutionalized or discredited and discarded (although these may have been subsequently rediscovered and revived). It seemed that as long as people sought to reduce maladministration, they would search for help and inspiration from any promising source (including administrative theory), extract what they wanted, and try repeatedly to implement reforms. Reformers might rest or even hide; they never gave up. Somewhere, however obscure, they would be found assaulting inertia, ignorance and incompetence.

Social Change and Administrative Reform

Although social change and administrative reform were closely linked, administrative reform was not desired so much for itself, as for its contribution to improving the general human condition. In the totality of social change, it was minor compared with technological invention, migration patterns, population changes and acculturation but a major factor in the adaptation of the organization society to ceaseless change. As scientists had just confirmed, change was part of the ceaseless movement of the universe even if not all of it could be explained. The idea of system, for example, had enabled scientists to comprehend the unity of the universe and the mechanics of universal change. The study of systems revealed how systems perpetuated themselves, adjusted to changing circumstances, and dealt with uncertainty and crisis. The analogy of systems could be applied to social and administrative arrangements. It provided useful pointers to their dynamics, the processes of maintenance and adaptation, the management of change and the absorption of innovation. Absorption without resistance could be considered change while absorption with resistance was reform. Thus administrative reform could not occur by default, only by deliberate facilitation.

How systems changed in time could be explained by models of their development or their life cycles. As change was assumed to be inherent and inevitable, systems passed through identifiable stages from birth to death. Studies of how systems developed should eventually reveal ways of speeding up or slowing down the development process and identifying the key variables at each stage. Confirmation was sought in induced modernization currently being applied in Third World countries. The idea was to accelerate the development of traditional societies and reduce the obstacles to their modernization. Modernity was held to consist of those features or characteristics of advanced (or developed or modernized) societies to which backward (or less developed or developing or traditional) societies aspired. Intervention was unavoidable if the process of development was to be speeded up and some stages actually omitted altogether. Particularly sought after was the capacity of the more advanced societies to generate and absorb continuous change and by maintaining uninterrupted growth allow the continuous expansion of human endeavors. Among the presumed benefits of modernization or development were the administrative state, the bureaucratization of social organizations, professionalization and managerialism. Clearly administrative reform had a key role in social change and development.

In modernized administration, everything changed and adjusted to cease-less change. So habitual was change that only unusual delays or denials of change attracted attention. Given natural conservatism, resistance to change was to be expected and anyway indispensable for stability. If people changed whenever something different appeared there would be chaos. They were more selective and cautious and usually had good reasons for hesitating. Once delay or denial occurred, tension would be generated, normal cooperation would be questioned and later withdrawn, and resistance would build. Usually persuasion, habitual deference and light sanctions were sufficient to overcome resistance though if it were particularly virulent, coercion might have to be used. Since the need for administrative reform arose from the malfunctioning of the natural process of change, administrative reform could be defined as *the artificial inducement of administrative transformation against resistance*. It was deliberate, contrived, irreversible and innovative. Three features – moral purpose (betterment, progress), artificial transformation and administrative resistance – made it distinctive. To succeed, opposition had to be overcome and to overcome resistance reformers had to demonstrate moral strength, energy, tenacity, organizing ability, and political skills. Unfortunately, too often the success of reform has been measured by the personal qualities, intentions, plans, support and progress reports of the reformers not by their actual achievements overcoming inertia and resistance and in demonstrably improving administrative performance. Achieving success is much more difficult than claiming success.

Perspectives on Administrative Reform

If administrative theories and social change theories had been a disappointment to guiding administrative reformers to successful intervention and implementation, perhaps something more practical could be learned from case studies of past reforms. Presumably, case studies would illustrate the richness of administrative reform and might reveal lessons that could possibly be combined into a general theory of reform or some generalized guidelines. Four case studies did indeed point to some lasting generalizations.

(a) The premodern bureaucratic empires brought out different class attitudes toward administrative reform (Eisenstadt, 1963). Rulers always backed reforms that would strengthen them and their control of government, but treated other reforms with great suspicion. The aristocracy had invariably sought to evade government interference, capture strategic public offices and corrupt administrative systems for their own advantage. The gentry and the urban literate welcomed the employment opportunities provided for them in the public sector generated by the government and, providing their special interests were protected, gave loyal service to rulers. In contrast, the peasantry, the bearers of the heaviest financial and military burdens, resented officialdom and actually benefited from maladministration, although they backed reforms that diminished arbitrariness and cruelty. The clergy, militia, professionals, and intelligentsia could go either way on governmental and administrative reform according to the dictates of self-interest as could the bureaucracy itself. Overall, reforms aimed at more effective administration, more equitable distribution of public goods and services, greater access to public employment, and professionalism, objectives still sought in administrative reform to this day. Reform was rarely self-evident; it had to be publicly articulated. Reformers were usually divided and often fell well short of their goals even when united. Failure was most likely where dictatorship prevailed and the bureaucracy lacked any service orientation. In strengthening administrative performance and bureaucratic power, reformers tended to diminish civil liberty and hitch education to bureaucratic needs. The lesson to be drawn was that administrative reformers had to be acutely aware of prevailing class attitudes and realize that perceived class self-interest would largely determine the line up of opposing forces. The chances of reform would depend on the distribution of power pro and con specific measures.

(b) The precontemporary Western bureaucratic states illustrated different strategic approaches in transforming absolute monarchy into representative, responsible government through bureaucratization and professionalization. Before the French Revolution, most reforms had been adopted to strengthen the monarchy when threatened by popular revolt or endangered by military defeat and invasion. All monarchies had reshaped their civil administration according to successful military organization. Immediately after the French Revolution, France had captured world attention when it had transformed the shaky apparatus of the *ancien regime* into an efficient instrument of public policy by way of the ideological and institutional changes that had been advocated by the revolutionaries and the practical organizational and legal reforms that had been implemented by Napoleon. Henceforth, in a military-like chain of command, public laws were to be impartially executed by publicly accountable, competent public servants in the furtherance of the general or public interest. Eventually, this became the credo of the modern administrative state. Meantime, other European countries had emulated France. Similar reforms had been imposed from above and institutionalized without necessarily incorporating the ideological underpinnings of the French Revolution. Where concessions had not been made to liberty, the reforms had made regimes even more repressive, domineering, rigid and corrupt until revolutionary ferment from below had forced concessions from above.

So long as the country succeeded in industry, trade and war, the British had continued to rely on amateurism and muddling through in public administration after bureaucratization and professionalization had taken place throughout continental Europe. As invasion and revolution had not been seriously envisioned, the British were more complacent about the need for a strong centralized administrative state. Their worst administrative deficiencies had been removed by some energetic administrative entrepreneurs to forestall more radical measures as administrative reform had followed closely behind societal reform accompanying the Industrial Revolution. In Great Britain, administrative reforms had been incremental measures, the minimum necessary to meet specific circumstances and the maximum acceptable to the Whitehall Establishment.

At least, the Americans had had the advantage of learning from British experience and at federal level starting off with a clean sheet designed for local conditions. After Jacksonian democracy, nothing had seemed to shake off amateurism and muddling through until the exploitation of public office had reached intolerable kleptocracy. Then wholesale reforms had been demanded – to take partisan politics out of public administration and public administration out of partisan politics, to cleanse government, and to apply the new American science of management to the public sector.

Clearly, administrative reform, being related to specific cultural environments, was not universally applicable and was an accompaniment to wider social changes taking place to avoid institutional rigidity that detracted from social betterment. To manage the public's business without resort to reform indicated a high tolerance for public maladministration and/or a remarkable capacity to absorb change through improvisation and loyal public service. No modern state could expect to progress without periodic bursts of reform to update public administration and increase government capacity to respond to changing public demands. Public bureaucracies rarely transformed themselves without external pressure and intervention.

(c) The newly independent states would obviously require preparation, wholesale institutional transformation and administrative cultures different from colonial administration. All would have initially to embark on comprehensive reform programs. The international community planned accordingly. Manuals were prepared and technical assistance readied, even though there had been little previous reform experience in these emerging states and independence would be taking place in most difficult circumstances. In fact, prevailing conditions were so uninviting that some new states just continued with their inherited administrative systems virtually unchanged while others improvised as best they could, going their own peculiar way regardless. But the majority did embark on ambitious reforms with considerable outside help. In any event, they were to attempt too much too quickly and fall victim to their own lack of administrative capability. There was insufficient political backing, social stability, discipline and restraint, resources and research. Colonial bureaucracies, where they had not already been dismantled, proved strong and resistant. Initial reform optimism evaporated when confronted with the realities. Disillusion set in. Whatever was tried, nothing seemed to make much difference; administrative performance did not improve, but deteriorated. Clearly, administrative deficiencies would continue to be a drag on national development. Reformers would have to keep trying their best for there were few alternatives for poor countries dependent so much on public sector performance.

(d) Automation showed how administrative reform was timeless, being related to social change, not least accelerating technology. Automation had direct impact on work, employment, organization and management and eventually it would affect all aspects of administration. Choices would have to be made between its technical advantages and its social dislocation. Thinking about the likely implications of automation should expose administrative deficiencies otherwise overlooked and reveal a growing need for properly coordinated information that could aid in successful prediction and advanced planning. Here was an area in which administrative reforms could be anticipated, planned and implemented in advance. In the absence of strategic planning, untold damage would be done and much unnecessary suffering occur. It was better to plan ahead than await the inevitable disasters that would occur by waiting and seeing, too late to act in time.

These cases seemed to indicate that certain generalizations about administrative reform could be drawn. Undoubtedly administrative reform was always controversial and problematic. The outcomes could never be accurately calculated and often they did not live up to expectations. Class and culture were important variables and to some extent the line up of forces pro and con could be anticipated at least in respect to specific reforms. The inertia and resistance in administrative systems was so great that reformers had to think in terms not of years but generations. Yet persistence would eventually pay off and reformed administrative systems were usually quite a cut above what had previously existed. In terms of social benefits, reforms were good investments. If these conclusions were hardly profound, they indicated that the common process of reform could profitably be examined in greater detail.

The Process of Administrative Reform

The case studies showed that administrative reforms followed a similar path or rather a series of distinct stages from conception to institutionalization or abandonment or eventual supersession. Their identifiable beginnings could be traced right back to a sense of wrong and awareness for remedial action or a flash of inspiration and vision of something better than existing outcomes and practices. To those who knew no better or had grown so accustomed to prevailing arrangements that they no longer recognized their shortcomings and deficiencies for what they really were or welcomed a quiet life to the upheavals, trials and tribulations of change, the very idea of reform would not occur and if it were to arise, it would be instinctively opposed. Reform ideas would occur only to the exceptionally gifted, rare in any society, capable of conceiving something superior, and the dissatisfied, the unhappy, the disgruntled, the aggrieved, the alienated, much more populous, prepared to articulate their complaints and demand better performance. Both sets perceived gaps between what was done and what could or should be done. Both sets could identify where administrative systems were obviously falling down on the job, incapable of doing more than they were doing let alone capable of taking on additional tasks, unable to anticipate let alone meet additional demands, and lax in adopting more effective methods. Since few administrative systems ever came up to such high standards, so virtually any system was capable of being improved and therefore reformed. But toleration of maladministration was generally high. On the whole, people put up with its inconvenience unless strangers, i.e. outsiders (who were different) heightened their awareness or the sufferings became too widespread or too intolerable whereupon people would start complaining first to themselves and then to anybody who might listen and respond. Growing public discontent and internal dissent made for greater receptivity to reform proposals.

But complaining was easier than the next step of diagnosing what was wrong and needed fixing which in turn was easier than the step after that of devising appropriate remedies. There was a natural tendency to look around and see what others in similar circumstances were doing. If they were doing better, it was easier to copy or imitate what they were doing rather than invent something new or more suitable. Even so, excuses could always be found to reject doing anything different and to create doubts whether foreign practices were desirable or transferable or workable in different circumstances. To overcome initial resistance, all reform proposals, however innocuous, required committed advocates wiling to persist and generate momentum for change, and the more complex and radical their reform proposals, the harder it was to convince the inexpert who usually preferred simple solutions. Reforms were more likely to be acceptable when tailored specifically to local conditions, implemented through existing channels and open to participation and modification by those most involved. As initial steps tended to be judged more critically than later steps, mistakes at the very outset could kill reform there and then. Reformers had to be ready and well prepared for any eventualities that might occur at this crucial stage to counteract expected opposition and take advantage of unexpected openings. While it was useful to resort to simple slogans and general catchwords, reformers should avoid subterfuge as usually deception was self-destructive when exposed.

Among the many factors making for success in gaining support and smoothing the way to implementation, the most important appeared to be the scope of reforms, the source of their support and the selected channels for implementation. The variations and combinations were many though certain universals seemed to stand out. (a) In the case of administrative reforms proposed by revolutionaries, firm political backing at the top was obviously indispensable as it probably was for all reforms, but especially those imposed from above. Often resistance mounted by vested interests and interlocking elites was underestimated but resort to fear and intimidation to reduce opposition would just as often backfire. Reform would obviously benefit from the ineffectiveness and discrediting of the previous regime and any compelling crises in the transition as it would from the direct linkages between the promised societal transformation and remodelled administrative systems. (b) Shock tactics to overcome bureaucratic inertia and organizational rigidity demonstrated the danger of going too far, too quickly and alienating the targets of reform. Instead of reforming the administration, the whole organization might unravel. (c) Legally imposed reforms showed the advantages of using law as a reform instrument but they also pointed to the technical difficulties (of drafting, promulgation and amendment) involved and the contradictions that often arose between intent and substance. They also warned that changing formalities was insufficient unless people's attitudes and behavior were changed too. In any event, the most difficult and hazardous of stages in the reform process was implementation. Throughout, reformers had to keep stressing the benefits of their reforms, to generate general confidence in their proposals, to exploit all available avenues of influence, and to master the political arts. The whole process was a costly gamble. Failure at any stage could set back the cause of reform for an appreciable time and make the next round harder.

Implementation was not the last step in the reform process. That was evaluation, proving that a prominent improvement in administrative reform had really taken place. Here, measurement was fraught with methodological difficulties. The performance of administrative systems was always hard to measure let alone the difference that might be attributable to reform which was only one contributor to change and not necessarily the most important. In the process of reform many alterations and compromises have to be made so that the end product or outcome may be quite different from that envisaged in the initial reform proposal. Long time lags occurred before reforms took full effect, sometimes as much as three generations of administrators. After the event rarely could all the facts be assembled and too many accounts relied too heavily on incomplete formal records and the prejudiced recollections of the participants. No doubt by this time other reforms had taken place to further confuse the situation. Nonetheless, the reform process should only be seen as being completed with some attempt at evaluation.

Obstacles to Administrative Reform

Administrative reform could not be abstracted from the multitude of events that criss-crossed it. A checklist of all factors that had to be taken into account would cover every aspect of human ecology. Nonetheless, certain obstacles seemed universal – intense social conflict, lack of resources, technology and enterprise, and high tolerance for maladministration. Where these prevailed, administrative reform was unlikely to succeed. Other obstacles that impeded reform undertakings included the following:

geographical: isolation, physical barriers, size of country, scattered settlement, poor communications, debilitating climate, low mobility;

historical: colonial legacy, biculturalism, traditionalism, inertia, past reform failures;

cultural: diversity, linguistic barriers, indiscipline, tribalism, religious fundamentalism, corruption, immobilism (or paralysis of public will);

economic: scarcity, monopoly, low savings and investments, lack of incentives, poor labor-management relations, low managerial skills, bureaucratism;

political: lack of consensus, rigid constitutional arrangements, weak and divided governments, insecure officials, entrenched bureaucracies, high turnover, personality clashes.

Wherever any combination of these obstacles existed, administrative reform was unlikely to succeed. Even when circumstances seemed more favorable, reform proposals could easily be upset. Many reforms failed due to circumstances beyond the control of the reformers. On the other hand, some reforms succeeded even in unpromising circumstances thanks to the skills of the reformers and even sheer luck. Fortunately, modern societies have come to appreciate their trailblazers to whose persistence against odds all have been indebted. If they had adjusted to the world as they found it instead of challenging it, they would never have changed it. Reformers had to be different, deviant (in a sociological sense), self-motivated, and exceptional to succeed, epitomized by Florence Nightingale's tussles with Whitehall (Woodham-Smith, 1955).

The Quintessence of Administrative Reform

Thus in the 1960s the prerequisites for a theory of administrative reform already existed. Further progress was being blocked by deficiencies in the study of administrative dynamics, lack of agreement over definition, incomplete evidence, major methodological difficulties, and the taboo that seemed to surround reform failures. Nonetheless there was growing consensus in the reform community (that is among those professionally engaged in reform schemes and academics studying reform as a distinct phenomenon within public administration) that reform could be studied in an orderly and systematic fashion, that its complicated nature could be unraveled, and that theories about it could be formulated and tested, although they would need to be placed in a larger framework of administrative dynamics and social change. What was most urgently required was an integrative framework that would cover the manipulative variables influencing the direction, tempo and quality of reforms, the costs of reforms, and reliable bases for diagnosis, formulation, implementation and evaluation. Ideally, it might be possible one day to program a computer into which all available administrative data could be fed and appropriate reform proposals would be printed out at the other end.

Meantime, it was possible to make a science out of administrative reform. Enough was already known to which further knowledge could be applied. Administrative reform refuted the notion that human society was governed by any hidden hand. What had been devised by humans could be altered by human intervention. It was concrete expression of mankind's desire to determine its own destiny. Administrators on their own initiative could devise their own improvements. True, to realize their proposals, they would have to exercise power (or influence those who did) and ultimately people's attitudes would have to be changed sufficiently to transform the prevailing administrative culture, but essentially administrative reform was no less than the application of the compelling idea of progress to a particularly conservative or slow changing area of human activity. Its importance had long been confirmed by historical evidence and contemporary research revealed it to be concrete, visible, frequent and deliberate, indispensable in keeping public administration in line with other social developments.

In essence, administrative reform was normative; in the search for social betterment, it repaid handsomely if done well. Reformers were idealists and utopians at heart, dismayed at what existed but ever hopeful of improvement. They didn't seek to overthrow the established order – as did revolutionaries – but to change it selectively, cautiously, experimentally, and pragmatically. They did not chase after unattainable perfection only improvements on the status quo, for which there was always room for more. Even when they failed, they sowed the seeds that awaited more favorable circumstances to germinate. They were truly inventive and responsible adventurers in the art of the possible.

This was all very well, but public administrators in the 1960s (as now) were realists, pragmatists; they dealt with the world as it was not as they would have liked it to be. They wanted more than exhortations to do better, untested ideas on improving performance, lists of questions they could neither fathom or answer, and nebulous advice that they "should combine in some measure the wisdom and sense of perspective of the historian and the penetrating acumen of the scientific observer, while putting into practice the skills and arts of appropriate and resolute action" (Bennis, Benne & Chin, 1961, 187). They wanted working maxims more on the lines of that first-rate administrative strategist, J.S. Mill:

> As a Secretary conducting political correspondence I could not issue an order or express an opinion without satisfying various persons very unlike myself that the thing was fit to be done. I was thus in a good position for finding out by practice the mode of putting a thought which gives it easiest admittance into minds not prepared for it by habit; while I became practically conversant with the difficulties of moving bodies of men, the necessities of compromise, the art of sacrificing the non-essential to preserve the essential. I learnt how to obtain the best I could, when I could not obtain everything, instead of being indignant or dispirited because I could not have entirely my own way, to be pleased and encouraged when I could have the smallest part of it; and when that could not be, to bear with complete equanimity being overruled altogether. (Krishnamachari, 1963, vi)

If they carefully combed the literature, they could find many operational principles (Mosher, 1967, 493; Caiden, 1969, 203). More were soon to be available (Backoff, 1974), demonstrating the crucial role of academic research in synthesizing practical wisdom, as long as everyone understood that the study of administrative reform conferred no expertise or relevant competence in reform work. The needs of administrative systems would continue to take precedence over the needs of their study, but further study might well

> quicken that sense of social inventiveness and responsibility which makes change not a burden but an adventure in the art of government and mutual adaptation in free societies. (Meynaud, 1963, 58)

Looking Ahead

Such was the state-of-the-art in the 1960s. All seemed much more straightforward than it really was. In their enthusiasm to ply their trade and sell their wares, reformers were convinced that the world would only benefit. Reforms had worked in the past. They appeared to be working in the present, or so everybody said. There was a great deal of administrative wrongdoing that could be put right if only reform were given a fair chance. Administrative theory had thrown up some pretty good pointers and the administrative sciences seemed to have the right tools in hand. Around the world, reformers had gained experience or were gaining experience and they did not lack for customers. Never mind that backstage they were divided over every issue and could rarely agree on fundamentals, that the administrative theories they relied on were already becoming outdated like their favorite instruments, that the rapidly changing world scene would confound their rather simplistic, set formulae, and that their diagnostic skills were not yet good enough to pinpoint with sufficient accuracy exactly what ailed administrative systems or which of their medicines were remedial not pure snake oil. The need for reform was so apparent by then that they glossed over these matters. Practice would make perfect.

But there were enough clouds on the horizon to warn administrative reformers to proceed with extreme caution. The heady successes in the West of democratizing postwar Japan and West Germany had not been repeated elsewhere. Communism had not raised productivity or reduced the administrative state. Many newly independent states had not been adequately prepared to manage their own affairs. Already, the performance of international organizations was disappointing. Perhaps the blame was largely political but not all of it. A booming global economy was lulling administrators into a false sense of security and dulling them to the requirements of administrative modernization. Reformers themselves were worried about the continuing bureaucratization of the world, where that was leading to and what part they played in fostering bureaucracy. They also realized that they were in a kind of treadmill: the more they worked at reform, the more their eyes were opened up to the need for more reform and the more questions they answered, the more they were leaving unanswered. They could not wait to see what the 1970s would bring. Whatever the coming decade had in store, they were sure it would bring greater action and greater recognition for administrative reform.

References

Backoff, R., "Optimizing Administrative Reform for Improved Governmental Performance", *Administration and Society*, Vol. 6, No.1, 1974, pp. 73-106.

Bennis, W, Benne, K., & Chin, R. (eds.), *The Planning of Change*, Holt, Rinehart and Winston, New York, 1961.

Caiden, G., *Administrative Reform*, Aldine, Chicago, 1969.

Eisenstadt, S.N., *The Political Systems of Empires*, Free Press, New York, 1963.

Krishnamachari, V., Forward to Special Number on Administrative Reforms Since Independence, *Indian Journal of Public Administration*, Vol. 9, No. 3, July-Sept 1963, vi.

Meynaud, J. (ed.), *Social Change and Economic Development*, U.N.E.S.C.O., Paris, 1963.

Mosher, F., *Governmental Reorganizations*, Bobbs-Merrill Co., Indianapolis, IN, 1967.

Woodham-Smith, C., *Florence Nightingale*, Penguin Books, Harmondsworth, 1955.

4. The Unrewarding Search for Communality

That administrative reform became prominent in the 1960s was no accident. The world of administration that could previously assume a certain sense of stability, that had coped with some of the most stressful events in human history, that was mastering crisis after crisis to reconstruct the international order after a devastating world war, was itself shaken by the unexpected. Its own offspring turned on it; the next generation rebelled against the establishment (established order, inherited institutional arrangements, orthodoxy, prevailing norms); and the establishment (established authorities) did not have good enough answers for it. Violent suppression of dissent would only widen the gap between the generations. The establishment had to rethink its own orthodoxy and come to terms with radicalism. Reform was the order of the day: bow to the inevitable, head off worse dislocation, and incorporate the best or most reconcilable of dissenters. In short, acknowledge that the world was changing fast and that the administrative state would have to change with it. Public administration would have to innovate, experiment and reform itself if it was to head off worse trouble when the offspring of the radicals would come of age in the late 1980s.

One of the few assumptions of the old administrative order that still held was the inevitability of bureaucratization and professionalization. The previous generation had embraced bureaucracy as the dominant form of social organization. It had also accepted forward planning as essential for all large organizations. But the new generation was becoming disillusioned with the Weberian *legal-rational* bureaucracy which no longer suited the times. Research was proving the Weberian model to be a mixed blessing and was reformulating it into the *rational-productivity* bureaucracy with emphasis more on expertise, action and results than position, form and procedures, more on a new breed of scientific, humanistic, proactive managers than the traditional, neutral reactive bureaucrats. There was flight from the abstract, static principles of the unproven managerial myths and contradictory proverbs of the past and an urge to reformulate administration on a more scientific, empirical, behavioral, dynamic basis geared to the real world.

The New Managerial Ethos

The real world now moved at a faster pace and was increasingly more complex and complicated. In the new turbulent global society, administration and management had become more important; getting things done properly and effectively, particularly new things and on a larger scale, had become harder. Big business was coming into its own as never before. It wanted results. Its aim was to improve performance: in profitability, productivity, market share, capital return, organization growth and in whatever other ways success was measured. It wanted managers who could get results, knew how to improve performance, made the right (or better) decisions, employed the latest scientific knowledge and techniques, reshaped organizations, overhauled procedures, streamlined operations, redesigned whole industries, and reformulated principles and processes to get into the future quicker.

Booming big business could afford business management education, training and research which pushed the new managerialism, the newly discovered techniques of game theory, management by objectives (M.B.O.), organization development (O.D.) and other alphabeticals that soon were to become managerial folklore, and the new fashionable concepts of the organization man, organizational health, planned change, organizational renewal, organizational diagnosis, self-analysis, and administrative innovation. Whenever something improved business performance, it was incorporated into practice and institutionalized as part of the new managerial ethos.

While big business strengthened itself through innovation, reform and revitalization, the new international superstructure established to deal with global problems, such as war, poverty, disease, illiteracy, malnutrition, genocide and racism, was trying to make an impact by helping those unable to help themselves. It was doing its best to prevent many newly independent states from sinking and to accelerate the development of poor countries. Specifically, the United Nations Public Administration Division (U.N.P.A.D.), the technical assistance missions of the three Western members of the U.N. Security Council (the United States, the United Kingdom and France) and the Ford Foundation had embarked on elaborate programs of administrative modernization in the Third World. These involved the replacement of expatriate administrators, the establishment of training in administration and management, long range institution building, the application of sound managerial concepts, and attitudinal change. They also included adequate organization and staff competence for national development plans, continuous managerial improvement, soundly designed operating systems, professionalized management, effective financial management, efficient organization and effective operations in the public sector. Clearly the new managerial ethos was intended to operate in big government as in big business.

Meantime, without international technical assistance, many countries were undertaking their own elaborate programs of administrative modernization and reform attuned to their own idiosyncracies. They were still wedded to legal-rational bureaucracy. They sought the basic managerial tenets of merit and competence, efficiency and economy, rationality and planning, and bureaucratic responsibility and responsiveness. Besides the better implementation of national plans, they also sought diminution of corruption, nepotism, overcentralization and overstaffing, and to this end established their own permanent organizations to undertake continuous administrative improvement. Many of the ideas and practices of the new managerial ethos entered their public sectors under the rubric of organization and management (O.&M.). International agencies issued guide-books and handbooks on establishing O.&M. services which were seen as prime facilitators of improved public management. This way, management improvement work in government was to be institutionalized. By the end of the 1960s there was hardly any country in which the government "had not established an O.&M. unit or similar institution as an instrument of management improvement" (United Nations, 1979, 1).

An example of what was being done was provided by the establishment of Developmental Management Services Units (D.M.S.U.s) in the Sudan Public Service. Following a United Nations mission which recommended in December 1972 a comprehensive administrative reform program, advisory management services were to be made available to public managers to improve organizational performance and increase public sector productivity. An O.&M. unit had been established in the Treasury twenty years previously but it had been largely ineffective. It had been revived in 1968 with better staff and better technical assistance. With the formation of the Ministry of Public Service and Administrative Reform in 1971, it had been transferred there. The new idea was to involve all public organizations directly in administrative reform instead of relying as previously on commissions and advisory bodies which had been "over-concerned with problems of organizational niceities [sic] and can be generally characterized as patching obsolete structures without considering the continuing adequacy or fitness of the structure and practices to Sudanese needs, capacities and aspirations" (Floate, 1976, 3). With the help of the Royal Institute of Public Administration under the United Kingdom's technical assistance program to Sudan, the Ministry of Public Service and Administrative Reform embarked on the planning, training (in Khartoum and London) and creation of D.M.S.U.s across the public sector in what was hoped would be a more sustained process of administrative improvement and development. D.M.S.U.s included O.&M. and much more in the way of management analysis (work study, A.D.P., O.D., operations research) that would eliminate unnecessary work, simplify work, increase efficiency and effectiveness, and improve the quality of public management in day-to-day operations under the control of line managers. This way, the public sector in the Sudan was to be reformed and revitalized from the inside according to the tenets of the new managerialism.

The limited impact of O.&M. units in administrative modernization was a cause of continuing concern, particularly in Western countries which had been the first to establish them in public administration. They did not touch fundamentals. Public administrators, untrained in the new management ethos, had continued to conduct public business as usual. They had not adopted modern business methods or modernized public business practices. They had ignored increasing public complaints about the bureaupathological tendencies of big government and discounted the humorous parodies of *Parkinson's Law* and *Murphy's Law* and the like which mushroomed in the 1960s and 1970s. In response, several countries had resorted to their traditional administrative reform device of the official inquiry. Among those that sent shock waves around the world of public administration were the Glassco Commission in Canada (1961-3) and the Fulton Committee in the United Kingdom (1966-8). The Glassco Commission was the most businesslike review yet of Canadian federal government administration, much more than commissions in the United States had done in adopting a strictly managerial stance and questioning cherished public administration concepts. But the Fulton Committee had gone on to attack the bedrock of the Westminster model of the civil service, the cult of the generalist administrator, now inadequate and obsolete for the most efficient discharge of government responsibilities, so advised its Management Consultancy Group. Although the Whitehall Establishment was able to ward off the Fulton Committee's challenge, it could not stop a "marked shift to the managerial view of administration," the drawing of analogies between business and public organizations, and the application of common management techniques (Leemans, 1976, 274).

Where big government had taken over big business, such commonality had supposedly been achieved. Leninism-Stalinism in the Soviet Union had created the totalitarian party-state bureaucracy that could indulge at will in social engineering and public management. A new technical intelligentsia had come to administer all public activities and to be measured by its results, its achievements, in the overfulfillment of planning targets. But without freedom of action, it had to devise ruses and subterfuges to conceal administrative deficiencies and to connive in evasion and corruption. Stalin's death had eased things and some reevaluation was permissible. At last, thorough-going reforms were contemplatable to overhaul a topheavy, cumbrous administrative system, to tackle institutionalized bureaupathology and to allow public managers greater freedom to manage. Khrushchev decentralized and devolved important administrative functions, dissolved planning agencies and enlarged the decision-making prerogatives of managers. He undertook major reorganizations in industry and agriculture "to push the experts and the specialists into the production process and to bring his administrators nearer to factory and farms" (LaPalombara, 1963,

259). Though the party-state bureaucracy resisted, continued scandals drew public attention to grave administrative deficiencies and pointed to the need for drastic reforms. By the late 1960s other East Bloc countries had come to the same realization but the Soviet Union prevented them from departing too far from its model. In China which had managed to depart, the Cultural Revolution set generations apart in violent confrontation and brought Mao's path into question. Not even there could the need for drastic administrative reform and improvement be denied as demanded by the logic of modernization and the results of the new managerial ethos.

The Transnational Inducement of Administrative Reform

These different reform impulses around the globe were separate. Each set of reformers had its own agenda. Few believed that much help could be gained from copying what anyone else was doing although they knew what others were about. They did borrow proposals and share information but usually kept their distance. The notable exception were the consultants and contractors for the U.N.P.A.D. and the United States Agency for International Development's (U.S.A.I.D.'s) International Cooperation Administration, mostly located in North America, many of whom had known one another from service in World War II and met frequently together formally at briefings and informally at various professional and academic gatherings. They shared common goals: the promotion of Western ideals, the modernization of the Third World and the improvement of Third World administrative systems. So it was natural for them to collaborate.

Their first attempt at collaboration on the subject of administrative reform arose out of a series of conferences organized by the Committee on Comparative Politics (C.C.P.) of the Social Science Research Council (S.S.R.C.) on the problems of modernization and democratization in developing countries sponsored by the Ford Foundation. Early in 1962 at Stanford University where the topic was "Bureaucracy and Political Development", the participants complained that too much attention had been paid to social and economic change, to the neglect of political change and the critical role of the public sector in national development. There were criticisms of transnational programs to improve administrative performance, particularly those that imposed the Weberian legal-rational model and American public management concepts on developing countries, that underestimated the survival power and capacity of traditional administrative systems, that ignored the political role of the public bureaucracy in stabilizing and integrating new states, and that improved administrative development at the cost of democratic political development by reinforcing already overpowering bureaucracies and overstressing planned, managed, publicly initiated economic development. For at least a generation, there would be a dearth of administrative talent that would continue to handicap development. If the bureaucracy did not restrain itself and reduce unfulfillable public demands, the political balance might be tipped permanently in favor of bureaucratic elites and military domination. Most reforms had already overcentralized administration and diminished the little creativity and innovation there had been. Further bureaucratic reform would have little impact on improving conditions for development.

This sobering analysis of transnational inducement of administrative reform was reinforced at another seminar held in mid-1963, organized this time by the Comparative Administration Group (C.A.G.) of the American Society for Public Administration (A.S.P.A.) on the topic of the relationship between administrative concepts and their sociopolitical context. Besides the general administrative reform programs, public bureaucracies in developing countries had been reshaped by new programs in public sector services. Recipient countries had realized that ostensibly neutral matters of means carried with them Western ideas at odds with national objectives. They had used the forms only to improve limited, technical operations (management) readily assimilable without fundamental changes (administrative reform). Adapting reform to indigenous needs had merely resulted in the adjustment of techniques at the periphery. Western approaches should be more concerned with ideology and thorough going societal changes not just management. Specifically, American efforts should in future encourage democratic, private and local government institutions and progress toward the rule of law, freedom of expression, and individual freedom, initiative and private enterprise.

In 1966 the Foreign Assistance Act was amended in this direction under *Title IX Utilization of Democratic Institutions in Development*. Its implications were discussed at several conferences, including a joint conference of A.S.P.A.'s Comparative Administration Group and S.S.R.C.'s Committee on Comparative Politics at Bellagio, Italy in July 1967 to explore the theoretical issues of the transnational inducement of administrative improvement, this time including multinational experience in administrative development (development of administrative capacity) and development administration (administration of national development plans and programs). Again it was emphasized that administrative improvement should not be pushed for its own sake, rather it should be wedded to the specific needs of each country in development administration. Unless reconciled with local ecology, universal formulae of administrative reform based on Western concepts were unlikely to work. Transnational efforts should aim to strengthen as many institutions, sectors and structures as possible, balance the power of bureaucracy with other institutional restraints, and transform instrumental bureaucratic management into institutional political leadership. Administrative reform was not just about management processes but also about political purposes and interactions directed at changing the behavior of the public bureaucracy. Its aims, sources, threats, impacts and benefits would differ according to the nature of the polity and bureaucratic power, bureaucratic perceptions and adaptability, and the specificity of bureaucratic annoyances. Case studies would demonstrate such profound differences in administrative cultures that would not permit the easy transnational inducement of administrative improvement and reform.

This prediction was substantiated at the Fifth General Assembly of the Eastern Regional Organization for Public Administration (E.R.O.P.A.) held in July 1968 in a seminar on "Administrative Reform and Innovations" which concluded that foreign management concepts, techniques and approaches had provided little assistance for development and development administration in South East Asia. Administrative reform had been good only on paper or had failed to measure up to expectations. There had to be more realistic consideration of the ecological and behavioral aspects of administrative reform which was not "simply a matter of management engineering, of applying O.&M. techniques" or ensuring economic and efficient management merely for system maintenance rather than "the pursuit of new developmental goals" (Lee and Samonte, 1970, 292).

> Administrative reform should encourage changes in the pattern of administrative behavior and decisionmaking that will stimulate greater initiative, discrimination, adaptability, and, above all, creativity and innovation. (Ibid, 294)

To this end, Asian governments had broadened participation in reform processes and sought wide based support, had relied more on local expertise than foreign consultants, and had introduced islands of excellence or innovational enclaves to serve as a vanguard of administrative modernization. To break with imposed Westernization, administrative reform should be redefined as "efforts to apply new ideas to administrative systems with a conscious view to improving the system for positive goals of national development" (Ibid, 7). Reform had a distinctive value dimension or remedial urge focused on the public sector. Each country would have to decide for itself what it wanted to achieve and how, relying on its own resources to blend the old with the new. To overcome obstacles to administrative modernization, changes would have to be made in its administrative culture well beyond the application of Western managerial concepts and techniques.

Enhancing Administrative Capabilities

The focus in administrative reform would have to be redirected, away from abstract public sector management processes toward realistic analysis of whole administrative systems in their societal context. The first systematic attempt to engage in this task was provided in the first half of 1971 with the appearance of a special issue of *Development and Change* edited by Arne Leemans. The contributors were aware, on the one hand, of the shortcomings of a strictly generic managerial or management science approach to administrative reform and, on the other, the significant advances that had been made in other relevant social sciences, particularly policy studies, behavioral and applied behavioral sciences, and organizational dynamics. They all stressed that reform efforts had to be adapted to the particular case. While many reforms had been too formalistic, too narrowly conceived, ill-suited and unrealistic, they had also been too risky in the unsettled circumstances, they had been given too low a priority in national plans and goals, and they had been allocated too few resources and too short time spans. But reforms had succeeded too. Rulers had implemented them. Reforms had been institutionalized. Although not all objectives had been attained, many had. Administrative reform had been partially achieved and could not be written off. Some rethinking was necessary.

The new thinking called for came in the second half of 1971 at the first global meeting of experts on major administrative reform organized by the U.N.P.A.D. The seminar was held at the Institute of Development Studies in the United Kingdom and it was aided by 23 technical papers and 33 country case studies. The definition of major administrative reform adopted was

> specifically designed efforts to induce fundamental changes in public administration systems through system-wide reforms or at least through measures for improvement of one or more of its [sic] key elements, such as administrative structures, personnel and processes...distinct from normal and continuing activities concerning administrative and management improvement...(United Nations, 1973, 2)

or major deliberate efforts to induce desired fundamental changes in public administration to achieve system-wide improvement of administrative capability for development (Ibid, 6). The seminar's objectives were to analyze national reform efforts designed to accelerate development in developing, i.e. undeveloped or underdeveloped or poor, countries, to identify factors critical in reform success or failure, to develop criteria for appraisal of reform efforts and to evolve guidelines for effective implementation of reform programs under different conditions. In opening the seminar, the chair, Lord Fulton (of the recent Fulton Committee in the United Kingdom), remarked that to match government problems, the public bureaucracy needed more sophisticated techniques and professional skills. It had to be more flexible and accommodating to changing times. It had to run more things and to preserve the public interest. It had to be an instrument of societal change and development, to innovate and to be deeply involved with societal changes around it. Thus, administrative reform had much wider objectives than managerial improvements of the O.&M. and managerial services variety and required substantially different approaches.

The seminar participants concentrated on the goals of administrative reform in developing countries, planning for administrative reform, strategies, substantive concerns, and implementation. The main goals should be "the development of greater administrative and managerial capabilities to achieve national objectives" (Ibid, 9), the transformation of public administration into an effective instrument for economic and social development, and more effective administrative use of science and technology. Effective, not efficient or cheap, government was sought, i.e. the administrative capability to foresee, define and overcome problems that gave rise to the need for administrative reform. To avoid perpetual crises, administrative reform plans, part of national planning, should generate information and discussion on improving administrative performance, clarify the major issues in carrying out reform programs, define the *modus operandi* and resources of reformers, and design specific programmatic approaches. In the discussion on strategies, the seminar dwelt on the need for institutionalization (through law, education, training, and organization), priorities, scope and leadership. As to substantive concerns, the seminar gave special attention to the machinery of government, personnel administration, public enterprises and decentralization. Throughout, the critical factor was held to be changing the attitudes of people within and without government.

When it came to substantive proposals, the U.N.P.A.D. seminar recommended further international cooperation for mutual understanding and learning and comparative analysis. Existing international efforts in institution building (islands of excellence), administrative training and education, technical assistance, and establishing regional centers of development administration, should be continued and strengthened. But what was really needed were new ways and means of effectively managing the problem of development, new effective interdisciplinary methodologies for increasing administrative and managerial capabilities and the transnational adoption of reform successes, and, if possible "ways and means of promoting research and development in administrative reform and innovation" (Ibid, p. 30) akin to business R.& D. in product design and marketing. Though the U.N.P.A.D. seminar had not given up on the transnational inducement of administrative improvement, it had abandoned administrative reform as organizational reform or organizational development in favor of comprehensive institutional reform, institution building, and systems engineering on a country specific basis, adapted to the peculiar circumstances obtaining in each country. The next step was to develop scientific guidelines, realistic formulas and operating rules for administrative reform.

Arne Leemans, who did not attend the U.N.P.A.D. seminar, took heed of these conclusions. He expanded the journal issue into a book (Leemans, 1976) and added a totally rewritten overview constituting the most comprehensive and updated theoretical framework yet of administrative reform (see Table 1). The title alone indicated a further departure from transnational inducement of administrative improvement through managerialism. Instead, the focus was on

Table 1: Leeman's Schematic Framework for Change in the Machinery of Government (Simplified and Adapted)

1. NEED FOR CHANGE
1.1 Fundamentally new political situations
1.2 New political demands
1.3 Institutionalization
1.4 Professionalization, specialization and differentiation, integration
1.5 Enlargement of scale
1.6 New values and attitudes, democratization and participation, confrontation

2. BARRIERS TO CHANGE
2.1 Regularity
2.2 Vested interests
2.3 Fear and insecurity
2.4 Blindness to defects
2.5 Limited resources
2.6 Complexity of large organizations
2.7 Monopoly
2.8 Sheltered bureaucratic elites
2.9 Political coolness
2.10 Constitutionalism
2.11 Need for consultation
2.12 Administrative due process

3. INDUCEMENTS TO CHANGE
3.1 Accumulation of changes
3.2 Tensions between environment and organization structure and processes
3.3 Tensions arising from innovations
3.4 Tensions between components and the whole organization
3.5 Tensions among components
3.6 Crises
regime change
violent dissatisfactions
environmental-war, depression, cuts,
maladministration-excessive annoyance

4. SYSTEM AND SUB-SYSTEM CONSIDERATIONS
4.1 Machinery of government as a system
4.2 Closed or open administrative systems
narrow unrepresentative elites
professionalization of civil service
closed career system
indoctrination
hierarchical command structure
4.3 The environment
static
pluralistic and differentiated
participative
turbulent

5. OBJECTIVES AND ACTORS
5.1 Multiple objectives
external-development
internal-cure of maladministration
5.2 Variety of key actors
5.3 Categories of actors and their roles
political office holders
bureaucratic office holders

6. REFORM STRATEGIES
6.1 Reform process
6.2 Rejection of universal strategies
contingency approach
mix approach
need for flexibility
6.3 Some polar sets of strategies
structural v. behavioral
noncollaborative v. collaborative
drastic v. piecemeal

7. PROCESS
7.1 Incentive
impulse
distance
annoyance
feasibility
7.2 Diagnosis
finding fault
devising remedies
7.3 Planned action
7.4 Implementation
7.5 Evaluation

8. MAJOR VARIABLES
8.1 Reform influence and power
8.2 Inertia
8.3 Availability of resources
qualified change agents time
personal
finance
methods and techniques
8.4 Costs and benefits of reform
8.5 Feasibility estimation
uncertainties
experience
scope and intensity
trustworthy information
complexity of situation
8.6 Political support
internal
external

Source: A. F. Leemans, "Overview," *The Management of Change in Government,* Martinus Nijhoff, The Hague, 1976, pp. 1-98.

the inadequate adaptation of the machinery of government "to internal and external needs, demands and opportunities" (Ibid, 5) and the relevance of much literature on organizational change, adaptation and innovation for big government. He viewed administrative reform as a species of the generic term administrative (or organizational) change. But he also recognized that in government no distinction could be made between changes in the public bureaucracy and changes in political executive organs. Further, the idea of improvement or betterment was ill-suited to objective analysis of the reorganization of the machinery of government. He adopted for his definition of administrative reform "*consciously induced and directed change in the machinery of government* " (Ibid, 8), i.e. sizeable change implying reorganization of broad scope and high intensity and conscious, deliberate, intended planned organizational change aimed at unfreezing the rigidities of an organization suffering from obsolescence. This way, he could cover the U.N.P.A.D. seminar on major administrative reforms, studies of reorganization in the public sector, and general literature on organizations, on which he drew for his framework that became a model of analysis for the next decade.

Leeman's model tried to subsume several linked concepts, namely, (a) modernization and improvement of public sector management and organization, (b) transformation of public administration to better effect national development, (c) planned purposive organization change (reorganization, restructuring) in public sector delivery systems, (d) innovations in the public bureaucracy, (e) enhancement of administrative capacity to cope with a turbulent environment and new government responsibilities, (f) the strengthening of development planning and implementation, and (g) increased professionalization of public officials and employees. Their mutual aim was to increase the effectiveness of government, to improve the quality of public sector decisions, to streamline the conduct of public business, to enhance client satisfaction and to contribute tangibly to the quality of life. They were all addressed to the future, to doing better tomorrow than today, to altering the status quo harmoniously and consistent with prevailing values, to achieving progress through missionary zeal and both institutional and attitudinal transformation, and to achieving stated objectives (productivity, economy and efficiency, vitality, effectiveness, accountability and responsibility, indigenization, ethnic representation, equity, social justice, coordination, etc.).

Jon Quah put these together into a comprehensive definition of administrative reform as "*a deliberate attempt to change both a) the structure and procedures of the public bureaucracy... and b) the attitudes and behavior of the public bureaucrats involved..., in order to promote organizational effectiveness and attain national development goals*" (Quah, 1976, 58). It applied to all organizations, both government and non-government, involved directly in the realization of national development. It included not only periodic comprehensive reforms but also (probably more successful) piecemeal, incremental reforms. The next step should be comparative studies of administrative reform concentrating on the goals and context of administrative reform, approach selected, attitude of political leadership, and the environment in which reform was being implemented. Coincidentally, major organizations around the world involved in administrative reform also arrived at this conclusion. Every year since 1976 somewhere around the globe there has been an international conference or seminar or workshop held for the exchange of ideas and experiences, adding concept papers and case studies that gradually increase knowledge and improve the state of the art.

In 1979, The United States which had just experienced President Carter's successful reform of the federal civil service, hosted an International Conference on Improving Public Management and Performance (I.C.I.P.M.P.), the largest of its kind since the 1971 United Nations seminar in the United Kingdom. More countries and international organizations attended than ever before but the gathering in Washington, D.C. was predominantly Western oriented, managerially inclined and informal in organization with an actual ban on speeches and the reading of papers outside plenary sessions, aimed at sharing experiences and identifying items for future international attention and action. Co-sponsored by the American Consortium for International Public Administration and the International Institute of Administrative Sciences, the focus was on producing better qualified public sector managers, a universal problem, and "maintaining an effective, competent, highly motivated, ethically-disposed staff of public servants" (Stahl and Foster, 1979, 10) but discussions ranged critically over public sector problems and promising administrative and managerial reforms as seen in the topics covered:

- energizing public service educational and training institutions
- developing public administration and management curricula
- planning public sector manpower and education
- educating and training in ethics and values of public responsibility
- improving management of public enterprises
- planning and managing public works infrastructure
- exchanging and utilizing international technology and innovative practices
- strengthening administrative capabilities of governments
- achieving better program management, performance and participation
- developing administrative policies and strategies for managing change
- managing sub-national regionalism, decentralization and devolution increasing efficiency in the public sector: improving productivity while controlling the growth of bureaucracy and expenditures
- dealing with problems of crisis management: famines, floods and other disasters.

The importance of this gathering was that it did set much of the agenda for administrative reform in the 1980s and that in so doing it marked the end of the search for communality in administrative reform. A common agenda could be devised but carrying it out was to be left to individual countries to decide for themselves.

At the minimum, the solutions and strategies must vary substantially in application to varying conditions. Each nation will ultimately have to be responsible for the adaptations and modifications necessary to fit its peculiar situation. (Ibid, 129)

Yet the whole purpose of the conference had been the *continuing* involvement and work by the international community in improving public sector management and performance. The expectation was that as a result of this successful conference there would be follow-up meetings, international cooperative ventures, investment in comparative research and strengthened international efforts to support national public sector improvement programs. The chilling economic climate and the current political challenge to the administrative state dashed any hopes. Cutback management was soon to reduce not increase international and cross-national cooperation and leave individual countries to their own devices. What was started in 1979, the culmination of at least a decade's effort at reaching common agreement in administrative reform, was brought to an abrupt halt. There would be no follow-up.

A Field of Many Colors

Even though countries were forced to turn inward and pursue their own separate paths to administrative reform, international efforts did not cease. They were considerably reduced and the prospects for communality declined accordingly. Nevertheless, I.C.I.P.M.P. in 1979 had recorded the practical advice of the day and had detailed an elaborate reform agenda. The international agencies continued to sponsor exchanges of experts on a quite modest basis. If they could not get participants together, they could reach them through publications. In the early 1980s the World Bank added a Management and Development Series to its Staff Working Papers which included comparative studies of mostly Third World experiences in managing development (Agarwala, 1984), national planning (Agarwala, 1984), managing state-owned enterprises (Shirley, 1983), corruption (Gould and Amaro-Reyes, 1983), decentralization (Rondinelli et al., 1983), strengthening local government (Cochrane, 1983), managing the public service (Ozgediz, 1983), training for public administration and management (Paul, 1983), and meeting the management challenge (Kubr and Wallace, 1983), all cautionary analyses of public sector problems and reform experiences. The International Monetary Fund included public sector related issues in its Occasional Papers on taxation in Sub-Saharan Africa (Aguirre et al., 1981), government expenditure (Tait and Heller, 1982), and government employment and pay (Heller and Tait, 1983). The Commonwealth Secretariat reported on its efforts to develop human resources among its (poorer) members, including better management, as did the International Labor Organization (I.L.O.), the Organization for Economic Cooperation and Development (O.E.C.D.), and the European Economic Community (E.E.C.). The U.S.A.I.D. got into the act with its policy paper on institutional development and its "new emphasis on assessing and restructuring patterns of behavior within institutions so that overall effectiveness can be improved" (U.S.A.I.D., 1983, 5).

The United Nations still continued its efforts to pin down more precisely the meaning of administrative reform and to provide operational guidelines for reformers and researchers. One of the most widely respected documents in the 1980s was its monograph *Enhancing Capabilities for Administrative Reform in Developing Countries* (United Nations, 1983). In it, administrative reform was defined as "the deliberate use of authority and influence to apply new measures to an administrative system so as to change its goals, structures and procedures with a view to improving it for developmental purposes" (Ibid, 1). Administrative reform excluded but overlapped with ongoing incremental management improvement in existing arrangements "by the adaptation of inherited structures, the redistribution of functions and responsibilities, the streamlining of administrative processes, and the revision of rules, regulations and orders governing the civil service" (Ibid, 1) and substantive programs of administrative change e.g., "the reorganization of ministries, departments, the civil service and personnel administration, finance and budgetary reform and management services" (Ibid, 2). Again, the intention was to distinguish reform from other strategies to enhance administrative capability, namely, institution building, socio-political change and management development services (O.&M.), and to differentiate reform from administrative change, modernization and improvement. In trying to incorporate both current and previous approaches, the document really did not clarify the situation but added more confusion in covering all aspects too briefly. As previously, the U.N. emphasized the different phases of administrative reform, the key role of rational planning of reform, the requisite institutional and organizational arrangements, and data collection (see Table 2). This time it warned about the division between practitioners and academics in public administration which was not productive for the overall improvement of administration. One way to bring them together was to increase their mutual involvement in the process of administrative reform.

Two attempts to do this were tried in Asia during the 1980s. The first was at the Tenth Annual Assembly of the Eastern Regional Organization for Public Administration (E.R.O.P.A.) held in Korea in October 1983 whose major theme "Social Change and Administrative Reform in Asia Towards the Year 2000" was divided into six major topics which obviously reflected the change in emphasis in administrative reform since the 1979 I.C.I.P.M.P.:

– perspectives on social change
– administrative reform towards decentralization and citizens' participation
– administrative reforms in budget systems (financial frugality)
– public enterprises and managerial improvement (privatization)
– public management, education and training in the region
– public ethics and accountability (corruption).

This time, the meeting did not encompass the whole world or the Western world, but concentrated on East Asian countries and their struggles to cope with global economic chills, the assault on the administrative state and continuing dissatisfaction with public sector performance. Even given common themes, few papers were comparative or drew conclusions that were not country specific. The exception was the integrative overview which outlined recent failures both in the study and practice of decentralization, decentralized development, and managing decentralized development. It pointed to the failure to learn from past administrative reforms and faulty reform strategies and raised many more questions than any of the papers had attempted to answer (Ro and Reforma, 1985, 223-234). It proposed as a partial but affordable solution – greater networking to encourage participants to deal with common issues, common problems, common approaches, and common strategies, to pool and share knowledge resources and research, and to devise common research frameworks that "could emerge as a starting point for systematic studies of comparative administration" (Ibid, 234). Clearly, whatever else E.R.O.P.A. had achieved in a quarter of a century, it had not achieved much communality.

The second attempt was at the U.N.'s international seminar on "Reforming Civil Service Systems for Development" held in Beijing in August 1985, attended by a mixture of academics and practitioners involved in civil service reform in thirteen countries and over 100 Chinese officials concerned with personnel and workforce management who discussed the seminar's report for its relevance to Chinese civil service reform. What they made of it has gone unrecorded but again it cannot be said to have advanced the cause of commonality. The country case studies followed no common or shared framework. The term "civil service" was used ambiguously and each paper focussed on something different. As a result, the discussions roamed all over the landscape. The seminar report seemingly felt obliged to cover every point made and every related issue, although not in any organized, systematic fashion. Nobody seemed to have heeded the seminar director's warning that "clarity of approach is particularly critical in the study and planning of a strategy of reform" (United Nations, 1985, 2). Numerous general suggestions were made about what ought to be done in civil service reform but no concrete proposals were detailed nor any hints to implementation. All the report could record was no agreement on this and no consensus on that and repeat in brief the findings of the 1983 U.N. document.

Table 2: United Nations Schematic Framework for Enhancing Capabilities for Administrative Reform in Developing Countries

1. RATIONALE
1.1 Newly independent states
1.2 Expanding role of government
1.3 Enhanced administrative responsibilities
1.4 Decentralization of government
1.5 Inadequate administrative performance
1.6 Need to change public service attitudes and behavior
1.7 Need for greater efficiency and effectiveness in delivery of public services
1.8 Inability to implement national plans
1.9 Failure to meet basic needs
1.10 Inadequacy of governmental policies and resources
1.11 Need to modernize methods, techniques and procedures
1.12 Bureaucratic rigidity
1.13 Overstaffing
1.14 Catalytic events
regime change
defeat in war
natural disaster
famine, etc.

2. APPROACHES
2.1 Relations between reform agent and target
authoritarian
participative
mixed
2.2 Content
ideological-socialization into political values and goals and public service norms
socio-psychological-provision of appropriate incentives to increase output
procedural-use of techniques (O & M, etc.)
institutional-establishment of new institutions such as decentralization, public enterprises and ombudsman
2.3 Substantive focus
reorganization of structures and functions
personnel administration
budgetary systems and financial and supply management
management development services
decentralization and local government
regional planning and integrated rural development
public accountability parastatals and mixed enterprises
urban administration
management of international economic and fiscal relations
corruption, etc.

3. PROCESS AND STRATEGIES
3.1 Stages
conceptualization
initiation
formulation
implementation
evaluation
3.2 Interrelationship between stages
3.3 Development and orientation
3.4 Comprehensive v. partial reform
3.5 Timing
3.6 Interaction of input and output

4. PLANNING
4.1 Critical phases
review of goals
problem identification and diagnosis
operational objectives
recommendations
choice and approval of strategy
implementation
monitoring
feedback
evaluation
4.2 Establishment of goals and strategies
national, sectoral and economic planning
public administration research and training
reform agencies
O & M organizations
changes in political system
international and external sources
4.3 More effective planning
focus, scope and content
clarity and specificity
comprehensiveness
integration with national planning
professional character
continuity, systemization and comprehensiveness
4.4 Planning for implementation interaction of input and output
creation of capacity for implementation
effective formulation
relevant design
leadership
staff
training
political, administrative and popular support
improved synchronization

5. ARRANGEMENTS
5.1 Organizational choices
reform agency
advisory commissions
coordinating mechanism
5.2 Location
chief executive or financial agency
permanent government agency
coordinating council
public administration research and training institute
5.3 Linkages
political
public administration research and training institutions
affected agencies
national planning and budget agency
central personnel agency
central auditing agency
legal system
5.4 Requirements
manpower
reform agency personnel
training
conditions of service
recruitment and selection
specialized expertise
consultants
international technical assistance and cooperation technology
finance
physical plant

6. DATA COLLECTION
6.1 Information system
level of information required
area of information
norms-goals, policies, programs, procedures, sanctions
resources-human, financial, material, technological
structures-differentiation, functional interdependence, authority, coordination, communication, evolution, control
behavior-identification, motivation, action-orientation, leadership, morality, conflict
productivity-efficiency, effectiveness, impact consequences
indicators of performance
6.2 Data collection for planning
fact finding
analysis
public vantage point
efficiency v. effectiveness
techniques for systematization and application
recommendations
final report
6.3 Implementation
monitoring
evaluation of results
reform agency involvement

7. CONSTRAINTS AND CRITICAL FACTORS
7.1 Political priorities and administrative problems
7.2 Time and timing
7.3 Confusion with management development
7.4 Selection of appropriate reform agency
7.5 Reform agency personnel competency and leadership
7.6 Feasibility and collaboration
7.7 Public administration R & D

Source: United Nations, *Enhancing Capabilities for Administrative Reform in Developing Countries,* Department of Technical Cooperation for Development, *ST/ESA/SER.E/31, 1983.*

If the Beijing seminar was any indication, this approach to communality was fruitless and stale. It was like riding the same roundabout over and over again. Not much advance had been made on the 1971 U.N. gathering at the Institute of Development Studies on a grander scale. Meantime, those doing administrative reform around the world had long taken the seminar's advice that "reforms have to be country specific" (Ibid, 1), including the Chinese hosts. This time, however, there was a follow-up meeting of experts convened by the U.N. in Beijing in 1989 to review and advise on the administrative reform programs that the Chinese had initiated after the previous seminar. Because of the political disturbances that had occurred in May, the Chinese would reveal next to nothing on what they had been doing except to say that their first phase had been successful. They just wanted to know from the experts what other countries had been doing and each expert participated in several private sessions. As one participant summed up the experience:

> There was some question as to the general value of the symposium although the Chinese continued to meet for five days following, indicating their feeling of usefulness. Some attendees considered that the Chinese were sufficiently far behind the management level of the symposium participants as to make difficult really meaningful professional communication. (*Global Network*, Fall 1989, 2)

Generalizing from these meetings and similar gatherings held during the 1980s, it may well be true that

> What works one place does not always work another because of different practices, different outlooks, and different constraints of capacity and funding. But what works in one place is very likely to work in quite a lot of places with appropriate modifications. It would be splendid if…we could find ways of getting not only the word about useful ideas around, but also the critical details of how to make them work in other places. Frequently, it is not just what you do but how you do it, that determines success. (Champion, 1986, 7-8)

References

Agarwala, R. (ed.), *The Japanese and Korean Experiences in Managing Development*, World Bank Staff Working Paper no. 574, Washington D.C., 1984.

Agarwala, R., *Planning in Developing Countries: Lessons of Experience*, World Bank Staff Working Paper no. 576, Washington, D.C., 1984.

Aguirre, C. A., Griffith, P. S., and Yucelik, M. Z., *Taxation in Sub-Saharan Africa, Part I: Tax Policy and Administration in Sub-Saharan Africa*, International Monetary Fund, Washington, D.C., 1981.

Champion, H., "State and Local Government: Where the Action Is," Second Annual Bollens Memorial Lecture, University of California, Los Angeles, 1986.

Cochrane, G., *Policies for Strengthening Local Government in Developing Countries*, World Bank Staff Working Paper no. 582, Washington, D.C., 1983.

Floate, N., *Management Services in the Sudan Public Services*, Directorate of Organisation and Administrative Reform, Ministry of Public Service and Administrative Reform, Khartoum, 1976.

Global Network, "Frey Briefs A.C.I.P.A. on Beijing Session," Vol. 10, No. 4, Fall 1989.

Gould, D. J., and Amaro-Reyes, J. A., *The Effects of Corruption on Administrative Performance: Illustrations from Developing Countries*, World Bank Staff Working Paper no. 580, Washington, D.C., 1983.

Heller, P. S., and Tait, A. A., *Government Employment and Pay: Some International Comparisons*, International Monetary Fund, Washington, D.C., 1983.

Kubr, M., and Wallace, J., *Successes and Failures in Meeting the Management Challenge: Strategies and Their Implementation*, World Bank Staff Working Paper no. 585, Washington, D.C., 1983.

LaPalombara, J. (ed.), *Bureaucracy and Political Development*, Princeton University Press, Princeton, N.J., 1963.

Lee, H. B. and Samonte, A. (eds.), *Administrative Reforms in Asia*, E.R.O.P.A., Manila, 1970.

Leemans, A. (ed.), *The Management of Change in Government*, Institute of Social Studies, Martinus Nijhoff, The Hague, 1976.

Ozgediz, S., *Managing the Public Service in Developing Countries: Issues and Prospects*, World Bank Staff Working Paper no. 583, Washington, D.C., 1983.

Paul, S., *Training for Public Administration and Management in Developing Countries: A Review*, World Bank Staff Working Paper no. 584, Washington, D.C., 1983.

Quah, J., "Administrative Reform: A Conceptual Analysis", *Philippine Journal of Public Administration*, Vol. 20, No.1, Jan. 1976, pp. 50-67.

Ro, C., and Reforma, M., *Social Change and Administrative Reform Towards the Year 2000*, E.R.O.P.A., Manila, 1985.

Rondinelli, D. A., Nellis, J. R., and Cheema, G. S., *Decentralization in Developing Countries: A Review of Recent Experience*, World Bank Staff Working Paper no. 581, Washington, D.C., 1983.

Shirley, M. M., *Managing State-Owned Enterprises*, World Bank Staff Working Paper no. 577, Washington, D.C., 1983.

Stahl, G., and Foster, G., *Improving Public Services: A Report on The International Conference on Improving Public Management and Performance*, U.S. Agency for International Development, Washington, D.C., 1979.

Tait, A. A., and Heller, P. S., *International Comparisons of Government Expenditure*, International Monetary Fund, Washington, D.C., 1982.

United Nations, *Enhancing Capabilities for Administrative Reform in Developing Countries*, ST/ESA/SER. E/31, New York, 1983.

United Nations, *Handbook on the Improvement of Administrative Management in Public Administration*, ST/ESA/SER. E/19, New York, 1979.

United Nations, *Interregional Seminar on Major Administrative Reforms in Developing Countries*, ST/TAO/M/62, New York, 1973.

United Nations, *Reforming Civil Service Systems for Development*, TCD/SEM. 85/7-INT-85-R61, New York, 1985.

United States Agency for International Development, *Institutional Development*, Washington, D.C., March 1983.

5. Administrative Reform Breaks Loose

Just when it seemed in the late 1970s that many international technical assistance experts in administrative reform in the Third World might be reaching substantial agreement over definition, scope, approach and feasibility, the ground was swept from under them. Governments all over the world plunged into administrative reform with a vengeance. This time, the initiative was taken by the developed countries. After being relatively passive for over a decade, content with piecemeal reforms and steady managerial improvements, they did an abrupt about turn as the world-wide recession took hold. They undertook wholesale administrative reform in an endeavor to improve public sector productivity and performance. Despite some cross-checking, it was not done in a concerted fashion but on a country-by-country basis. The new reformers involved deliberately broke with the past and embarked on a radical change in direction in reshaping public administration and management.

At an International Round Table on Public Administration held in 1983 in Tokyo, Japan's Minister for Administrative Reforms remarked that administrative reform had become "a hot subject all over the world," as indeed it was. That meeting was attended largely by representatives of Western democracies which were, like Japan, carrying out sweeping reforms of their administrative systems. The Tokyo meeting, arranged by the host country, was a rare attempt to bring the Western Bloc together to share ideas and exchange information on government reorganization. At the same time, several East Bloc countries were also revitalizing their centrally directed economies and public bureaucracies without apparently paying much attention to what anybody else around the world was doing. As a result, the 1980s were eventful years in administrative reform at least at national level even if each country pulling in different directions undermined previous efforts at communality. It was a decade in which administrative reform broke loose from its preoccupation with forms and processes and delved deeper into the structural and institutional shortcomings of public administration.

This latest rush to overhaul administrative systems and rejuvenate public organizations around the globe had been prompted largely by a world-wide decline in public finances and the need for governments to get more for less. The 1980s were to prove a difficult decade for governments. The slowdown in economic activity accompanied by persistent public pressures for increased government intervention to reverse the situation pushed governments into large scale borrowing, unprecedented public indebtedness, high rates of inflation, frequent devaluations, and harsh financial policies imposed under the pressure of the International Monetary Fund (I.M.F.). Governments had to cut back, reduce expenditures, staff, investments and services and demand higher productivity and better performance from their sluggish public sectors. To improve their competitive international economic position, governments were forced to redefine their role and strategies. All blamed the dead hand of bureaucracy, especially the poor performance of public bureaucracies and the daily annoyances of irksome restrictions, cumbrous red tape, unpleasant officials, poor service and corrupt practices. Government, itself, had become too big, had taken too much on itself beyond its capacity to realize, and had allowed public expenditures and public employment to grow without adequate investigation and examination to the uses they were put and to the outputs obtained from the burgeoning administrative state.

The reexamination of the role of government that took place lifted administrative reform well beyond traditional concerns. In Japan,

> The first consideration in administrative reform is what the government should do: in short, how the public and private functions should be shared, how the responsibilities… of governments or the quasi-governmental organizations such as public corporations should be shared, and how the government should function, that is, whether the government should do everything by itself, and whether and how the public sector should entrust certain functions to the private sector…(Plowden et al., 1983, 104)

Only second was the reexamination of the functioning of the administrative system, followed by pressing resource problems in energy, social security, and science and technology, and the merging of political and administrative cultures which had prompted reckless government spending and the privatization of public ethics.

Similar views were being expressed in post-Mao Zedong China where serious doubts about excessive statism had been raised in Mao's own "Twenty Manifestations of Bureaucracy," in the post-Stalin Soviet Union where reform sentiment was to culminate in Gorbachev's reconstruction (*perestroika*) policy, in the revamping of the British administrative state under Prime Minister Thatcher, in Brazil's debureaucratization program and in the I.M.F.'s economic restructuring programs. In all these cases the primary concern was the remapping of the state itself, the redefinition of its boundaries, before turning to the administrative, bureaucratic, managerial and professional features that needed to be redesigned. Unlike previous technocratic administrative reforms, these were more ideological and politically partisan in nature. Beyond the competence of public officials, the quality of state performance included the institutional competence of the administrative state: its definition of the public interest and social objectives; its capacity for policy making and public leadership; its ability to adapt to changing circumstances; its sensitivity, responsiveness and responsibility to its many different publics; its strict compliance with public ethics; its incorporation of the best available technology; its respect for public accountability and controls; and its attention to direct public participation and self-help, self-management opportunities. The dead hand of bureaucracy had to be replaced by a new invigorating concept of public management and clear proof that public organizations were value for money.

Privatization and Coproduction

The failures of capitalism before the Second World War had induced governments thereafter to manage their economies, plan economic activities, sponsor public enterprises, and run major industries. For a time, collectivization and nationalization appeared to meet public objectives better than superseded private organizations. But, in time, their performance fell below expectations, productivity declined and public enterprise was often not any improvement over private enterprise. The social costs of forced collectivization proved prohibitive. Public enterprises exploited their monopoly position. Detailed public management of the economy failed to safeguard public investments or provide sufficient incentives to raise performance. Many economic regulations proved unenforceable and were largely ignored. In reality, a private enterprise underground market economy returned, allowing some consumer choice and self-regulation. The less dogmatic Marxist states acknowledged this and allowed a greater degree of liberalization. Then the spread of television revealed to all that the collectivized economies were being out-performed by the liberal economies. Without abandoning cumbersome, inflexible and coercive economic direction, the gap between them would widen. It was left to more pragmatic leaders in China and the Soviet Union to justify in ideological terms economic reforms and the attendant administrative reforms that would encourage greater private initiative, self regulation and consumer choice.

The term "privatization" took on a more precise meaning when Prime Minister Thatcher assumed office in 1979 on a populist platform centered on "rolling back the state", resisting the power of public sector employees and reducing public expenditures. The financially strapped British government, under pressure from the I.M.F to put the economy on a sounder basis, decided to denationalize several state-owned enterprises where ready private purchasers could be found. This would give it a beneficial injection of sorely needed finance and relieve it of the burden of managing marketable public goods and services. For many years the nationalized industries had not given much capital return on the large public investments made in them. The previous government had opted for public targets for capital needs, return on investment and higher productivity. The Thatcher government opted for market forces and decided to privatize as many public enterprises as it could by selling majority shares in some, selling off others altogether and generally reducing their monopoly status. The Thatcher government's success enticed other governments around the world to divest themselves similarly of public enterprises, particularly in telecommunications, airlines, public housing, hotels and bus services. To speed the transfer of publicly owned and managed industries into private hands, the United States Agency for International Development and the World Bank, among international bodies, provided technical assistance. As a result, governments everywhere have since been reexamining what businesses they ought not to be in and devising various ways of transferring public enterprises into private hands under public supervision.

Privatization shifted state-owned enterprises into the private sector, automatically reducing the size of government, state controls and the public budget. It relieved governments of their detailed management and possibly contentious subsidies. It enabled the new owners to offer their wares at market rates, streamline operations and rid themselves of publicly protected feather bedding. Their example of improved economic efficiency, client satisfaction and investment returns put pressure on the whole public sector to reconceptualize operations. Privatization appeared to reverse the prospects of several unprofitable government ventures, to improve performance, and to reduce industrial disputes. On the other hand, it also involved the sale of undervalued public assets to private parties which have not always proved capable of operating them at previous performance levels. It has not relieved governments from having to determine what criteria other than economic efficiency, should be applied to economic enterprise. In poor countries, privatization has been more of a mixed blessing with several scandals associated with the sale of public enterprises and their failure under private management. Already saddled with unprofitable enterprises that their governments could not sell, they have had to rescue the failures of privatization and co-ventures where self-styled expert private partners have used public capital in unsuccessful pursuit of untested markets.

As a middle ground between direct delivery and privatization, governments have preferred to contract with other public bodies or private parties. Governments have increasingly resorted to contracting with other public bodies or devising joint delivery arrangements or transferring operations to special public authorities. Such intergovernmental arrangements have largely been responsible for increasing the actual number of government organizations. General purpose governments have contracted specific services to other government organizations which could concentrate on delivering services more efficiently on a user cost basis, more as a private business yet still be publicly accountable. Consequently, complex government has become even more complicated, government even more fragmented, and the delivery of public goods and services even more dominated by professional managers, with the profusion of intergovernmental arrangements and interlocking jurisdictions.

Closer to privatization has been the contracting out not to other public bodies but to private enterprise, in the absence of which the government itself would have to perform all operations and provide a reserve capacity for contingencies. While governments have always contracted for readily available "on the shelf" items, it has become more common practice to contract out for services and one-of-a-kind items unavailable in the market place for which the government is the sole purchaser (Gilbert, 1983). Often governments have only the vaguest idea what they want; nobody knows whether a certain service or item can be supplied to expected specifications or at all. Such forms of contracting out have created non-market delivery systems solely dependent on public funds with a strong contractor interest in sole source supply (monopoly), higher returns (waste), loose supervision (low accountability) and follow-on contracts (political lobbying). Yet as governments try to shrink the public sector or divest themselves of detailed management or boost non-governmental enterprise, contracting out has become more popular. It has gone so far in the United States that some local governments contract out all key services – police, fire protection, social welfare, public works – while others make their own municipal agencies bid against private contractors. The U.S. federal government has even been encouraging public employees to form their own private companies to contract for newly privatized activities. The aim of all these experiments has been to reduce public expenditure without curtailing service quality, although this aim has often been defeated by fraud, waste and abuse.

In all these experiments, the public have been passive onlookers. But as public resources have diminished, so governments have sought to cut costs by relying more on voluntary participation in public organizations to take over some of the work load and by encouraging people to do more things for themselves instead of looking to government to do things for them. Despite bureaucratic and professional opposition, governments have also attempted fitfully to devolve some activities to communal organizations and various public-private partnerships. Here, the public have been encouraged to share in the public service delivery through privately financed participation, hopefully reducing public alienation and making citizenship more meaningful (Levine, 1984). Such coproduction has so far worked only on a small, local scale and has relied heavily on private funding, local self interest and community organization. However, the potential of coproduction for generating private inputs into government is likely to lead to novel partnerships in the future as governments endeavor to shift production of public goods and services off the machinery of government into private, voluntary and non-governmental organizations. It will open a whole new frontier in administrative reform especially in countries anxious to reduce bureaucratic centralism.

Debureaucratization

Privatization and coproduction were part of a larger effort to reduce statism and to get government off the people's backs, generally to reduce government intervention and bureaucratic controls. Such streamlining and simplification of public bureaucracy – termed debureaucratization – also sought to put an end to the methods devised by people to evade government controls and cut through the bureaucratic maze. It was expected that eventually debureaucratization would improve public trust and confidence in government and minimize people's need to use intermediaries to deal with the public bureaucracy on their behalf. Debureaucratization viewed government from the public's standpoint with the overarching twin objectives of eliminating bureaucratic dysfunctions or bureaupathologies (not the bureaucracy itself) and transforming the mindless bureaucrats of the imperious state into caring public servants of the community.

Debureaucratization incorporated virtually the whole gamut of administrative reform:

improving public policy making and government decisions
streamlining the machinery of government
deconcentrating power and authority
increasing public sector productivity
devising measures of performance and insisting on better performance
tackling bureaupathologies, such as fraud, waste and corruption
adopting up-to-date information and administrative technology
simplifying and rationalizing administrative processes
reducing unnecessary red-tape, feather bedding and paper work
devising organizational innovations
diversifying public service delivery systems
providing and ensuring greater public accountability
allocating scarce resources more rationally
providing incentives for cost consciousness and public savings
reducing public debts
improving forecasting and simulation
deregulating marketable services
consolidating fragmented units
emphasizing effective consultation and coordination
enforcing financial management controls
attracting and retaining better qualified public employees
transferring and retraining surplus employees
educating public managers to manage
retuning public employee skills
improving public sector working conditions
demanding higher professional standards and stricter discipline

speeding up operations
stressing public ethics and norms
restoring public confidence in public institutions
investigating and responding to public complaints
allowing greater direct public participation in public administration
educating public officials and public on how to behave with one another.

All these elements had supposedly been contained in the National Debureaucratization Program in Brazil, a model for other countries in Latin America. The program had been based initially on a survey of all contacts between citizens and officialdom over a lifetime to find out what could be eliminated altogether or simplified, and on another similar survey for small businesses only (Carneiro, 1982). While it operated, every area of federal government administration was reviewed, several hundred legal documents were revised and millions of documents were eliminated. Regulations were modified or discontinued, and new information technology reduced red-tape. Some activities were decentralized to quicken decision making and attempts were made to humanize public administration.

The task in Brazil was truly overwhelming and the momentum of the program dwindled because the disposition both of officials and public towards each other failed to change appreciably (Belmiro et al., 1986: Joao, 1984). Public administration was still seen as management of the public with decisions imposed from above and afar while the public still viewed their over-centralized government as out of touch, too exploitive and self serving. Although the program eventually fell victim to old habits of mind, bureaucratic inertia and political downgrading, it did make a welcome dent in Brazilian public administration. Its main thrusts – deregulation, decentralization, modernization, personalization, and greater public accountability and participation – were repeated elsewhere in Latin America as in Mexico's Administrative Simplification Program and Peru's debureaucratization schemes and also around the globe with mixed successes.

Deregulation outside Brazil has gone well beyond lifting irksome government restrictions on business activity, which was one of the major objectives of the Brazilian government, to revising all statutes and official instructions so as to reduce generally the volume and weight of legal rules and constraints on social activities and restore the value of law crippled by excessive red-tape, regulatory overkill, and ineffective legalism. Deregulation had two major aims. One was to reduce unnecessary restrictions on individual liberty, to lower the excessive cost of social resistance to the proliferation of regulations, and to avoid the real danger of individual suffocation, i.e. to lighten the load of regulation. The other was to restore the efficacy of the regulatory process by eliminating unnecessary red-tape imposed on the public to obtain required documents such as birth, marriage and death certificates, driving licenses, land titles and labor permits, by speeding up and simplifying procedures through newly available technology, by reducing costs of conducting business with the government, by pruning outdated, redundant, superfluous and pointless rules and by codifying the rules and revising them so that they were known, understandable and followed and less subject to constant alteration.

The whole effect of deregulation was to demystify the law, open up the rules making process, reduce state intervention in society, and diminish bureaucratic rules for self-defined social norms. Importantly,

> ...the rule of law is increasingly becoming an *operations management technique* to be tested in the furnace of efficiency; its value in the future will depend less on its intrinsic normative power than the quality of the methods which have gone into its formulation and the relevance of its content...law [will be] no more than an instrument *at the service* of efficiency [rather than efficiency being advanced through the law]. (Chevallier, 1988, 17)

This change in approach brought about by deregulation was expected to result in profound changes in the relations between the governors and the governed in the future.

> The job of public policy is not to tell people what to do but to create a context which will allow them to find for themselves what to do, and hence create more. It is not a matter of imposing objectives, but of helping people achieve theirs and discover new ones. (Crozier, 1987, 314)

Most probably, deregulation will undoubtedly improve even further face-to-face contacts between public officials and members of the public.

Improvement of face-to-face contacts would not have been achieved without the willingness of central authorities to delegate much more to local offices, standardize operations and procedures, and maintain more of a general supervisory stance. Such decentralization of authority has not come easily after decades of centralization but it was inevitable as the increase of detailed paper work threatened to paralyze government altogether (Bayley, 1974; Graham, 1980). The aim has been to relieve the center of detailed minutiae and to reduce routine matter that is passed along instead of being decided locally. Local officials have been encouraged to decide more for themselves and to consult more locally in reaching their decisions. Unfortunately, central officials have been reluctant to relinquish their control of details and their hold over local officials. The problem has not so much been structural as behavioral, emanating from decades of bureaucratic buck-passing and paper-shuffling.

Almost universally, the revised education and training of public officials have encouraged them to be more proactive, enterprising, creative, sensitive, responsive, human and humane. More attention has been paid to civility in conducting public business and to the provision of proper facilities for people who have business to conduct with government. Helpfulness should characterize dealings with the public who should be informed of their rights and helped to obtain their legal entitlements. Their complaints should be treated with respect and dealt with promptly. These prescriptions have been translated into budget requests for the redesign of public buildings, the legitimation of public relations, advertising and information campaigns, and the establishment of information and complaint offices. They have led to greater use of mass media for public education programs, open houses and exhibitions and a willingness to allow the public to see the inside the public bureaucracy.

Reorganization

Once reorganization of the machinery of government used to be considered the primary need in administrative reform. And governments did indeed reorganize only to be disillusioned when their expectations of economy, efficiency, productivity, effectiveness and responsiveness did not materialize. Often the managerial prescriptions in regrouping administrative units, redistributing functions among them and other structural transformations, did not pay off at all and they were not worth the cost of the political upheavals involved or the time and effort. In short, reorganizations were a "source of frustration and disillusionment" (Fain, 1977, ix). No matter what might be done, administrative problems persisted; reorganizations had little impact on costs, efficiency and control (Boyle, 1979; Kaufman, 1977; Szanton, 1981); they were more useful as policy tools, signals of intention, means of redistributing power. In short, reorganization came to be recognized as "a domain of rhetoric trading, problematic attention, and symbolic action" (March and Olsen, 1983, 291) in which administrative and management theory clashed with real politick, "iron triangles" fought over turf, political trading and bargaining resulted in unworkable compromises or the sacrifice of administrative reform, and reorganizations became garbage cans.

> …reorganizations tend to become collections of solutions looking for problems, ideologies looking for soapboxes, pet projects looking for supporters, and people looking for jobs, reputations, or entertainment. (March and Olsen, 1989, 82)

Consequently, reorganization had been administratively – if not politically – relegated as a strategy of administrative reform. Nonetheless, in the 1980s governments continued to reorganize and rearrange in the belief that bureaucratic performance would be improved thereby.

Where once the focus of reorganization had been the consolidation of small units and on the integration of minor activities, it was now recognized that the consolidation of units created massive impersonal organizations that lost touch with the publics they were supposed to serve and that the integration of similar activities was endless – given the multiplicity, diversity and complexity of contemporary government activities. Instead, there has been a search for decentralizing activities that could and should be better performed at a more local level, closer to their intended publics, and for restructuring regional and local governments to allow for greater direct public participation. Overcentralization had produced much needless bureaucracy and paperwork with too much public business being funneled to the center where channels tended to get clogged, decisions delayed and details just lost altogether. Several countries began seriously reviewing relocating the central government away from a choked capital city or at least relocating major administrative units out of the capital city to less crowded towns, thereby deconcentrating public employees and geographically spreading public investments. But few schemes have been implemented because of the costs and because few senior officials have been willing to leave the capital. Similarly, schemes to devolve central government on special regional governments have not gone far, this time because the regions have lacked sufficient resources and the central government has not wanted to create political rivals (Rowat, 1980).

Decentralization has not been just a reaction to overcentralization but has also been a genuine attempt to facilitate effective popular participation in national development and to improve local delivery of government services, particularly in rural areas of poor countries. Much of the impetus has been prompted by international agencies, especially the United Nations' Development (formerly Public) Administration Division which has recognized the failure of national planning to consider rural needs sufficiently. Actually, more concern has been expressed in decentralizing national administrations and in incorporating local representative institutions than, as formerly, in creating several layers of autonomous regional and local governments, although multi-layered governmental systems have been established where they did not previously exist. Nonetheless, "the majority of decentralization programs have been seen as attempts to *decentralize the national government*, rather than to establish a second tier of government" (Conyers, 1983, 105). The actual degree of decentralization has been quite limited (and has rarely contributed to rural development) and local popular participation has been low (Saxena, 1980).

Many countries, rich and poor, have been experimenting with local government reorganizations and how they fit with decentralized national government organization; with redistribution of governmental activities among the different tiers; with the size and number of local government authorities; and with various forms of community organization and public participation. They echoed the sentiments of French President Mitterrand to give the state back to the people with a "new citizenship" for the individual, a new division of economic power, and new influence for submerged ethnic and cultural minorities. But in reality, the reforms have been much less radical, although they have increased local government's influence in national policy making (Keating and Hainsworth, 1986). It has proved difficult for centralized governments to relinquish any power and supposedly autonomous tiers have been highly dependent on central governments for subsidies. In Europe, Denmark, Sweden and the United Kingdom achieved a radical overhaul of their systems. But elsewhere, reorganization for decentralization has been largely cosmetic. Local government has been reorganized not reformed, with central government authority usually prevailing over local proposals (Rondinelli et al, 1983).

Effective Public Management

Rather than attempt dramatic reorganizations, governments have been trying to achieve the same results by shaking up the top management of public organizations, the senior officials who set the style and tone for conducting public business, and who almost universally have been much criticized for being unduly privileged, unworldly, arrogant, unenterprising, and "badly trained, lacking in expertise and devoid of the managerial skills necessary in an era of complex interventionist government" (Greenaway, 1984, 67). Big government needed more than competent bureaucrats; it needed more effective managers who were imaginative, energetic, ever alert to remove the dead hand of bureaucracy and revitalize managerial systems that had "become so rigid, stultifying and burdened with red-tape" that they crippled government performance, made public administration cost ineffective and irresponsible, and frustrated the dedicated" (National Academy of Public Administration, 1983, vii). Specifically, a new philosophy was required that emphasized mission over control, managerial qualities and skills, a new freedom for public managers to manage, a new leadership "more concerned with broad management policy and experimentation with innovative management approaches, linked to evaluation and reporting of agency managerial performance than detailed operational controls" and with "greater emphasis on pressing for innovation, research, the redesign of outdated systems, and the attainment of managerial excellence" (Ibid, viii).

Before "a more robust breed of public servant" (Greenaway, 1984, 80) could emerge under a transformed system of public management, governments had to go outside the public sector to supplement the internal supply and seek managerial talent from all walks of life. The bureaucratic elite had always been leavened by a sprinkling of capable, proven outsiders who could move in and out of government and could also move around government, energizing and revitalizing inert bureaucracies, insisting on higher performance standards, being free to manage, that is, to set objectives, determine priorities, designate targets, and make their own decisions as how best to improve performance. The model for this new style of effective public management has been the Senior Executive Service (S.E.S.) established by the U.S federal government following the passage of the Civil Service Reform Act of 1978 (Bowman, 1982; Dillman,

1986; Godwin and Needham, 1981; Ingraham and Ban, 1984). The S.E.S. was to be

> a general civilian officer corps, staffed by highly trained and broadly experienced men and women who could be shifted from assignment to assignment as the needs of government required. In return for higher pay, performance bonuses, and enhanced career opportunities, S.E.S. members were to forgo many of the protections of the traditional civil service system and be held to higher standards of performance. The S.E.S. would, in brief, create the vigorous, competent, and spirited bureaucracy that democratic government requires (Twentieth Century, 1987, 29).

All senior positions were grouped into a single personal rank class with a fixed percentage quota for non-careerists. Incumbents could be shifted around but they would be evaluated annually according to individual and organizational performance. Although consistently poor performers could be removed or retired, half of S.E.S. careerists would be eligible for annual cash bonuses (up to 20 per cent of base salary) and exceptional performers could be placed in special meritorious ranks with a one-time cash bonus.

Other countries have adopted similar principles, namely, opening up closed career systems, banding senior officials together to overcome departmentalization, remuneration based on annual performance ratings, bonuses (incentives) for superior performance, and possible demotion and removal. In practice, the hopes of civil service reformers have been dashed because the initial base salaries were kept too low and turnover has been high as identifiable good performers have been induced (even seduced) to leave public service. In the face of departmental opposition, mobility within has been low, while the executive training that was supposed to accompany appointment has rarely materialized. The performance appraisal and bonus systems have proved difficult to apply to technical specialists. But the real block has turned out to be accusations of politicization of senior positions as governments have relished their new freedom to pick and choose bureaucratic chiefs at will. Furthermore, although the whole conception was based on the reform of managerial systems that would permit the new breed of public managers to manage, these reforms have been slow to emerge, leaving in place rigid, counterproductive, dysfunctional practices which choke individual innovation and initiative.

Value for Money

The central theme behind most recent reform campaigns has been that government does not give enough value for money. Privatization would reintroduce market principles and economic efficiency. Debureaucratization would eliminate unnecessary, parasitic and unproductive government activities. Reorganization would improve government performance and improve service delivery.

Effective public management would increase productivity and reduce incompetence. All would give better value for money. But they failed to deal adequately with overspending and waste – due primarily to the lack of incentives in public budgeting to save public money. Bureaucratic performance, so mythology would have it, has tended to be measured by outlays and staff size, not by effectiveness and opportunity costs. Something had to be seriously wrong when governments which could not cover expenses piled debt upon debt. Past budget reforms, such as P.P.B.S. and Z.B.B., which had promised to stop the rot, had done no such thing.

The economic crisis of the 1970s forced governments to insist on cuts all around. Some way had to be found to control runaway government expenditures, rising inflation and mounting debts. So cutback management became the order of the day – to cut budgets or at least cut estimates and claims, cut staff or at least freeze establishments, cut services or at least postpone things that did not have to be done right away (Levine, 1984). The opportunity was taken to do some things that had been politically unpopular or had been resisted by public employee unions, now much weakened by the economic situation. Programs were terminated and organizations reduced – sometimes cosmetically by transferring the activities to non-governmental organizations – but largely with the least harmful effects by putting off long term public works, reducing maintenance, inducing early retirements, diminishing reserves, lowering real conditions of employment, leaving vacancies unfilled, and generally enforcing austerity. Governments sought to reduce, not eliminate, their debts and deficits. They added another step in the budget process, that of prepreparation, rather than reform the budget process itself. Prepreparation set overall spending and borrowing limitations beforehand, later to be translated into broad budgetary ceilings and (reduced) program targets. This new step was a centralized, top down integrated rationing process involving

> the use of tight fiscal norms and targets to constrain spending demands, strict enforcement of budget ceilings and the use of baselines to set cutback targets, the conversion of multiyear budgets from program plans into spending controls, and greater attention to the preparation phase of budgeting (Schick, 1986, 216).

In this way the objectives of budget reforms – multiyear cycles, programic content, prioritizing requests, performance appraisal and baseline auditing – were achieved in substance not form, although the deeper intractable problems of public budgeting directed thinking toward more radical reforms in process.

The budget imperative of more for less did accelerate the adoption of other administrative reforms. Wherever possible, government organizations were made individually more financially self-contained and reliant through self-financing by way of user fees and other charges more in line with the actual costs of delivery. In this way, government organizations became more aware of their expenses and the public more aware of the real costs of public services.

Although attempts were made to reduce entitlements and other universal legal rights to public services for people who did not need them or could afford to pay for them on a commercial basis, proposals were dropped where such cuts were interpreted as rolling back the welfare state or a failure to maintain the level of private sector employment. Other targets for reform were overspending and seepage of public funds through fraud, waste, and corruption, i.e. the diversion of public funds to people for whom they were never meant. Retired public servants, such as Leslie Chapman in the United Kingdom (Chapman, 1978), and inquiries led by business persons, such as the Grace Commission in the United States, suggested that significant savings could be made if the loopholes were blocked. Similarly, public funds could be boosted if the government's collection of money was improved, not only including loans never collected but also taxes which had been avoided and evaded. Finally, along with prepreparation in the budget process, preauditing was also boosted. Even before money was allocated, claims and requests were to be audited for their public worth and value, not just for their legality and appropriateness. Altogether, government auditing was tightened, with previously exempt public organizations now included. In the United Kingdom, a new Audit Commission was specifically established for local governments and empowered to undertake "value for money" studies.

The "value for money" approach in administrative reform was greatly assisted by the upsurge of policy analysis and public productivity research (Dillman, 1986; Miller, 1984), dispelling doubts that much government performance could not be measured and evaluated. Their impact has been to switch attention from process to substance, "from tasks to goals" (Bonwit, 1989) from general government arrangements to specific improvements in individual public organizations (Brown, 1979; Hawker, 1981; Tierney, 1981). Social security insurance schemes were transformed by new information technology. Competition and technology prompted reforms in public businesses such as mail delivery, telecommunications and airlines. Government has had to change, and government administration and management have had to change accordingly. The overall impact of substantive reforms has been to lift the gloom and pessimism about government and the governability of modern society which was widespread with the onset of the economic crisis (Rose, 1979) to guarded optimism a decade later that the state was capable of adaptation.

A New Realism

While these administrative reforms proceeded with reasonable success, the more ambitious comprehensive reforms faltered and proved a great disappointment in poor countries which had pinned such high hopes on them. While the National Debureaucratization Program in Brazil dwindled in impact, until it was killed in

1989, its imitators in other Latin American countries could not even match the N.D.P.'s initial successes and administrative reforms may have made things worse, not better (Perlman, 1989). In Africa, administrative reform initiatives collapsed in one country after another, victim to political corruption, bureaucratic inertia, and social disharmony (Chikulo, 1981; Williams, 1987). Bureaucratic resistance largely defeated reform campaigns in the Indian subcontinent (Khan, 1979; Maheshwari, 1981; Tummala, 1979; *The Indian Journal of Public Administration,* 1985; *Public Administration and Development,* 1989) while political corruption and political turmoil often upset reform programs elsewhere in Asia (De Guzman et al, 1982; Khan, 1980; Krannich, 1980). As in the past, the administrative systems most in need of reform could not muster the political support, administrative capacity and public participation for effective implementation, while those possibly least in need among the more wealthy countries were able to do so (Al-Saigh, 1986, Mayo-Smith and Ruther, 1986).

The comparative success of administrative reform in the richer countries could, of course, be attributed to political determination, administrative expertise and public pressure, always essential ingredients in administrative reform. But there were other important supporting factors. For a start, the world economic situation challenged the voracity of the public sector which the preceding decades of economic growth and high employment rates had encouraged. The change in economic fortunes forced a reconsideration of public expenditures, the role and the size of the public sector, and the productivity and economic performance of public organizations. Something had to be done to reassure a critical public that the public sector was really pulling its weight. But action was not along traditional reform lines at all. Grandiose schemes for wholesale transformation were replaced by incremental, quickly attainable substantive improvements. Privatization did not abandon the welfare state or public enterprise; it only denationalized profitable public businesses. Debureaucratization did not abandon the administrative state; it only removed unnecessary red-tape and public regulation. Decentralization did not abandon big government; it only attempted to relocate routine decision making. Effective public management did not abandon career systems; it only sought to introduce a higher priority for managerial talent. Value for money did not abandon budget processes; it only added an extra preliminary process to cap public expenditures. Behind them, however, was the threat of more radical reforms that would have been introduced had the public bureaucracy resisted such incremental reforms.

More important, it was recognized that the reform of public bureaucracy had in practice to "be implemented by and within that same bureaucracy" (Smith and Weller, 1978, 310-311). The public bureaucracy was consulted and involved throughout the reform process. The public bureaucracy was not seen as the inevitable enemy but as a willing partner, having talented, experienced professionals who knew where the problems were and what could be achieved with minimum dislocation. While there were reactionaries among them who resented any suggestion that the public bureaucracy was less than perfect, there were also radicals frustrated by the system and full of ideas how to make the system work better. Governments tapped their ideas and sided with them, shifting the weight of the system on the side of the desired changes. Also governments realized that as long as they minimized any personal damage pertaining to victims of reforms, public officials had the good sense to go with the times to meet the challenges presented. The fact that governments were able to function so well given general belt-tightening was testimony to bureaucratic resilience. While outside critics might use this as evidence of previous slack, more knowledgeable insiders realized that the public bureaucracy had responded despite an appreciable degree of demoralization that boded ill for the longer term. In the meantime, the public bureaucracy had been positioned in a different and more desirable direction.

In this realistic reappraisal of public sector performance, a number of myths were exposed. Government could not be run like a business although it could be more businesslike (Calista, 1986; Campbell and Peters, 1988; Garson and Overman, 1983). What government had to do was quite different from business and how it went about doing what it did also had to be different. The public sector had a logic of its own. Furthermore, given its context and limitations, the public sector performed much better than often realized. Indeed, its productivity may have been rising at a higher rate than private sector productivity and it was often managerially more enterprising and creative. Outside criticism had been exaggerated, and if it was continued, might prove to be a self-fulfilling prophecy. Panaceas for government ills could not be found in political abstractions or business practices or purely managerial prescriptions or constant harassment of public officials. They could not be conjured up from foreign administrative cultures or from general manuals of management or even from neighboring public organizations. The post office was as different from mental health treatment as the foreign service was from tax collection or the operation of transportation services was from public schools. Realistic reform required a pragmatic experimental approach, perhaps confined to one specific public activity or one set of public organizations or one class of public employees. While outside experts, public inquiries, new laws, new organizations, new people and new coordinating mechanisms could make a difference (Wilenski, 1986), reform success depended on the everyday operations of government and the hundreds of thousands of permanent officials who handled public business daily to devise for themselves better ways of doing their jobs. In short, it seemed better to encourage and solicit reforms from the inside than to impose them from the outside.

The Limitations of Reform

Although each country had gone about reform in its own peculiar way, as might be expected given the diversity of administrative cultures, no country had been uninfluenced by what has happened elsewhere. When country A had decided to overhaul its administrative system, its neighbors had followed suit. When country B had published the results of its investigations, so they had been studied on the other side of the globe. Reformers everywhere avidly searched for proposals they might themselves adopt, for tips on what seemed to have worked elsewhere, and for evidence that bolstered their case. They carefully reviewed the successes of reform campaigns and concentrated on achievable, measurable goals, always aware of the inherent limitations of their reforms. They did not aim to change governing principles or essentials but to strengthen them (Calista, 1986), although at the end of the 1980s, they were being pushed into more radical if not revolutionary proposals.

The new generation of reformers deliberately tied administrative reform to policy changes and political reforms but with a quite conservative or conserving intention. By making government more effective, government could do more. By giving better value for money, public expenditures could go further. By freeing the public of needless bureaucracy, people could devote themselves to more important tasks. By improving public sector performance, government could be more responsive to national aspirations. Streamlining, modernization, cutback management, debureaucratization and the like were not ends in themselves, but means to making the public bureaucracy more economic, more productive, more efficient, more effective, more adaptive, more innovative, more accountable, for better serving the public.

By using the system in place, the reforms had guarantees of system supports, adequate resources, and opportune timing. But this strategy could only work where the existing system was already performing reasonably well and where the people who directed it were politically sensitive, professionally sophisticated and self-interested in identifying with the reforms. Unfortunately, in many countries, it was the system itself that was grievously faulty and no amount of tinkering around with it could overcome built-in deficiencies. Governments had to devise more radical administrative reforms, bypassing the public sector altogether with their strengthening of private producers, voluntary and non-governmental organizations or bypassing the public bureaucracy altogether by relying more on outside advisors, appointing non-career persons to top administrative positions and imposing stronger political, legal, financial and managerial controls on task oriented executives.

These reform experiences of the 1980s confirmed more than ever that a crusading spirit was still essential in administrative reform. A burning spirit of righteous indignation was crucial to overcome bureaucratic inertia, political indifference and public apathy. And as many countries and reformers had found, idealism was all too easily crushed in the daily frustrations of reform programs. In any event, imperfections would remain even if the reforms were successful (Feldman, 1981). Reforms could only control not cure the ills of public administration. They exposed maladministration and proposed alternatives that promised to reduce it but they could not guarantee good administration nor prevent the reappearance of maladministration. But even if they failed at any point in time, the effort kept the flame of idealism alive without which no reform would ever succeed.

References

Al-Saigh, N. M. (ed.), *Administrative Reform in the Arab World: Readings*, Arab Organization of Administrative Sciences, Amman, 1986.

Bayley, L. G., *Local Government: Is It Manageable?,* Pergamon Press, New York, 1974.

Belmiro, V., Castor, J. and Franca, C., "Administracao Publica no Brasil: Exaustao e Revigorameto do Modelo," *Revista de Administracao Publica*, Vol. 20, No. 3, 1986, pp. 3-26.

Bonwit, B., "Reform of Public Administration: From Tasks to Goals," *International Review of Administrative Sciences*, Vol. 55, No. 2, 1989, pp. 211-228.

Bowman, J. (ed.), "Civil Service Reform", *Review of Public Personnel Administration*, Vol. 2, No. 2, Spring 1982, pp. 1-4.

Boyle, J. M., "Reorganization Reconsidered: An Empirical Approach to the Decentralization Problem," *Public Administration Review*, Vol. 39, No. 5, September/October 1979, pp. 458-465.

Brown, R.G., *Reorganizing the National Health Service: A Case Study in Administrative Change*, Blackwell/Robertson, Oxford, 1979.

Calista, D. S., *Bureaucratic and Governmental Reform*, JAI Press, Greenwich, CT., 1986.

Campbell, C. and Peters, G. (eds.), *Organizing Governance, Governing Organizations*, University of Pittsburgh Press, Pittsburgh, 1988.

Carneiro, J. P., *National Debureaucratization Program: Three Years of Debureaucratization*, National Debureaucratization Program, Brazil, 1982.

Chapman, L., *Your Disobedient Servant*, Chatto and Windus, London, 1978.

Chevallier, J., Introductory Report of the Research Committee on Law and Science of Administration, Budapest Round Table, International Institute of Administrative Sciences, 1988.

Chikulo, B. C., "The Zambian Administrative Reforms: An Alternative View," *Public Administration and Development*, Vol. 1, No. 1, January-March 1981, pp. 55-65.

Conyers, D., "Decentralization: The Latest Fashion in Development Administration," *Public Administration and Development Vol.* 3, No. 2, April-June 1983, pp. 97-109.

Crozier, M., *Etat Modeste, Etat Modern: Strategie pour un Autre Changement*, Paris, 1987.

DeGuzman, R., Pacho, A., and Legada, R. T., *Institutional Organizational Arrangements for Planning and Implementation of Administrative Reform*. College of Public Administration, University of the Philippines/E.R.O.P.A., Manila, 1982.

Dillman, D. L., "Personnel Management and Productivity Reform: Taming the Civil Service in Great Britain and the United States," *International Journal of Public Administration*, Vol. 8, No. 4, 1986, pp. 345-367.

Fain, T.G. (ed.), *Federal Reorganization: The Executive Branch*, Bowker, New York, 1977.

Feldman, D., *Reforming Government*, Morrow, New York, 1981.

Garson, D., and Overman, S., *Public Management Research in the United States*, Praeger Publishers, New York, 1983.

Gilbert, C. E. (ed.), "Implementing Governmental Change," *The Annals of the American Academy of Political and Social Science*, Vol. 466, March 1983, pp. 9-205.

Godwin, P., and Needham, J., "Reforming Reform – Challenging the Assumptions for Improving Public Employee's Performance," *Public Personnel Management*, Vol. 10, No. 2, Summer 1981, pp. 233-243.

Graham, L. S., "Centralization versus Decentralization in the Administration of Public Service," *International Review of Administrative Sciences*, Vol. 46, No. 3, 1980, pp. 219-232.

Greenaway, J. R., "Bureaucrats Under Pressure: The Thatcher Government and the Mandarin Elite", *Teaching Politics*, Vol. 13, No. 1, Jun 1984, pp. 66-83.

Hawker, G., *Who's Master, Who's Servant? Reforming Bureaucracy*, Allen and Unwin, Sydney, 1981.

The Indian Journal of Public Administration, Vol. 31, No. 3, July-Sept 1985, Special Number on Administrative Reforms – Revisited, T. Chaturvedi, (ed.), pp. 459-1189.

Ingraham, P. W., and Ban, C., *Legislating Bureaucratic Change: The Civil Service Reform Act of 1978*, State University of New York Press, Albany, 1984.

Joao, B. O., *Desburocratizacao e Democracia*, Papirus, Sao Paulo, 1984.

Kaufman, H., "Reflections on Administrative Reorganization," In *Setting National Priorities: The 1978 Budget*, edited by J.A. Pechman, Brookings, Washington, D.C., 1977.

Keating M., and Hainsworth, P., *Decentralization and Change in Contemporary France*, Gower, Aldershot, 1986.

Khan, M. M., "Administrative Reform," *Indian Journal of Public Administration*, Vol. 24, No. 2, April-June 1979, pp. 170-180.

Khan, M. M., "Ruling Elites and Major Administrative Reforms: The Case of the Pakistan Civil Service," *Indian Journal of Political Science*, Vol. 41, No. 4, December 1980, pp. 729-760.

Krannich, R. L., "Administrative Reform and Role Responses in Thailand," *International Journal of Public Administration*, Vol. 2, No. 3, 1980, pp. 263-296.

Levine, C., "Citizenship and Service Delivery: The Promise of Coproduction", *Public Administration Review*, Vol. 44, March 1984 Special Issue, pp. 178-187.

Maheshwari, S., *Administrative Reform in India*, MacMillan, New Delhi, 1981.

March, J.G., and Olsen, J.P., "Organizing Political Life: What Administrative Reorganization Tells Us about Governing," *American Political Science Review*, Vol. 77, No. 2, June 1983, pp. 281-296.

March, J.G., and Olsen, J.P., *Rediscovering Institutions: The Organizational Basis of Politics*, Free Press, New York, 1989.

Mayo-Smith, I., and Ruther, N. L., *Achieving Improved Performance in Public Organizations: A Guide for Managers*, Kumarian Press, West Hartford, CT., 1986.

Miller, T., *Public Sector Performance: A Conceptual Turning Point*, The Johns Hopkins University Press, Baltimore, 1984.

National Academy of Public Administration, *Revitalizing Federal Management: Managers and their Overburdened Systems*, Washington, D.C., 1983.

Perlman, B., "Modernizing the Public Service in Latin America: Paradoxes of Latin American Public Administration," *International Journal of Public Administration*, Vol. 12, No. 6, 1989, pp. 671-704.

Plowden, W., et al., "New Directions in Administrative Reform," *International Review of Administrative Sciences*, Vol. 49, No. 1, 1983, pp. 96-109.

Public Administration and Development, Vol. 9, No. 3, June-August 1989, Special Issue: South Asia: Policy Developments and Administrative Changes Since Independence, O. Dwivedi (ed.), pp. 245-330.

Rondinelli, D. A., Nellis, J. R., and Cheema, G. S., *Decentralization in Developing Countries: A Review of Recent Experience*, World Bank Staff Working Paper no. 581, Washington, D.C., 1983.

Rose, R., "Ungovernability: Is There Fire Behind the Smoke,?" *Political Studies*, Vol. 27, No. 3, September 1979, pp. 351-370.

Rowat, D. C. (ed.), *International Handbook on Local Government Reorganization*, Greenwood Press, Westport, CT., 1980.

Saxena, A. P. (ed.), *Administrative Reforms for Decentralized Development*, Asian and Pacific Development Administration Centre, Kuala Lumpur, 1980.

Schick, A. (ed.), *Perspectives on Budgeting*, American Society for Public Administration, Washington, D.C., 1986.

Smith, R., and Weller, P. (eds.), *Public Service Inquiries in Australia*, University of Queensland Press, St. Lucia, 1978.

Szanton, P. (ed.), *Federal Reorganization: What Have We Learned?,* Chatham House, Chatham, N.J., 1981.

Tierney, J. T., *Postal Reorganization: Managing the Public's Business*, Auburn House Pub. Co., Boston, 1981.

Tummala, K. K., *The Ambiguity of Ideology and Administrative Reform*, Allied Publishers, Bombay, 1979.

Twentieth Century Fund, *The Government's Managers*, Priority Press Publishers, New York, 1987.

Wilenski, P., "Administrative Reform – General Principles and the Australian Experience", *Public Administration*, Vol. 64, No. 3, Autumn 1986, pp. 257-276.

Williams, R., *Political Corruption in Africa*, Gower, Aldershot, 1987.

6. In Pursuit of Betterment

Administrative reform is never far from the forefront of the contemporary administrative state. Nor should it be, given that the ability of modern technology to produce abundant public goods and services at reasonably affordable costs has far outstripped the capacity of administrative systems to deliver them efficiently, equitably and humanely. It is not for lack of knowledge that people want or preventable disasters occur. Rather it is because social systems fail and the fallible humans who compose administrative systems fall below expectations. When knowledge, technology and administrative know-how combine mankind can reach great and even greater heights. In less than one century, the administrative state has helped to double the average expectancy of life, eradicate preventable diseases, diminish hunger, sickness, ignorance and poverty, and generally given hope to the underprivileged in society. On the other hand, public maladministration can leave deep and deeper misery in its wake and most people know how frustrating it is to deal with insensitive, uncaring and incompetent bureaucrats. It is the vision of what could be contrasted with the evidence of what is that fuels administrative reform.

Unrealized Potential

Administrative reform is based on certain premises, rarely articulated by administrative reformers who believe them self evident. The first is the imperfectability of human institutions. No matter how much mankind improves itself, it can always do better. Nothing is yet perfect. Perfection is still beyond mankind's reach; human institutions are far from reaching their potential. Indeed, there are glaring imperfections that cry out for improvement and drastic change. Mankind is still experimenting with what works and what does not work. Only the exceptionally privileged can be content with the status quo and even they must have fears about the state of world affairs. It seems that for every two steps forward, mankind slips back a step and more. Progress is painfully slow. While in recent centuries economic prospects may have improved, humanity is still beset with religious hatred, racial discrimination, social dissent and national rivalries that threaten to end civilization altogether and perhaps all human life on the planet. Further, many of the worst disasters to befall mankind in recent years have been manmade and preventable (epidemics, poisons, oil spills, nuclear plant failures, chemical plant explosions, narcotics consumption, terrorism) and the growing destruction of the environment is solely manmade. All human arrangements are obviously capable of improvement, no matter how well they may or appear to be performing.

The second premise behind administrative reform is that large organizations, particularly large public organizations, tend to become overly conservative, if not complacent. Success breeds fixation rather than flexibility. Organizations stick to well proven formulae. They prefer administrative systems that work reasonably well rather than risk all on unproven innovations or uncertain changes. They do this even though conditions overtake them and seemingly everyone else can see that they are heading for trouble. Postmortems consistently reveal how often obvious warning signs were ignored and how frequently disconcerting reality was distorted to fit into comforting preconceptions, until it was too late to head off the disaster that was bound sooner or later to occur. Certainly, large organizations tend to become sluggish and much organization theory assumes that they naturally tend to entropy.

> …even excellent institutions run by excellent human beings are inherently sluggish, *not* hungry for innovation, *not* quick to respond to human need, *not* eager to reshape themselves to meet the challenge of the times. (Gardner, 1968, 2)

Public organizations seem particularly prone to caution and narrow or tunnel vision because (a) they are inherently subordinate institutions, dependent on the will (or lack of will) of their political overseers and they can only go at a pace acceptable to an apprehensive public; (b) they are publicly responsible and must judge to the best of their ability how the public will react and what is best in the public interest which means that they cannot go too far ahead of the public; (c) to ensure public accountability, they are so regulated and cumbrous in operation they cannot take high risks jeopardizing public safety and security; and more questionably (d) the people attracted to serve in them are possibly less entrepreneurial and innovative or their administrative systems impede the creative, the dynamic, and the agents of change, that is, public employees seem to relish the security of working for the government and value highly the familiar and unchanging. In any event, there is much reluctance to allow public servants to play fast and loose with national security, public safety, economic well-being, political compromise and social harmony, even should they be right. Cautious organizations cannot realize their full potential and often fail to recognize opportunities staring them in the face.

A third premise is that given the highly conservative disposition of most public organizations, innovation permeates too slowly. Even when a better way of doing things has been found, there is reluctance to try it. Always, somebody else has to demonstrate the effectiveness of innovations. Always, the evidence has to be examined and reexamined until any shadow of doubt is removed. Always, it takes considerable time, effort, energy and conviction to incorporate innovations. In the meantime, the outmoded and the outdated persist and they are perpetuated unless firm and drastic action is taken all the way down the line to see that things are changed. Likewise, there is a considerable gap between research and application. Even when research proves that administrative processes are wrong or bad or ineffective and suggests feasible alternatives, the findings are often denied by those too wedded to the status quo to change their ways or discounted by those too complacent to question what they do and what they could do differently. In any event, there is a gap, often a widening gap, between what is being done and what could and should be done. Worse still, their employees seem unaware of any gap and when made aware they are at a loss to know what to do about closing it.

> Most ailing organizations have developed a functional blindness to their own defects. They are suffering not because they can't *solve* their problems but because they won't *see* their problems. They can look straight at their faults and rationalize them as virtues or necessities. (Gardner, 1968, 42)

As these three premises have rarely proven incorrect, administrative reform has found a permanent place in the study and practice of public administration and management as governments strive to improve their own performance and tap the unrealized administrative potential of public organizations. Administrative reform is becoming increasingly institutionalized. Public administrators the world over are being educated and encouraged to be their own reformers. Public organizations are expected as a matter of course to keep up with the state-of-the-art, to promote innovation and to adopt professionally accredited research recommendations. Public professions are establishing governance systems that maintain professional standards by penalizing professional malpractices, insist on ever rising professional entry standards, and publicize advances in professional practice. Public inspection and audit agencies have taken upon themselves the duty not only of pointing out errors and mistakes but of suggesting ways and means by which errors and mistakes might be reduced. To all this momentum for administrative reform, it is becoming more commonplace for governments to appoint special, separate bodies whose major function is to promote administrative reform through research, investigation and experimentation. In addition, major international organizations have shifted their attention to improving their own delivery systems and encouraging member countries to increase their administrative capabilities and strengthen their managerial performance. A sign of the times was illustrated in the World Bank's sixth *World Development Report* (1983) where the focus was on measures necessary for improving management performance as central to achieving further economic development and more efficient use of scarce resources.

Administrative reform has thus moved up in government priorities, and for fairly obvious reasons that governments have to do more with less. The world-wide recession has diminished funds available for new investment and capital maintenance, particularly large scale public works, local government services and public utilities. Governments have had greater difficulty making ends meet and they have been reducing the number of people they employ and cutting back on their conditions of employment. Where governments have been unable to eliminate or drastically reduce their activities, the emphasis has been on trying to maintain the current level and quality of public goods and services while reducing costs. The aim has been to get greater value from public expenditure and higher productivity from public organizations. To realize greater potential from administrative systems, administrative reform has been disguised in more publicly appealing slogans as “privatization”, “cutback management”, “streamlining”, “modernization”, “simplification”, and “redeployment”. Under this guise all kinds of administrative reform plans and proposals have been revived, revised and implemented. Changes that had long been needed have been carried out. In such a receptive climate, much more radical proposals have been aired, preparing the way to a great deal of necessary house-cleaning and tidying up that had been long postponed. Political ideologues have been seizing the opportunity to pose fundamental questions about the nature and size of the administrative state, the need for so much administrative regulation, the efficiency of public monopolies, the productivity of public services, and the competence of public servants.

Such fundamental issues have long been raised by administrative reformers. In recent years they have been getting more of a response, sometimes not to their liking at all. Extreme anti-statist ideologues have seized upon their criticisms of public maladministration, exaggerated them and entered battle to do away altogether with the governmental or *public* provision of goods and services. More moderate ideologues want to retain the warfare state and some of the regulatory state but abandon the welfare state. Business executives, also armed with well-founded criticisms of the public sector, claim that all that has to be done is to run government like a business and to convert public organizations into business organizations, overlooking the obvious point that the aims, structure, activities and responsibilities of government are quite dissimilar to business and require quite different operating procedures, as business executives quickly find out when they are called upon to run public organizations. Every conceivable crank, guru, philosopher-king, and expert has been touting pet nostrums as administrative reform, without caring about or knowing or understanding the logic of public administration, in a universal quest to better the human condition.

Administrative Reform For What?

One of the major difficulties in preventing everyone and anyone who wants to better the human condition from advocating *administrative* solutions is the failure to separate ends from means. It is commonly though mistakenly believed that any improvement in means should result in an improvement in ends. After all, defective administration, poor management and inappropriate implementation obviously detract from performance and expected results and outcomes. In the same way, people believe that improved decision-making will make for better decisions, or improved policymaking will result in better policies. After all, defective decision making makes for poor decisions and poor policymaking produces bad policies. But just because bad means make for bad ends, it does not necessarily follow that good means make for good ends or, in the case of administrative reform, better means make for better ends. Nonetheless, administrative reformers link ends and means together. They believe that improvements in means will benefit the ends, just as night follows day. Administrative reform is not so much desired for itself but for the anticipated benefits that will occur in achieving better results. More people will share to a higher degree for a longer period with less difficulty, effort and resources. As the World Bank implied, better management should use scarce resources more economically and effectively to generate greater economic development.

The same understanding was implied in the United Nations' definition of administrative reform "as the deliberate use of authority and influence to apply new measures to an administrative system so as to change its goals, structures and procedures with a view to improving it for development purposes" (United Nations, 1983, 1). Jon Quah had previously gone so far as applying administrative reform only to organizations that were involved in realizing development objectives (Quah, 1976, p. 58). In this, he had followed Jose Abueva but without the latter's distinction between manifest or declared goals (indigenization, economy, streamlining, etc.) and undisclosed or undeclared goals (political control, empire building, spoils). Yehezkel Dror pointed out that administrative reform was multi-goal oriented, usually a mixture of intra-administrative goals primarily concerned with improving administration and extra-administrative goals dealing with the societal roles of administrative systems, including even purely political functions (Leemans, 1976, p. 130), and questioned whether they had any necessary connection to vague, abstract terms such as national development. Henry Kariel urged that emphasis be placed on extra-administrative goals.

> If we desire societies to be well administered; if furthermore, we realize it is merely question-begging to urge greater administrative efficiency; and if finally, we know we cannot reasonably speak of administrative reforms without defining the goals we wish to

realize, we cannot evade the attempt to define the ideals to be sustained by the machinery of the state. (Braibanti, 1969, 150)

Administrative reform should attempt to make the administrative arena approximate human ideals. He wanted no contradictions between ends and means.

As a result, ends and means are confused and fused. Administrative reform is justified not for itself but for its expected impact on furthering societal goals, such as national development, and advancing human endeavors. Thus, administrative reform proposals for international organizations promise to advance their activities – the end to hostilities, the resettlement of refugees, more food and better diets, safer air travel, uninterrupted communications, release of political prisoners, and so forth. Among its benefits are supposed to be:

- reduced human suffering, misery, pain, hunger, and poverty
- prevention of wars, physical violence, needless destruction of life and property
- conservation of nonreplaceable natural resources and preservation of unique cultural amenities
- protection of individual rights and liberties
- enhancement of life opportunities and the quality of life, social justice, and equity
- reduction of unused and underutilized productive capacity, waste, pollution, preventable deaths, overcrowding
- elimination of artificial barriers among peoples.

In short, administrative reform is valued for its potential or anticipated contribution to human progress or the quality of life. As such, it can contain every conceivable matter of public interest somewhere on the planet. The administrative aspect is merely the pretext to advance whatever cause people desire. It serves to demonstrate concern, clarify values, reaffirm ideology, challenge authority, test power, reorder priorities, remake policies, reenforce programs and symbolize action, i.e. its externalities not only deal with the benefits that are supposed to flow from better administration but also with the political gains that might result from pushing administrative reform as a challenge to the status quo.

A good illustration can be seen in Taiwan which has been subject to the single party authoritarian rule of the Kuomintang (K.M.T.) since freedom from Japanese occupation in 1945. As in mainland China, the people were impoverished and submissive until after the 1960s rapid economic growth brought into being a high social mobility, a strong, widening middle class, a redistribution of population, a shift in social values, a new experience of consumerism, and a growing desire to be free of government restrictions and controls and party networks based on lineage, religion and communal bonds. The K.M.T. establishment failed to incorporate the expanding middle class which desired a more open political system and rallied to the *Tangwai* movement that capitalized on middle class resentment of bureaucratic red-tape, unresponsive public enterprises, urban ills (over crowding, traffic jams, illegal parking, inadequate public amenities), pollution, and a tainted legal system. Administrative reform was a justifiable demand as public officials ignored complaints in the mass media about government inefficiency, waste, corruption, illegality, differential and deferential law enforcement, lagging public utility services, inadequate public infrastructure, and growing inequalities.

Behind the call for administrative reform was the desire of the middle class to have stronger input into public policy, greater political representation, alternatives to the officially sanctioned K.M.T. line, and more stress on private rather than government initiatives. The upward mobile wanted democratization, liberty, the impartial rule of law, and responsive public administration. Continually frustrated, *Tangwai* promoted mass organization and in 1986 established the Democratic Progressive Party (D.P.P.). In response to this new political challenge, the K.M.T. changed its line, adopted new policies, and introduced administrative reforms in such areas as environmental protection, social welfare and labor relations "to meet the demands of predominantly middle class civic organizations and public interest groups" (Chu Yun-Han, 1989, 18). In Taiwan, administrative reform had been backed initially as one way of opening up the political system. But once the political system had been opened up, political reforms required administrative reforms for their effective implementation. These in turn led to modifications and improvements in long standing governmental practices, including even the traditional civil service examinations and in-service training. Yet while these measures might still enable the public sector to attract talent they could not offset the growing attractiveness and superior compensation of the private sector and they probably would continue to lag behind rapid social and political transformations in Taiwan (Chen Wentsung, 1989), demonstrating the close ties between administrative reform and societal reforms.

Because of the extensive activities of the contemporary administrative state and the difficulties of distinguishing between the substance of administration and the objectives of administration, the internalities of administrative reform are no less ambitious. They deal with every aspect of the modern state, which in totalitarian regimes covers virtually everything, and all the petty details of modern management, anything and everything that might contribute to the better performance of public institutions and organizations and to the advantage of their clients and employees. Even a list of what might be termed strictly house-keeping aspects of the administrative state soon spills over into larger social issues such as the scope of government, the quality and nature of pre-employment education and training, the nature of industrial relations, the rights and duties of citizens, social ethics, the distribution of wealth, the incidence of taxation, social structure and so forth (see Table 1). Since they

Table 1: Major Concerns of Administrative Reformers

Governments

roles, functions, activities, aims, content, courage, quality, performance, suitability, adaptability
image, status, prestige, attractiveness, capacity, stability, readiness, quickness, harmony, integration
effectiveness, policymaking, information processing, consultation, advisory channels, public relations, outreach
size, structure, co-ordination, redundancy, scope and reach, communications, control, enforcement
costs, income, expenditure, debt, loans, financial management, reserves
employment, composition, capacity, quality, competence, competitiveness, stature, retention, mobility
construction, maintenance, aesthetics, mechanization and automation, location and siting
record-keeping, archives, paperwork, information processing
humanness, responsiveness, sensitivity, values (truthfulness, equity, etc.)
proactiveness, strategic management, forward planning, future capacity
breakdowns, bottlenecks, counterproductivity, illegitimacy, illegality, criminality, immorality
contracting out, contractual performance, contract supervision and administration

Organizations

objectives, goals, targets, social purpose, public need, policies, clientele, constituency, effectiveness
legitimacy, legal status, jurisdiction, authority, power, autonomy, monopoly, independence, accountability, law abidingness, regulations
inter-organizational relations, competition, coalition-building, public relations, contracting, industrial relations
size, form, structure, concentration, centralization, delegation, overlapping, duplication, coordination
functions, activities, diversification, compatibility, specialization, departmentalization, standardization
resources, capitalization, mechanization, factor mix, information retrieval, planning, reserves, supplies, stores
leadership, participation, representation, supervision, rules, controls
decisionmaking style, problem solving, conflict resolution, restrictive practices, communications (frequency, direction, credibility)
division of labor, work flow, interlocking processes, organization and methods (O.& M.), research, management services
record-keeping, accounting, auditing, property management, reports, budgeting, economy
staffing, recruiting, promotion, training, classification, compensation, incentives, security, safety, employment, turnover
culture, norms, ethos, ethics, discipline, sanctions
productivity, efficiency, adaptability, flexibility, competitiveness, survivability, innovativeness

Groups

permanence, unity, cohesion, compatibility, interdependence, conformity, congruence, conflict
autonomy, dependence
rank order, status, prestige
composition, openness
morale, loyalty, identification
norms, self-control, standards, targets, productivity, discipline

Individuals

rights, duties, obligations, loyalty, dependability, commitment
skills and aptitude, ability, health, competence, dependability, capacity, qualifications
knowledge, experience, articulation
judgment, values, ethics, responsibility, reliability
attitudes, beliefs, opinions, ambitions, aims, will, expectations
enthusiasm, incentive, drive, creativity, originality
job satisfaction, mobility

cannot be divorced and separated as a purely technical matter, administrative reformers use changes in public sector arrangements for their impact outside the public sector. By altering public sector requirements, they force far reaching changes in education, health, law and business. By making models out of public sector arrangements, they force other organizations to follow, as in the case of safety standards, non-discriminatory employment practices and arbitration procedures. Although the objectives of administrative reform are ostensibly to improve public sector administration, they are supported for their wider societal implications. Again, administrative reform is used as a lever for reforms that are not strictly administrative or for administrative changes beyond the public sector, that would bring the reformers' notion of a better world or their vision of the Good Society that much closer to reality, assuming that they act out of honorable, disinterested motives.

While reformers usually profess to good intentions, their acts may worsen the human situation. There are those who seek to improve administrative systems to carry out evil and wickedness, to create better killing machines, to perpetuate slavery, in short, to use administration for bad not for good, who see it as a purely technical instrument to be used for any objective. And there are those who seek to corrupt administrative systems, to aggrandize themselves, monopolize public office, enrich their families, destroy rivals, reward friends, punish opponents, and generally act perversely. Every so often, they succeed. They undo the good that has been done. They derail progress. They set the clock back. Each time this happens – and it happens all too frequently – the well intentioned reformers have to regroup and try again. Administrative reform is very much like pushing a large stone uphill. Left to itself, administration tends to slide backwards, even without the efforts of those who would gladly roll it downhill for their own evil designs.

The Folklore of Administrative Reform

Progress upwards can be measured against the ideals that well-intentioned administrative reformers have formulated and refined over the years and to which reference is constantly being made. These ideals cluster around the sixteen major areas of administrative reform.

1. Scope and activities of the administrative state
   overwhelming public need
   no other body as capable, competent and willing to meet need
   public interest requires non-private supply and delivery
   incentives to ensure continuous, affordable, private supply and delivery
   productivity, performance and worth

2. National planning, agenda setting, performance indicators
   imperative to anticipate and forecast immediate future
   proactive measures to deal with known future events
   allocation of guaranteed resources and reserves to priority concerns
   feedback for continuous adjustment

3. Organization and structure of the machinery of government
   strengthened control and coordination of diverse units
   reliable and dependable performance
   quick, effective action and conflict resolution
   economy of effort, resources, time
   responsible, responsive, sensitive exercise of public authority
   efficiency

4. Rule of law
   constitutional and legal limitations on public power and arbitrariness; law abidingness
   accountable exercise of discretionary authority
   public's right to know; access to information
   administrative due process

5. Public policymaking
   appropriate, highest possible quality; clear guidelines formation
   adequate supporting information, counsel and evaluation
   operability

6. Program execution
   state-of-the-art, professional delivery
   continuous monitoring
   adaptation to changing circumstances
   accessibility
   equity

7. Public budgeting and financial administration
   compatibility with national planning and public policy
   least waste; frugality
   detailed tracking of all monies and authorization of all transactions
   value for money

8. Public employment
   competence
   ideology of public service
   fair employment practices
   comparability of conditions
   resolution of disputes

9. Public regulation
   demonstration of real need
   impartial implementation and enforcement
   safeguards against abuse, failure and supersession
10. Public capital
   preservation and maintenance
   better utilization
   beautification
11. General services
   standardization and consistency
   instant availability
   quality performance
   best deal
   greater mechanization
12. Public enterprise
   demonstrated superiority over private enterprise
   positive impact on economic policy
   adequate return on investment
   fair pricing policies; non-exploitation of natural or legal monopoly
   consumer satisfaction; marketing
13. Public management practices
   more effective leadership and enterprise
   O.& M. principles
   debureaucratization
   paperwork reduction
   streamlining, simplicity and convenience
   productivity; elimination of feather-bedding
   discipline
14. Public ethics
   honesty and integrity
   professionalism
   humanitarian
   prevention of corruption, fraud, and misconduct
15. Public participation
   voluntarism
   coproduction
   complaint handling mechanisms
16. Institutionalization of administrative reform
   designated authority

research
training and education
innovation and experimentation.

Together these ideals constitute the folklore of administrative reform. They are articles of faith, principles of exhortation, emblazoned slogans, the closest to communality so far attained in administrative reform. They cover most of the territory and each has been fairly well explored, well enough to convince administrative reformers that this is the way to go. They promise improvements over the status quo and fortified they do seem to hamper back sliding. Moreover, they provide safe and secure ground on which to launch attacks on public maladministration.

In their zeal to do battle with their opponents, administrative reformers tend to get rather carried away. Folklore is after all folklore. It is not science, not until put through the same vigorous testing and substantiation. While over the past century, much progress in this direction has been achieved, much more testing has to be done. This has not stopped administrative reformers from overselling their wares. After all, to convince others, they must first convince themselves of the value of the product and then convey their enthusiasm to potential buyers. Naturally, they make the best case they can, and nothing helps like a few embellishments here and a few distortions there, "a certain shrillness…a little bombast to catch the eye of the consumers of reform," notably seen in the overselling of budget reforms which caused Allen Schick to comment, "The overselling of new ideas is a chronic problem in American public administration. Apparently, innovations cannot be successfully marketed unless they promise more than they can deliver" (Calista, 1986, 262). And to some extent reformers can get away with this because their product is largely untested. Nobody knows how it will perform in practice in a particular instance until it is tried, when, of course, it is too late to start over again should it fail to meet expectations. No product can be guaranteed to work in every circumstance.

When specific reforms fail to perform as promised and certainly when they fail to perform at all as every so often happens, the credibility of administrative reform itself is undermined. The going is made so much harder for the next set of reforms and reformers. This is especially true of reforms and reformers who focus on the perfectibility of public administration, the ideal administrative system, instead of contenting themselves with reversible imperfections. Success in administrative reform goes to those who keep their feet on the ground even if their heads are in the clouds. While there is a place for idealism in administrative reform, and a very necessary place, effective reformers have to be pragmatic. They have to settle for what they can get which is most unlikely to be what they originally set out to achieve. The best they can hope for is limited success.

Limited Success

Two examples from among many successful reforms show how reformers can improve government performance or at least prevent further deterioration, even if they do not achieve everything expected of them and expected from themselves. Both are drawn from the United States, one reform setting out to reduce needless government paperwork and the other attempting a quick turnaround of a badly performing public agency. All governments have been plagued with excessive paperwork but have rarely been able to do much about the problem. When the U.S. federal government began to get seriously troubled at the beginning of World War II, the Federal Reports Act of 1942 established some guidelines against the needless collection of information and made the Bureau of the Budget (B.O.B.) responsible for vetting agency plans to collect additional information. These measures did not prevent agencies from collecting more and more information thought justified in their operations or the propensity of Congress to exempt as much as 80 percent of federal paperwork from the clearance process. The growing expansion of paperwork added to government costs and increasingly irritated the public and small businesses. Not much formal objection was taken until the public lost confidence in big government in the early 1970s and began to have serious doubts whether all that information was really needed and was worth the cost and bother.

The Watergate scandal provided the lightning rod for the general reaction against federal government snooping activities. The Ford Administration identified paperwork reduction as part of its general policy of regulatory reform. President Ford wanted "an end to unnecessary, unfair and unclear regulations and to needless paperwork" while Congress appointed a Commission on Federal Paperwork which pushed hard for paperwork reduction (Weiss, 1989, 103). The Office of Management and Budget (B.O.B.'s successor) instigated a Forms Reduction Program to reduce the number of agency reports, a Burden Reduction Program to reduce the hours spent completing reports, and an Information Collection Budget to limit information requests. It also ordered sunset provisions on all reports to ensure regular reviews and reconfirmed justification and it restricted data collection from small businesses. The Carter Administration was just as eager to cut red-tape and paperasserie. It strengthened O.M.B.'s paper work reduction measures and O.M.B. was ordered to implement the recommendations of the Commission on Federal Paperwork. All these efforts culminated in the Paperwork Reduction Act of 1980 (which replaced the Federal Reports Act of 1942) so that by the time the Reagan Administration took office "most of the underbrush of paperwork burden" had been cut away (Ibid, p. 107) at least for the time being.

During the 1980s the overall paperwork burden began to grow again. Between 1982 and 1987, only 6 percent of some 20,000 information collection requests were disapproved by O.M.B.'s new Office of Information and Regulatory Affairs as being unnecessary or without practical utility. This small number had largely been the result of agencies establishing their own systematic reviews. Nevertheless, the thoroughness of the review process had caused increasing delays and same agencies felt that there had been a general chilling effect thereby reducing the availability of certain types of information which they considered necessary, credible and accurate. Furthermore, governmental insistence on annual reductions in the information collection budget which determined the maximum number of hours an agency could require the public to spend annually responding to its information collections, had reduced collections to the "bare bones" and was becoming counterproductive. Agencies were finding ways of getting around the legislation while the process was being manipulated to reduce the quality of information collected and to prevent ("redline") the collection of desired information (U.S.G.A.O., 1989, 14). In short, the original paperwork reforms of 1980 now required overhauling and reforms of their own, particularly the decentralization of paper work reviews and better resolution of what was meant by "unnecessary" as opposed to burdensome or unwelcome disclosure.

Meantime, not far from Washington, D.C., the corrupt Pennsylvania Department of Transportation (PennDOT), a wasteful and immobile bureaucracy in charge of a deplorable state highway system, was being turned around and revitalized, after a newly elected governor appointed the previous chair of the Transportation Advisory Committee to head the agency in 1978. The new head had been responsible for several critical analyses of highway and fiscal policies and was familiar with the agency's problems. The situation was deplorable. The highway construction program had been halted, maintenance was virtually at a standstill, most of the workforce was unqualified and beyond the agency's chain of command, and the whole system was in shambles (Poister and Larson, 1987). Yet in less than four years, the agency was turned around. The new management team adopted a strategic management approach (and implemented both M.B.O. and P.P.B.S.), ended political interference and patronage with a merit system, eliminated graft and corruption, captured complete control over the agency through a centralized program management committee, reorganization, reshuffling and streamlining, raised productivity, made large cost savings, and shifted expenditures. The team professionalized management and strengthened management systems, mounted an aggressive marketing and public relations campaign, and cultivated political support to gain infusions of additional funds. When the "do more with less" approach began to wear thin, the team adopted more employee oriented slogans such as "productivity through people" and "PennDOT – We're Making a Difference" to develop an administrative culture stressing productivity and excellence. Although the initial momentum could not be maintained, PennDOT was reinvigorated and transformed but PennDOT's problems reemerged in the late 1980s under new financial restraints and yet another change in management teams. The reforms could not be fully sustained. As so often happens, success had been only partial or temporary. The same story could be repeated over and over again about other acknowledged administrative reforms. Victories involved compromises or the original circumstances which brought about public maladministration reoccurred or reform pressures just could not be maintained beyond a certain point.

The reasons why reforms are never completely successful as contemplated are many and well known, and are no different from the usual restraining factors on government performance, political, bureaucratic and technical.

> Public policy makers and managers work in complex political and bureaucratic environments, responding to a multiplicity of competing goals, suffering from "information overload," and never armed with sufficient staff, time or financial resources to meet all the demands placed on them. Responsibility and authority are fragmented among multiple agencies, among different levels of government, and between the public and private sectors. Services are fragmented among programs with overlapping but different goals. Even within a single agency or program, there is disagreement over what would constitute 'high performance': disagreement over goals, disagreement over priorities, disagreement over the most important measures of performance. Policy makers and managers lack information on current performance and lack information on how to achieve higher performance. Given the constraints, uncertainties and disincentives they face, policy makers and managers tend to place relatively low priority on improving the performance of the agencies and programs for which they are responsible. (Wholey et al., 1989, 1)

If all these obstacles constrain government performance, they certainly handicap administrative reformers.

Reformers must look back from whence they started before they (and their critics) complain how far off they are from their original goals. Administrative systems take considerable time and patience to assemble into acceptable working models. Trial and error is the process; gradually administrators learn what to do and what to avoid. However, whatever is done will never satisfy reformers for that is the nature of reformers not to be content with what others accept. Yet to improve those systems, to make them work better, also requires time and patience, also involves trial and error, also means settling for what one can get rather than what one envisions.

> How can we make people understand that if they expect all good things instantly, they will destroy everything? How do we tell them that they must keep unrelenting pressure on their social institutions to accomplish beneficial change but must not, in a fit of rage, destroy those institutions?....(Gardner, 1968, 5)

If administrative systems were capable of instant transformation, they would not be what they are and what people, however begrudgingly, admire in them – their stability, their reliability, their dependability, their trustworthiness and their ability to function under normal circumstances. The process of reform cannot be speeded up unnaturally without damaging the reforms.

Assessment of administrative reform depends from which direction it is approached. If one is searching for the perfectibility of public administration, if one compares what is achieved (or achievable) against the unreachable ideal, then administrative reform is most disappointing. As Robert Miewald points out, "if one simply compares the wildest hopes (and some of those hopes were wild indeed)" with what actually happens, then most reforms must be counted as failures (Calista, 1986, 261). Reform from this perspective of completeness does not succeed anywhere. Nothing dramatic happens. No miracles occur. No public organization is transformed out of recognition. Human behavior does not change that significantly. The same old practices seem to be perpetuated even if the laws are changed and the people replaced. Certainly reformers often end disappointed, disillusioned, disenchanted. They feel cheated when halted prematurely. They bemoan all unfinished business.

If, on the other hand, one is searching for any improvement in the status quo, any reduction in public malpractices, then administrative reform works. Almost every day in every public organization, things are done that otherwise would not have been done without the presence of administrative reformers. Actions are different. Attitudes do change. Eventually, behavior too changes. Sometimes, the differences are imperceptible; they can only be seen over generations of public administrators. Other times, they can be readily demonstrated. Laws that protect human rights put the authority of the state behind them and mobilize the whole apparatus of the administrative state to protect rather than abuse those rights. Training that teaches people skills they never had before makes them different people who have to be treated differently. The example of one person can flow through a whole organization, making it a different place in which to work and a different organization to deal with. So too can those program planners who search for alternatives to government delivery and who redesign service delivery to provide for intergovernmental agreements, private contracting, coproduction and self-help, franchises, subsidization, volunteerism and vouchers (Ruchelman, 1989). These may be puny results in themselves but collectively over an appreciable time, they mount to much more. Progress may be slow, much slower than reformers would like, probably much too slow for the needs of the time, but it is made.

The ultimate key to administrative reform, to improving public sector performance, is in changing the administrative culture. Changing laws, overhauling organizations, elaborating guidelines, employing education and training, instituting new procedures – these will not work unless they change the attitude, behavior, and conduct of the administrators, indeed, of all public officials, that is, the way they all view the public and their responsibilities and duties, the objectives they set for themselves, the manner in which they conduct their business, even the way they view time, authority, service, and the Good Society. Inevitably, the pursuit of betterment in government and administration is bound up with such matters as the role of the state, the mobilization of community resources, the image of the public sector, accessibility to public office, performance criteria of public organizations, and the adaptive capacity of governmental systems to respond to changing public expectations. None of these is ever fully resolved. What unites reformers is not so much agreement on what constitutes good as a common desire to reduce bad, i.e. to end public malpractices, and to rid public office of unworthy incumbents.

> Most human arrangements that fall short of their goals do so not because of stupidity or faulty doctrines, but because of internal decay and rigidification. They grow stiff in the joints. They get in a rut. They go to seed... when the people in them go to seed...provided they are not too gravely afflicted with the diseases of which institutions die – among them complacency, myopia, an unwillingness to choose, and an unwillingness on the part of individuals to lend themselves to any worthy common purpose. (Gardner, 1968, 39-41)

For reformers, administrative reform is such a worthy common purpose, not because they will personally gain (for rarely they do) but because everyone will ultimately gain when the sicknesses which afflict administrative systems are remedied.

References

Braibanti, R. (ed.), *Political and Administrative Development*, Duke University Press, Durham, N.C., 1969.

Calista, D. (ed.), *Bureaucratic and Governmental Reform*, JAI Press, Greenwich, CT., 1986.

Chen Wen-tsung, "Testing for Talent", *Free China Review*, Vol. 39, No. 12, Dec 1989, pp. 4-14.

Chu Yun-Han, "The Search for Common Ground", *Free China Review*, Vol. 39, No. 11, Nov. 1989, pp. 12-19.

Gardner, J.W., *No Easy Victories*, Harper Colophon Books, Harper & Row, New York, 1968.

Leemans, A. (ed.), *The Management of Change in Government*, Institute of Social Studies, Martinus Nijhoff, The Hague, 1976.

Poister, J., and Larson, T., "The Revitalization of PennDOT: Strategies for Effective Public Management", Paper presented to 48th National A.S.P.A. Conference, Boston, MA, 1987.

Quah, J., "Administrative Reform: A Conceptual Analysis", *Philippine Journal of Public Administration*, Vol. 20, No.1, Jan. 1976, pp. 50-67.

Ruchelman, L., *A Workbook in Redesigning Public Services*, State University of New York Press, Albany, 1989.

United Nations, *Enhancing Capabilities for Administrative Reform in Developing Countries*, ST/ESA/SER.E/31, New York, 1983.

U.S. General Accounting Office, *Paperwork Reduction: Mixed Effects on Agency Decision Processes and Data Availability*, GAO/PEMD-89-20, Washington, D.C., 1989.

Weiss, J., "The Powers of Problem Definitions: The Case of Government Paperwork", *Policy Sciences*, Vol. 22, No. 2, 1989, pp.97-121.
Wholey, J. et al., *Improving Government Performance*, Jossey-Bass, San Francisco, 1989.
World Bank, *World Development Reports*, Washington, D.C., 1978 – .

7. Administrative Malpractices

Administrative reform has two major concerns. One is improving on what exists, that is, the pursuit of betterment imbedded in human aspirations to attain heights never before scaled and to realize or approximate near perfection in human arrangements. Its success can be measured by the steady improvements in the state of the art of administration, organization and management. In rich countries, most public arrangements now hum along at such a satisfactory level, that they are taken for granted and rarely questioned. Public administration in them ensures that things governments want done do get done reasonably well. Indeed, it works so well that most people don't have to think about it at all until they run foul of it or emergencies shatter their complacency. Otherwise, when it falters, it somehow detects its malfunctioning and institutionalized fail-safe procedures kick in for instantaneous correction. Their well-being would be impossible without such high levels of performance.

But public administration does go wrong, sometimes horrendously wrong, even in the most prosperous societies and most advantageous circumstances. Things don't get done at all or done so badly that everybody gets upset. Malfunctioning goes undetected for too long. The fail-safe devices do not operate or prove to be inadequate. This is the second of administrative reform's concerns, that of correcting administrative wrongdoing and deficiencies, i.e. maladministration. No matter how well-performing an administrative system may be, how pleased people might be with it and how difficult it is to conceive of improving it, somewhere things are wrong, mistakes are being made and justifiable grievances are being ignored. Moreover they may have been wrong for some appreciable time. Indeed, the whole endeavor may be one big mistake being perpetuated for no good reason. But the fact is that much administrative wrong occurs, warnings go unheeded, evidence is suppressed, correctable errors are ignored, and too little is done too late to avert avoidable tragedy.

As administrative malpractices are part and parcel of everyday life in modern society, for hardly a day goes by when people do not get irritated or annoyed or upset at some administrative malpractice or other, stories about bumbling bureaucrats and administrative snafus are legion around the world, each one more bizarre than the last (*U.S. New & World Report*, 1979). One would expect that obvious administrative malpractices would be a popular topic among administrative reformers and that correcting them would be of more immediate concern than devising grand schemes for future improvement. But this has not been the case. Perhaps administrative reformers have been realistic in recognizing that in the trillions of administrative actions that occur daily, a certain percentage no matter how minute will go wrong and that by concentrating on individual instances, the more important patterns they may make may escape attention. Perhaps investigating the wrongdoing of administration is not as appetizing as its right side and some social stigma may sick to researchers who harp on the bad rather than the good of government arrangements. Despite major efforts that went into identifying bureaucratic dysfunctions in the 1950s, there are precious few thorough studies of particular dysfunctions. No typology of administrative pathologies and morbidities appears in any major academic text on administration, organization and management or even in books that purport to explore the phenomena of counter productive organizational behavior (Brown, 1987).

One of the major obstacles is picking out gross errors of human judgment that can be attributed largely to *administrative* practices. Human activities and arrangements are so complex and complicated that everything is mixed up with everything else, the administrative with the non-administrative. Listen to a sample of excuses given by public administrators when things went wrong.

"We just followed orders. No, we did not question them. It was not permitted."

"We were given an impossible task. We were doomed from the very beginning. We did what we could but nothing would have succeeded."

"The job was too big and expectations were far too high, anyway quite unreasonable. It could never be done."

"We were never given adequate or proper resources. We were let down all the time."

"We were not given sufficient time. Deadlines were unrealistic and timetables too optimistic."

"It was an act of god. Nobody could have known or anticipated what happened."

"We were misinformed. Nobody told us. We never knew. They lied to us."

"We cannot change human behavior. People are like that. What else do you expect?"

They were not to blame. The fault was somewhere else or somebody else's. The totally unexpected and unpredictable intervened. No matter what they would have done, they could never have succeeded. In truth, administrators are often placed in impossible situations as when administrative solutions are offered for non-administrative problems or technical experts on whom they rely do not turn out to be so expert. But they are not placed in impossible situations as often as they claim. They are guilty. They have failed. Their performance was not good or not good enough. They did not correct what was obviously going wrong. Their job was to see that things did not go wrong and when they did go wrong to take the blame unless they could prove conclusively that somebody else was at fault.

Administrative Disaster

Everybody likes to take the credit for successes; nobody does for failures. When things go really wrong, people distance themselves. They make themselves scarce and they hide the facts through elaborate cover-ups. The nature of public administration is such that oftentimes no one is to blame but all collectively are to blame for what was done or what was not done. The blame goes to those who were in charge, i.e. to those who would have taken the credit had things worked out otherwise. When a country wins or loses a war, who gets the credit and who gets the blame? The heaviest responsibility is put on those who made the initial decision to enter into war, those who marshalled the country's resources for war, those who led the fighting forces in war, and those who actually fought in the war. Administratively, the finger would be pointed at those who assisted in making the key decisions and those who implemented them or saw that the decisions were implemented. It would be the administrators, managers, and supervisors and their closest advisors who would be held most administratively responsible and blameworthy, because they were in a position to make a difference, to support or to object to what was being done, to do things differently, to evaluate, alter, protest, to go along or not go along. As the same criteria can be applied to all social activities, administratively when things go wrong, it is possible to identify whose fault it is without blaming everyone or no one. If they did not know, they should have known or made it their business to know unless deliberately excluded from knowing or deceived. Their role is to accept the blame, produce the facts, take immediate action to minimize harm, and to reorganize to prevent any recurrence.

All have their daily brush with administrative malpractices which inconvenience, annoy, offend and intrude. People get so used to them that they no longer recognize them for what they are. People accept them and accommodate to them; people don't take them personally and shrug them off. Life is too short to fret over them. People may react more strongly to some that are particularly irksome with a mild protest or complaint but they do not expect that anything will be done about them. But every so often, people or some people will be sufficiently annoyed, bothered or hurt, that they do react strongly: they do protest and complain. They do expect corrective or remedial action. When nothing is done, they take offense and go on the offensive. These do become whistle-blowers, telling their tales to whoever will listen, persisting even against measures to silence them, and undergoing personal indignities to warn society of wrongdoing or upcoming tragedy (Truelson, 1987).

But even the horror stories told by whistle-blowers rarely amount to true administrative disasters that boggle the imagination when they do come to light. How could they have happened? Who could have been so dumb? Why didn't people do as they were instructed to do? Why didn't they follow procedures? Why didn't they ask obvious questions? Weren't they aware of the inevitable consequences? Here is gross maladministration from which few large scale organizations, public and private, have been spared. Most multinational corporations have made incredible errors of judgment, costing their shareholders and their customers huge losses. They have invested unwisely, located in the wrong places, designed faulty products, provided unsafe working conditions, produced for non-existent markets, acted wickedly, destroyed unnecessarily, and generally engaged in disgraceful practices. Models of excellence to be emulated have collapsed into models of failure to be shunned.

Not a day goes by when somewhere an administrative scandal is exposed which has had preventable disastrous results following a long period of neglected warnings. For instance, failure to follow routinized safety procedures and to inspect whether such routinized operations were actually being carried out has resulted in spacecraft, airplane and train crashes, ferry and boat sinkings, nuclear plant accidents, chemical explosions, oil spills, toxic poisoning, epidemics, auto and bus accidents, collapsed buildings and bridges, crushed spectators, and diseased patients, with considerable loss of innocent lives. Failure to audit finances and to see whether any accounting operations were actually being carried out has resulted in huge diversions of loans, fraud, kleptocracy, tax evasion, money laundering, smuggling, conspicuous consumption, vote buying, colossal theft, currency and stock manipulations, ruinous investments, and speculation, with considerable loss of hard earned monies. These administrative disasters occur so frequently with such harm and involve so many people that they cannot be ignored or brushed off as some freak, isolated, rare occurrence.

Administrative Self-destruction

Such self-destructive mistakes occur too frequently to attribute them to chance or accident or occasional weakness. Can they be inherent in large scale administration? Christopher Hood has sought to classify and explain some of the key mechanisms of such counter-intuitive behavior that contrive to defeat administrative effectiveness (Hood, 1974). He identified at least five distinctive types of administrative failure: –

overkill or diseconomy: results are achieved at unnecessary high cost
counter productive: results are contrary to those desired
inertia: nothing happens in response to stimulus

ineffectiveness: responses evoked merely rearrange inputs and outputs achieving little or nothing
tail chasing: the more is supplied, the more is demanded

and eight mechanisms involved: –

under- and over-organization: red-tape (ritualized procedures) and bribery (corruption)
wastage: revolving door employees
big stick syndrome: self-defeating controls and threats
negative demonstration: actions trigger antagonistic or perverse responses
time-lags: delayed responses (fighting yesterday's war)
reorganization: structural changes as symbolic responses, tokenism leaving substance untouched
suboptimization: component units defeat overall purpose; conflicting objectives; lack of coordination
professional fragmentation: shuffling problems and costs around.

His was a step toward identifying administrative diseases based on policy failures mostly in British public administration.

In a more light-hearted vein, Thomas Martin consolidated all the then laws of administrative behavior or rather of administrative misbehavior (kludgemanship) in the world of bureaucracy (blunderland) in which "almost every effort of almost every bureaucrat in almost every bureaucracy is counterproductive, nearly always producing results contradictory to those predicted and planned..." (Martin, 1973, 128). He cited gems already assimilated into English managerial parlance such as:

Murphy's Laws
If something can go wrong, it will.
When left to themselves, things always go from bad to worse.
Nature always sides with the hidden flaw.

Parkinson's Law (1957)
Work expands to fill the time available for its completion.
Officials multiply subordinates, not rivals.
Officials make work for each other.
Expenditure rises to meet income.
Delay is the deadliest form of denial.

The Peter Principle (1969)
In a hierarchy every employee tends to rise to his maximum level of incompetence.

and their many corollaries and variations, together with famous quotes applied to administration such as Lord Acton's "Power tends to corrupt and absolute power corrupts absolutely" and Gresham's "Trivial matters are handled promptly – important matters are never solved".

More seriously, Robert Kharasch investigated the laws of institutional behavior or rather of federal agency misbehaviors, blunders and gamesmanship and concluded that their malfunctioning was systematic, consistent and accelerating such that "Our great institutions are out of control" (Kharasch, 1973, 245). Peter Drucker came to similar conclusions and stated that "malperformance is increasingly being taken for granted...All we really expect now...is more expenditure, a bigger budget, and a more ineffectual bureaucracy" (Drucker, 1980, 103). Whereas Kharasch attributed malfunctioning to self-justificatory axioms that could be combatted by sixteen rules of institutional design, mostly tough minded managerial axioms, Drucker blamed "six deadly sins in public administration":–

giving lofty (unspecified) objectives without clear targets which could be measured, appraised and judged
doing several things at once without establishing and sticking to priorities
believing that "fat is beautiful," i.e. that abundance not competence got things done
being dogmatic, not experimental
failing to learn from experience and feedback
assuming immortality and being unwilling to abandon pointless programs.

Whereas Kharasch believed that public organizations were programmed for failure and could be programmed for success, Drucker was more sanguine. Avoiding the sins would not guarantee performance and results but at least it would be a prerequisite as "most administrators commit most of these "sins" all the time, and indeed, all of them most of the time" due to the cowardice of practitioners and the lack of concern with performance by theorists.

William Pierce went further in listing comprehensive types of bureaucratic failure besides malperformance (Pierce, 1981). He listed corruption (theft of materials, misuse of time on the job, bribery, misuse of office, conflicts of interest), misallocation of resources, technical inefficiency (waste, diseconomies, poor management, inappropriate investments, lack of innovation), ineffectiveness (useless activities, quiet ineffectuality, bad advice, egregious errors), subservience to clients, lack of coordination, conflicting objectives, spoils system, displacement of mandated objectives, favoritism, foot-dragging, arbitrariness, and inflexibility. His study was based on eleven cases of administrative failures in U.S. federal government, variously attributed to inadvertent legislation (written without forethought), ambiguous goals, inappropriate sanctions, incompetence, incompatible tasks, interorganizational conflict, defective management, turnover, excessive workload, and haste to spend. He put forward 75 hypotheses each beginning with "Failure is more likely...", under fifteen headings:

A. Hierarchical control	(5)
B. Control problems	(10)
C. Information	(11)
D. Measurement of output	(1)
E. Preferences and abilities of bureaucrats	(3)
F. Coordination	(5)
G. Structure of the organization	(7)
H. Interest groups in the political process	(7)
I. Political mechanisms of control	(11)
J. Bureaucratic influence on policy	(1)
K. Legislative control	(3)
L. Bargaining among agencies	(1)
M. Professional control	(6)
N. Incentives	(1)
O. Human side	(3)

He went beyond fairly standard American public organization theory by combining these hypotheses within major themes relating to miscommunication, immeasurable outputs, technical difficulties (environmental uncertainty and task complexity), ineffectual coordination, disregard of costs imposed on others, political problems, governmental turbulence, role conflicts, incompetent personnel, non-accountability, and inappropriate mandates. Presumably all these factors were recipes for administrative disaster if left uncorrected.

Maladministration

The breakdown of individual policies, programs and organizations did not constitute an indictment of a whole administrative system. They could always be aberrations although none of the quoted analysts thought so. They implied that whole administrative systems could self-destruct. Studies of post-colonial administrations in several newly independent states had indicated that systemically sick administrations did exist, which caused the societies they served so badly to fail to develop and even deteriorate. Unless they were turned around and turned around quickly, their future was bleak. John Montgomery had gone some way in the mid-1960s to catalogue complaints against such obstructive administrative systems:

> …resistance to change, rigid adherence to rules, reluctance to delegate authority, sycophancy toward superiors, "target" mentality, indifference to the standards of efficiency, ignorance of the purposes behind regulations, generalist-elitist orientation combined with hostility toward technology…insistence on status and prestige symbols, "formalism" or adherence to traditional relationships while desiring to appear modern; and…job-stocking and overstaffing, corruption, xenophobia, and nepotism. (Montgomery and Siffin, 1966, 262)

But these were often-heard criticisms of public bureaucracies the world over and read remarkably similar to those of William Robson:–

...an excessive sense of self-importance on the part of officials or an undue idea of the importance of their offices; an indifference towards the feelings or the convenience of individual citizens; an obsession with the binding and inflexible authority of departmental decisions, precedents, arrangements or forms, irrespective of how badly or with what injustice or hardship they may work in individual cases; a mania for regulations and formal procedure; a preoccupation with particular units of administration and an inability to consider the government as a whole; a failure to recognize the relations between the governors and the governed as an essential part of the democratic process. (Robson, 1964, 18)

and he quoted from the 1944 Parliamentary committee on civil service training:

...over devotion to precedent; remoteness from the rest of the community, inaccessibility and faulty handling of the general public; lack of initiative and imagination; ineffective organization and waste of manpower; procrastination and unwillingness to take responsibility or to give decisions. (Ibid)

Could there be a theory of public maladministration? Although individual administrative maladies have been identified for many centuries, no one has ever tried to combine them systematically. The closest attempt was made by F.H. Hayward who referred to common criticisms made of professionalism or the dangers of professionalism or professional depravity (Hayward, 1917). Since government service was also a profession, public administration shared them:–

perversity – professionalism became the enemy of the ends which it should serve and resisted innovations

treason – professionalism opposed the great aims of humanity as a whole in mistaken defense of its own procedures

self-seeking – professionalism sought to acquire power, privileges or emoluments for itself

cultivation of complexity and jargon – development and retention of complicated and laborious methods of work and jargon, the tendency to create work and jargon as means of maintaining or expanding professional importance

fear of definiteness – professionalism opposed definition and preciseness because they would allow standards by which it could be judged

hatred of supervision – particularly from the uninformed general public

self praise – vanity, exaggerated claims made for past professional achievements

secrecy – professionalism resisted prying eyes

uncreativeness – improvements mostly came from the laity and were opposed by professionals

abuse of power – professionalism was unchivalrous, tyrannical or cruel towards the weak in its care

malignity – professionalism waged a war of slander and spite against innovators, suggesting they were defective, unpractical, weak, unbalanced, without judgment, ignorant, hasty, plagiarizers, and motivated by self- seeking, self-achievement or private gain. (Warner, 1947, 63-65)

In these respects public administrators were the same as everybody else and they were subject to the same failings.

But the study of public maladministration as such had to await the spread of the institution of ombudsman from its native Scandinavia into the English-speaking world. Here, after 1960, was an organization established by governments to receive and investigate public complaints against government administration, a veritable gold mine of information about public maladministration. In 1973, Sir Kenneth Wheare chose maladministration and its remedies within British government administration as his topic for the Hamlyn Lectures (Wheare, 1973). But his main interest in so doing was focusing on comparative jurisprudence and showing how remedies for maladministration in Europe were superior to those in the United Kingdom. He did state that maladministration was present in all social organization, that the more administration there was, the more maladministration there would be, that while maladministration was difficult to define, most people could describe it by examples (illegality, corruption, ineptitude, neglect, perversity, turpitude, arbitrariness, undue delay, discourtesy, unfairness, bias, ignorance, incompetence, unnecessary secrecy, misconduct, and high handedness). The best that could be done was to quote an ombudsman's definition of maladministration: "administrative action (or inaction) based on or influenced by improper considerations or conduct." Bernard Frank elaborated on this position in his view of the ombudsman as an office to prevent:

...injustice, failure to carry out legislative intent, unreasonable delay, administrative error, abuse of discretion, lack of courtesy, clerical error, oppression, oversight, negligence, inadequate investigation, unfair policy, partiality, failure to communicate, rudeness, maladministration, unfairness, unreasonableness, arbitrariness, arrogance, inefficiency, violation of law or regulation, abuse of authority, discrimination, errors, mistakes, carelessness, disagreement with discretionary decisions, improper motivation, irrelevant consideration, inadequate or obscure explanation, and all the other acts that are frequently inflicted upon the governed by those who govern, intentionally or unintentionally. (Frank, 1976, 132)

Based on actual complaints investigated by the British version of the ombudsman, Geoffrey Marshall concluded that maladministration was both a matter of instinct and an acquired technique (Marshall, 1975). Facetiously, he suggested 15 maxims for the potential maladministrator, which give the flavor of administrative gamesmanship: –

- Don't volunteer written explanations of decisions
- Don't allow access to technical, legal or other advice received
- Frequently change policies randomly

- Arrange for high position turnover so that different people deal with the same case
- Delay acting on favorable jurisdictional points until after expiry of possible client remedies
- Ensure overlapping responsibilities without easy coordination
- Don't record (but misfile) correspondence
- Don't volunteer assistance
- Leave uncertainty about conclusions reached and next steps
- Draw out consultation
- Refer to being overworked
- Jumble communications
- Keep files moving
- Open multiple files without cross-referencing
- Arrange for occasional erroneous release of libellous internal memoranda.

Again, these are all singular rather than institutionalized instances of maladministration. None of them include crimes committed by people in organizations either on their own behalf against organizational norms (theft, violation of trust, fraud, tax evasion, embezzlement) or at the behest of their organization (genocide, torture, murder, robbery, coercion, terror, intimidation, crimes against humanity, etc.) (Smigel and Ross, 1970).

A novel experiment was tried in the early 1970s at the Institute of Administration at the University of Ife, Nigeria, where 72 Nigerian civil servants wrote case studies of malpractices. Factor analysis pointed to six leading causes preventing initiative – corruption and lack of integrity, community conflict and aggression, inefficiency, sectarian conflict, misconduct and indiscipline, and bad authority relationships. Specific cultural items – "rumor, accusations, denunciations, suspicion, intrigue, threats, blackmail, coercion, malice and inequitable treatment of individuals without cause" – suggested a paranoid personality in "a social climate of pervasive anomie, distrust and lawlessness" (Bowden, 1976, 392). As Yoriba culture was "dysfunctionally distorted toward a schizoid-paranoid form of culture personality," there could be little room for initiative where suspicion, intrigue and insecurity was combined with the stultifying effect of authoritarianism in which deference was paid to age and rank. Here was a culture of maladministration akin to repressive authoritarianism found throughout history and depicted in its modern form by Franz Kafka before being exemplified in Nazism, Stalinism and Latin American fascism.

Bureaucratization

Institutionalized maladministration is not attributed so much to authoritarian cultures or psychotic individuals as to increasing reliance in human arrangements on the bureaucratic form of administration, i.e. the process of bureaucratization. The critics of bureaucratization range ideologically from extreme Left to extreme Right but they all have one thing in common – they do not like contemporary society or certain dominant aspects of it. They blame the process of bureaucratization and the bureaucratic form of administration which they see as being inherently defective and a curse on modern society. They dislike bureaucratization altogether or for what it does to society, organization and individuals. They object variously to authority, technocracy, meritocracy, materialism, consumerism, capitalism, state power, complexity, mass culture, elitism, large organizations, self-serving administration, impersonality, complexity, legalism, specialization, careerism, formalism, dependency and anything else they attribute to bureaucratization. They seek to reverse the process of bureaucratization, that is, to turn back the clock to before the organizational society or to advance the clock to a debureaucratized (or post-bureaucratic) society, to liberate people from organization, to eliminate rule by officials, to reduce administration by experts, to minimize public sector administration, to make organizations less dysfunctional and to get rid of administrative diseases.

Bureaucratization, according to it critics, has been a wrong step for humanity. To reform bureaucracy, to improve it, to make it work better, would only make things worse. It should be replaced altogether with alternatives that are not inherently bad. The critics think this way because they see beyond bureaucracy, beyond instrumentality, to the ultimate goals and objectives of society (O'Leary, 1988). For the Left, bureaucratization has been associated with exploitive capitalism, public bureaucracy and the administrative state have been seen as handmaidens for capitalism, and bureaucratic organizations have been viewed as counter productive for genuine democratization. For the Right, bureaucratization has been associated with creeping socialism, public bureaucracy and the administrative state have been seen as handmaidens for the socialist state, and bureaucratic organizations have been viewed as counter productive to liberty and enterprise. Neither has envisaged bureaucracy in its future and neither has come to terms with bureaucratization. Both have distorted history and contemporary reality to fit preconceived notions of naive simplicity. Big government and big business are more allies than enemies in the contemporary world and they are both more or less bureaucratic in operation.

The New Right says that is just the trouble; they are too cozy, too interdependent, too self-aggrandizing, too unaccountable, too secure, too complacent, too inefficient, too unproductive, too illiberal, too uncompetitive, too stagnant. Big government should be reduced, privatization expanded, free markets (and free choice) restored, and individual self-reliance boosted, even if it increases economic inequality and reduces political liberty. The New Left agrees; they are too bourgeois, too self serving, too corrupt, too coercive, too alienating, too stifling. Big government should be decentralized, public organizations made more representative, self-management encouraged, demarchy[1] boosted (Burnheim, 1985), even if private enterprise is increased and the political monopoly of the Communist Party is ended. Both the New Right and the New Left propose radical if diametrically opposed solutions. Both want to get rid of the administrative state and any possibility of bureaucratic government (Peters, 1981) because they do not want bureaucrats to rule or fill power vacuums. The New Right would prefer to rely almost exclusively on private initiatives and market forces while the New Left would prefer autonomous self governing communities. Neither really tackles the challenge of contemporary bureaucracy or bureaucratization.

Less politically motivated opponents of bureaucratization do believe that they have better solutions and that they can reverse the process of bureaucratization. They do not associate bureaucratization with either capitalism or socialism but with the evolution of a global economy, industrialization, urbanization and the need to deliver uniform goods and services on a larger and larger scale. The scale will continue to grow but the model of production, the techniques of administration, and the nature of organization will be transformed by technology, especially information technology. The rigid hierarchical structure of bureaucracy will be replaced by more flexible, participatory, temporary organizations beyond bureaucracy (Bennis, 1973) as machines replace human labor altogether in the post-industrial world. The adhocracy of the future (Toffler, 1971) would be smaller, less hierarchical, more professional, less routinized, more innovative, providing more creative, meaningful, stimulating work and more collaborative, personalized, responsive management. Computers spell the death of bureaucracy. They will reduce the number of clerical functionaries and blue collar workers, ensure the accurate dissemination of information, eliminate much job fragmentation, place people into electronic networks, minimize paperwork, decentralize decision-making, broaden effective participation, and free people from economic serfdom.

Once the realm of futurizing and science fiction is entered, it is anyone's guess what the future may hold. Far from correcting the undesirable fruits of bureaucratization, they may well be exacerbated. So far, there has been no sign of their reduction. Bureaucracy has not declined. Big has not turned out to be so ugly. On the contrary, as people wake up to their rights all over the world and raise their expectations, so they insist on constitutionalism, rule of law, equal consideration, due process, equity, protection, access, competence, regularity, quality, fairness, responsibility, accountability, openness, and those other factors that have promoted bureaucracy. Bureaucratization may well have peaked. That will not be known just yet. In the meantime, the process of bureaucratization has

---

1 A society served by autonomous specialized agencies staffed by experts but run by continuously changing statistically representative samples of the adult population.

transformed the way people work and live. There have been great gains and heavy costs. Undoubtedly some cherished values of the past – self-reliance, individual initiative, independence, integrity, the work ethic, altruism, competitiveness – have suffered in the process of bureaucratization and bureaucracy has been carried too far in some areas, but this does not mean that other equally cherished values have not gained more and that bureaucracy cannot be readjusted (Hummel, 1982). On the other hand, bureaucracy does carry within it a high propensity for maladministration.

Bureausis and Bureaucratic Dysfunctions

Bureaucratization has transformed the way people work and live. For many, the change has not been easy. A few have never accepted the change. They hate bureaucracy, all bureaucracy, and resent it. Because the source of criticism is external to bureaucracy, Victor Thompson termed this anti-bureaucratic, non cooperative behavior "bureausis," whose basic ingredient was "immaturity, the dysfunctional persistence of childish behavior patterns" (Thompson, 1961, 170) by people unable to adapt to the complexity, impersonality and impartiality of modern organizations. These bureautics resist answering personal questions as an invasion of their privacy, have low powers of abstraction and need to personalize the world, feel powerless and alienated because they want to be the center of attention everywhere and want instant gratification. They find intolerable the rationalism, orderliness, impartiality, and impersonality of bureaucracy. As other avenues of employment decline, they are employed in bureaucracies where they behave with the same non-cooperation, personalization, alienation and suspicion, which spill over in the way they treat others inside and outside the organization, and so give rise to justifiable complaints about maladministration.

Apparently everybody else can adjust to being small cogs in a large impersonal organization and accept the fact that they lose control over personal destiny, lose their freedom and independence, and realize the need to get along and conform as good organizational/bureaucratic people. But bureaucracies generate tension and insecurities and in reducing them, people also indulge in behavior which is dysfunctional to the organization; they indulge in "bureaupathic behavior" (Ibid, 24) such as dramaturgy (or creating a favorable impression), aloofness, ritualistic attachment to routines, petty insistence on turf, appearance of busyness, resistance to change, and excessive protection (the paperwork proof). These do not advance organizational goals but reflect the personal needs of individuals; they are self-serving behavior patterns. Harry Levinson disagreed (Levinson, 1972). His research on the psychological problems of individuals at work (which resulted in accidents, absenteeism and alcoholism) led him to conclude that the way an organization was managed impacted the mental health of people who worked in it. “Logically, then, an important mode of preventing emotional distress was to understand organizational malfunctioning…” (Ibid, ix). In short, maybe the organization was more to blame than the individual.

That bureaucracy had inherent dysfunctions had long been known. Its unanticipated dysfunctional consequences had been subject to much sociological analysis. Karl Marx had identified the maintenance of the status quo, promotion of incompetence, alienation, lack of imagination, fear of responsibility, and rigid control over the masses. Robert Michels had recognized that democratic participation was technically impossible in complex organizations. Max Weber perceived that bureaucracy threatened democracy by demanding the sacrifice of freedom. But it was Robert Merton in the 1930s who first emphasized dysfunctions that impeded effectiveness when conflicting or displacing organizational goals i.e. means became ends in themselves (Merton, 1936). He later identified rigidity (1940), while Phillip Selznick (1949) added bifurcation of interests and Alvin Gouldner (1954) punitive supervision. These and other dysfunctions (mediocrity, officiousness, stratification, gamesmanship) sabotaged bureaucracy.

Studies of over-bureaucratized organizations such as multinational corporations, armed forces, prisons, legal systems, mail services, and welfare agencies indicate how the functional elements of bureaucracy – specialization, hierarchy, rules, managerial direction, impersonality and careerism – if overdone turn dysfunctional and counter productive, alienating employees and clients. Its virtues become vices.

Specialization → job differentiation, position classification, simple task performance, productivity → boring routine, soul destroying work, indifferent and careless performance, escapism, soldiering, flawed output, doctrine of the minimum, detachment,sabotage → low productivity

Hierarchy → concentrated authority, direction, coordination, accountability → fixed jurisdiction, limited perspectives, narrow responsibility → turf battles, suboptimization, self-contrived barriers, status differentiation → information filters, self justification, manufacturing needless work, self-protection → isolated, self indulgent elites, fragmented power, vacuums → irresponsibility, ignorant leadership

Rules → standardization, uniformity, consistency, equity → red-tape, rigidity, legalism, ritualism → transposition of goals, process as end, incomprehension → substitution of informal norms, contradictions, cross purposes → corruption → arbitrariness, discrimination, injustice

Managerialism → leadership, smooth working, harmony → forced promotions, loss of expertise, misuse of talent → jargon, artificial measures of success, passing on incompetence → lack of proprietary interest, technical ignorance → followership, mismanagement

Impersonality → objectivity, impartiality, equality → dehumanization, insensitivity, callousness → burnout, uncaring, indignities, suffering, degradation → servility, intimidation, coercion, inhumanity

Careerism → competence, loyalty, concentration → socialization, self-protection, limited experience → self-perpetuation, narrow vision, assumed progression → no incentives, mediocrity, time-serving.

An organization can start out with all the virtues of bureaucracy and soon decline with all its vices, a process which James Boren described as *mellownization* "as dynamic action is replaced by dynamic inaction" (Boren, 1975, 7).

Jack Douglas believes that contemporary bureaucracies go through cycles similar to those experienced by ancient dynasties. They begin dynamically and grapple with real problems directly, simply and successfully. They have vigorous administration and entrepreneurial bureaucrats uplifted with ideas and bounding confidence bending the rationalistic, legalistic forms to achieve their goals. Because they work or work better than any predecessors people demand more and get hooked on entrepreneurial bureaucracy. They grow, adopt increasingly formal-rational methods of recruitment and administration and become increasingly distant from the people, and stiffling. Their efficiency declines and they subvert their resources and power, becoming corrupt and usurpatory, succumbing to machinations that eventually give way to self-serving, change resistant, devious, ineffective and corrupt bureaucrats. They decline into bureaucratic factionalism, inertia, "the fluorescence of (useless) reform movements" (that mostly rationalize their appeals for more power, money and personnel), irresponsibility, and self-directing fiefdoms, invoking rebellion by the populace and conquest by new entrepreneurial bureaucrats who repeat the cycle. He compared the dynamism of the Roosevelt New Deal social welfare bureaucrats such as Harry Hopkins with contemporary social welfare agencies:–

> …some of the bureaucrats are still dedicated, at least when they begin, but they soon burn out from the immensity of the rules, the relative inflexibility of the regulations. and the apparent uselessness and unprofitability of all their efforts…Careerism, alienation, factionalism, inefficiency, and displacement of goals are their most important products. (Douglas, 1989, 407-8)

He largely blamed the informational pathologies inherent in bureaucracy, such as the divorce of income from expenditure and inputs from outputs, the lack of marketing price and profit signals, the absence of proportioned feedback, information distortions and blockages, the emphasis on conformity, the propensity for sabotage, hyperinflexibility, elongated chains of command, enfeudation, conspiracy to defraud and deceive, disinformation, and sheer size. But they are not the only bureaupathologies that attack administration.

Bureaupathologies

These vices, maladies, and sicknesses of bureaucracy constitute bureaupathologies. They are not the personal failings of individuals who compose organizations but the systematic shortcomings of organizations which cause individuals within them to be guilty of malpractices. They cannot be corrected by separating the guilty from the organization for the malpractices will continue irrespective of the organization's composition. They are not random, isolated incidents either. While they may not be regular, they are not so rare either (see Table 1). When they occur, little action is taken to prevent their recurrence or can be taken as in the case of anorexia (debilitation) and *gattopardismo* (superficiality) (Dunsire and Hood, 1989). They are not just physical either; organizations also suffer definite mental illnesses or neuroses too – paranoid, compulsive, dramatic, depressive, and schizoid (Kets de Vries and Miller, 1985). To correct them, wholesale changes are needed, i.e. administrative reform. But how are bureaupathologies to be tackled? Who knows of them? Who can identify them for what they are? Who can attempt a cure? And what happens when cures are attempted?

The greatest obstacle for administrative reformers to overcome is that of bureaucratic complacency and inertia. Bureaupathologies often create a comfortable, serene and relaxed atmosphere in which work is performed after a style and everything on the surface looks fine (Levin, 1970; Warwick, 1975). But dig below the surface, as ombudsman and whistleblowers reveal, and maladies abound and persist. The people in the diseased organization agree that what is being done is unsatisfactory and capable of considerable improvement. As individuals they all welcome change and reform. They may even be agreed on the specific changes they would like to see made. Plans may have been made, guidelines readied, staff prepared, but they are still waiting for a more opportune moment that never seems to arrive. Or they have kept abreast of discoveries in their field and are keen to try some new ideas. But nobody is prepared to take the first step and the same ideas are discussed repeatedly without any action being taken. Or some people do take upon themselves the responsibility for initiating change and design suitable, feasible, doable proposals, which they know beforehand are acceptable. But they never hear again what happened to their proposals. Nobody knows why. They have been lost in the works.

Table 1: Common Bureaupathologies

- Abuse of authority/power/position
- Account padding
- Alienation
- Anorexia
- Arbitrariness
- Arrogance
- Bias
- Blurring issues
- Boondoggles
- Bribery
- Bureaucratese (unintelligibility)
- Busywork
- Carelessness
- Chisling
- Coercion
- Complacency
- Compulsive
- Conflicts of interest/objectives
- Confusion
- Conspiracy
- Corruption
- Counter-production
- Cowardice
- Criminality
- Deadwood
- Deceit and deception
- Dedication to status quo
- Defective goods
- Delay
- Deterioration
- Discourtesy
- Discrimination
- Diseconomies of size
- Displacement of goals/objectives
- Dogmatism
- Dramaturgy
- Empire-building
- Excessive social costs/complexity
- Exploitation
- Extortion
- Extravagance
- Failure to acknowledge/act/answer/respond
- Favoritism
- Fear (of change, innovation, risk)
- Finagling
- Footdragging
- Framing
- Fraud
- Fudging/fuzzing (issues)
- Gamesmanship
- Gattopardismo
- Ghost employees
- Gobbledygook/jargon
- Highhandedness
- Ignorance
- Illegality
- Impervious to criticism/suggestion
- Improper motivation
- Inability to learn
- Inaccessibility
- Inaction
- Inadequate rewards and incentives
- Inadequate working conditions
- Inappropriateness
- Incompatible tasks
- Incompetence
- Inconvenience
- Indecision (decidophobia)
- Indifference
- Indiscipline
- Ineffectiveness
- Ineptitude
- Inertia
- Inferior quality
- Inflexibility
- Inhumanity
- Injustice
- Insensitivity
- Insolence
- Intimidation
- Irregularity
- Irrelevance
- Irresolution
- Irresponsibility
- Kleptocracy
- Lack of commitment
- Lack of coordination
- Lack of creativity/experimentation/innovation
- Lack of credibility
- Lack of imagination
- Lack of initiative
- Lack of imagination
- Lack of performance indicators
- Lack of vision
- Lawlessness
- Laxity
- Leadership vacuums
- Malfeasance
- Malice
- Malignity
- Meaningless/make work
- Mediocrity
- Mellownization
- Mindless job performance
- Miscommunication
- Misconduct
- Misfeasance
- Misinformation
- Misplaced zeal
- Negativism
- Negligence/neglect
- Nepotism
- Neuroticism
- Nonaccountability
- Noncommunication
- Nonfeasance
- Nonproductivity
- Obscurity
- Obstruction
- Officiousness
- Oppression
- Overkill
- Oversight
- Overspread
- Overstaffing
- Paperasserie
- Paranoia
- Patronage
- Payoffs and kickbacks
- Perversity
- Phony contracts
- Pointless activity
- Procrastination
- Punitive supervision
- Red-tape
- Reluctance to delegate
- Reluctance to take decisions
- Reluctance to take responsibility
- Remoteness
- Rigidity
- Rip-offs
- Ritualism
- Rudeness
- Sabotage
- Scams
- Secrecy
- Self-perpetuation
- Self-seeking
- Self-serving
- Slick bookkeeping
- Sloppiness
- Social astigmatism(failure to see problems)
- Soul destroying work
- Spendthrift
- Spoils
- Stagnation
- Stalling
- Stonewalling
- Suboptimization
- Sycophancy
- Tail-chasing
- Tampering
- Territorial imperative
- Theft
- Tokenism
- Tunnel vision
- Unclear objectives
- Unfairness
- Unnecessary work
- Unprofessional conduct
- Unreasonableness
- Unsafe conditions
- Unsuitable premises and equipment
- Usurpatory
- Vanity
- Vested interest
- Vindictiveness
- Waste
- Whim
- Xenophobia

In such inert organizations, the people are not lazy. On the contrary, they work hard and keep busy coping with daily demands. Everybody appears to be fully occupied, carrying out their set tasks and observing the directions issued to them. Each is loyal to the organization, each approves of its mission, each is keen to do a good job. All are aware of its shortcomings and deficiencies. They know of its mistakes and errors and can recount horror stories they know about. Between them, they have a pretty good idea how it can be improved, and they personally are willing to try something different to improve its performance. Yet, somehow little changes. The same old patterns and routines are preserved, the shortcomings and deficiencies are perpetuated, mistakes and errors are repeated. When the organization does change, it moves slowly, incrementally, and predictably, and then not always in the right direction. It fails to adjust in time to changes in its environment. It becomes insensitive to criticism. It appears not to know or want to know what is really going on. Everything stays pretty much the same. Nobody knows why. Nobody admits responsibility. Nobody confesses error. Nobody ends wrongdoing. It is as if the organization has a mind of its own, a mind closed to any other way of doing things. In fact, by failing to anticipate, recognize, avoid, neutralize or adapt to pressures that threaten its long term survival, it is in a serious state of decline threatening enormous social repercussions to the economy and society, and to the individuals dependent on it for products and services and jobs (Cameron et al., 1988; Weitzel and Jonsson, 1989). A dose of organizational development might rejuvenate it (Guy, 1989) or a good demotional shake-up may suffice to reinvigorate it (Golembiewski, 1983) but already it may be too blind to recognize threats, too inert to decide on a remedial course of action, too incompetent to make and implement the right actions, too crisis ridden to accept the need for major reform, and even too far gone to save. It is beyond rescue. Maladministration harms, but bureaupathologies eventually kill.

References

Bennis, W. *Beyond Bureaucracy*, McGraw-Hill, New York, 1973.

Boren, J. *Have Your Way With Bureaucrats*,, Chilton Book Co., Radnor, PA., 1975.

Bowden, E., "Maladministration: A Thematic Analysis of Nigerian Case Studies in the Context of Administrative Initiative", *Human Organization*, Vol. 35, No. 4, Winter 1976, pp. 391-394.

Brown, D., *Management's Hidden Enemy and What Can Be Done About It*, Lomond, Mt. Airy, MD., 1987.

Burnheim, J., *Is Democracy Possible?*, Polity Press, Cambridge, 1985.

Cameron, K.S., Sutton, R.I., and Whetten, D.A. (eds.), *Readings in Organizational Decline*, Ballinger Publishing Co., Cambridge, MA, 1988.

Douglas, J., *The Myth of the Welfare State*, Transaction Publishers, New Brunswick, N.J., 1989.

Drucker, Peter, "The Deadly Sins in Public Administration", *Public Administration Review*, Vol. 40, No. 2, March/April, 1980, pp. 103-106.

Dunsire, A., and Hood, C., *Cutback Management in Public Bureaucracies*, University of Cambridge Press, Cambridge, 1989.

Frank, B., "The Ombudsman and Human Rights Revisited," *Israel Yearbook on Human Rights*, Vol. 6, 1976, Tel Aviv University, pp. 122-156.

Golembiewski, R.T., "The Demotion Design: An Option for Forward-Looking Organizations," *National Productivity Review*, Vol. 2, No. 1, Winter 1982-1983, pp. 63-70.

Gouldner, A.W. *Patterns of Industrial Bureaucracy*, Free Press, Glencoe, IL., 1954.

Guy, M.E., *Organizational Decline to Organizational Renewal*, Quorum Books, New York, 1989.

Hayward, F.H., *Professionalism and Originality*, Allen & Unwin, London, 1917.

Hood, C., "Administrative Diseases: Some Types of Dysfunctionality in Administration," *Public Administration*, Vol. 52, No. 4, Autumn 1974, pp. 439-454.

Hummel, R., *The Bureaucratic Experience*, St. Martin's Press, New York, 1982.

Kets de Vries, F.R., and Miller, D., *The Neurotic Organization*, Jossey-Bass Publishers, San Francisco, 1985.

Kharasch, R.N., *The Institutional Imperative*, Charterhouse Books, New York, 1973.

Levin, A. *The Satisficers*, The McCall Publishing Company, New York, 1970.

Levinson, H. *Organizational Diagnosis*, Harvard University Press, Cambridge MA., 1972.

Marshall, G., "Technique of Maladministration", *Political Studies*, Vol. 23, Nos. 2-3, 1975, pp. 305-310.

Martin, T., *Malice in Blunderland*, McGraw-Hill, New York, 1973.

Merton, R. "Bureaucratic Structure and Personality", *Social Forces*, Vol. 18, 1940, pp. 560-568.

Merton, R. "The Unanticipated Consequences of Purposive Social Action", *American Sociological Review*, Vol. 1, 1936, pp. 894-904.

Montgomery, J., and Siffen, W.J. (eds.), *Approaches to Development: Politics, Administration and Change*, McGraw-Hill, New York, 1966.

O'Leary, B., "The Limits to Bureaucide: A Critical Analysis of Three Visions of Debureaucratization", Paper presented to the Round Table on Administration Without Bureaucracy, International Institute of Administrative Sciences, Budapest, 1988.

Parkinson, C. Northcote, *Parkinson's Law*, Houghton Mifflin, New York, 1957.

Peter, L., and Hull, R., *The Peter Principle*, William Morrow & Co., New York, 1969.

Peters, B.G., "The Problems of Bureaucratic Government", *Journal of Politics*, Vol. 43, No. 1, February 1981, pp. 56-82.

Pierce, W.S., *Bureaucratic Failure and Public Expenditure*, Academic Press, Harcourt Brace Jovanovich Publishers, New York, 1981.

Robson, W., *The Governors and the Governed*, Allen & Unwin, London, 1964.

Selznick, P. *T.V.A. and the Grass Roots*, University of California Press, Berkeley, 1949.

Smigel, E.O., and Ross, H.L. (eds.), *Crimes Against Bureaucracy*, Van Nostrand Reinhold Co., New York, 1970.

Thompson, V. *Modern Organization*, Knopf, New York, 1961.

Toffler, A., *Future Shock*, Bantam Books, New York, 1971.

Truelson, Judith A., "Blowing the Whistle on Systemic Corruption: On Maximizing Reform and Minimizing Retaliation," *Corruption and Reform*, Vol. 2, Spring 1987, pp.55-74.

U.S. News & World Report, Sept. 3, 1979, "Where Bureaucracy Really Runs Riot," pp. 31-2.

Warner, R., *The Principles of Public Administration*, Pitman, London, 1947.

Warwick, D., *A Theory of Public Bureaucracy*, Harvard University Press, Cambridge, MA., 1975.

Weitzel, W., and Jonsson, E., "Decline in Organizations: A Literature Integration and Extension", *Administrative Science Quarterly*, Vol. 34, No. 1, 1989, pp. 91-109.

Wheare, K., *Maladministration and Its Remedies*, Stevens & Sons, London, 1973.

8. Doing Something Different

At any particular moment, blunders are being committed somewhere in every administrative system and there are always people around who sincerely believe that something different (and better) could be done. To improve matters alterations are constantly being made. Until administrative reform became institutionalized in several countries in the early 1960s, administrative reforms were distinct periodic events. Now reform is more of a continuous ongoing activity, part of a perpetual war against maladministration that blights so many lives in contemporary society. But administrative reforms should not be confused with run of the mill changes, the minor tampering and adjusting that naturally occurs, or innovations. Their scope, radicalism and impact are usually of a much greater order and unlike most innovations they are premeditated, deliberate, planned overhauls that run into considerable opposition; they are rarely popular. They are intended to shake up inert bureaucracies, to battle vested interests, to tackle systemic shortcomings and failures, and to alter some aspects of the prevailing administrative culture. If nothing else, they are ambitious, defiant acts of courage against those who firmly believe that "you can't change the system". They aim no less at the modernization of administration as a dynamic force for human progress, the improvement of productivity and effectiveness, the strengthening of accountability and controls to ensure the public interest, the reconstruction and redesign of outmoded systems, and the revitalization of sluggish, inert, incompetent, corrupt, defective public organizations.

Undoubtedly, administrative systems are difficult to transform along these lines. They are not built to be easily changed. Their virtues are permanence, continuity, reliability, dependability, solidity. They are designed to systematize, routinize, socialize, and enforce. Their very success makes people reluctant to depart from what works (or has worked) well or change a proven formula; they are given the benefit of any doubt. They have built-in technical inflexibilities, commitments and time lags. Norms tend to stick, and are bolstered by collusion, connivance, self-interest, indifference, timidity, and dogmatism; once set, they become part and parcel of future expectations and planning. The whole works in such a way that people prefer what they already know or have become accustomed to against anything new. Hence, the pessimism that lurks behind attempts at challenging the status quo that in itself reinforces the many constraints and limitations that already exist on administrative reform.

Just because things go wrong does not mean that anything different will be done. Habit is difficult to break and rather than change, people may even reinforce "what has always worked before". But self-correction just does not work for major shortcomings and failures in administrative systems. Things continue to go wrong and obviously so. More and more complaints are registered, annoyances build up, criticisms cannot be ignored. Patchwork solutions are tried but prove inadequate; the rot continues and frustrations mount. Eventually, people with different ideas persist, pressure and push and gain a hearing. At last, there is resolution to take drastic action, for nothing less is needed. Drastic means not just different but dramatic. Deliberate attention is drawn to a change in direction, to a definite even definitive turning point, to putting the stamp of legitimation on what is decided, to mobilizing system supports to doing something quite different. From this point onward, administrative reform has its opportunity.

Whatever is decided, a series of integrated or associated actions is about to be taken. Minimally, even symbolic actions such as retitling means that letterheads will have to be altered, correspondence redirected, files reorganized, and addresses reidentified. But administrative reform, if done properly, involves much more – changing legislation and regulations, redesigning organizations and structures, overhauling processes and procedures, reformulating policies and programs, altering documents and forms, and retraining and reeducating both employees and clients. The task is quite daunting, daunting enough that to promise much is to promise too much. To condemn beforehand in the system those who have to work out all the details because of their alleged wrongdoing is to court disaster. It merely stiffens resistance and insults their intelligence, loyalty and competence.

To mark the break with the past, reformers do tend to exaggerate the benefits expected from the new era about to dawn, and worse still, promise things that no administrative system, no matter how well performing, even perfect, could deliver, such as ending poverty, providing absolute equality, eliminating all corruption, and guaranteeing everyone complete self-fulfillment. To justify their claims, they blacken current practices and, particularly in the public sector, indulge in wholesale condemnatory public service bashing, thereby undermining morale, loyalty, self-respect, and security. In so doing they create self-fulfilling prophecies by the reactions provoked. In 1947, a Cabinet committee on civil service manpower in Britain recognized this when it stated "no organization can long sustain morale or attract the right type of recruit if it is publicly or privately stigmatized as consisting of parasites on the community or unjustly criticized in other equally opprobrious terms" (Hennessy, 1989, 170). Long before the spate of public service bashing occurred globally in the late 1970s, this was academically confirmed.

If the nation wishes to reduce bureaucracy, it must cease beating the bureaucrats and involve them in the process of creating a less threatening, less cumbersome, more satisfying, and ultimately less expensive work environment...Reforms involving decimation of agencies or other meat cleaver tactics only serve to vindicate the inveterate fears of the bureaucrats and to bolster the protectiveness of their...allies. (Warwick, 1975, 215)

So many details are involved in administrative reform that obstruction can occur at any point. Reformers can be tripped over so easily by non-cooperation and delay. There is already enough inertia and resistance in the system without deliberately provoking needless suspicion and resentment, not to say dumb insolence.

Fundamental Decisions

Administrative reformers have at the very outset to make fundamental decisions, the outcome of which will dog them and their reforms forever afterward. Astute judgment is required; unwise and inappropriate decisions doom reform.

(a) Timing. A symposium of administrative reform experts organized by the Organization for Economic Cooperation and Development in 1979 warned that rarely should "reform be undertaken merely for symbolic or public relations purposes... only when genuinely needed...when the timing is right" (O.E.C.D., 1980, 13). But no time is ever ripe for reform. It always comes at the wrong time. Since there is no right time, reformers should not wait in the hope that the opportune time will come; a more favorable moment is the best they can hope for when circumstances are not at all inviting. On many occasions they have no choice. Crises arise that demand action, ready or not. Fear that something worse may yet befall also prompts action. In short, there is no time like the present unless the odds are overwhelmingly against a fair hearing in which case reform is probably a hopeless cause anyway short of a miracle. Much depends what else is of higher priority or urgency occupying people's attention. Administrative reform rarely rates high, so that when it does at last receive some attention, the opportunity has to be seized; it is not likely to recur quickly. Reformers have to work hard to ensure that reform does get attention and a higher priority than usual, that plans are readied in time when the opportunity presents itself, and that reforms are allowed sufficient time for implementation and adequate time for a fair evaluation. Clearly preference is for constant administrative adjustment and attention and continuous adaptation but even in the best of circumstances, more fundamental overhauls are necessary and as the 1979 O.E.C.D. symposium of experts concluded "should not be attempted too frequently and should be initiated only on a highly selective basis" (Ibid, 14).

(b) Scope. As all human activities intermesh, administrative reform inevitably spills over into political, economic and social reform en route to substantive results. There are no neat lines separating different social systems, least of all different administrative systems, and administrative reform will minimally affect policymaking, law enforcement, and public behavior, if not eventually politics, industrial relations, the distribution of wealth, education, legal institutions and mass media. One of the major weaknesses of administrative reformers has been their failure to discern the boundaries of their intent and to bring about changes in closely related aspects without which they cannot achieve their goals (Leemans, 1976, 132). For example, the decentralization of budget making may appear to be confined to the techniques of financial management, but it involves the relocation of decisionmaking, the transfer of power, the realignment of political forces, the redefinition of political responsibility and financial accountability way beyond the restructuring of budget sections, the retraining of budget staff, and the redesign of budget instruments. The reformers have to decide themselves the proper boundaries; they should not draw them too widely to make reforms unmanageable or too narrowly as to make them easy to be blocked. Grandoise, comprehensive reform efforts often breed "midspread cynicism among the clientele and lost morale and momentum among the change agents" (Lee, 1970, 187).

(c) Priorities. To tackle the major areas of administrative reform concerns all at once and to do it properly is probably beyond the capability of any administrative system. Choices have to be made which are the more important areas, where changes would have the greatest impact, what is doable, and whether to start with the hardest or most serious problems or leave them until later when reform would have achieved some momentum. There is no universal formula; each situation has its own logic. Although some progress has been made in recent years, Leemans' description of the state of the art still rings true today as it did in the mid-1970s. Methods to diagnose maladministration are too defective and theories to design optimal arrangements are still not good enough for absolute reliability. Reformers "have few reliable theories and methods available and consequently it is difficult to estimate the feasibility and effectiveness of change instruments and methods or to predict their outcome" (Ibid, 47). Reformers have to be flexible and continually reevaluate and revise their plans. It is best to hasten slowly and to experiment at first on a small scale. Some aspects of administrative reform are more divisible and self-contained than others and these – public enterprises, budgeting, personnel management, ethics – might best be tackled separately. The O.E.C.D. symposium advised looking for areas that had the greatest potential results or the greatest chance of success or the greatest multiplier effect. Within the chosen area consideration should be made as to how much change could be digested in a given time and whether new administrative machinery should be created to bypass what exists (O.E.C.D., 1980, 17).

(d) Involvement. Who is going to tell who what has to be done? Who has to be involved to see that what has to be done is done? Who is willing to be involved? When nobody knows what has to be done, outside experts have to be invited to diagnose and prescribe. Somebody has to evaluate what the experts prescribe and decide on a course of action. If those at the apex of government are not consulted or given a front role, then those below may not consider reform to be important enough to bother with. So key politicians and senior administrators must be involved, however reluctantly. Then the bodies most affected by the contemplated reforms should be brought in to gauge their reactions, draw on their knowledge and get them to be stake-holders in reform, to own the reforms, to identify themselves with the reforms, and to support the reforms all the way. The key opponents of reform should also be involved if only for the purpose of defanging to say nothing of the possibility of cooptation.

There is no end to who might be involved. Undoubtedly it would be most beneficial to have everybody who ought to be and could be involved actually involved. But this is rare. Politicians do not show much interest in administrative matters which they take very much for granted and they are usually ignorant about the pros and cons of specific reforms and whether or not they will actually work. In administrative reform they prefer not to take the lead, to wait and see what the political fallout is likely to be, and to side with reforms that promise immediate rather than long term impact. On the whole, they tend to tolerate maladministration, to leave administration alone and to reverse whatever their political opponents have done, unless for some reason (such as personal administrative experience) they have a keen interest in the subject and are administrative reform advocates. Otherwise, they quickly lose interest and settle for whatever compromises can be obtained. They want what can be achieved in a few years; they cannot wait the generation or so that lasting radical reforms require to succeed. They soon abandon the quick fixes that don't work and become impatient with reforms that do not show immediate improvements.

Senior administrators also tend to stand on the sidelines, unless they personally have much to gain or lose in reform outcomes. They are already at the pinnacle of their careers; they may be over the hill and on the way out; they are already so overworked that peace and quiet is preferred to the rough and tumble of administrative reform. In any event, they have made it through the system and they are not so critical of a system which brought them to the top. Experience has tempered and diluted the criticism of their youth or as they would put it, they have become wiser, more realistic, more comprehending (although reformers would interpret this quite differently as their becoming complacent, lazy, defensive, blind, and stubborn) and they would have seen past reforms tried and abandoned. Rare at the top is the results-oriented entrepreneurial bureaucrat, the crusading reformer, the idealistic missionary: more common is the safe task-oriented bureaucrat, the organizational politician, the empire builder and domain protector, all of whom are self-interested, and when they gang up against reform, they are almost unbeatable. Reformers often wish the defensive administrators and the uninterested politicians could be left out but both hold too strategic positions to be excluded.

(e) Situational imperatives. The opportunity for reform usually arises suddenly and without premonition. Those involved don't have much time to think; they have to act on whatever is ready to go. Yet every reform requires hard decisions on how to proceed. First, the objectives have to be clarified – whether the intention is to improve the end products of the administrative system (programic content and performance) or to streamline and simplify the administrative system itself (organizational design and engineering) or to change the methods and mode of operation (managerial technology and behavioral techniques) or any combination of these. Thereafter, the reform campaign is determined by the following choices:

Aim: legitimacy, simplification, economy, productivity, efficiency, effectiveness, client satisfaction, equity, employment;

Perspective: outside looking in or inside looking out, top-down or bottom-up, control or choice centered, procedure or results oriented, coercive or collaborative, short or long term;

Focus: comprehensive or narrow, macro or micro, whole or partial, ends or means, inputs or outputs, formalities or realities, structural or behavioral, fundamental or marginal, drastic or piecemeal;

Concerns: fact or opinion, small or high investment, high or low resource commitment, high or low risk, shock treatment or incrementalism, token or stiff resistance, existing or new instruments.

What all these choices boil down to is whether the reformers seek to reform from the outside or revitalize from the inside and how far they want to go. Often the urgency of the situation predetermines any choice. There may be no time to go outside or nobody capable of revitalizing from the inside.

Reform or Revitalization

During the 1976 presidential campaign in the United States, both major parties promised to reshape, reorganize and reform the federal bureaucracy to make it a more economic, efficient and effective instrument of government. Jimmy Carter made much of the fact that as an outsider to Washington, he would be better able to undertake sweeping changes in the machinery of government. Immediately on taking office, he appointed several blue-ribbon committees containing federal officials most likely to be involved to suggest and implement apposite administrative reforms. He impressed urgency on them. Soon they came up with an impressive list of what might be done to streamline the operations of the federal government, improve the delivery of federal services, and upgrade federal management performance.

With the clear support of mass media, President Carter moved quickly to prepare appropriate legislation and to win support from Congress, the federal bureaucracy and other concerned parties, something that previous presidents had often failed to obtain. By midterm (1979), he had achieved probably the most important set of civil service reforms for several decades as well as other significant changes in federal government organization. Nonetheless even to get this far, he had had to compromise and to modify his original stance. His much heralded administrative reforms fell well short of expectations, certainly well short of what most experts had suggested was long overdue. Still they were significant steps in the right direction and hopefully more reforms would follow.

But the reform momentum stalled there. More pressing issues crowded out further plans for reform. Getting that far had cost much political capital and had so antagonized the Washington establishment that the president had jeopardized his political future. Whatever the reason, President Carter decided not to pursue further reforms but to pin his hopes instead on a Presidential Management Improvement Council that would encourage and aid the federal bureaucracy to improve itself without external imposition. This was a decided change in approach – from reform to revitalization. At the time, many thought that the president had shot his bolt and had been forced to compromise with the Washington establishment, that as a newcomer to Washington he had overestimated the ability of the president to reform the federal bureaucracy and had underestimated the strength of bureaucratic resistance to reform. He had had to learn the hard way that more effective results would come out of revitalization than reform. Stronger presidents than he had failed in the past to prevail, preferring in the end to manipulate the system rather than change it. They had not reformed or revitalized. President Carter had at least attempted both, achieving some success in reform and launching initiatives in revitalization that were to be strengthened and compounded by his successor. President Reagan also understood the compelling need for both approaches in contemporary administrative systems.

The times are so turbulent that high-level administrators of large scale organizations are so caught up in the rush of everyday business that they rarely have time to sit back and review their organizations to see whether they can make improvements. They rely on consultants and institutionalized mechanisms to warn them of potential troubles and to advise them what should be done differently. They consider themselves fortunate to accomplish what they do, much less keep up with the state of the art. The limitations on governmental organizations are such that Michel Crozier harshly concluded that public bureaucratic systems "resist change as long as they can" and "move only when serious dysfunctions develop and no other alternatives remain" (Crozier, 1964, 196), i.e. that reforms would have to be imposed on them. What must be done is to convince high-level administrators (or whoever has the final say) that changes are imperative, and that administrative experts must work out the details with those who will have to implement them. One simply cannot rely on the people running the system to change it themselves or to assume the initiative. They will try to evade the task or tinker with non-essentials or resort to symbolic rather than substantive action.

This has been the traditional approach to administrative reform. Insiders cannot be trusted to do what has to be done. Outsiders have to impose their proposals on reluctant recipients. The impression created has been that insiders are overly conservative, lacking in initiative, and hostile to change. The reality has been otherwise. Insiders have always been at the forefront of reform, constantly urging reforms and seizing the initiative when permitted to do so. External consultants have been fed proposals and rehearsed. So-called independent inquiries have been manipulated all the way to arrive at predetermined recommendations. Behind the facade of externally imposed reform, insiders have changed things the way they wanted them changed. Even without such cover, they have quietly transformed operations from within as required. Nevertheless, what they could achieve on their own has been limited. They have had to ally themselves with outsiders to overcome their conservative peers.

But externally imposed reform has been disappointing. True, it has generated much publicity. Indeed, the great bulk of literature on administrative reform consists of accounts of public inquiries, reform proposals, reform arrangements, new laws, reorganizations, and battles over reform. Precious little recounts follow through on what really did happen in the end and how reform was frequently blocked or gutted or diluted by intransigent vested interests. The end results contrast so much with initial expectations that this approach to reform has been highly suspect for good reason. First, many of those who decide on reform are themselves strangers to the situation to whom reform is just another chore, another assignment. Such is mobility today, that few people stay long enough to get a proper feel or grasp what is at stake or care enough about what happens after they have moved on, unless reform is their full time occupation. Second, many of those on whom the burden of implementation falls are similarly disposed. They have their own personal agendas and cannot be entirely disinterested about reforms whose very nature is seen as an indictment of them. Naturally they are resentful, certainly suspicious, but they may also have a superior grasp of the situation to realize that the proposed reforms may worsen not better the status quo. Third, many public organizations in existence for a long time are institutional not instrumental. They just do not take orders but they have a dominant voice in what orders are made. They are entrenched in the social fabric. Taking them on administratively is taking them on politically.

Reform represents a threat not only to them but also to their allies, clients and the general public accustomed to their arrangements who will rally to their side. Fourth, many public organizations are considered experts in their field. To find equivalent or superior expertise outside is difficult. When two sets of experts disagree, who can decide between them? When the outsiders may have been denied the evidence that substantiates their case who can challenge the official version of events? Fifth, reforms are at the mercy of any determined band of resistant insiders. Until they are convinced to change or they are removed from the situation, nothing much different will happen. The trouble is that the least reform-minded organizations are the hardest to reform but the most likely to need reform. Sixth, reform becomes progressively harder as the easiest targets are eliminated and as passions aroused by obvious malpractices diminish, particularly when the issues get more difficult for the public to understand and more removed from personal concerns. As administrative systems improve, they become more difficult to reform.

In these circumstances, revitalization or self-reform, the process of self-renewal, has much to commend it. For a start it has had considerable success in the private sector where organizations have greater independence and autonomy in running their affairs and where management has greater flexibility in altering arrangements and greater incentives to improve administrative systems. Revitalization is "the process of initiating, creating, and confronting needed changes" to enable organizations to be viable, to adapt to new conditions, to solve problems, and to learn from experience (Lippett, 1969, 1). They monitor their administrative performance on their own initiative, continuously, with or without external assistance. They develop their own in-house capacity for reforming themselves to avoid stagnation. The benefits of revitalization are so obvious that it should be a given in any self-respecting organization. As the managerial ethos spreads, as it has done since World War II, then revitalization can be increasingly taken for granted in both private and public sectors.

Yet revitalization has some serious drawbacks for the public sector. Compared with externally induced reform, it is by nature less bold, less visionary, less inclusive. By confining itself to one organization, this approach fails to deal with inter-organizational problems in the public sector and administrative shortcomings that go beyond any specific public organization. It relies unduly on the interest, talent and capability of people within the organization and is restricted to how they define their problems and view the world. They may be unable to go beyond traditional (and notoriously conservative) professional perspectives and they may not place sufficient value on the unorthodox or the innovative. They may not pay sufficient attention to external criticism and participation. They may disfavor the ideas of those low in the organization's hierarchy in deference to the perceptions and attitudes of those high in the hierarchy. Nobody may want to offend anybody else or to admit that the problems stem from incompetent top management. The organization may not possess the necessary tools to carry through a thorough reform program. It may not want to stand out or do things differently from others. Revitalization may be seized as an opportunity for managerial or union manipulation. Finally, there is always the inherent problem, at least in conservative bureaucracies, of self-fulfilling prophecy where the organization decides in advance what will or will not work and predetermines the results. Only those reforms acceptable to the organization are even considered and they are dropped at the first signs of serious internal opposition. For the public sector, organizational self-reform is just too narrow.

On the other hand, there are advantages which cannot be lightly dismissed. For a start, administrative reform is at least tried. It does not remain forever in the recommendations of a distinguished public body that disbands as soon as it has completed its inquiries. It is operationalized and decisions to proceed or halt are made by identifiable persons who are held accountable for their decisions and must justify their choice. This is particularly advantageous in the case of institutional bureaucracies, which can block externally opposed reforms, and public organizations, such as the military, the police, and the secret service, which are often sheltered from outside pressure and where only the views of peers may be respected. It is also advantageous in the case of complex administrative arrangements where more than a superficial or general knowledge is required. The fact that reforms are self-induced eliminates a crisis or panic approach and aids association and identification with (even loyalty to) reform efforts. Organizational dynamics can be used on the side of reform, not against it. Revitalization can tap accumulated experience and perhaps channel suppressed frustration of internal critics, dissenters and mavericks into positive contributions to change. Determined reformers know what they want, can insist on getting their way, can monitor and control reform efforts, and can evaluate progress. With a proper understanding of individual needs, concerns, and anxieties, they can reduce fear, antagonism, and resentment but if there is opposition they can persist. Opponents cannot wish them away or evade them. The issue has to be faced and mutually resolved.

Reform and revitalization complement one another. To rely exclusively on one or the other would be a mistake. Hovering over every public organization that fails to perform adequately there must lurk the threat that it can be abandoned altogether, split into several parts, or confronted with competitors if it does not reform itself. To determine whether public organizations are performing adequately in the public interest, the government must always have the power to receive public complaints and petitions concerning their operations, to conduct independent inquiries, to run spot checks at any time, to inspect their operations and audit their accounts, and generally reserve the right to intervene in the conduct of their affairs. Members of the public should be encouraged to conduct their own investigations and reviews of public organizations and bring to the attention of the community any disquieting features that may be discovered. Clients and employees should have the right to complain to an independent body against suspected wrongdoings of public organizations, to have their complaints competently investigated, and to receive compensation in the event that their complaints are found justified.

If these are correct conclusions, then President Carter's administrative reform strategy has much to commend it. He opened the process to be as inclusive as possible in the short time span he set for himself. He dispensed with the more costly, time-consuming brains trust approach of the Hoover-type public commissions whose detailed, comprehensive and principled reports often tend to be politically and administratively impractical in favor of more manageable representative task forces that would focus on the feasible and the acceptable. In so doing, he sacrificed scope for action. At the outset he threatened to impose far-reaching changes on an intractable federal bureaucracy while promoting official participation and self-revitalization, clearly implying that if official cooperation were not forthcoming, he would marshall political support for severer measures. Until the Washington establishment could accurately gauge the new president's political strength, he held the upper hand and it was obviously more politic for the federal bureaucrats to go along with self-imposed changes which they could tolerate rather than accommodate unsuccessfully to externally imposed reforms. Once he had achieved some success, President Carter switched to revitalization through management improvement, thereby abandoning the larger struggle of revamping the whole machinery of federal government and venturing no further than politically feasible at the time. His successor decided that a more uncompromising and unorthodox approach through budget reallocations and managerial accounting would force necessary internal reforms and improvements where he wanted them. He resorted to blue ribbon commissions and task forces only where he sought policy advice. Once his mind was made up, he employed new machinery and self-correcting devices to promote revitalization while using central administrative agencies (particularly the Office of Management and Budget and the Office of Personnel Management) to impose reforms on the bodies within their jurisdiction.

Reform Instruments

The range of reform instruments available to governments and to those urging governments to adopt reforms continues to increase. To the traditional key instruments – consultants, public inquiries, law, education and training, research – have been added mass media investigative reporting (ranging from titillating exposures of scandal to serious in-depth research), permanent administrative reform organizations (ministries, commissions, sections, offices) which concentrate on continuous reform and improvement as their sole responsibility or in conjunction with other administrative functions, suggestion schemes, performance audits, ombudsman offices, hot-lines (direct confidential telephone contacts), independent commissions against corruption, fraud and other white collar crimes, whistle-blowing protection, productivity councils, work quality circles and similar self-participatory devices for improving outputs, freedom of information and codes of ethics. These are all devices for drawing public attention to administrative deficiencies, mobilizing public opinion behind reform, investigating bureaupathologies, designing reform policies and proposals, assigning on-going responsibility for reforms, marshalling supports and resources for reform, and generally monitoring the progress of reform. No longer is there any excuse for not knowing what to do and how to proceed. It is only a question of willingness.

Direct action. The late 1980s saw spontaneous outpourings and demonstrations by people demanding political and economic reforms. They massed in the streets, held up posters, chanted slogans, and called for sympathetic strikes and work stoppages, formed human chains linked by clasped hands, and organized boycotts. They could only be terrorized out of existence, as in China. Elsewhere, regimes caved in to their demands, particularly in Eastern Europe. Reforms quickly followed and behind them administrative reforms. But rarely was direct action responsible directly for administrative reforms confirming a longheld belief that reforms follow not lead social changes. Nonetheless, the impressive victories scored could make direct action an instrument for administrative reform in the future, because mass media dramatize pent-up frustration and hatred of the status quo and publicize reform proposals. Skillful reformers are likely to reconsider direct action and opt for the publicity it achieves to draw attention to their cause and to undermine official resistance and inertia.

Strengthening legal controls. The rule of law and the independence of the judiciary still provide the major reinforcement of administrative reform. Confronted by legal and judicial sanctions, public administrators have to abide with the reforms. Besides various Human (or Civil) Rights Acts, the number of laws and court rulings that enforce administrative reforms on reluctant public organizations has been growing since the hallmark Administrative Procedures Act of 1946 in the United States, a model of its kind to ensure open, fair, equitable and humane conduct of public business. Among other noteworthy U.S. federal government legal instruments are the Budget and Accounting Procedures Act of 1950, Civil Service Reform Act of 1978, Economic Opportunity Act of 1964, Equal Access to Justice Act of 1980, Ethics in Government Act of 1978, Federal Tort Claims Act of 1946, Federal Managers Financial Integrity Act of 1982, Freedom of Information Act of 1966, Inspector General Act of 1978, Intergovernmental Cooperation Act of 1968, Right to Privacy Act of 1974, and Sunshine Act of 1976. The 1976 sunset legislation in the state of Colorado has not been copied at federal level (Kearney, 1990), nor have all kinds of model legislation and codes governing public personnel administration, public financial management, public employee ethics, the institution of ombudsman, intergovernmental relations, industrial relations, occupational safety and health, public accounting and auditing, delegated legislation, administrative tribunals, public enterprises, regulatory commissions, and so forth (Rosen, 1989). The fact that they exist and are well known in professional circles makes the task of reformers easier as designs of appropriate legal instruments are available and can be modified according to local circumstances.

Mass media. It used to be that mass media avoided administrative reform. Quality newspapers would summarize reform documents and occasionally comment on public maladministration while popular newspapers would report sleaze in government and indulge in public service bashing. After the successful investigative reporting of Watergate, mass media give more attention than ever before to public administration, a reflection of its increasing importance in everybody's life. Direct visual impact makes even a greater impression and administrators have to respond immediately to criticism and complaint. Maladministration now sells and mass media invests more effort into exposing it. Global networks make everyone familiar, for instance, with official corruption in Japan, the Philippines, Korea, Germany, Greece, and the U.S.S.R., accidents and disasters attributed to faulty administration everywhere, and public service deficiencies in Africa, Asia and Latin America. Even countries that have tried to block international telecommunications have not prevented their inhabitants from learning eventually about what was wrong and what could be done to improve matters. Mass media are a new principal ally of administrative reform.

Consultants. The United Nations family of organizations, the World Bank and the International Institute for Administrative Sciences have continued to support global initiatives in administrative, managerial and organizational reform and to arrange for international experts in the field to visit member countries. The major world powers still offer technical assistance although not so much in administrative reform as they used to do and private foundations have virtually abandoned the field altogether. Their place has been taken by multinational corporations in management, accounting and auditing. Help is now readily available at a price. Not only is it costly, but the multinationals have their own agenda and their consultants, as with all other international consultants, may not be experienced or skilled enough in public sector administration to master specific situations quickly to proffer much realistic advice in administrative reform. Increasingly, governments have been employing management experts and successful business leaders from their own private sectors to conduct overviews of public sector organizations. These consultants are familiar with the local situation from first hand contact and they do understand the prevailing administrative culture, although they may not be as impartial as they claim.

Public inquiries. There has been no diminution in English-speaking countries of royal commissions and other suchlike independent committees of inquiry, task forces and blue-ribbon commissions to examine a particular problem, to gather relevant information and conduct investigations, and to produce a report setting out their views and what should be done. Governments use them to restore public confidence in public institutions damaged by poor performance, to conduct open, fair and impartial post mortems of failures, and to help them make up their mind. But because of their political nature, they can be manipulated to reach foregone conclusions, to rubber stamp (i.e. legitimize) what has already been decided, to delay action until the problem at issue has been forgotten by the public, to obfuscate and equivocate, and to educate. In administrative reform, they have performed all these functions (Hanser, 1965; Rhodes, 1975; Wraith and Lamb, 1971). They have also stimulated much needed research, provided long term policy agendas, opened up the inner workings of administration to public view, brought new perspectives to bear on familiar issues, and promoted political consensus. Certainly, the world of public administration has been transformed by the Northcote-Trevelyan (1854) report and other British inquiries, and the Brownlow Committee report (1937) and the postwar Hoover Commissions (1949, 1955) of the United States. Perhaps there have not been in recent years inquiries of such international import, but at national level there certainly have been and will continue to be, even in countries like Japan and South Korea that once would never even contemplate *public* inquiries of state administration before.

On the other hand, recent public inquiries have been disappointing. Where they have been bold, they have offended; where they have not, they have watered down their proposals into blandness.

> All administrative reform committees tend to combine radical and critical diagnosis with relatively moderate prescriptions. Brave words are not followed by equally brave deeds, because while such committees must show a proper sense of urgency and indignation about the shortcomings of bureaucracy, their conclusions must in practice be implemented by and within that same bureaucracy. (Smith and Weller, 1978, 310-311)

Other critics believe they may have outlived their purpose, certainly "committees of wise laymen who can with a degree of leisure consider a problem area" (Chapman, 1973, 187). Nonetheless, there was a whole spate of them in the 1970s in the United Kingdom and Australia. Clearly they filled a political vacuum although they did not seem to result in much remedial action. They generated much publicity and attention for a while and then they were quickly forgotten except by academics and succeeding inquiries which repeated much the same exercise. They illustrated all the pitfalls involved in having proposals generated by one set of people left to be adapted and implemented by another. Many had spent too long on their work, for by the time they reported, the reform momentum had already petered out or the government had changed and was now unwilling to act. The wrong people had been picked, not up to the task or divided or uncompromisingly radical or too busy elsewhere. Their working methods had been slipshod or they had been given insufficient resources to do a proper job. A growing body of literature now provides a legal guide (Hallett, 1982) and many pointers how to increase their effectiveness (Bulmer, 1983). They still provide a necessary sanction on occasions to keep high standards in public life and public administration, to get to the bottom of a matter and to galvanize administrative reformers.

Ombudsman. If public inquiries have been overused, then the ombudsman office has been underused for administrative reform purposes. Since 1960, the ombudsman and ombudsmanlike offices have spread beyond Scandinavia onto all continents with very few casualties. While seen essentially as an avenue for the redress of grievances against administrative wrongdoing and a citizen's defender, it is also an instrument for tackling bureaupathologies. The investigation of a ceaseless flow of complaints enables the ombudsman to know every manifestation of maladministration, to discern regular patterns of misconduct and to publicize wrongdoing. Experienced ombudsman office staff are well qualified to comment on administrative practices and to suggest improvements. Some have powers to initiate their own investigations of malpractices and others work behind the scenes to improve administrative practices. But with few exceptions, they have been peripheral to administrative reform; they could be used to greater effect to diagnose and propose. They are permanent offices working within administration yet independent and not identified with the administration, and they have both political and public backing.

Performance audits. Another strengthened organization within the administration with full powers of independent investigation is the audit office which also since 1960 has gone well beyond financial balance sheets and the legality of expenditures into matters of economy and efficiency, program and policy evaluation, cost-benefit analysis, effectiveness audit, official norms and corrective action (Geist, 1981). Indeed, over the last two decades, there has been a significant improvement in the state-of-the-art of public accounting and audit which during the period linked Management by Objectives (M.B.O.), Planning-Programming-Budgeting Systems (P.P.B.S.), and performance budgeting into truly integrated financial management systems through program analysis and evaluation and performance measurement. When planning, budgeting, and accounting were finally linked, it became possible to separate investment from operating costs, to measure operating costs in terms of expenditures, to separate expenditures from changes in working capital, to correlate program elements and responsibility centers, and to break expenditures down into categories useful to operating managers (Anthony, 1971). Once this occurred, financial accounting and audit took on a completely new aspect and opened the way to new financial management information systems (mechanized and automated), standardized budgeting definitions and formats, forward planning and estimating, input and output measurements and matching, full disclosure of costs and liabilities, the streamlining of financial budgeting operations, program evaluation (Wholey et al., 1989), productivity measurement and improvement (Torpey, 1988), social indicators (U.S.O.M.B., 1974), the separate professionalization of government accountants, much improved financial reporting, strong financial controls, and a transformed role for public auditors in ensuring greater efficiency and effectiveness of public services (Brown, 1988).

Two models in particular seem to indicate the shape of things to come. The United States General Accounting Office has changed from financial compliance auditing to program effectiveness auditing, from oversight and accountability to advice on policy, legislation and future action (Mosher, 1979), trying to show what is being accomplished against Congressional intent but falling well short of assessing government priorities or funding requirements. It has made advances in efficiency auditing, productivity measures and performance indicators. In the United Kingdom, since 1983 the Audit Commission for Local Authorities has been obliged to judge the economy, efficiency and effectiveness of local governments and has conducted value for money (V.F.M.) audits as part of the national government's program of administrative reform. It has been evaluating the management of local governments, devising performance indicators (and the necessary backup research), comparing the results of local governments, and generally acting as an initiator of administrative reform.

Both countries have embarked on productivity improvement programs to strengthen their international competitiveness and have taken to comparing public and private sector performances. In the United Kingdom the Financial Management Initiative (F.M.I.) obliged ministries to develop performance measures against clear objectives, and their progress has been monitored by the Treasury, the National Audit Office and the Public Accounts Committee (of Parliament). In 1985 some 500 output and performance measures had been developed, a number that quadrupled within four years in the quest for performance targets (although there was some doubt whether they were actually being used in practice). In the United States similar work has been conducted by various federal government agencies, such as the National Commission on Productivity (1970-1974, then National Commission on Productivity and Work Quality 1974-1978, National Productivity Council, 1978-1980), Civil Service Commission (later Office of Personnel Management), Office of Management and Budget, General Services Administration, and the U.S. General Accounting Office, and consolidated first in 1982 in President Reagan's Reform '88 program, then the President's Council on Management Improvement in 1984 and the President's Productivity Improvement Program in 1986 to achieve a 20 percent productivity increase by 1992. The Productivity Improvement Program necessitated a measurement system to determine standards of quality, timeliness and efficiency and procedures for the collection and reporting of data resulting from application of productivity measures under Executive Order 12552 monitored by O.M.B. in partnership with P.C.M.I. These efforts have disabused any doubts whether or not a substantial part of public administration performance is measurable (Miller, 1984). Once measured, there could only follow demands for improvement (Berkowitz, 1988).

Inspectors General. To protect themselves from administrative malpractices, despots used to employ general inspectors to roam around in the government to act as their watchdogs, informers, troubleshooters and ombudsman. Military services retained the office to promote discipline and remedy abuses but civil services transformed the office beyond recognition. Some countries like the Soviet Union retained it as an independent watchdog of the people against government malpractices though burdening it with legal and audit functions as well. The concept was revived in the late 1970s in the United States in response to the need for independent offices to detect and prevent fraud, waste and abuse and promote economy, efficiency, effectiveness and integrity in federal government programs and operations. Each office, required by statute, is headed by an inspector general (I.G.) appointed by the president with Senate approval to conduct audits of agency operations, review proposed laws and regulations to determine their impact on the economy and efficiency of agency operations, and detect wasteful practices and significant fraud and abuse problems. Audits evaluate agency performance while investigations deal with alleged wrongdoing and possible remedial action. Soon after taking office, President Reagan established the President's Council on Integrity and Efficiency (P.C.I.E.), not to be confused with the President's Council on Management Improvement (P.C.M.I.) established in 1984 after the President's Private Sector Survey on Cost Controls (Grace Commission), to coordinate and combine the efforts of the IGs to combat program abuse and vulnerability through government-wide projects. Among its priority interests have been improved loan, cash and financial management systems, increased controls in automated information systems, the effective use of investigative techniques and civil fraud remedies, long term computer matching, and generally strengthening accountability.

Whistle-blowing. The Inspectors General provide hot-lines for tips from whistle-blowers where wrongdoing may be going undetected because of internal conspiracy. In fact, whistle-blowing was institutionalized in President Carter's Civil Service Reform Act of 1978 where whistle-blowers were supposedly provided statutory protection. But organizational vilification and retaliation against such untrustworthy employees ("squealers") are probably too effective to provide them any real protection (Truelson, 1986) even though they have revealed serious illegalities, flagrant fraud, waste and abuse, and life threatening health and safety violations. Protection of such brave souls who defy overwhelming pressures to conform and go along with administrative malpractices is a new and valuable instrument of administrative reform (Jos et al., 1989). Clearly the other instruments, as powerful and effective as they appear to be, do not detect serious wrongdoing and fail to get to the heart of the matter.

While new instruments are being devised, the older instruments can hardly be ignored. Budgeting has probably become one of the most effective administrative reforms in recent years. The linking of resources, objectives and results, has the potentiality of molding budgeting into a performance contract. This indeed has been the intention in the United Kingdom (Financial Management Initiative), Canada (Increased Ministerial Authority and Accountability), Australia and New Zealand and in some Western European countries (Schick, 1990). Doing something different in budgeting means doing better budgeting to obtain better management results for better government performance (Prechand, 1990). True, it also involves trying new gimmicks which may not improve public budgeting practices at all but worsen budgeting problems (U.S.G.A.O., 1989). The problem with all reform instruments, all reform strategies, and all reforms is that doing something different does not guarantee any better results. Indeed, reforms may not only turn out to be little improvement on the status quo, they may be detrimental. They may result in a big fuss over nothing because the whole process of reform itself is so vulnerable that most reforms rarely come to anything. The fault is not so much in the conception but in the doing.

References

Anthony, R., "Closing the Loop Between Planning and Performance", *Public Administration Review*, Vol. 31, No.3, May-June 1971, 388-398.

Berkowitz, M. (ed.), *Measuring the Efficiency of Public Programs: Costs and Benefits in Vocational Rehabilitation*, Temple University Press, Philadelphia, PA, 1988.

Brown, R.E. (ed.), *Accounting and Accountability in Public Administration*, American Society for Public Administration, Washington, D.C., 1988.

Bulmer, M., *Social Research and Royal Commissions*, Allen and Unwin, London, 1983.

Chapman, R.A. (ed.), *The Role of Commissions in Policy-Making*, Allen and Unwin, London, 1973.

Crozier, M., *The Bureaucratic Phenomenon*, Phoenix Books, The University of Chicago Press, 1964.

Geist, B., *State Audit*, Macmillan, London, 1981.

Hallett, L.A., *Royal Commissions and Boards of Inquiry*, The Law Book Company, Ltd., Sydney, 1982.

Hanser, C.J., *Guide to Decision: The Royal Commission*, The Bedminister Press, Totowa, N.J., 1965.

Hennessy, P., *Whitehall*, Secker & Warburg, London, 1989.

Jos, P.H., Thompkins, M.E., and Hays, S., "In Praise of Difficult People: A Portrait of the Committed Whistleblower", *Public Administration Review*, Vol. 49, No. 6, Nov./Dec. 1989, pp. 552-561.

Lee, H.B. "An Application of Innovation Theory to the Strategy of Administrative Reform in Developing Countries," *Policy Sciences,* Vol. I, No. 2, Summer 1970, pp. 177-189.

Kearney, R.C., "Sunset: A Survey and Analysis of the State Experience," *Public Administration Review*, Vol. 50, No. 1, Jan-Feb, 1990, pp. 49-57.

Leemans, A. (ed.), *The Management of Change in Government*, Institute of Social Studies, Martinus Nijhoff, 1976.

Lippitt, G., *Organization Renewal*, Appleton-Century-Crofts, New York, 1969.

Miller, T.C. (ed.), *Public Sector Performance: A Conceptual Turning Point*, The Johns Hopkins University Press, Baltimore, 1984.

Mosher, F.C., *The G.A.O.*, Westview Press, Boulder, Co., 1979.

Organization for Economic Cooperation and Development, *Strategies for Change and Reform in Public Management*, Public Management Series 1, Paris, 1980.

Prenchard, A. (ed.), *Government Financial Management: Issues and Country Studies,* International Monetary Fund, Washington, D.C., 1990.

Rhodes, G., *Committees of Inquiry*, Allen and Unwin, London, 1975.

Rosen, B., *Holding Government Bureaucracies Accountable*, Praeger, New York, 1989.

Schick, A., "Budgeting for Results: Recent Developments in Five Industrialized Countries," *Public Administration Review*, Vol. 50, No. 1, Jan/Feb 1990, pp. 26-34.

Smith, R., and Weller, P. (eds.), *Public Service Inquiries in Australia*, University of Queensland Press, St. Lucia, 1978.

Torpey, W.G., *Federal Productivity: A Management Challenge*, Byrd, Richmond, VA., 1988.

Truelson, Judith A., *Blowing the Whistle on Systemic Corruption*, Ph.D. dissertation, University of Southern California, School of Public Administration, 1986.

U.S. General Accounting Office, *Managing the Cost of Government Proposals for Reforming Federal Budgeting Practices*, GAO/AFMD-90-1, October 1989.

U.S. Office of Management and Budget, Statistical Policy Division, *Social Indicators, 1973*, U.S. Government Printing Office, Washington, D.C., 1974.

Warwick, D.P., *A Theory of Public Bureaucracy*, Harvard University Press, Cambridge, MA., 1975.

Wholey, J.S. et al. (eds.), *Improving Government Performance*, Jossey-Bass Publishers, San Francisco, 1989.

Wraith, R. and Lamb, G., *Public Inquiries as an Instrument of Government*, Allen and Unwin, London, 1971.

9. Guarding Against Failure

Most administrative reforms fail. Reform movements and reformers begin well enough but usually find that they cannot get much beyond a sympathetic hearing, symbolic backing, and polite formalities. Thereafter vested interests and bureaucratic inertia continue to defy reform intentions. Even though maladministration is freely acknowledged, the conditions that give rise to it are not altered enough to make a real difference. Laws are changed, structures reorganized, people moved around, manuals altered, and instructions revised, but the same behavior patterns are continued. The administrative culture – its beliefs, values, priorities, norms – is hardly touched. History is littered with unsuccessful reforms which rarely get revived. Most notable, for example, in recent years have been national economic planning in Third World countries (Caiden and Wildavsky, 1974) and program budgeting in poor countries (Agarawala, 1983). It appears that conception is easier than action and successful action is exceptional. For this reason, most attention in the literature has been placed on the relatively few successes, thereby giving the appearance that reform is easier than it is. In reality, most suggestions for betterment are rejected and most reforms are blocked altogether or compromised into pale images. Implementation is the Achilles' heel of administrative reform: it is the filter and reformers "who focus on the decision and neglect the implementation process do so at their own peril" (Grindle and Thomas, 1989, 241). A strategic plan of implementation must accompany any decision to reform (Ibid, 243).

Reform fails mainly in implementation not for want of creativity, inventiveness, concern, or trying. Where reformers are outsiders to the administrative systems they seek to improve, they often have no power, position and status to influence those who can change things or they have no access to people who do have influence or they have no impact on those who have to be convinced. Reformers know only too well that organizations are blind to their defects or rationalize them as virtues or necessities (Gardner, 1968, 42). Even institutionalized reform bodies discover that they exist on sufferance and that without imposing sanctions few organizations really act on their proposals; much of the time they are just spinning their wheels without accomplishing much at all. Administrative reform moves painfully slow, much slower than political and economic reforms. None of the current crop of major administrative reform proposals is exactly new except perhaps the rollback of the administrative state, corporatization and privatization. The so-called managerial revolution has taken well over two centuries to establish itself. Debureaucratization is almost as old.

So too is the mechanization of administrative processes although its pace has quickened. What is new is automation although even that is two generations old already. Progress is slow. It is surprising how many countries still lack elementary administrative professionalization and suffer from anachronistic administrative processes and primitive methods. It may take a generation or two yet in them before lasting reforms take effect.

When reformers do at last get an opportunity to effect significant changes, they often miss their chance by proposing inappropriate, complex, unrealistic, unaffordable or inoperable reforms, by failing to explain themselves properly or clearly so that their reforms are misunderstood and misinterpreted, and by allowing their opponents to attack them personally rather than the substance of their reforms. They dogmatically stick to a wrong position. They too readily assume that everyone sees what they see and knows what they know. They are insufficiently prepared for their opponents' distortions and mendacity that can be quite breathtaking in audacity. They see themselves as being helpful, obliging, well-intentioned, benign not as threatening, dangerous, offensive. They tend to get carried away by their own enthusiasm, energy, and dreams. Above all, they tackle administrative problems as if they were capable of being solved purely by management science or scientific management which is rarely the case in government.

Belief in scientism still runs strong in much management education despite the disappointments and frustrations experienced in transforming the administrative systems of newly independent states. Even by the end of the 1960s, it was evident that the scientific management approach to administrative reform had failed. Administrative reform programs in several states had never even been tried because chronic instability in them had preoccupied administrators with firefighting and improvisation. Almost every state concerned had underestimated how much time and resources had been needed and many reforms had been abandoned before they had had any impact. Resistance and inertia had proven stronger than anticipated; entrenched administrators had killed moves in new directions. Administrative reform had been thwarted by political instability, economic scarcity, social conflict, cultural confusion, and incompetence.

A basic flaw had been the failure to appreciate the difference between reforming instrumental and institutional bureaucracies. It had been all too readily assumed that as all organizations were instrumental bureaucracies, they could be reformed from the outside and from the top, with everything else following suit. But most public organizations had long evolved into institutional bureaucracies. They had built up their autonomy, become used to working independently, and cherished their ability to determine their own administrative arrangements. They resented imposed reforms from the outside and from the top as unwarranted intrusions, just like long established professions.

> Professions are subject to the same deadening forces that afflict all other human institutions: an attachment to time-honored ways, reverence for established procedures, a preoccupation with one's own vested interests, and an excessively narrow definition of what is relevant and important. (Gardner, 1968, 42)

Instead of being meekly obedient as expected, institutional bureaucracies and public professionals fiercely resisted and mustered their own power bases to force reformers to back down, and to leave them alone to govern themselves. Thus,

> Reforming institutional bureaucracies is political rather than managerial. No standard formulas can be applied. Reformers...have to abandon consistency and uniformity. They have to tackle each institutional bureaucracy on its merits; for each, different concessions will have to be made and different compromises struck. For each, the process of transformation will take different forms over varying time periods (Bjur and Caiden, 1978, 362).

They won't change if they believe they don't have to. They have to feel threatened; they should never be allowed to assume that they are indispensable or unassailable or omnipotent. They are vulnerable as long as they need to maintain legitimacy and keep intact the image they foster about themselves. Shaking the public's faith in them forces them to reevaluate themselves. They, too, can be reformed if reformers recognize the political process and avoid twelve common pitfalls in the process of implementation.

1. A Bad Start

Unless a situation is really desperate, it is virtually fatal to undertake anything blind. Reform is not revolution; it is not expected to sweep away everything that exists and replace it with something entirely new. To a greater or lesser extent, what exists will continue but altered in some important respects. Complete overhaul and refurbishment is impractical while coercion is likely to be counter productive for the longer run. Besides the imperative of strong and binding political commitment and the welcome identification with reform efforts by top political leadership, voluntary support and cooperation from the potentially reformed should be sought. They must be convinced that the reforms are feasible and practical and will indeed improve on existing arrangements. All this implies thorough knowledge on the part of the reformers on what they are about. Minimally, they need to know the basic facts about the reform situation, the pros and cons about their own proposals, the likely lineup of forces, and some range of possible strategies. Beyond this, it would be desirable to have a historical appreciation of the situation, some account of previous reform attempts, character assessments of influential people in the reform process, and adequate feedback on progress. A good deal of this knowledge is specific to the situation and can only be obtained firsthand. But it is surprising how many reformers neglect their homework. They rediscover the wheel; that is, they use most of their resources in needless repetition of what has already been done. In the end they exhaust their resources before they get to implementation or, worse still, their ignorance of the situation nullifies whatever they do.

Sometimes, the reformers find themselves identified as insiders, clearly the administrative elite, and whatever they do is seen as a front, a superficial survey, a white-wash job, an excuse to pay off administrative or political scores. They are seen as tools of the very administrative system they are supposed to reform. This is particularly risky in the case of formal public inquiries where those appointed to investigate accept too much and assume too much about the situation. They concern themselves with ritualistic reforms and marginal changes that will not affect anything important. They do not delve deeper or tackle the real problems. They accept the limited terms of reference given them and refuse to go beyond them even when the evidence demands a broader slate. They ignore leads and refuse to accept uncomplimentary evidence. They close their ears to criticism and condemnation. They confine inquiries to those who are responsible for the status quo and ignore everybody else. In this case, their narrow perception of the situation and their prejudice on the side of the establishment, rather than their ignorance, undermine the worth of their work whose superficiality was probably intentional.

These initial defects may be exaggerated during the process of inquiry. Convinced that they are right, the would-be reformers provoke hostile reaction from witnesses who want to broaden their vision or save them needless work. When witnesses suspect that the reformers are not listening to them, they withdraw their support and go on the offensive. Much the same reaction occurs when the reformers try to spring surprises or conduct their inquiries with undue secrecy. Rumors abound, and gossip spreads suspicion and antagonism. The final damaging touches spring from premature leaks of findings or the absence of any forethought by the reformers as to the method of release and presentation of their proposals and the possible reaction to them. In this situation, the reforms may be stillborn.

A good beginning is worth much. It can carry a controversial reform program through difficult stretches. Hence it is incumbent on reformers to know the reform situation in detail, to avoid accusations of prejudice and bias against radical change, and to conduct their inquiries with an open mind and with due regard to the impression they are making on those whose cooperation will be needed at a later stage. Just as important, they need to provide administrators with whom they come into contact with an optimistic work ethic. If the reformers do no more than this, they can be proud of their accomplishment, for from this will flow administrative changes in due course, even if their substantive reforms are not immediately implemented. Obviously, reformers should practice what they preach, and apply to themselves what they want others to do.

2. Imitation Not Innovation

No administrative system is identical with any other. In each situation, reform is an innovation – it is doing something for the first time. No matter how many times a particular change may have been successfully introduced elsewhere, there is no guarantee that it will work in a particular place. Reformers need to tailor their proposals to the specifics of each situation. Unfortunately too many imitate, not innovate. Imitation in itself is not wrong. Most reforms are imitative; most reformers copy somebody else. Few are truly creative. But in introducing a reform, some original thinking is required. On too many occasions it is sadly missing. Administrative systems cannot be treated as if they were intricate pieces of machinery to which universal mathematical formulae or engineering methods can be applied when they go wrong. They are alive, and the individuals who compose them react in unexpected ways to the new. Just as in business, reformers may have to change their own assumptions and engage in break-away thinking (Mitroff, 1988) and innovation (Lee, 1970).

The commonest faults are repetition and abstraction. Reformers delve into previous attempts at reform and rediscover voluminous reports studded with reform gems. Convinced of their continuing aptness, the reformers merely repeat the proposals, perhaps adding a few of their own, altering a phrase here or there, and rewriting the justification to suit the latest thinking. So the same reforms are proposed for many years without any practical effect. This process is not reform but ritual affirmation of administrative precepts. The real mission of the reformers is to find out why nothing was done previously, whether the current circumstances are more encouraging for adoption, and what should be done to get effective action if past proposals are still deemed appropriate. In this, ritualistic affirmation of administrative precepts has its place and performs a valuable ideological service, but it cannot substitute for applying new ideas.

Repetition also occurs with international reports and textbooks but in this case the shortcoming is abstraction. Universal prescriptions are obviously wide generalizations employing abstract or sophisticated language. Their terms are subject to misinterpretation or mistranslation in different cultural circumstances. For instance, countries are encouraged to replace political patronage with "the merit system" in making appointments to public offices. But there are various kinds of merit system and the word "merit" has many different meanings, not always associated with achievement rather than ascription. If confined strictly to entrance by academic examination in strict marking order, the great majority of the world's population without requisite access to the necessary education is automatically excluded from public service. If extended to practical tests for actual work in public employment, many higher level jobs would be confined to technically but not necessarily administratively competent persons. Looking back over history, societies which never employed a merit system nevertheless achieved remarkable administrative feats in building large cities and public works, governing huge empires, directing large armies, and constructing the wonders of the world and great religious shrines. In short, the imitation of abstract principles, however well meaning and intellectually appealing, ignores the problems of application to specific situations.

Repetition and abstraction rarely impress. Many people involved in the reform situation would be aware of past proposals and universal prescriptions. The reformers are not suggesting anything that is not already known. Outside support is not really needed in carrying out reforms. Most people know *what* to do. What they want to know is *how* to do it. If the reformers cannot provide something novel, practical, attainable, or refreshing, they will be ignored. At the present time, several countries have broken continuity with the past in their deliberate societal transformation, and many others have not been able to keep abreast of the knowledge explosion. In their case, reformers who articulate or generalize what others are doing perform a valuable service. So do the information services of international bodies, research missions of interregional associations, staff exchanges between universities and the whole host of international cooperation aids. But without specificity, their value is much diminished.

3. Incorrect Diagnosis

Effective results spring only from realistic appraisals of the reform situation, not imitation of some other situation. But without the facts, no diagnosis is possible and even with the facts, the diagnosis may be incorrect because of faulty interpretation. Reformers do go astray. Facts are confused with opinions (and vice versa); they are muddled and confused; they are overlooked. The reformers get sidetracked from their main purpose into the byways of scandal or intellectual fascination. They allow common misconceptions to prevail. They accept too much without question. For these and other reasons, an incorrect diagnosis may kill reform prospects. But administrative situations are usually so complicated that a wrong diagnosis cannot be easily detected. Only in implementation are doubts confirmed. Unfortunately the implementation of reforms to correct wrongly diagnosed faults worsens the situation; incorrect treatment may be worse than leaving well alone.

Usually major faults occur because an administrative system is trying to do things that it cannot do (unattainable objectives), or the administrative arrangements do not permit the administrators to do what they have to do (obstructive structure), or some component is not doing its expected job (inadequate performance): –

Unobtainable Objectives
(a) The objectives are unknown, undefined or abstract.
(b) The objectives are ideals, perfections, beyond mankind's current capability.
(c) Inadequate constraint is responsible for trying to do too much at one time.
(d) Excessive caution widens the gap between prospect and performance.
(e) Subsystem optimization erodes system optimization.
(f) Abnormal burdens are placed on administrators without adequate societal supports.
(g) The administrative culture or infrastructure is incapable of supporting administrators in fulfilling public expectations.
(h) Administrative objectives conflict with other societal objectives.
(i) Policies contradict objectives.

Obstructive Structure
(a) The number of components is inadequate, there being too many or too few.
(b) The arrangement of components is unsuitable for the task (being too hierarchical, too collegial, or outmoded).
(c) Relationships between components are needlessly complicated.
(d) Communications break down.
(e) Foreign models are copied without adequate appreciation of supporting infrastructure.
(f) Incompatible and uncooperative components are not separated and no machinery exists to reconcile them.

Inadequate Performance
(a) Constituents do not know what is expected of them and do not perform to expectations.
(b) Constituents lack the necessary qualifications and conditions to perform their tasks.
(c) Constituents are composed of disloyal and otherwise unsuitable members who sabotage cooperative efforts.
(d) Constituents lack incentives for effective performance.
(e) Talent is wasted.
(f) Service orientation is displaced for self-convenience.
(g) Scientific management and management sciences are inadequately employed.
(h) No provision is made for self-evaluation, error correction and adequate learning experience.

Correct diagnosis involves sorting out these system shortcomings and rating them in importance for action before deciding on a reform program.

4. Hidden Agendas

Much less frequent than incorrect diagnosis are the occasions when the reformers are rightly suspected of hidden intentions. Ostensibly their purpose is to review existing arrangements and propose remedies for observed deficiencies. In reality they have different objectives, public and personal. The opportunity is used to silence critics for the duration by occupying them on apparently important work. It is also used to take people away from their permanent positions while their offices are reshuffled. More sinister, evidence is sought for a purge of inefficient, disloyal, disliked or feared administrators. These hidden intentions are usually soon discovered and warnings flash along the grapevine. Less provable is the use by reformers of their position to gain publicity, direct public attention to themselves, and generally seize the opportunity for career advancement, without caring too much about effective reform. If performance is a criterion for promotion, then these ambitious reform sympathizers who do get things done may prove more beneficial than more reform-devoted but less effective persons.

5. Indecisive Approach

How much the reformers decide to reveal of their work and intentions is a strategic consideration concerned with the best way of pushing reforms through. Many reform attempts have failed because the reformers could not agree among themselves as to the scope of reform programs, the magnitude of change implied in them, the rate of change preferred, and the comprehensiveness of specific proposals. In trying for compromise, they have appeared indecisive, uncaring, unconcerned. Opponents have shifted attention away from their proposals to their consensual methods and slow decision-making style. Yet a bold approach, sweeping proposals and urgent action may not augur well for success. Just as shock tactics may backfire, so comprehension may detract from adoption. Ambition is not necessarily the best formula for success in administrative reform.

In steering a careful path between indecision and abrasion, reformers make other mistakes. They neglect to consider the divisibility of their proposals, that is, to separate those that could stand by themselves should the whole package be rejected. They overlook the possibility of revocability after adoption. The longer the reforms take to make an impact the more likely they may be dropped as patience wears thin and opponents organize. They disregard the incompatibility between their reforms and the values and norms of those charged with implementation and sometimes fail to realize the inconsistency and ambiguity of their own proposals. In concentrating on the long term and ignoring short term interests, the reformers do themselves harm, as they do when they recommend complex rather than simple reform instruments, large-scale rather than small-scale resources, extraordinary rather than routine methods, coercive rather than persuasive techniques, and optimal rather than satisficing results.

6. Faulty Planning

Administrative reform is a preparation for an inaccurately predictable future. Before they design a reform program, the reformers have some conception of what they want and expect to happen. They proceed on the assumption that they might as well attempt the maximum at the outset if they later have to modify their ambitions. It is almost inconceivable that they proceed without some kind of a plan, if only a conceptualization of the reform ideas into practical proposals. They usually express their objectives, identify their main difficulties and outline some ways of overcoming resistance, but they may prefer to play down the difficulties and hide their intentions by avoiding specific commitments to retain maximum flexibility. Contingency plans endeavor to cover the following elements:

- identification of the reformers and their principal supporters and an appeal to the noncommitted for backing
- attestation of the worth, feasibility, practicality, and acceptability of the reform proposals
- evidence where similar proposals have worked
- estimation of favorable outcomes
- points anticipating opposition and distortion
- promises of rewards for supporters and possible threats of penalties on opponents
- hints of access to adequate resources
- reevaluation of chosen instrumentalities.

These constitute the program as far as most people are concerned.

While the program outline may be impressive, the planning behind it often is faulty. Insufficient time and background material are largely to blame. So too is personal incompetence. The reformers fail to formulate both broad and specific objectives related to the reform situation. They disregard operational objectives in setting the direction and scope of reforms and defining the basis for the consideration of alternatives. They refuse to spell out the choice of criteria for the selection of strategies and reforms, and consequently omit evaluation of foreseeable consequences. They may overlook the constraints of the situation and omit some crucial dominant factors. Clearly,

The more innovative and far-reaching changes need the most careful implementing. They require the most re-training of people, the most explaining, the greatest patience and often will cause the greatest change in human relationships. Generally, these are also the changes that require the most testing...(O.E.C.D., 1979, 26)

Yet, often this sage advice is ignored. All these factors constitute missing links in the planning of reform.

7. Narrow Vision

The number and variety of reform instrumentalities increase with the enlargement of administrative concepts and the progress of administrative technology. The main instrumentalities – public inquiries, law, institution-building, reorganization, professionalization, budgeting, and scientific management – remain popular. In recent decades, they have been joined by mechanization, debureaucratization, education, training and executive development, organizational development, management sciences, and decentralization. More recent are privatization, management consultancy, data storage and retrieval, institutionalized clientele protection, and policy sciences. Yet reformers themselves remain unduly conservative in their choice of instrumentalities. They stick to predominantly favored methods such as the superimposition of new watchdogs, the introduction of new laws and law enforcement machinery, the replacement of top personnel, and the establishment of research and development facilities for continuing improvement.

While in general they cannot be faulted, in actual reform situations they need to be more enterprising in their selection of instrumentalities and more experimental in techniques. For instance, the establishment of an investigatory body to propose reforms for implementation by operating units, a common reform proposal, once activated may well signal the end of further interest as attention switches to other matters. Without top level support, the reform body may not be taken seriously by operating units, irrespective of the quality of its work. Operating units take their cue from elite attitudes. If the country's leadership takes little interest in administration, downgrades administration in national priorities and is ambivalent about reform, then reform agencies find themselves conducting technical exercises with little impact on administrative performance. This is not so true of ad hoc task forces which depend less on elite support than professional acceptance. In time, enthusiasm dies and the agencies, playing for safety and security, switch from macro-reforms to technical trivia and limited experiments.

Their competence depends to a large extent on their ability to attract and retain creative talent as centers of administrative leadership. The necessary conditions include a critical mass of congenial reform-minded individuals open to new ideas, ready to articulate and push reforms, exposed to varied organizational experiences, and rewarded for continuous innovation. These reform leaders should possess a trained intellect and certain qualities such as a passion for human development, propensity to organize and a spirit of experimentation. The reform agencies should provide an innovative atmosphere – stimulus and incentives to produce, sympathetic leadership willing to back staff efforts, an open, accessible, encouraging management, free flow of information, decentralized decision-making, and an organized system of acknowledging, rewarding and publicizing innovations. A major fault of such agencies is that they themselves fall far short of these conditions. But then again if they met these conditions, there would be much less need for reform in the first place.

To cover up defects, reformers tend to explain away their lack of impact and rationalize their shortcomings. By taking a narrow view of the administrative function, they refuse to tackle policy, law or morality. By adopting a purely investigatory-advisory role, they refuse to interfere in day-to-day operations. By disclaiming any special expertise, they refuse to enter into open controversy or back tough-minded staff. Such antics convince their opposite numbers in operating units that they are weak and wishy-washy interferers. They boast about their weapon of publicity (i.e. exposure) but they rarely use it. When they do go public, nobody else takes any real notice and their releases are usually forgotten within days. Further, their very existence may discourage alternative arrangements and thwart further reform prospects. Meantime, operating units evade implementation without themselves engaging in self-correction and innovation.

8. Inability to Command Resources and Internal Support

Reform is an investment, requiring substantial resources of time, energy, creativity and finance. Whereas the reformers may have sufficient for their needs, the operating units may not be able to divert or attract sufficient for implementation. Usually at the outset the reformers get all that they request. They can pick administrative talent, contract with expert consultants, invest in research materials and generally gather sufficient resources to get off the ground. In time, they too run into difficulties as they try to keep the initial momentum going. But they are not so badly off as the operating units presumably already lack sufficient reform resources. Now extra demands are placed on them at the very points where they are weakest. Their staff have to work out the practicalities of reform and adjust to any attendant dislocations. Whatever goodwill exists cannot substitute for time, energy, creativity and finance. Without additional resources, the extra demands may not be met at all (the reforms are ignored) or met perfunctorily (the reforms are paid lip service) or sacrificed (the reforms are adopted at the expense of operational standards).

Even with sufficient resources, reforms are likely to be doomed by lack of internal goodwill or support. Without winning over the potentially reformed, i.e. those who will be expected to adopt, assimilate and routinize the reforms, only perfunctory implementation occurs at best.

> Every employee involved in the change needs to be made aware of the reasons for the change, the problems which the change is designed to correct or minimize and how the change is to be made. The change needs to be explained in great detail. (O.E.C.D., 1979, 27)

The more they feel they have an important role in reform, the more they will identify with it and make a sincere effort to make it work. Half-hearted implementation is also likely to be prevented if those involved have an opportunity to raise questions and make suggestions of their own and this way brought into the reform campaign as active and willing partners. At least their involvement should reduce risk aversion, and identify unforeseen obstacles, defense mechanisms being employed and the common motives for resistance, some of which may be groundless and others compensated for, so that resisters can be won over (Kets de Vries and Miller, 1985).

9. Absence of Feedback

Once the chosen strategy and instrumentalities are put into operation, the next task in implementation is keeping track of what is happening to the reform program and determining whether the reforms are taking effect as anticipated. The problem is simplified if the reform advocates are also the adopters and implementors. *Self-initiative* is obviously the best course in administrative reform for there is minimum need to consult outsiders, obtain elite support, wage public campaigns, convince conservative functionaries, and devise special channels for feedback. "Every administrator his own reformer" is a good slogan but somewhat idealistic in that the administrators may be the cause of inadequacy, or they may not be competent reformers, or they may not have the time, energy and will to devote to reforms when pressing issues of the moment have to be decided. Nevertheless, it is desirable to encourage self-initiative in administrative reform, to decentralize decision-making to enable the people most affected to decide for themselves without inordinate delay, and to emphasize error-correction at the point of action.

In the absence of self-initiative, feedback is indispensable. Yet too often reformers think their job finished when the operating units have acknowledged the reforms and decided to implement them. But though the operational responsibility is not theirs, if they are really committed to reform, their hardest task has only just begun – that is, to keep at the operational units until the reforms are successfully assimilated. Feedback only becomes a problem when mutual confidence between involved parties does not exist, reform processes are secret and the reformers don't really care what happens after adoption. The reformers may be content with any change in the status quo along the lines of their original conceptions, accepting any departures as the price of reform, or they may be uncompromising, not resting until satisfied that they have gone as far as possible and exhausted every avenue. The perfectionists among them will want of course to investigate the consequences both good and bad of unforeseen factors and to estimate the possibilities of using the transformed situation as a springboard for further reforms.

10. Little Monitoring

To some extent feedback is an indispensable part of monitoring performance, but there may be feedback without monitoring and monitoring without feedback. In feedback without monitoring, the reformers may take the word of the operational units and supplement their reports with informal contacts. The operational units do not have special monitoring facilities. In monitoring without feedback, the operational units are careful to monitor reform efforts for their own purposes but do not bother (or care) to report their findings back to the initiating reformers. Major reforms probably need both feedback and monitoring. The operating units may mistake or misinterpret reform intentions. They may misunderstand reform requirements. They may change reform directions. They may just go through the motions without effect. Worse still, lower levels in the operating units may deliberately sabotage reforms or passively resist any change. Monitoring, unlike feedback, ensures that original intentions are followed and that departures are corrected.

11. Evaluation Ignored

Once a cut-off point in time has been decided, assessment of reform efforts can be made at several different levels. The outcomes can be compared with original conceptions, ostensible reform objectives, real intentions, declared compromises and modifications, and possible outcomes. Apart from varying conceptual difficulties, each of these requires different feedback mechanisms. Appraisal is not the exclusive right of reformers and reformed. The final judgment should be with the clients and consumers of the end-products of the administrative system.

Unfortunately evaluation of this kind is the most neglected aspect in reform implementation. Given inarticulate public opinion, administrative secrecy, autocratic institutions and sporadic, isolated and uncoordinated efforts to improve performance, there is rarely any strong public movement in favor of administrative reform in any country. People who would like to see better public administration often do not know what to do or how to make their wishes known. While people cannot shut administration out of their lives, it shuts them out. Successful administrative reform should allow for public participation both in administration and administrative reform.

12. Goal Displacement

At least three possibilities for goal displacement have been identified in passing: use of administrative reform inquiries to distract critics, the use of such inquiries by reformers for career advancement, and the operational unit's ability to block reform. These can be considered the inner politics of administrative reform implementation. There is also the outer politics of administrative reform. Although the goal is ostensibly *administrative* reform, there are usually more important issues at stake. Reorganizations involve a deliberate transfer of power. In government, administrative reforms may strengthen the law and order functions at the expense of national development or divert resources from traditional functions to new government activities. Likewise, civil service reform may be a device to broaden or narrow entry into the political elite, curb or extend governmental spoils, reshape the educational system, and transform occupational images and status. In short, administrative reform is only a pretext or lever for political, social, cultural or economic change, and in certain circumstances it may be a very effective device with which to achieve other objectives.

At any point of administrative reform the genuine administrative goals of the initiators may be replaced by other goals. The chosen reform agency, for instance, may find itself responsible for national planning, economic regulation or social integration because of its centrality, its high status, its effective working relationships throughout the governmental structure, and its high quality, innovative and energetic personnel. It may be one of the few bodies capable of getting anything done. It finds itself responsible for all kinds of government policies and programs which it never envisaged at the outset. It becomes the channel for overseas funds and foreign aid. It assumes responsibility for security, performance audit and recruitment for the public sector. Reform gets further and further pushed into the background as it is transformed into another operating agency. Likewise, operating agencies, seeing that they can obtain more funds for administrative reform, embark on large reform schemes which are merely fronts for obtaining more operating funds, enlarging their programs, expanding their activities and increasing their overall standing in the governmental system. They also seize the opportunity of reform to implement postponed projects and rejected policies. Again, reform is a secondary consideration.

Even if the goals are displaced, and administrative reform deemed a failure by the reform initiators, it is no disgrace. The whole process may enhance performance. First, reform proposals challenge bureaucratic inertia and conservative administrators. Although defence mechanisms may temporarily suppress change, things can never quite be the same and peace tokens have to be made if the situation is to be kept in hand. Second, reform programs attract enterprising administrative talent and provide valuable experience for a new generation of administrative aspirants. Third, reformers promote badly needed administrative modernization which is likely to set off a chain reaction in functional reforms as changes in techniques, skills and attitudes in specialized fields seem more attainable than possibly the harder changes to carry through in administration. Fourth, constructive progressive forces find openings for their respectable creative talent in empirical problem-solving, particularly the kind presented in administrative reform. Sensitive elites seek to enlist their aid to prevent their joining extremist political and social movements. Fifth, there is little inventiveness in outmoded systems, obsolete institutions, inert bureaucracies, useless arrangements and conservative attitudes, and any effort to transform administrative systems is to be commended in the face of official indifference, technical ignorance, political intransigence and public apathy.

Learning From Failure

These twelve common pitfalls in the implementation of administrative reform drive home important lessons for potential reformers embarking on their own particular voyage of discovery apart from the fairly obvious points that (a) political support is imperative and to embark on reform without it is foolhardy, (b) reformers should know beforehand whether their reforms are feasible and economical, and (c) they should not leave out people who know most how the reforms could be implemented.

- A good beginning is essential and requires thorough homework where possible, an appearance of independence and commitment, open-mindedness, and model decorum.
- Innovativeness means tailoring reforms to specific conditions and avoiding needless repetition and abstract prescriptions.
- Diagnosis should be correct and focused on attainable objectives, facilitating structures and suitable performance.

- Hidden intentions should be avoided lest exposure doom reform.
- Reformers have to be decisive and maintain the upper hand.
- Reformers have to plan carefully and replan as circumstances change.
- Reformers should be bold and imaginative.
- Reformers have to muster sufficient resources to realize reforms.
- Reforms should be monitored at all times.
- Reforms should be evaluated by the reformers, the reformed and the public at large.
- Goal displacement should be avoided.

These seem obvious enough and warn reformers to proceed at risk. Little can be taken for granted. Reformers have to be on watch for all these pointers at all times. The slightest relaxation can prove fatal.

If reformers have to avoid doing too little or not enough, they also should guard against doing too much, too quickly, too often, lest saturation psychosis sets in and administrators neglect their primary tasks and "become increasingly impatient with the imposition of administrative reforms and the proportion of time required for their introduction and operation", eventually leading to administrative immobility and revolt against all administrative innovations (Lambramboise, 1971, 303). To offset such risks, reformers could well adopt methods of radical practice in being realistic, making limited demands, relying on negotiation and genuine deals rather than confrontation, and assuming "a posture of active patience "(Friedmann, 1979, 172).

On the other hand, protests by administrators that reform is too fast or too elaborate or too distractive also indicate that reform efforts need also to be measured less by their quantitative or even qualitative contributions to improved administration but according to their contribution to problem solving, creativity and innovation, and societal transformation, which is bound (and intended) to place abnormal stresses on administrators in their concern with system design and system building. The conflicts between administrative reformers and line staff are inevitable because they define problems differently, they see situations from different perspectives, and they hold different assumptions about the feasibility and consequences of reforms. Whether the conflicts can be contained, the line staff won over to reform, and the reformers complete their work satisfactorily depends also on what lessons reformers care to derive from experiences of other reformers and reforms around the globe (Table 1).

In the global society, every country has to be concerned with events elsewhere. Only a handful have tried to isolate themselves and all by 1990 had rejoined the world community. Every state now looks closely at its neighbors and at those considered to be the most successful internationally. Thus when Japan gained pre-eminence in the late 1970s, other countries sought the secret of its success, studied its administrative culture, and attempted to copy its managerial practices. Likewise, envious glances have been made at South

Korea, Taiwan, Singapore and Hong Kong. But much of the world still looks to the United States and Western Europe for its inspiration, just as the East Bloc looks to the Soviet Union and China, the Commonwealth countries to the United Kingdom, Latin America to Spain, Portugal and Brazil, and the ex-French colonies to France, and what they do in any field is closely watched. In public administration certain other countries have a following of their own either internationally or regionally and these variously include Sweden, Canada, Egypt, India and Australia. What these fashion leaders do, sooner or later others follow. Generally, renewed interest is being shown in comparative studies and lessons that might be learnt from other countries' experiences (Crozier, 1988).

In administrative reform, it has long been realized that every country is different, that no administrative culture is identical to any other even if certain characteristics are shared, and that each administrative reform situation is unique. Reformers can, however, borrow, copy, reshape, and modify reforms and they can derive tips from what others do. Where reforms have succeeded, one can study diagnosis, obstacles, mistakes and resistance. There is something to be gained from every reform attempted. For instance, in budget reform the failures of implementing P.P.B.S. and Z.B.B. taught reformers what to discard as inoperable and what might be tried differently. Whenever elaborate administrative reform investigations are conducted around the world, their findings are circulated and closely examined. Many are discarded as being too idiosyncratic but others receive international attention for possible action. While there is no guarantee of success, looking at other people's experiences at least guards against possible failure.

After all, reforms are costly investments (and costlier political investments when they go bad). They require scarce resources which poor countries cannot afford at all or only sparingly and always begrudgingly. In this respect, richer countries are fortunate. Not only can they probably find the resources for reform when they need to but they probably enjoy excess administrative capacity, i.e. built-in reserves and greater administrative capabilities as well. Unfortunately, although since the 1960s available global resources have increased, they are maldistributed and they still fall almost everywhere short of administrative reform requirements. There has not been that much slack around anywhere and it has not been possible to conjure up the requisite resources at short notice. Political leaders everywhere have to be careful not to squander what they have by repeating the mistakes of others.

On the other hand, in recent years a new generation of leaders has been assuming power, leaders not scarred by the memories of the First World War or even of the Great Depression. They are not so obsessed by the past that they cannot think of the future and prepare the way by adopting long overdue reforms now. They are more prepared to challenge the administrative arrangements they inherit. They recognize administrative failings and shortcomings and are not so

Table 1: Most Frequently Cited Administrative Reform Proposals: 1970-1990

Australia	Royal Commission on Australian Government Administration (Coombs) 1976 Review of New South Wales Government Administration (Wilenski) 1982
Brazil	Under Secretariat for Modernization and Administrative Reform 1964 National Debureaucratization Program 1979
Canada	Royal Commission on Government Organization (Glassco) 1962 Operational Performance Measurement Systems (O.P.M.S.) 1975 Royal Commission on Financial Management and Accountability (Lambert) 1979 Committee on Personnel Management (D'Avignon) 1979
China	Third Plenum of C.C.P. Central Committee 1979 Zhao's administrative reform program 1982
France	Ministry of Civil Service and Administrative Reform
Japan	Provisional Commission on Administrative Reform (RINCHO) 1981 Administrative Reform Promotion Committee (GYOKAKUSHIN) 1983
Soviet Union	Gorbachev's reconstruction (**perestroika**) policy 1986
United Kingdom	Committee on the Civil Service (Fulton) 1968 Committee on Personnel Social Services (Seebohm) 1968 Central Policy Review Staff 1970 Local Government Act 1972 Privatization program 1979 Efficiency Scrutinies (Rayner) 1979 Financial Management Initiative 1982
United States	Congressional Budget and Impoundment Control Act of 1974 Civil Service Reform Act of 1978 Cutback management programs 1978 Paperwork Reduction Act of 1980 President's Council on Integrity and Efficiency (P.C.I.E.) 1981 President's Private Sector Survey on Cost Controls (Grace) 1983 President's Council on Management Improvement (P.C.M.I.) 1984 Reform '88 program 1984

reticent from publicly admitting them. They are more open to suggestions and they are more willing to experiment with alternatives that promise better public sector performance. Though they are still wedded ideologically to different paths to national development, they are more pragmatic when it comes to administrative means. Universally, they have been disappointed in time-honored methods of running the administrative state and they are prepared to take on their own entrenched bureaucracies to which they attribute much of the blame for sluggish public administration. In this, they have shown an unaccustomed boldness and propensity to try anything that seems promising in reinvigorating not just the administrative state but the wider society too.

References

Agarwala, R., *Planning in Developing Countries: Lessons of Experience*, World Bank Staff Working Papers, No. 576, Washington, D.C., 1983.

Bjur, W.E., and Caiden, G.E., "Administrative Reform and Institutional Bureaucracies", in S.K. Sharma, ed., *Dynamics of Development: An International Perspective*, Vol. 1, Concept Publishing, New Delhi, 1978, pp. 365-378.

Caiden, N. and Wildavsky, A., *Planning and Budgeting in Poor Countries*, John Wiley and Sons, New York, 1974.

Crozier, M., *How to Reform the State?: Three Countries, Three Strategies: Sweden, Japan, United States*, La Documentation Francaise, Paris, 1988.

Friedmann, J., *The Good Society, 1979*, The Massachusetts Institute of Technology, Cambridge, MA., 1979.

Gardner, J., *No Easy Victories*, Harper Colophon Books, New York, 1968.

Grindle, M.S., and Thomas, J.W., "Policy Makers, Policy Choices, and Policy Outcomes: The Political Economy of Reform in Developing Countries," *Policy Sciences*, Vol. 22, Nos. 3-4, November 1989, pp. 213-248.

Kets de Vries, F.R., and Miller, D., *The Neurotic Organization*, Jossey-Bass Publishers, San Francisco, 1985.

Lambramboise, H. L., "Administrative Reform in the Federal Public Service: Signs of a Saturation Psychosis," *Canadian Public Administration*, Vol. 14, No. 3, Autumn 1971, pp. 303-325.

Lee, H. B., "An Application of Innovation Theory to the Strategy of Administrative Reform in Developing Countries," *Policy Sciences,* Vol. I., No. 2, Summer 1970, pp. 177-189.

Mitroff, I., *Break-Away Thinking: How To Challenge Your Business Assumptions (and Why You Should)*, John Wiley & Sons, New York, 1988.

Organization for Economic Cooperation and Development, *Strategies for Change and Reform in Public Management*, Paris, 1979.

10. Reforms in the East: Retreat from Bureaucratic Centralism

Authoritarian regimes devoted to comprehensive planning or bureaucratic centralism probably best illustrate how in the contemporary state administrative reform impacts the wider society and vice versa. Political leaders in them as elsewhere have to make the crucial decisions governing the scope and boundaries of reform, its timing, the specifics and when to change reform policies and strategies if reforms do not work out as anticipated. Even when they delegate such matters to subordinates, there is no telling when they may decide on their own to take charge of administrative reform and dictate even petty details. And when they do delegate authority, they only move decisions one step back into offstage infighting among party and bureaucratic functionaries. The politics of administrative reform is still not removed; it is merely assumed by lower ranking public officials who have their own vested interests in how well both state and party perform in pursuing national development objectives, controlling the affairs of state, strengthening their position in society, and retaining the active support of the masses who are their followers, clients and servants. Furthermore, they command directly by far the major portion of available resources and indirectly the rest if need be without too much difficulty. They do not have to heed the niceties of democratic liberalism to reallocate power, resources and priorities virtually overnight. When determined on reform, they can move much quicker. What they have to worry about is whether they can still carry the rest of society with them, whether the long tail of the administrative state will wag as instructed, and whether, once the people taste reform, they can hold back the floodgates and prevent themselves being swamped by pent-up expectations.

The most startling reforms in recent years have come from probably the least expected direction, that of the East Bloc of countries which have ideologically been against the whole notion of reform. As bearers of Marxism ("the science of social revolution") they have been against reforms and reformism which Lenin saw as concessions made by the ruling class to stem or weaken the revolutionary struggle to split the forces and energy of the revolutionary class. Their Communist Parties had no such reformist illusions. They were revolutionary parties (Kagarlitsky, 1990). In their rejection of capitalism, private property, competition, inequality, exploitation of labor, pluralism, bourgeois values and imperialism, Communist ideologues had envisioned a socialist republic based on public property, collective enterprises and state guidance and a transition period of the dictatorship of the proletariat led by the Communist Party which would work to eliminate capitalism and bourgeois values. The party would substitute pride of labor and contribution, cooperation, equity, sense of community and brotherhood, sharing and civic virtues.

Accordingly, in the East Bloc countries, the Communist Party had led the revolution and established itself as a monopoly over most social organization, including the state, government, military, police, judiciary, bureaucracy, state enterprises, mass media and education, in a highly centralized administrative state governed by an elaborate planning apparatus. In them, national development has for several decades largely depended on state initiative and enterprise, on a dominant public sector, on a work force largely composed of public employees, and on state management of people's lives. Party and state have been so intertwined that they have been virtually indistinguishable. Although formally the rule of law, checks and balances, representative institutions, direct participation, individual rights and integrative consultative mechanisms have been legally enshrined, informally the party leadership has exercised absolute power through party channels and bureaucratic centralism, thereby constituting a privileged "statocracy" (Kagarlitsky, 1988).

In time, the party leadership became in turn party dominance and then party tyranny, and in some countries even attempted party hegemony based on patronage and nepotism. The leaders enjoyed exceptional privileges of rank, exacted tribute from the masses and slid into protected kleptocracy. The rigid planning system responsible for the minute details of millions of items could not adjust to turbulence and caused much waste, inefficiency, and ineffectiveness. It was accompanied by a huge underground economy and together they institutionalized corruption. There were large surpluses of unwanted items, and huge scarcities of necessities such as food and consumer goods. Since the state provided almost everything at least officially free or at highly subsidized rates and employment was compulsory, the best course of action for the alienated masses was to go along, connive like anybody else, and hope personally for party promotion. They had long disregarded Lenin's strictures that the sole condition for their salvation was to "keep accurate and conscientious accounts; conduct business economicially; not to loaf; maintain strict discipline at work" (Eaton and Lvov, 1990, 4). Instead, as there were few incentives to produce and few quality control checks, there was labor waste and indiscipline, much mismanagement and incompetence, much squandering of natural resources, and much disregard for safety and environmental deterioration. In short, East Bloc economies performed poorly (Bergson, 1989).

To disguise the rot, censorship was strict and disinformation was common practice. Most people lived quiet lives of desperation and resentment. As the whole system of bureaucratic centralism performed more and more abysmally, so things got worse not better and no amount of official propaganda could disguise the fact. People did not know what to believe anymore and grew increasingly disillusioned with the system. But they knew no different and had been brought up on the horrors of the past before the revolution and the evils and dangers of alternative systems. Bureaucrat-bashing was one of the few tolerated forms of popular expression and relief, but even there one had to be careful not to offend anyone in particular lest quick retribution descend. For how long could self-deceit on such a scale last? Who would be the first openly to challenge the system? What would be proposed to change bureaucratic centralism? The answers came with the deaths of the revolutionary heros, Stalin in the Soviet Union and Mao Zedong in China, with the imposition of reforms from above, and with the begrudging change of the official party line.

The earliest diagnoses suggested that the command administration mechanism was basically sound but required a return to Lenin's strictures, that is greater discipline, improved planning and better investment and social policies. Reforms were implemented on these lines but with almost everyone in the system having job security, they had little impact and failed to combat corruption, cronyism and stagnation. Mass protests were suppressed and all attempts to move the system into another (more liberal) course were ruthlessly crushed; the basics were not to be questioned. But slowly as things worsened, the basics were seen as being after all unsound or at lest unsound for the turbulent times inaugurated by the world energy crises. Central planning, state ownership of the means of production and the monopoly of the Communist Party were not healthy after all. Better results might be forthcoming outside state action and bureaucratic centralism. What was needed was a good dose of decentralized individual and group effort and employee collectives and cooperatives interacting in real markets, i.e. the reforming of Communist ideology in favor of market socialism and practical reforms that would revitalize every office, factory, farm, school and home.

So wholesale economic reforms were launched, difficult to implement without systematically undoing bureaucratic centralism. Further, greater economic freedom could not properly work without greater political freedom and greater ties with the West. Old-style totalitarian Communism was increasingly irrelevant; its policies had failed and its ideology was outdated. But could the alienated masses be energized without abandoning Communism altogether? The die-hards thought not; they refused to let go of bolshevik ideology and unnecessary concessions to bourgeois concepts. Awakened liberals (and anti Communists in general) wanted to sweep the whole system away overnight and westernize as quickly as possible. In between, the reformers tried to find a compromise, something that was neither East or West but different. It was they who surfaced in leadership positions and made reform respectable as the path to socialism. But they soon found "it may be easy, although bloody, to set up a Stalinist centrally planned economic system, but it is very difficult to dismantle it and replace it with one that is market oriented" (Goldman, 1990, 44). They were forced to be societal transformers not mere economic or administrative reformers.

A Stitch in Time?

By 1990, reform had become the official policy in most East Bloc countries, if only to ward off counter-revolution or disintegration and chaos. The Marxist-Lenin-Stalin system which had been tried for at least two generations had not succeeded, not when compared to liberal democracies whose people were undeniably better off, more innovative, and more secure. The failure could no longer be blamed on external factors but upon leaders who had imposed their dogma in defiance of facts. At last, the truth could be revealed. Repressive police states had inhibited spontaneity and creativity. Centrally controlled economies had allowed no freedom of choice, provided no incentives to excel, and fostered societal corruption that in turn reinforced inequality. The Communist Party leadership had designated priorities without concern for individual choice, individual preference, and individual rights and had imposed its decisions through a totalitarian administrative state that had suffered from every conceivable form of bureaupathology and public maladministration. The recipients had protested against such regimentation however they could – through defection, escapism, passivity, rebellion. Now, as their discontent mounted and found open expression, the system was in danger of unravelling. The party leaders were still unwilling to admit defeat or to abandon the system altogether. They sought not so much political or social reforms that might defeat the revolution but economic and administrative reforms that would perpetuate it, turn the system around, make it more modern, more productive, more efficient, more viable. They wanted reforms that would not turn the clock too far back and would not change the fundamentals too quickly so they would lose control, position and credibility.

Nobody forecast how quickly the dictatorship of the proletariat led by the Communist Party would crumble. The turning point came in June 1989 which witnessed some key events that unleashed mounting reform pressures shaking the whole East Bloc to its foundations. In China, the old-line revolutionary autocratic leadership brutally crushed student demonstrations for democracy in Beijing, just as its predecessors had done countless times before, this after a decade of post-Mao reforms which had freed part of the economy and supposedly had sensitized public administration. The whole world was shocked at the cruelty of the repression, no less other East Bloc countries. They realized that unless they made concessions to mounting dissent and gave in to justifiable demands for reforms, they would have to resort to similar measures to preserve not the dictatorship of the proletariat but the dictatorship of an enfeebled party leadership which had lost touch with the people and could only fault the corruption of individuals within the system, not the corruption of the system itself.

In the Soviet Union, Premier Ryzhkov, in the spirit of Gorbachev's *perestroika* (reconstruction) and *glasnost* (openness), confessed that because of poor planning and overspending, the government was unable to raise the standard of living, ensure national security and finance further development. Only radical economic reforms could reverse the decline. The government would economize, reduce military expenditures, cut back on the bureaucracy, shift from central planning and management of the economy to market socialism (wherein state-owned profit maximizing enterprises would compete fairly with co-operatives and private enterprises in free money markets), increase investments in food production, reduce the growth of heavy industry, and increase the incomes of the poorest. As in China, reforms previously introduced to preserve the system were causing opponents of the system to bubble to the surface but instead of coercion and repression, they were now to be acknowledged, respected and given a responsible place within the system, even at the cost of abandoning major features of the system. The Soviet Union was still not prepared to go as far as Poland where the first election in 40 years giving people a genuine choice, resulted in a resounding defeat of the Communist Party's candidates. There, too, people had lost confidence in the government to deal with the country's problems, to attack corruption and to be responsive to its citizens, and they had lost much of their respect for the party and for Communism as an ideology.

Within a year, Eastern Europe had been transformed, the political map of Europe had been changed, and the Cold War was being terminated. After forty years, the Iron Curtain had been lifted, the Berlin Wall had been breached, Communist Parties had lost their monopoly of power and governments were openly admitting that their economic systems were in a state of advanced collapse. No longer would the *nomenklatura* be allowed to manipulate the system uncontested and run the churches, universities, town councils and factories. In Poland, Czechoslovakia and Hungary, coalitions dominated by non-Communists ruled and the Hungarian and Polish Communist Parties had renounced Marxism and changed their names, East Germany had been reunited with West Germany and had agreed to abandon bureaucratic centralism for liberal capitalism, Bulgaria had rid itself of tyrannical Todor Dhivkov as had Romania of the Ceausescus, and even Albania was ending its self imposed isolation and embarking on internal reforms. New freedom of movement had seen unprecedented travel across open borders. New freedom of expression had seen unprecedented mass protests, demonstrations and strikes, causing changes in political leadership and promises of free elections. Soviet President Gorbachev had ruled out force against East Bloc neighbors, had urged East Bloc Communist Parties to compromise and yield power where they had lost public confidence, had encouraged other East Bloc countries to democratize, to decentralize their state managed economies and to de-Stalinize their societies, and had advocated a commonwealth of all European countries, both East and West. Truly a revolution of expectations was taking place that was bound to result in sweeping political, social and administrative reforms.

Throughout history, administrative reforms have followed shocks to the system. In every country, reforms have resulted from disasters and failures attributed to administrative shortcomings. But reforms in the East Bloc have not been the result so much of a sudden, unexpected, unpredictable shock caused by specific events as the dawning realization that the whole edifice so patiently constructed over several generations was flawed and would not realize the dreams of its founders and most faithful supporters. Patching it up here and there only delayed the inevitable a little longer; it only perpetuated coercive totalitarianism, stifling *immobilisme*, official lawlessness, production for production's sake, low productivity, poor quality goods and services, wastefulness and incompetent management (Desai, 1989; Prybyla, 1990). To avoid slipping further back, it had to be reconstructed into a different model of democratic socialism with radical changes in every area of social life and confidence in the civic maturity of the people. In Gorbachev's own words, it was "either democracy or social inertia and conservatism" (*Pravda*, Feb. 26, 1987).

> People will judge our policies, will judge reconstruction... by the tangible results in improving the work conditions and lives of the millions: by how much more sensibly production work is organized, how much fairer people's pay is, whether housing construction has speeded up, whether stores, household services, city transport, medical services, and hospitals have improved, and whether the moral climate in a party organization or a work unit has got better. (*Pravda*, Jan. 30, 1987)

What he meant by this was not a renunciation of the principles of the revolution but their restoration, not a return to capitalism but to humane socialism, not the abandonment of socialism but its renewal. He wanted an irreversible end to state controls imposed by Stalinism and "bureaucratic Stalinization" (Cohen and Heuval, 1989, 15).

Perestroika (Restructuring)

The latest round of reforms differed in several respects from those that had preceded it. This time, it was backed if not instigated by the Soviet Union which had deliberately intervened and crushed previous reforms in the East Bloc that it had opposed. It was not largely confined to the economic sphere but embraced sweeping societal changes that were also needed to make economic reform effective. It was not based on presuming a centrally managed society but on promoting genuine pluralism, competition and self-management. It had to overcome public disinterest (from people who had seen so many reforms fail and who had been led astray so many times before) and hard line resistance from entrenched vested interests who had the most to lose. It took place under crisis conditions and suffered from resource deficiency, particularly time, administrative competence, and well formulated plans. It was probably riskier than any before because if it succeeded, it could well be the end of Communism altogether. If it failed, all that 1917 stood for might be swept away, or to preserve 1917, Stalinism might be reimposed bereft of its world-revolutionary ideology and rhetoric, its expansionist foreign policy and its large internal *gulags*. *Perestroika* represented the widest departure yet from Stalinism.

De-Stalinization began with Khrushchev who like Gorbachev had also wanted to "get the country moving again" after some years of *immobilisme*. He had sought to reinvigorate society and the economy to make Communism more popular at home and abroad. He had revised Marxist-Leninist ideology. He had promised material abundance for all, ambitious public service programs and greater personal rewards. He had declared an end to oppression (by releasing political prisoners, curbing secret police power and revising legal codes), greater democratization and popular self-government, and had reduced privileges for the *nomenklatura*. He had replaced Stalinist hardliners with younger "dynamic, fresh-minded, professionally qualified cadres" and he had announced a new policy of *glasnost* or openness and self-criticism "to learn the real state of affairs in many spheres, to stimulate debate on issues like economic reform, to promote a cultural revival, to help him purge opponents, and to impress the west with the pace and extent of change" (Reddaway, 1987, 22). He had campaigned against drunkenness and shirking and had clamped down on corruption. Administratively, he had sought to improve managerial effectiveness, decentralized control and worker self-management. Though by the early 1960s, Khrushchev had failed, his successors pursued similar policies of de-Stalinization with no greater success, all of which predisposed observers to be skeptical of further "efforts to make more efficient, responsive, open and also honest the incredibly massive and stolid bureaucracy of the Soviet system" (Galbraith, 1987, 53). After all, bureaucratic centralism and administrative controls ("bureaumania") had been strengthened in the 1960s and 1970s, despite the emergence within party leadership of a strong reform faction which eventually was victorious in 1985 (Cohen and Heuvel, 1989).

The first real reform breakthroughs came under Andropov at the July 1983 Party Plenum where problems of the battered economy were openly raised. That was followed in July 1983 by Tatiana Zaslawskaya's "Novosibirsk Report" which recommended greater individualism and greater decentralization of planning and management. Andropov responded by instituting a new round of reforms to improve bureaucratic centralism, economic incentives and labor discipline to combat the underground economy. But the situation continued to deteriorate until the accession of Gorbachev in March 1985. He was determined to end economic stagnation by revitalizing the system, altering the pattern of state investments, setting ambitious technological targets, modernizing industry, enforcing discipline, and inspiring people to work harder. He began with a series of experiments and reorganizations, financial incentives and managerial initiatives, subcontracting and enhanced organizational autonomy that showed that mere tinkering around with bureaucratic centralism would not suffice. Half measures would not work (Aganbegyan, 1989).

In his rousing address to the January 1987 Party Plenum, Gorbachev went over by now familiar ground but this time he called for comprehensive reforms aimed at providing "for flexible, efficient, decentralized implementation of centrally determined objectives through the use of tightly controlled 'socialist markets'" whose centerpiece was to be a new Law on State Enterprise under which

> enterprises were to become fully self-financing and largely self-managing. There was to be an expanded role for workers in decision-making and more direct control over most of its investment activity. Central planning was to be focused on long-run strategic and developmental issues; it was to provide general suggestions and guidelines, rather than to command specific performance. "Socialist markets" were to replace the direct allocation of supplies and products; price formation was to be thoroughly reformed and made more dependent on market forces; the Party was to step back from the day-to-day management of economic affairs. The plan called for a complete revamping of the financial system, including new commercial banks. Finally, foreign trade was liberalized, formally allowing greater direct interaction between Soviet organizations and the world market; through joint ventures, foreign capital was admitted into the Soviet economy. (Ericson, 1990, 36)

Gorbachev promised he would mobilize the masses against the dead hand of bureaucracy, reduce both party and state hierarchies, devolve and decentralize decision-making, strengthen popular self government, and encourage entrepreneurship. This time, he presented a more realistic program for *uskorenie* (accelerated economic growth):

* modernization of technology and production methods; restructuring of agriculture, industry and commerce; increased research and development; productivity measures and incentives;
* more open society; greater self-criticism; freer expression; more factual reporting; *glasnost*;
* democratization; more representative elected assemblies; greater choice of candidates; less ready exercise of police powers; greater incentives for self-initiatives; greater public participation in decision-making;
* entrepreneurship; self-financing; foreign investment; joint enterprises; special economic zones; autonomous cooperatives; private ownership; reconstructed pricing system; markets; profit incentives; reduced central planning; reduced public middle management; reduced subsidization; fair competition; contrac-

tual freedom; some legalization of industrial action; more user fees, fewer free public goods and services;

* separation of party and state; party to be pulled out of of day-to-day administration; state organizations to be more independent of party; reduced party directives; realistic self-management;
* decentralization of economic decision making; more self- financed local projects;
* reorganization of the machinery of government; reduction in number of ministries and departments; streamlining; simplification; curtailment of empire-building;
* retrenchment of state and party managers; cutback management; debureaucratization; some privatization of small state enterprises; retraining and redirection of surplus employees;
* some deregulation; strengthened complaint channels; some judicial review and increased legalism, strengthened due process;
* reduction of indiscipline, corruption, shirking, slacking, drunkenness, parasitical activities;
* general assault on public bureaupathologies, particularly insensitivity and indifference.

The unfreezing of the Soviet economy in this way would encourage other Communist countries to choose their own particular paths to democratic socialism, some no doubt more autocratic and more conservative, and others more radical and more liberal, perhaps even more capitalistic. All would be racing against time to prevent decay, recapture the popular imagination and restructure their economies more in keeping with the global society, in which unification would be founded on diversity instead of a single ideology.

To explain his stance to the West, Gorbachev outlined his ideas in greater detail (Gorbachev, 1987). From the mid-1970s, the country had began to lose momentum, economic failures had become more frequent, and unresolved problems had multiplied, so that the economy lost ground to other countries because of the high cost of production, waste of resources, energy and manpower, poor quality products, gross mismanagement and parasitical attitudes.

> Eulogizing and servility were encouraged; the needs and opinions of ordinary people, of the public at large, were ignored. In the social sciences scholastic theorization was encouraged and developed, but creative thinking was driven out of the social sciences and superfluous and voluntarist assessments and judgments were declared indisputable truths. (Ibid, 21)

In this "everything goes" atmosphere,

> At some administrative levels there emerged a disrespect for the law and encouragement of eyewash and bribery, servility and glorification, working people were justly indignant at the behaviour of people who, enjoying trust and responsibility, abused power, suppressed criticism, made fortunes, and in some cases [indulged in crime]. (Ibid, 23)

To put the economy in order, tighten up discipline, raise the level of organization and responsibility, and to catch up in areas where the country lagged behind, *perestroika* was needed – a profound structural reorganization of the economy, reconstruction of its material base, new technologies, investment policy changes, higher standards of management, and openness to activate the human factor, to take notice of people, the public, to energize them, wake them up, make them truly active and concerned, get them involved, to renovate society, lift the individual spiritually, give moral strength, and to ensure that everyone felt as if he were master of the country.

> We are seeking to make the whole intellectual potential of society and all the potentialities of culture work to mold a socially active person, spiritually rich, just and conscientious. An individual must know and feel that his contribution is needed, that his dignity is not being infringed upon, that he is being treated with trust and respect. (Ibid, 30)

Administratively, the aim was to ensure the transition from an excessively centralized management system relying on orders, to a democratic one, based on the combination of democratic centralism and self-management.

> The reform is based on dramatically increased independence of enterprise and associations, their transition to full self-financing, and granting all appropriate rights to work collectives. They will now be fully responsible for efficient management and end results. A collective's profits will be directly proportionate to its efficiency. (Ibid, 33)

Perestroika meant mass initiatives, priority to the social sphere, denunciation of management by injunction and by administrative methods and the overall encouragement of innovation and socialist enterprise, and resolute struggle against red-tape and illegality. It was to be more than statism with a human face (Oliver, 1988); it was to be a return to non-statist initiatives under the guidance of representative democracy. By going back to the principles of 1917, Gorbachev was risking the reemergence of all the forces that had provoked the revolution, that had led to the subsequent civil war, and that had brought Stalinist absolutism and Soviet imperialism, and a painful, destabilizing, disrupting, and possibly violent transition from bureaucratic centralism to democratic socialism.

To reform on such a scale would be difficult under the best of circumstances and would invariably be accompanied by "big oscillations, contractions, resistance and conflicts" (Stojanovic, 1988, 166) and reverses. Any unanticipated events could stop reform dead in its tracks. If the masses were not won over, *perestroika* would fail. If it had to rely on the *nomenklatura*, it would be unlikely to bring about any fundamental redistribution of power, rights, freedom, wealth and control of property (Cohen and Neuvel, 1989, 123). Gorbachev's brave words did not halt the continuing economic slump and declining living standards, environmental blight, housing shortages, poor public services and health care (Schultz and Rafferty, 1990), rising crime, growing black markets and speculation, the stubbornness of the *serokratiia* (aging mediocrities), increased deficit spending and inflation, and the obstructions of the command-and-administer system. Already by the late 1980s,

> Various agencies are simply ignoring new laws designed to force state enterprises from Moscow's tutelage, contriving new directives in the guise of reform, denying licenses to aspiring cooperatives and individual firms or suffocating them with excessive taxation and regulations, devising technicalities to deprive peasants of their new right to lease land, and imposing more restrictions on local markets. (Cohen and Neuvel, 1989, 26-27)

The system was responding sluggishly at best to Gorbachev's initiatives. Among the public a new slogan was *borba idyot* ("the struggle goes on") denoting the public's unwillingness to kow-tow to bureaucratic centralism commonly summed up in the phrase "they pretend to pay us, and we pretend to work" (Brumberg, 1989, 39).

Gorbachev capitalized on popular discontent by moving ahead with political reforms that he rightly predicted would increase pressures for economic reforms on the lines of market socialism. He did not anticipate that the new political liberalism would release suppressed centrifugal political and social forces and pent up resentment against continued economic stagnation. The threatened social costs of transition – dislocation, inflation and unemployment in particular – added to worsening shortages and gloomy economic forecasts following from the failure of the ambiguous Law on State Enterprise and the jeopardized law on co-operatives (*The Economist*, 1990, 11-12). In 1990, Leonid Abalkin, deputy prime minister for economic reform, pushed for an end to half-hearted reforms toward decentralized socialism that were neither here nor there and only increased popular discontent. He called for radical measures toward a more privatized economy with a legalized market system, the breakup of state monopolies, the expansion of cooperatives and private enterprises and ownership, more realistic prices, and a capital market. His opponents predicted that such measures if not spread over several years and watered down would result in an explosion of public wrath. A compromise of sorts was made at the 28th Congress of the C.P.S.U. in July 1990 and later in the Shatalin economic reform program that promised to liberalize the Soviet economy by March 1992. Party discipline had held but at the cost of transferring more authority from the party to the state and some checks on even more radical measures. Repressive mechanisms had still not been abandoned and at the back of everybody's mind was whether authoritarianism would be reimposed if chaos threatened. After all, the country that had previously moved away from bureaucratic centralism, China, had already experienced similar problems and had backed off temporarily from abandoning or dismantling it any further because of the dysfunctions of the strengthened illegal "shadow economy".

Administrative Modernization in China

The most populated country in the world, "the poor man of Asia," has been trying for most of this century to catch up with everybody else. It had been left behind under a centuries-old feudal regime in which public administration was bureaucratic management of the people *par excellence* and the public bureaucracy was overbloated, privileged, corrupt, wasteful, and inefficient. So detested was it that the very term "bureaucracy" (*guanliao zhuyi*) in China is derogatory, denoting an unmindful, unrealistic, aloof entity, giving orders without investigation, and bureaucracies are known as degenerate organizations. "Healthy, responsible, efficient organizations are…called "organs" (*jigou*) or "offices" (*jiguan*)" (Burns, 1983, 694). Mao Zedong described bureaucracy in his 1967 "Twenty Manifestations of Bureaucracy" (*Guanliao Zhuyi de er shi Zhong Biaoxian*) as authoritarian, elitist, lazy, talentless, corrupt, irresponsible, deceitful, nepotistic, and bureaupathologic. Other Chinese leaders have been equally forthright and condemning in their criticisms of the cumbrous, underemployed, unproductive, parasitic administrative state that has ruled over China for centuries and has remained unchanged in major respects for even longer (Harding, 1981).

Mao Zedong tried to tackle the bureaucracy several times, beginning with the 1952 Three Anti's Campaign directed against bureaucratism, corruption and waste, and the Five Anti's crusade against bribery, tax evasion, fraud, stealing government property and using government secrets for personal advantage, and ending with the bloody Cultural Revolution (1966-1976). The Communist Party's attempts to substitute communal self-management (mutual aid teams, cooperatives, production teams, brigades, communes) as social control mechanisms nearly brought the country to economic ruin, and certainly left public administration in a shambles. Although the machinery of government was simplified and streamlined, and the bureaucracy was purged, the institutionalized style of public management was barely touched. Laws, structures, and people may have been changed, but bureaucratic behavior, values and attitudes remained much the same. There were still too many government offices duplicating each other's functions, staffed by poorly paid, poorly educated and trained, poorly managed aging staff, operating with antiquated tools and equipment in poor accommodation in altogether depressing, discouraging conditions, and supposedly practicing open, participative, people-oriented leadership but more often continuing traditional secretive, authoritarian, self-interested, arbitrary and smug mannerisms, neither of which were exactly results oriented administrative styles. If anything, the Cultural Revolution had made the situation much worse by terrifying public officials into inaction, disrupting organizations, replacing experienced with ill-prepared, inexperienced administrators, and reducing state performance.

The coincidental deaths in 1976 of Mao Zedong, Zhou Enlai and Zhu De shook the party into remedial action. The surviving leadership, more pragmatic, having been both beneficiaries and victims of the system, (Tsou, 1986, 303), resolved under Deng Xiaoping on the modernization of the Chinese economy and society and "changing" all methods of management, actions and thinking "inconsistent with modernization" (Falkenheim, 1980, 5). While paying lip-service to Mao's thoughts and deed, egalitarianism was to be abandoned; so too was collectivization in agriculture in favor of a new (household) agricultural responsibility system, part of a "socialist commodity economy" incorporating a modified, controlled market system. Privatization was to be extended into other economic sectors. The major emphasis was to be placed on technological modernization, increased economic output, and administrative reform. The new leadership knew only too well the dead hand of bureaucracy and realized that economic enterprise was probably being stifled by state regimentation and control. Even apart from freeing some of the economy from state direction, administrative reform of itself should also improve economic performance by reducing structural rigidities, institutionalized inertia, statist mentality (and the bureaucratic centralism that went with it), and official misconduct. Furthermore, administrative management (*xingzheng guanli*) would be separated or distinguished from economic management (*jingji guanli*) so as to reduce the "problem of 'over-administration' resulting from reliance on inappropriate organizational forms and methods which compel 'the mechanized adaptation' of economic activities to 'administrative convenience, administrative channels and administrative systems'."

> The result is to "confuse the flow of economic materials," disrupt "rational economic ties," and cause "man-made disruptions and blockages." Such systems further lack both flexibility and accountability, and "bearing responsibility neither for profits or losses" engender waste and sluggish- ness. (Ibid, 7)

Overreliance on administrative power had resulted in economic mismanagement.

The reformers had no master plan, no blueprint, no set design other than "socialism with Chinese characteristics" among them competition, enterprise, inequality, and marketing. The first item on their agenda was to reconsider the authoritarian role of the state in the economy and to remove state intervention where it restricted economic growth. This meant the reduction of bureaucratic centralism, overregulation and state management of economic enterprises, an end to the confusion between political and economic spheres, party and state organization, and between economic and administrative management, and state divestment of business enterprises. The second item was decentralization, deregulation, indirect controls, and autonomous management. The third item was emphasis on economy, productivity, efficiency and effectiveness as administrative values and insistence on competent, professional management. Deng sought models from around the world but did not flinch from risking experimentation. Specifically, state enterprises would be managed on a more businesslike basis and subject even to collapse and bankruptcy as in a market system. State planning would be enhanced as a more realistic central control mechanism linking supply and demand with enterprises now having the right to reject output targets for which no corresponding input or supply plan was available (Ibid, 10). New product trusts would be established to enhance technological innovation and product quality. Indirect banking and fiscal controls would replace direct administrative controls in a new economic system. The state would provide a planned framework with incentives and sanctions in which freed, autonomous enterprises would operate to maximize returns, thereby encouraging unproductive and underproductive teams to improve their performance.

Reform from the top was consistent with traditional Chinese deference to authority and people were relieved to be rid of an overweening bureaucratism. Deng set no timetable and did not get rattled when things did not go as intended. He was patient and accommodating even when new found economic freedom and consumerism (from the beginning of 1979) strengthened foreign influences and increased demands for political freedom. In the countryside, increased production occurred together with diversification of products, enhanced capital construction, better land utilization, and greater mechanization and mechanical standardization, though things by no means proceeded smoothly. In the towns, rationalization improved productivity, the trusts worked reasonably well, and free enterprise responded extremely well despite restraints. Reverses were blamed on the Gang of Four but after Zhao Ziyang was appointed in 1981 to speed the reform program, the economy improved so that China became almost self sufficient in food, the number of consumer goods increased, and construction boomed. Indeed by the late 1980s, the "Socialist Planned Commodity Economy" began to overheat. Programs to move further toward a market economy had to be abandoned when they accelerated inflation, produced economic dislocation and promoted corruption, although in 1989 the Shenzhen Special Economic Zone adjacent to Hong Kong was empowered to proceed to a market economy.

Meantime there has been no comparable improvement in the unreformed state bureaucracy despite several attempts to modernize it and the realization of a new local government system. In 1979, the Criminal Code was amended to outlaw certain prevalent forms of corruption (embezzlement, kickbacks, fraud, speculation, smuggling, bribery) but yet another campaign failed to deter widespread, endemic, systemic corruption. In 1982 the central machinery of government was reorganized to improve public policymaking, reduce overstaffing, simplify procedures and strengthen accountability but reorganization did not seem to make a significant impact. Nor did periodic purges of undesirables from public office, although tougher disciplinary measures against incompetents and improved management training after 1983 were reputed to have had a positive effect. At least, government had gotten out of the detailed management of economic enterprise and had turned the economy around. Retrenchment had begun to elevate a younger generation within the state bureaucracy even if officialdom was still too large, clumsy, confusing, and corrupt.

But while progress had not been as dramatic as in economic reform, administrative reform had taken Chinese bureaucracy away from the chaos of the Cultural Revolution. The rule of law had been partially restored. Party cadres and local bosses could not take the law into their own hands or not so easily. Both the fourth Constitution of the People's Republic of China (Article 5) and the Constitution of the Communist Party formally subordinated the party to the law. The merging of party and government bureaucracies at local level in the late 1950s which brought about so many abuses in the Cultural Revolution, was ended in 1979 with their structural reseparation and the reestablishment of village and township governments after 1983. At the same time, joint office holding was discouraged and some limitations were placed on party office tenure. Clear differentiation was made between the power and functions of government and party bureaucracies (Chunmei, 1986) with the former being allowed greater latitude and responsibility for policy implementation, although in reality the party still involved itself in public administration at all levels of government. Such party involvement reduced the impact of the formal decentralization of government decision-making meant to reduce over-centralization. Administrative reforms aimed "at distributing macro-decision-making power to the local governments and micro-decision-making power to the enterprise" (Ibid, 133) separated village government from local enterprises (communes, co-operatives, development corporations), clarified the respective roles of urban government and urban enterprises, decentralized decision-making down the governmental chain of command and rationalized the machinery of government through reorganization, retrenchment, restructuring and relocation. Although advances had been made in personnel management too, even a sympathetic observer had to record that "the old style, old administrative procedure and old methodology remain" (Ibid, 140).

> Although overlapping agencies have been merged or have been eliminated, they tend to live on and to function under new titles and with their old divisions of labour. The red-tape thus remains as long as ever. (Ibid, 141)

The Chinese system of governmental administration has been a classic case of bureaucratic inertia. Although the country created the world's first civil service system, it held on to it for too long and has been unable to modernize it in keeping with the sweeping changes that have been taking place in Chinese society. The Chinese bureaucracy has strongly and successfully resisted imposed reforms designed to reduce its status power and position, to curb such long cherished practices as tolerated corruption (*tanwu*), nepotism, *guanxi* (influence peddling or use of connections), expectation of tributes, and protected tenure, to tackle its rigid structure, obsolete practices, surplus employees and waste of talent and to rid public administration of the many servile, decadent, thieving, embezzling, bribe-taking, bumbling, complacent, lazy, and incompetent officials who staff the state apparatus from top to bottom.

With the failure of the valiant 1982 reforms to make any appreciable impact, yet another attempt at administrative modernization was launched in 1988 on several fronts. First, the government took stronger action against corruption even at the highest levels and instigated yet another public ethics campaign to remind public officials (both party and state employees) of their duties and obligations, public responsibilities and moral leadership. The reestablished Ministry of Supervision (which had lapsed from 1959 to 1986) was strengthened throughout the whole state apparatus to investigate and prevent corruption. Anti-corruption centers were set up with hot lines all over the country to receive complaints and new part-time neighborhood supervision committees were created to act as local ombudsman offices. Public offices were requested to make their procedures and processes known to their clientele (Yan, 1989).

Second, the government recognized the imperative need for administrative and managerial training and education for public officials. Besides the 230 or so management cadres institutes across the country that had been established to train 27 million Chinese officials including a unique joint Sino-U.S. business management project at Dalian, Liaoning province, the Organisation Department set up the Chinese Training Center in 1988, and the new National Administrative Institute offered its first training course in November 1988 although it did not officially open until late 1989. At the universities public administration courses, which had lapsed from 1952 until 1981, were revived and Chinese textbooks on public management soon followed (Chow, 1988).

Third, civil service reform was given priority although it was realized that the intended creation of a proper merit system might take as long as thirty years and progress would be slow. Nonetheless a start would be made through cutback management of the 4 million civil servants and an overhaul of recruitment and selection methods to be based on the principles of openness, equality and competition, piloted by the high ranking Central Personnel Group which did not flinch from seeking international advice. The new Ministry of Personnel, established in 1988, would have the difficult task of reducing the *nomenklatura*, separating political officials from career public servants, revamping the recruitment, promotion, classification, appraisal and remuneration systems in the career services, and generally maintaining and improving public sector conditions of employment (Burns, 1989). The painstakingly revived "Provisional

Regulations on State Civil Servants" was attempted first in a few selected departments, provincial governments and city governments. If successful, the new public personnel merit system would be gradually extended and finally nationalized although "cadres working in the Party apparatus, enterprises, institutions and mass organizations will be managed separately according to specific rules yet to be drawn up" (*China News Analysis*, 1989, 2) and would not be part of civil service reform.

The contrast between the successes of economic modernization and the failures of administrative modernization has been startling. Similar imbalance has been evident within the public bureaucracy among regions, functions, programs and organizations. Not surprisingly, the public grew increasingly perturbed by the incongruence between economic freedom and political direction, open, thriving special economic zones and backward traditionally regulated regions, private profiteering and public austerity, wealthy entrepreneurs and impoverished workers, official propaganda and social reality. They became upset, depressed and confused. They could not understand why the same goods were priced differently depending whether they were sold in state or private markets or why the government allowed unscrupulous entrepreneurs and bureaucrats to shift goods between public and private sectors for personal profit, groups that have long been notoriously corrupt in manipulating the system to their advantage in cornering most things of value in a backward society (Oi, 1989).

Such disparities were bound to occur during transition and could have been anticipated. But it seemed to the common people that just as in the discredited Chinese empire, so their post-Mao leaders seemed out of touch with them, insensitive to them, too distant from them to comprehend their inner thoughts, too used to instant obedience to listen to public grievances. They had been so intent on creating wealth that they had ignored more compelling problems, such as food and energy shortages, mounting foreign debt, rising crime, overpopulation, resurgent illiteracy, squalid working conditions, all of which pointed to ineffectual government, empty rhetoric, increasing polarization, and growing dissent. Admittedly, when chaos threatened, the leadership drew back and froze modernization and reform. Political demonstrations were violently suppressed, economic reformer Zhao Ziyang was dropped and reform leader Chao Tzu-Yang was purged, bureaucratic centralism was reimposed, and yet another campaign against official corruption launched, as the regime struggled to retain its grip and control events rather than have events control it as seemed to be happening elsewhere in the East Bloc. In Premier Li Peng's own words at the opening of the 1990 National People's Congress, "we must intensify dictatorship by the socialist state apparatus…[and] and be on the alert to promptly crush infiltration and subversion by foreign and overseas hostile forces and crack down on all sabotage by hostile elements at home." Unwillingness to adopt a market system and the continued absence of the rule of law brought a relapse into bureaucratic centralism with new economic problems added to the old (Prybyla, 1990, 16).

In the decade after Deng Xiaoping had launched his bold reforms at the 11th Central Committee of the Chinese Communist Party in December 1978, he had achieved at least two of his four objectives (the institution of a contract responsibility system in rural areas to replace collective farming and the revival of individual business in the urban areas) but had only mixed success with the other two (the devolution of greater authority to state enterprises and the reform of the irrational price system), still creditable given his original starting point. What he had not anticipated was rising inflation and unemployment, growing inequality between the privileged (people with official connections, profiteers and speculators, party entrepreneurs, and affluent peasants) and the common people, foreign sanctions and economic retaliation against political repression, the failures among individual businesses, and persistent bottlenecks in energy and transportation (Chu-Yuan, 1989) and an austerity program that brought the economy to the edge of recession in 1990. Nevertheless, his target of quadrupling economic output by the end of the century would easily be met and would not go the way of the 1958 Great Leap Forward which had not depended so much on market discipline, after-tax profits, revenue-sharing, and foreign exports. Deng's pragmatic managers may have replaced Mao's ideological mobilizers (Li and White, 1988) but seemingly not their administrative culture. Leviathan was as repressive as ever, the people as self-interested as ever, and the Chinese version of Communism ("socialism with Chinese characteristics") had become nationalist, atheistic, unsentimental Confucianism posing as social public morality in a poor country desperately trying to catch up with the rest of the world, but on its own terms which did not embrace capitalism, liberalism and pluralism.

The Bird Cage Theory and Market Socialism

The Chinese veteran revolutionary, Chen Len Yun, who had opposed both Mao's radicalism and Deng's economic reforms, likened markets to a "bird" that should be allowed to fly but within the "cage" of socialist central control. Until the reforms were frozen in 1989 and the cage reimposed, Westerners were beginning to think of the Chinese economy more as an aviary than a bird cage. Zhou Zhiyang, an economic planning official, explained: "We want the bird to fly but not to fly away" (*The Korean Times*, October 19, 1989, 5). He was anticipating the dilemmas of all East Bloc reformers. On the one hand, they wanted to abandon hardline Communism but on the other they did not want to replace it with Western liberal capitalism.

East Bloc reformers have admitted that the dictatorship of the proletariat led by the monopolistic Communist Party still headed by the original revolutionary generation and its chosen heirs had long been declining in legitimacy. It had saddled new generations with a rigid, dogmatic, stagnant corrupt totalitarian state which had alienated the masses, discouraged initiative and handicapped development. It could not cling to power solely on the basis of its claim to historical truth. The people had to be freed, trusted, respected, to be invigorated, activated, energized, concerned, involved, to be spiritually enriched, to be democratized, in Gorbachev's own words. Their enthusiasm, which had been destroyed by bureaucratic centralism and unresponsive administrative planning, had to be rekindled by allowing them to participate, contribute, profit, progress, consume, and enjoy the fruits of their labors. But not too much, too far, too quickly and not by abandoning the party, the central tenets of socialism, collective interests, and the gains of the revolution. The weaknesses of Communism should not permit the counter-revolutionaries to return nor should they be interpreted as the inevitable failure of Communism. Mistakes could (and should) be corrected and the ultimate aim of democratic socialism could be achieved along different (but *not* capitalist) lines.

It is quite conceivable that the East Bloc will eventually abandon Communism and socialism. No doubt some countries like the former East Germany will probably do so where Communism had been imposed on the masses without winning over their hearts and minds. No doubt some Communist Parties as in Hungary and Poland will renounce their aged revolutionary generation and rename themselves to denote a break with the past. No doubt some Communist Parties as in Italy and France out of power will revise and overhaul their platforms to avoid the mistakes committed by Communist regimes and to incorporate the new thinking of East Bloc reformers. None of this implies that all will eventually switch to liberalism and capitalism. More likely, they will try variations of the bird cage theory. They will attempt to get the best out of both worlds. They will probably use the administrative state to restrain license, libertarianism, individualism, exploitation and excess and to impose national interests, collective obligations, social welfare, and equal opportunity. Then they will be confronted with problems similar to those experienced by the Chinese reformers, namely:

* **price reform** – dual price system, underpricing and overpricing, inflation (caused by deficit budgets, penned up purchasing power, compensation exceeding productivity increases), corrupt arbitrage; scarce capital; subsidization; collapse of demand; credit;
* **enterprise reform** – increased autonomy and responsibility, uneven and disparate enterprise, local monopolies, managerial enrichment, unemployment, bankruptcies, defective management; incentives; differential regional impacts; bottlenecks; financial discipline; special case of agriculture;

* **internationalization** – foreign trade and investment, convertible currency, technology transfer, political concessions, free trade zones; consumerism, external influence;
* **ideological confusion** – reinterpretation of Marxism, redefinition of socialism, legitimacy, credence;
* **political liberalization** – human rights, free association, free speech, openness, freedom of thought, ingratitude, opposition, defiance;
* **strategy** – gradualism, compromise, incrementalism, unfulfilled raised expectations, austerity; short sharp shock or long troubled transition; (Harding, 1989)

and the dilemmas inherent in reforming centrally planned economies such as markets, controls, contract management, performance targets, profits, ownership, credits, wages, taxes and macroeconomic policy (Wolf, 1990).

The East Bloc has been attempting to move away from highly centralized, bureaucratic control of resource allocation to a more decentralized market system while still retaining strong political control over the economy and state ownership of most capital. It has yet to go all the way to market socialism because markets are still not trusted (Hewett, 1989, 16). Markets operate but are carefully regulated and controlled by a highly centralized, bureaucratic planning apparatus. Government (and party) officials intervene when they are not supposed to and newly autonomous enterprises exploit market opportunities before price controls are lifted. Privatization gives corrupt state enterprise managers exceptional opportunities to become owners and well connected government and party officials to obtain public or state assets at bargain prices to open their own businesses. Political and administrative determination of economic policy continues persistent imbalances in factor and product markets and seemingly does not prevent economic absurdities, poor quality products and services, and a vast underground economy. So many exceptions to the rules are allowed as a result of political pressures that there are no consistent economic policies and distortions are legion. So instead of getting the best of both worlds, the mixed systems get the worst, what Jeremy Paltiel terms "Mexicanization" (Caporoso, 1989, 275) or state patrimonialism.

Take, for example, the agriculture industry in Poland which in the late 1980s accounted for over one quarter of the economy. Some 70 percent of farms were in private hands as they had been since the Communist takeover in the 1940s but they were supplied by state agribusiness monopolies that also distributed their produce. The agribusinesses in turn were governed by central economic planning. Unfortunately most private farms were too small to turn a profit. But the mixed system compounded their problems. Farm equipment was scarce, maldistributed and unsuitable. Tractors had been allocated to the regions that least needed them. Western farm staples, such as wagons, sprayers, mowers, balers, spreaders, pick-up trucks and loaders were rarities as were silos and refrigerated trucks. So most farms had to rely on horsedrawn vehicles and wooden implements. Even if they had mechanical tools, spare parts were scarce at state-run distribution centers where broken parts had to be turned in before a new part could be obtained. Otherwise, local agricultural supply committees had to approve all purchases and these favored the state-run farms which anyway had automatic allocations, not much good when supplies were generally unobtainable. Consequently, productivity was low and around 40 percent of that was lost because of poor storage. Consumers routinely boiled milk because it was usually contaminated. Food processing plants awaited traditional start up dates although crops were already rotting in the fields. To improve the situation, farms would have to be consolidated (thereby depriving large numbers of elderly substance farmers of their income and reducing the incomes of part time farmers who had other jobs), the state-owned agribusinesses would have to be broken up and privatized, central planning would have to be disbanded, and food prices would have to be increased to provide greater incentives for production. Instead, the vested interests opposed all changes and prevented reforms, turning a blind eye to illegal markets, corruption and finagling. In this case, only complete privatization in 1990 could restore economic logic.

Or take the financial plight of Hungary with soaring deficits and a large foreign debt at the end of 1989. The I.M.F. demanded economic restructuring and reforms, including the closure of 50 loss-making state owned enterprises, a 20 percent cut in state subsidies and a balanced budget. The closures would certainly raise unemployment and the withdrawal of subsidies would increase food prices by up to 25 percent. Proposals to increase public sector housing rents by 50 percent and to impose a tax on mortgages had already been rejected. Yet if Hungary did not tighten its belt, then it would be unable to service its debt or obtain new loans. The government decided on a rapid privatization program and a selloff of public property, hoping to eat into rising inflation and unemployment.

In Czechoslovakia where consumers fared much better than in Poland and Hungary and the economy was in better shape than most East Bloc countries, the government was not prepared to move straight to a free economy because of its fears of destabilization. It might abandon central planning but not a strong central authority and it might gradually deregulate but any transition would result in a decline in economic efficiency. It had on hand huge stocks of unsold and unsalable goods ordered by central planners but not wanted; nobody would buy such junk. Under Communism, its per capita national income once 10 percent higher than Austria had declined to 30 percent below with virtually no investment to modernize its industries and public infrastructure yet with one of the world's worst industrial pollution which had lowered life expectancy and decimated forest lands.

Even Yugoslavia which had kept its political distance from the East Bloc and had avoided much bureaucratic centralism, also had serious economic problems despite once being the leader in political and economic reforms in Eastern Europe. Its citizens had been the most free, possibly the wealthiest and most innovative. Yet in 1989, it found itself behind other East Bloc countries. It too had runaway inflation, large foreign debts, useless public projects (e.g. a nickel-alloy plant in Macedonia never used), regional inequalities (300 percent as between Slovenia and the poorer Serbia) and a Communist Party that no longer was holding the country together. It was trying to work its way to a freer economy without abandoning its socialist tenets, but this "tinder box of Europe" was apparently disintegrating into regional factions. These examples could well mean that

> The inefficiencies and imbecilities of socialist economies are so complex and interconnected that reform can come to seem a hopeless task. Clearly, it is politically and administratively impossible to put everything right at once. And yet, it might seem, unless you put everything right at once nothing will work...(*The Economist*, 1990, 21)

Part of the problem was that economists knew both worlds well but they had been of little help in devising strategies for the transition from one to the other and in comprehending the nature of mixed systems and how they differed from the pure or ideal models on either side. Immediate or instantaneous transition was impractical and would be chaotic, although some countries, seeing the mess made of mixed systems, believed they did not have much to lose by a "big bang". Otherwise, transition has to proceed in stages.

> But, how many stages? Over what time period? With what coming in which stage? Are there "clusters" of systemic changes which make sense? Is there a logical order of progression for the clusters?...What sort of unemployment and retraining system should be in place, and when? What sort of bureaucracy is needed to ensure a smooth transition? (Hewett, 1989, 19)

And to what end? What shape will economic decentralization take?

> Typically reformers are clear that enterprises will only economize on resources and genuinely strive to ascertain and satisfy customer needs if they are forced to finance their operations and service debts out of receipts. That implies a banking system acting as the major mechanism for financial intermediation. But how will the state exercise its ownership rights without unduly interfering in enterprise operations, effectively blunting the force of market incentives? If somehow that problem is worked out and profit-maximizing enterprises are operating with – among other things – the right to hire and fire, and the right to set their own prices, then how will this version of socialism differ from some of the social democratic versions of capitalism? (Ibid)

Perhaps, the reformers are pursuing will o' the wisps, mixed systems of decentralized socialism "inherently prone to micro economic inefficiency and macro economic instability" (*The Economist*, 1990, 16) or just slightly more collectivized versions of Western mixed welfare economies.

The emergence of mixed systems has given rise to studies to explain how and why they differ from more traditional orthodox ideal polar systems. These accept that they are a new fact of public life, a new phenomenon in organization theory and practice and they cannot as yet be fitted into traditional studies (Hankiss, 1990). They show that mixed systems do achieve what they were designed to do, that is, they do increase productivity, efficiency and effectiveness, they show greater enterprise, initiative, and verve, they reduce bureaucratic centralism and the dysfunctions of central planning, they get things done quicker and cheaper, they provide greater incentives and rewards and they reduce bottlenecks and delays. On the other hand, they make for greater external dependence, inequality, opportunism, immorality and corruption, they involve value ambiguity and confusion, they encourage the formation and perpetuation of paternalistic hegemonies and fiefdoms, they result in tax evasion, financial deceit, fragmentation, spoils, and subsystem optimization, subinfeudation (Boisot and Child, 1988, 514), and nepotism, and they dampen long term objectives and risk-taking.

In mixed systems, enterprise managers are given the responsibility for performance but denied legitimate authority for activating it. They are caught between "the competing claims of a tax-maximizing state and a welfare-maximizing workforce" (Ibid, 517). They cannot release themselves from the grip of government bureaucracy and act entrepreneurially and their rationality, discretion and internal cohesion is destroyed. Indeed, "inability to codify an economically rational and unified set of enterprise objectives...opens the door to constant renegotiations and the personalization of power relationships between superior and subordinate organizations" (Ibid, 521). The presence of fiefdoms and clans (as opposed to bureaucracies and markets) makes administrative reform even more difficult than otherwise it would be. There is likely to be more resistance from competing vested interests, more conniving at avoidance and evasion by institutional fixers, more variety and more oddity in the administrative system, and more sympathy with authoritarian administrative traits that block reforms unacceptable to the clearly identifiable political establishment.

The central issue is whether reforms of bureaucratic centralism are possible without ending in a complete muddle which may feed counter-revolution or if carried through to their logical conclusion, the self-liquidation of Communism. Half-hearted measures have failed in the past. More radical systemic reform which "is a very arduous and usually painful undertaking, a wrenching institutional, intellectual, and moral experience" (Prybyla, 1990, 9) may be attempting the impossible, namely, the reconcilation of administrative command and free markets without privatizing property, freeing prices, ending job security, changing the bureauratic mindset, embracing bourgeois values, and liberalizing politics. Perhaps there can be no middle ground between plan or market and that the whole attempt by socialist ideologues to develop mixed systems may be close to a waste of time (Ibid, 13) and the equivalent futility as trying to square the circle. Only the next decade will tell, if the reformers can still stay in business. Meantime, continued economic decline fed political, social, ethnic and religious unrest. On the one side, diehards were insisting on reimposing authoritarian Communism and on the other there was a distinct possibility that public dissent might boil over into counter-revolution, chaos and anarchy and a return (or reemergence) of popular authoritarian fascistic governments. Much depended on whether reforms enabled a *peaceful* transition to capitalism or socialism or whatever mixed systems might pragmatically emerge out of all the experimentation.

References

Aganbegyan, A., *Inside Perestroika: The Future of the Soviet Economy*, Harper and Row, New York, 1989.

Bergson, A., *Planning and Performance in Socialist Economies: The U.S.S.R. and Eastern Europe*, Unwin Hyman, Boston, 1989.

Boisot, M., and Child, J., "The Iron Law of Fiefs: Bureaucratic Failure and the Problem of Governance in the Chinese Economic Reforms", *Administrative Science Quarterly*, Vol. 33, No. 4, December 1988, pp. 507-527.

Brumberg, A., "Moscow: The Struggle for Reform", *The New York Review*, March 30, 1989, pp. 37-42.

Burns, J.P., "Chinese Civil Service Reform: The 13th Party Congress Proposals," *The China Quarterly*, No. 120, Dec. 1989, pp. 739-770.

Burns, J.P., "Reforming China's Bureaucracy, 1979-82", *Asian Survey*, Vol. 23, No. 6, June 1983, pp. 692-722.

Caporaso, J.A. (ed.), *The Elusive State: International and Comparative Perspectives*, Sage Publications, Newbury Park, CA, 1989.

China News Analysis, (Hong Kong), N. 1383, April 15, 1989.

Chow, K., "Public Administration as a Discipline in the People's Republic of China: Development, Issues and Projects," paper presented at the National Conference of the American Society for Public Administration, Portland, Oregon, April 1988.

Chunmei, Y., "Current Administrative Reform in China", *International Review of Administrative Sciences*, Vol. 52, No. 2, June 1986, pp. 123-144.

Chu-Yuan, C., "A Troubled Economy", *Free China Review*, November 1989, pp. 49-52.

Cohen, S., and Heuvel, K. (eds.), *Voices of Glasnost: Interviews with Gorbachev's Reformers*, W.W. Norton, New York, 1989.

Desai, P., *Perestroika in Perspective: The Design and Dilemmas of Soviet Reform*, Princeton University Press, Princeton, N.J., 1989.

Eaton, J. and Lvov, Y., "Soviet Business: A Micro Analysis," a draft monograph of the U.S.-U.S.S.R. Joint Research Project, University of Pittsburgh, Pittsburgh, 1990.

The Economist, Vol. 315, No. 7652, April 28, 1990, "Perestroika: Ready to Fly? A Survey." 22p.

Ericson, R.E., "What Is To Be Done?" *The New Republic*, March 5, 1990, pp. 34-38.

Falkenham, V.C., "Administrative Reform and Modernization in PostMao China", *Pacific Affairs*, Vol. 53, No. 1, Spring 1980, pp. 5-28.

Galbraith, J.K., "Can the Russians Reform?", *Harper's Magazine*, June 1987, pp. 52-55.

Goldman, M.I., "Gorbachev the Economist," *Foreign Affairs*, Vol. 69, No. 2, Spring 1990, pp. 28-44.

Gorbachev, M., *Perestroika*, Collins, London, 1987.

Hankiss, E., "In Search of a Paradigm," *Daedelus*, Vol. 119, No. 1, Winter 1990, pp. 183-214.

Harding, H., Address to S.I.D.-D.C. Chapter Luncheon, October 17, 1989, reported by S. Von Oehsen, "Harding Presents Dilemmas Reforming Socialist States Face", *Development Connections*, Newsletter of the Washington Chapter of the Society for International Development, Vol. 10, No. 3, Dec. 1989, pp. 1-2.

Harding, H., *Organizing China: The Problem of Chinese Bureaucracy: 1949-1976*, Stanford University Press, Stanford, 1981.

Hewett, E.A., "Economic Reform in the U.S.S.R., Eastern Europe, and China: The Politics of Economics", *A.E.A. Papers and Proceedings*, Vol. 79, No. 2, May 1989, pp. 16-20.

Kagarlitsky, B., *The Dialectic of Change*, Verso, New York, 1990.

Kagarlitsky, B., *The Thinking Reed*, Verso, New York, 1988.

Kovacs, J.M., "Reform Economics: The Classification Gap," *Daedalus*, Vol. 119, No. 1, Winter 1990, pp. 215-247.

Li, C., and White, L., "The Thirtieth Central Committee of the C.C.P.: From Mobilizers to Managers", *Asian Survey*, Vol. 28, No. 4, April 1988, pp. 371-399.

Oi, J.C., "Market Reforms and Corruption in Rural China," *Studies in Comparative Communism*, Vol. 22, No. 2/3, Summer/Autumn 1989, pp. 221-233.

Oliver, D., "'Perestroika' and Public Administration in the U.S.S.R.", *Public Administration, Vol. 66, Winter 1988, pp. 411-428.*

Prybyla, J.S. (ed.), *Privatization and Marketizing Socialism*, The Annals of the American Academy of Political and Social Science, Vol. 507, January 1990, Sage Publications, Newbury Park, 1990.

Pye, L.W., "Political Science and the Crisis of Authoritarianism," *American Political Science Review*, Vol. 81, No., 1, March 1990, pp. 3-19.

Reddaway, P., "Gorbachev the Bold", *The New York Review*, May 28, 1987, pp.21-25.

Schultz, D.S. and Rafferty, M.P., "Soviet Health Care and Perestroika," *American Journal of Public Health*, Vol. 80, No. 2, Feb. 1990, pp. 193- 6.

Stojanovic, S., *Perestroika*, Prometheous Books, Buffalo, N.Y., 1988.

Tsou, T., *The Cultural Revolution and Post-Mao Reforms: A Historical Perspective*, The University of Chicago Press, Chicago, 1986.

Wolf, T.A., "Reform, Inflation, and Adjustment in Planned Economies," *Finance & Development*, Vol. 27, No. 1, March 1990, pp. 2-5.

Yan, G., "Corruption and Clean Government Drive in China." paper presented to the Thirteenth E.R.O.P.A. Conference, Katmandu, Nepal, December 1989.

[illegible], A.C., "Administrative Reform and [illegible]", [illegible] Affairs, Vol. 58, No. 1, Spring 19[illegible], pp. [illegible]

[illegible] "Chinese Economic Reform" [illegible] Argument [illegible], pp. [illegible]

[illegible], "[illegible] the Economists", Foreign Affairs, Vol. 6[illegible], No. [illegible], 1990, pp. [illegible]

[illegible], Collins, London, 1937

[illegible], "In Search of a Paradigm", [illegible], Vol. 19, [illegible]

[illegible], "Address to [illegible] D.C. Chapter [illegible]", [illegible] Newsletter of the Washington Chapter of the Society for International Development, Vol. 10, No. 4, [illegible] 1989, pp. 1-3

[illegible]

[illegible] New York, 19[illegible]

[illegible] New York, 19[illegible]

[illegible] 1990, pp. [illegible]

[illegible] Central Committee of the [illegible]

[illegible]

[illegible] Health Care in [illegible]

[illegible] Planned [illegible]

[illegible] paper presented in [illegible], Nepal, [illegible] 1989

11. Reforms in the West: Changing Administrative Values

Western Europe was the cradle of the modern administrative state and most of the key features of modern public administration were institutionalized first in Western European countries. Ever since, it has been the major inspiration of administrative experimentation and reform and its administrative exports can be found all over the world. Despite the excesses of Nazism and Fascism, people still continued to put great faith in the ability of the administrative state to deal with most societal problems providing it was placed under strict constitutional, legal and political controls to safeguard individual freedom and rights. Between 1950 and 1975, they believed they had found the happy medium of the mixed enterprise, social democratic welfare stare, until growing structural unemployment became apparent and world-wide recession squeezed their economies. Rising unemployment increased the welfare bill which was resented by those paying taxes out of their shrinking real incomes. Inflation, industrial unrest and structural readjustment further divided haves from have-nots while overloaded, stressed governments groped with stagflation, rising political dissent, terrorism, indebtedness and international instability.

After a generation of coping quite well, things seemed to be falling apart. Perhaps post-industrial society was becoming ungovernable. Governments could not command sufficient resources to meet all their commitments let alone their promises. Public confidence in public institutions was declining fast and weird fringe groups were defying convention. Government was now being seen not as part of the solution but as part of the problem. Increased public intervention had been permitted because it was supposed to result in increased public benefits. Instead, it seemed that rising public expenditures were being spent on needlessly expensive overheads, parasitic bureaucrats, wasteful programs, and inefficient public organizations. After all, neither the warfare or the welfare state had emphasized efficiency, effectiveness and value for money. Perhaps greater benefits might be gained by redirecting resources to more productive and efficient private organizations that could better service the public directly.

Whatever government was in office faced the dilemma whether to react along fairly well-established lines that had been developed since postwar reconstruction or to strike out in bold new directions. The opposition could always promise something radically different but if brought into government or taking over government, would it be capable of doing something different or would it marginally adjust what everyone had grown used to? The balance was held by floating middle class voters who would not go for something too radical, like market socialism or anything more left wing than that, such as industrial democracy (which meant more power to militant trade unions) or centralized planning or more nationalization, state enterprise and state intervention, but would not give up full employment underwritten by public spending, state welfare, social reforms and a free labor movement. They might welcome lower taxes, less welfare, less state regulation and intervention but how far would they be willing to roll back the state altogether, to reduce the public sector and expand private enterprise, decentralize state activities and privatize many state ventures? How many would embrace the rising anti-statist sentiment that called for smaller if not small anorexic government and tight restraints on leviathan (James, 1987) and used butcher-shop metaphors (Reich, 1987, 112) to radically cut the administrative state? Nobody knew, only that the electorate was so dissatisfied with worsening economic fortunes, it was prepared to dump whoever was in power, even long reigning governments such as Sweden's Social Democrats who had held office since 1933. Actually in most of Western Europe, few were willing or able to depart much from the status quo, except in the United Kingdom where the need was probably the greatest and where the demands for a stronge managerialist approach to the public sector was the highest (*Governance,* 1990).

Tackling the Whitehall Establishment

Nowhere were problems more compelling than in "the sick man of Europe," the United Kingdom, and nowhere were the doomsayers more prominent. There seemed to be no end to the decline of Albion in world circles and nobody seemed able to stop the rot. The country found itself in a tail-spin that no matter what governments did, things continued to slide further and further downhill. Productivity barely improved; strikes crippled trade and output; indebtedness rose. In 1976, the British pound sterling was in crisis and the International Monetary Fund laid down severe conditions for rescue. It was not just the powerful Treasury that was blamed for the debacle but the whole Whitehall Civil Service Establishment.

For many decades there had been complaints against Whitehall particularly by the British left but administrative reform had always been considered an internal affair of the Whitehall Establishment, partial, incremental, accommodating. The 1854 Northcote-Trevelyn Report had caused a temporary flutter but no sharp break with the past as the ranks quickly closed up again. No radical government had been able to shake up Whitehall, not even the Atlee Labour Government (1945-1951) or the Wilson Labour Government (1964-1970), which had appointed the Fulton Committee (1966-1968) and been presented with a radical enough set of proposals to shake up Whitehall. However, Whitehall had managed to outmaneuver the Fulton Committee which had not gone far enough in recognizing that civil service reform alone fell far short of a thorough review of the whole operation of the administrative state in the United Kingdom (Hennessy, 1989). When reform did come, it came not from the radical left but from the radical right in 1979 in the person no less than Conservative Prime Minster Margaret Thatcher. She was resolved to end the prevailing consensus about the role of the state and embark on radical reforms – to roll back the state, reduce state intervention, diminish the public sector, overhaul the machinery of government and reform Whitehall, i.e. no less than a transformation of British administrative culture as a crucial ingredient of the reconstruction of British society.

During Britain's gloomiest days in the 1970s, Whitehall had been accused of everything from committing treason (the spy scandals) to being an unworthy ruling class (Kellner and Crowther-Hunt, 1980). A retired civil servant told of thwarted attempts to save public money within and gained notoriety (Chapman, 1978). Public imagination was later fired by a popular T.V. series, *Yes, Minister* which first appeared in January 1980, about how civil servants supposedly ruled their political masters. This point had been made countless times before by outgoing Cabinet ministers, and repeated by one of the Thatcher Government's incoming ministers as follows:

> I had general advice on every political issue – but no analysis of how each part of the machine operated, why it operated in that way, and how much it cost...If options are called for, the usual response is to submit the least attractive in political terms, the easiest to achieve in administrative terms, and with the minimum effect on those putting them forward...(Kellner and Crowther-Hunt, 1980, 286-7)

The Thatcher Government was determined to break free from Whitehall's grip by taking full command of public policy, devising its own options and generally diminishing the role, functions and size of the public bureaucracy. It was finally to end political ineffectiveness in administrative reform and development.

Mrs. Thatcher did not consider herself part of the Whitehall Establishment and was contemptuous of it. She came from a middle class business background which valued commerce and competitive capitalism, self-reliance and self-initiative and scorned undeserved privilege, coddling and the cult of the aristocratic amateur. She was a conviction not a consensus politician and surrounded herself with like-minded advisors who shared her view that Whitehall was a morass of waste, bureaucracy and over-government, and that Britain's prestige and position in the international community could only be restored by ending the middle-of-the-road policies so beloved by the Whitehall Establishment. Instead, she wanted people in office not just committed to changing Britain but capable of doing so in radical, unconventional ways by rolling back the state, restructuring and modernizing the British economy, privatizing public enterprises, extending private ownership, reducing the power of trade unions, and confining the public bureaucracy to managing programs. In the 1979 election campaign she showed her deep prejudice against the Whitehall Establishment and cleverly mobilized public opinion behind her promised shake-up.

Immediately upon her election, the major outlines of what was to be in store for Whitehall included:

* an immediate freeze on public sector hiring and possible reduction in public sector employment by as much as 20 per cent
* a cutback management survey to reduce unnecessary functions, activities, programs, and work
* privatization of public business enterprises and public property to raise needed cash
* restructuring of the machinery of government, public enterprises, and public health and social services
* overhaul of the tax system
* contracting out
* civil service reform.

Although this plan had been influenced by New Right thinking, it was more of a pragmatic response to the economic situation that the country faced. The government needed money to pay rising debts. It needed to make economies. It wanted to put public enterprises on a more commercial market oriented basis and farm out government activities to private contractors. It wanted to free government from bureaucratic shackles and take charge of the country. It wanted to shake up Whitehall and replace those who had led Britain down the wrong path with others who could find a better path. It wanted a different mind-set in Whitehall. Obviously such a bold and sweeping transformation could not be executed overnight and at first the Thatcher Government proceeded cautiously as it readied measures for the most dramatic administrative reforms in British history.

(a) Retrenchment. The original freeze on new hiring in the civil service was only an expedient and it had at first only marginal effect. Its real impact was psychological. The government showed that it meant business. The freeze was announced without prior consultation with the public service unions as had been customary. It was coupled with a noticeable decline in the real income of public employees and a falling behind in comparison with the private sector, as a result of the government's rejection in 1980 of the fair comparability pay system that had been in effect for a quarter of a century. Further, before pay negotiations could open cash limits were to be placed on the civil service wage bill within which any settlement had to be contained as a move to encourage productivity and cut staff. Clearly in future material rewards would be much higher outside public employment. In fact, public sector employment was about to experience a sharp drop in status and prestige, an exodus of talented, experienced employees now much in demand by private sector organizations, difficulty in attracting capable newcomers to a "deprivileged" profession, and persistent industrial unrest leading to long and bitter strikes.

The initial reduction of 3 per cent was followed by a series of longer term labor force reduction targets. Central government agencies were required to identify ways of cutting their staffs by 10 per cent, 15 per cent and 20 per cent. Annual labor ceilings were incorporated into the supply estimates from 1981 onwards. On its reelection in 1983, the Thatcher Government set new targets for retrenchment according to cash-based public expenditure planning which did not take into account inflation, thereby limiting staff ceilings. After 1980, the Treasury reported annually on how reductions in staffing had been achieved. By 1986, 20 per cent of central government jobs had been eliminated through streamlining, privatization, contracting out (hiving off) of work, dropping or materially curtailing functions, and greater efficiency through changes in operation (Harrison and Gretton, 1987, 169). Thereafter, the targets set were regularly surpassed, making an unprecedented cut in the size of the British civil service (Ibid, 173), although public sector employment overall achieved such cutbacks only with a certain slight of hand (Dunsire and Hood, 1989).

(b) Raynerism. Mrs. Thatcher brought into the Cabinet Office a chief executive of one of Britain's most successful businesses, Derek Rayner, to conduct a series of detailed efficiency scrutinies into the work of government departments. Rayner had previously fought against paperasserie and red-tape (Rayner, 1975) and in the previous Conservative government he had been head of defense procurement. He brought with him a reputation for dynamic management and a strong appreciation of economy, productivity, efficiency, effectiveness and value for money. His surveys were to go beyond the usual management services' approach and cost-reduction exercises. They were to be government activity reduction inquiries which had to answer three questions: "What is it for? What does it cost? What value does it add?" It was quite apparent that in Whitehall managerialism had been neglected, that initiatives were stifled and that cost-consciousness was largely absent. In a Cabinet paper in April 1980, Rayner urged more emphasis on managerial abilities and initiatives to eliminate waste, first to get rid of needless paperwork, then improving the way government activities were performed, and then changing the education and experience of career civil servants to become real managers (Hennessy, 1989, 595). Convinced that Whitehall contained much talent that was being wasted, and that insiders were best equipped to examine the resources being used, the scrutinies were to be cooperative and participative directed at getting results. By the time Rayner returned to business toward the end of 1982, some 130 scrutinies had saved

16,000 positions and some £200 million in operating costs. He was succeeded by another successful business figure and government confident, Robin Ibbs.

By that time, Raynerism had been institutionalized in the Efficiency Unit attached to the new Management and Personnel Office in the Cabinet Office, and the Financial Management Initiative Unit, a joint Treasury-M.P.O. body consisting of three officials and four outside management consultants to examine on-going proposals for improving management and financial accountability under the Financial Management Initiative of May 1982. The function of the Efficiency Unit was to promote scrutinies rather than to conduct them, scrutinies designed to increase productivity and make the civil service more cost conscious. In Rayner's own words,

> ...The purpose of each scrutiny is action, not study. It is therefore:
> * to examine a specific policy or activity, questioning all aspects of the work normally taken for granted;
> * to propose solutions to any problems and to make recommendations to achieve savings and increase efficiency and effectiveness; and
> * to implement agreed solutions, or begin their implementation, within 12 months of the start of the scrutiny (Harrison and Gretton, 1987, 12).

By 1985, some 300 scrutinies had identified possible savings of £600 million a year but as it took between two to five years to implement the savings, it was estimated by the National Audit Office that by April 1986 some £1 billion had been saved for a total scrutiny cost of £5 million.

The scrutinies had led to widespread changes in management and management information services rooting out "the absurdities, anomalies and plain fossiled [sic] practices" (Hennessy, 1989, 601). The scrutiny process was later extended to quangos and local government services but again without the more advanced human services management practices that Rayner personally advocated. They were lost on Ibbs' Efficiency Unit which revised the rules to accentuate annual management improvements, value for money and managerial initiatives not just in the running costs of government but also in government policies and programs under the new Financial Management Initiative (F.M.I.) policy.

(c) Privatization. Of all Thatcher Government reforms, privatization has caused the greatest stir in public administration around the world and generated its own literature. For over a century, Britain had experimented with public enterprise and for thirty years it had taken over several bankrupt industries and companies. Privatization began as a means of divestment (load-shedding) and raising cash where domestic buyers could be found for government shares. It came to mean many other things, including a neo-liberal ideology of getting government out of production altogether (Veljanovski, 1987) and public choice among multiple providers of public services. At issue was whether the state should have any part in the production of industrial and commercial goods and services, whether their prices should be set solely by the market, and how much of the economy should be in public hands. The Thatcher Government preferred a minimal role for the state and resort to more indirect means to control public utilities and natural monopolies. Its objective was to halve the 10 per cent of the G.D.P. in the hands of government owned enterprises and to switch about £10 billion in capital assets and over 600,000 jobs to the private sector before 1990, something it would have achieved had its denationalization of the water and power industries not been delayed.

The Thatcher Government concentrated on the denationalization of public enterprises and the sale of public owned housing to tenants. It began in its first year by selling off 5 per cent of British Petroleum and other small holdings, in Ferranti and Fairey Engineering, for example. In the second year, it sold off over half of British Aerospace and the following year Amersham International, Cable and Wireless, National Freight, and British Sugar Corporation, raising £1.276 billion in three years, and thereafter the rate increased with the sale of Britoil, Enterprise Oil, Inmos, Sealink, Jaguar, Trustee Savings Bank, Associated British Ports, and British Telecom for £4.194 billion in the following three years. The National Bus Company was split up and sold off in pieces. British Telecom was sold off in one piece to face competition from Mercury, a subsidiary of Cable and Wireless, under the regulatory Office of Telecommunications (OFTEL). British Gas was also sold off in one piece under the regulatory OFGAS in 1986 and others to follow were aircraft and defense related industries, British Airways, British Airports Authority, Rolls Royce, Short Brothers, Unipart, Royal Ordinance Shipbuilding and parts of British Steel and British Leyland. This way, the Thatcher Government rid itself of major administrative headaches running state owned industries, shifted economic power and enterprise from the state to the private sector, and enlarged private ownership and investment. Privatization had reduced public sector borrowing requirements and government involvement in enterprise decision-making, eased problems of public sector pay determination, and widened share ownership but whether it had succeeded in improving performance, competition and economic efficiency was debatable (MacAvoy et al., 1989).

The Thatcher Government also encouraged public sector organizations to contract out whatever they could to private business and to privatize public housing and land. Except in such areas as office maintenance and cleaning, street cleaning and garbage collection, hospital laundry, and catering, the response was disappointing. In contrast, the sale of public owned housing and other property assets was greeted enthusiastically. In the first six years (1979-1985) sales netted over £8 billion, increasing owner occupancy from 56 to 62 per cent.

Altogether by 1989 the Thatcher Government had raised some £70 billion from sales of public assets. It was about to double that with the privatization of the power industry alone in electrical regeneration, transmission and distribution facilities with 130,000 jobs. Critics maintained that public assets had been sold off too hastily, too cheaply and without sufficient attention to the nature of markets and ownership (Vickers and Yarrow, 1988). But already, privatization was being pursued for a new enterprise culture rather than government income and decontrol. What was involved was the undoing of nationalization, public monopoly and public sector unions, and public welfare dependency, for wider private ownership and competition, self-improvement through thrift, hard work and personal responsibility, self-reliance, personal independence and freedom, i.e. a "people's capital market," and the promotion of popular capitalism. Privatization was being continued to change attitudes and political behavior, not necessarily to improve individual enterprise performance (Vernon, 1988, 40-41) achievable in other ways. Nonethless, the chief executives of the newly privatized companies thought that privatization had been traumatic and beneficial with marked gains in performance, productivity and managerialism (culture change and competiteveness) but not necessarily in improved returns on capital, sales or growth (*The Economist,* 1990, 57-58).

(d) Restructuring public enterprises. In the case of those public enterprises that had not been privatized, notably the Post Office, British Coal, British Rail, British Steel, British Waterways Board, and London and Scottish regional transportation, the Thatcher Government had done much to end monopoly, improve the rate of return on assets, reduce borrowing and increase productivity and efficiency. Thus, their debts were reduced from over £2 billion in 1978-9 to under £400 million in 1986-7 (Whitehead, 1988, 28). Most nationalized industries had been subject to review either by management consultants (mostly by one of the large multinational management and accounting companies) or after 1981 by the Monopolies and Mergers Commission. Particularly critical reports on the coal and steel industries had been delayed. Otherwise, much more information on nationalized industries became public knowledge. It showed persistence of incremental budgeting, weak investment forecasting, low productivity and poor service. The Post Office had done quite well but British Rail had not done as well as expected. Overall, the nationalized industries had been revitalized and in the 1980s they had increased their productivity at a higher rate than the private sector.

(e) Restructuring government. Although at first it seemed that local government authorities were to be freed of many central government restrictions and allowed greater financial and administrative discretion within broad central government guidelines, the Thatcher Government actually increased centralization to reduce overall public spending and pursued policies reducing the powers and prerogatives of local governments. It strongly opposed devolution. It eliminated a complete tier of elected government in metropolitan areas including the powerful London County Council. It established the local government Audit Commission in 1982 to scrutinize local authority costs and services (and to highlight local authority deficiencies). Most importantly, it radically altered central government financing of local government services by imposing strict limits on local government ability to raise and spend money, cutting financial support to local government and penalizing local governments which spent more than the Thatcher Government wished. The 1984 Rates Act brought rate capping, the first time that the central government had ever restricted local rate revenues. By 1987 about one-fifth of all current spending was under direct central government control. The 1980 Local Government Planning and Land Act had already capped capital spending or so it had been intended although poor drafting had allowed local governments to exploit the rules to avoid or shift the incidence of prescribed expenditure. More controversially, in Scotland it abolished the traditional rates (property tax) system and replaced it with a community charge (poll tax), and then in 1990 extended the new poll tax system to England and Wales. This time it seemed to have overreached itself politically and it was forced by adverse public opinion to slightly modify the new system. Nonetheless, undoubtedly local government had become less independent while the power of central government had been "restructured rather than reduced" (Parkinson, 1987, 169).

There had been no preconceived plan at first behind all these changes other than to reduce state expenditures by diminishing the role of the state and making public sector organizations more efficient. But once these changes had been made the Thatcher Government could prescribe a broader based policy for local government than improving their performance and making them more financially responsible in a national context. It had encouraged local authorities to sell public housing to tenants but why should local authorities be in the housing industry altogether? For problem areas, the central government would establish Housing Action Trusts and housing accounts in local authorities would be separately administered. Future central government subsidies would have to be traded off. This way, local authorities would be encouraged to get out of the housing industry altogether or find alternative sources of housing income from the private sector. Similarly, local authorities would be pressured out of running the schools directly, and new city technology colleges would be established outside local jurisdiction. Local authorities would be compelled to adopt competitive tendering for all kinds of general services such as refuse collection, street cleaning, vehicle maintenance, office cleaning, and catering and operated by direct service organizations with separate trading accounts which made prescribed rates of return. They would have to overhaul their operating procedures, internal structures and management capacities to ensure clear accountability and improved performance. Underlying these reforms was the expectation that the public would demand clear demonstration of better performance, that the public would participate more directly in local government administration, and that competitive tendering would result in greater efficiency (Jeffries, 1989). Meantime, the central government would continue to retain its tighter grip over local government.

(f) Civil service reform. Mrs. Thatcher had little love for the public bureaucracy in general and the Whitehall Establishment in particular. She believed that civil servants exercised too much influence over public policy and that the public sector unions were much too powerful. From the start, the Thatcher Government sought to put both back in their place. It reduced the power of the trade unions and asserted its authority in public sector industrial relations by linking concessions to productivity gains, defeating and punishing strikers, and undermining national pay bargaining through regional differentials. As to civil service reform, it brought in outsiders to policy-making positions and reshuffled senior civil servants around. It strengthened the Cabinet Office against traditional Treasury control. It set out to refute the myths of *Yes, Minister*. When in 1981 the Treasury reabsorbed the Civil Service Department which had been originally created to implement the Fulton Committee recommendations, management and organization, overall efficiency and personnel policy, including recruitment and training, were reserved for a new Management and Personnel Office (M.P.O.) within the Cabinet Office. The M.P.O. sought to open up top positions to high flyers and "can-dos," to put emphasis on performance and results, not style and appearances, and to launch a "new professionalism which will secure better value for money…focusing on performance and outputs and individual responsibility for securing desired results" (Fry, 1988, 1). M.P.O. was reabsorbed in the Treasury in 1987.

Plans had already been devised by the Efficiency Unit to reshape the structure of the civil service more upon Swedish lines with a small core of policy-making departments (ministries) sponsoring a number of attached or contracted free-standing management agencies that would be held accountable for operations according to set policy and resource guidelines but free to devise their own arrangements and "to recruit, pay, grade and structure in the most effective way" (Efficiency Unit, 1988, 9). The civil service had become "too big and diverse to manage as a single entity" and was "bound to develop in a way which fits no single operation effectively". Decisions were "structured to fit everything in general and nothing in particular" and seen as "a constraint rather than as a support" (Ibid, 5). The practical disadvantages of a unified civil service outweighed the advantages, especially beyond Whitehall.

* The work of each department had to be organized to enhance the efficient delivery of policies and services.
* Departmental staff had to possess relevant experience and skills for their tasks.
* Real and sustained pressure for improvement had to be exerted continuously.

Within every department, agencies should be established to carry out government activities within a set policy and resources framework, such agencies could be public *or* private and their management held vigorously to account for their results. Within the strategic controls set by the department, properly trained agency management should have as much independence as possible in deciding how their objectives were met.

> The central Civil Service should consist of a relatively small core engaged in the functions of servicing ministers and managing departments, who will be the 'sponsors' of particular government policies and services. Responding to these departments will be a range of agencies employing their own staff, who may or may not have the status of Crown servants, and concentrating on the delivery of their particular service, with clearly defined responsibilities between the Secretary of State and the Permanent Secretary on the once hand and the Chairman or Chief Executive of the agencies on the other. (Ibid, 15)

Such were the recommendations of a Rayner-type scrutiny into improved civil service management.

This "major onslaught on the conventional organization of the civil service" (Fry et al., 1988, 429) was to begin immediately with the identification and hiving off of distinct executive units such as the Employment Services, Her Majesty's Stationery Office, Driver and Vehicle Licensing Directorate, Meteorological Office, and Royal Parks whose business would be to manage programs not make or scrutinize public policy. The objective was to hive off some 75 per cent of the civil service by 1992 and to explore the possibilities of increasing that figure by tackling notoriously resistant ministries, such as Defence and Social Security and converting them to a business management approach. If successful, such fragmentation would mean abandoning a unified career civil service and central management controls, undermine industrial unionism even further, and create a two-tier structure of a core civil service with job security and career prospects and a peripheral civil service employed on a wide range of conditions (Fry et al., 1988, 435), a peripheral service headed by management experts fully indoctrinated with the new management culture. By mid-1989, some seven agencies had been established, another thirty identified and ten other possible candidates mentioned. But already questions were being raised whether the plan had been thoroughly thought through and whether it might not run into the same problems experienced in Sweden in undertaking large scale organizational and cultural change (Fudge and Gustafsson, 1989) and "the need to reconcile Parliament's ultimate control with the need to give managers freedom to manage" (*Govenance* 1990, 196).

(g) A management culture. Mrs. Thatcher held firm views of government in which politicians ruled with the best available advice from whatever quarter and public administrators managed and were held directly accountable for their performance. The government decided objectives, priorities, and targets and allocated resources accordingly. The administrators delivered results in the most economical and effective ways. This view had been shared by Derek Rayner in his efficiency scrutinies and by John Hoskyns, another close policy advisor who had planned the 1982 election campaign and the administrative reforms thereafter (Greenaway, 1984, 71). Both called for a different mindset in Whitehall and a more robust breed of public managers altogether. The traditional administrative culture that prized intellectuality and political gamesmanship was to be destroyed by deliberate demoralization (Richards, 1988, 5) and then reconstructed into a new managerial belief system. The Efficiency Unit would use its surveys to illustrate what should be done, to persuade civil servants to adopt managerialism, and to implement model management systems across the board.

In 1982, the Thatcher Government introduced its Financial Management Initiative (F.M.I.) to ensure that managers at all levels had a clear view of their objectives and means to measure performance in relation to those objectives, a well-defined responsibility to make the best use of their resources including a critical scrutiny of output and value for money, and information, particularly about costs, training and access to expert advice needed to exercise their responsibilities effectively (White Paper, 1982). The idea behind this seemed to be that "if you get the budgeting process right, and provide people with the information, skills and advice to exercise their budgeting role, you get good management," i.e. management was seen as a question of control through budgets which fastened "responsibility and accountability for the achievement of budgeting targets on line management" (Harrison and Gretton, 1987, 25).

Three principal mechanisms were established to achieve F.M.I.'s objectives, first, the provision of top management information systems, second, the installation of decentralized budget control systems within departments, and, third, the development of performance assessments of both operations and personnel, as part of the evaluation of efficiency and effectiveness. The top management information systems were modeled after the successful management information system for ministers (MINIS) originated by the Minister for the Environment, Michael Heseltine, when he took office in 1979. Decentralized budget control established a hierarchy of cost centers operating under M.B.O.-type guidelines, and assessment of efficiency and effectiveness was to be done by developing performance indicators. To help departments implement F.M.I., a small Financial Management Unit – a joint venture between the Treasury and the Management and Personnel Office – was set up (and in 1985 succeeded by the Joint Management Unit) and soon encountered problems usually connected with efficiency budgeting (Metcalfe and Richards, 1987).

The F.M.I. was followed by efforts to obtain information about detailed administrative costs, to allocate responsibility and accountability to cost-center managers ("let the managers manage") and to devise performance indicators, set targets, and hold departments to those targets and generally to turn civil servants into public managers thereby linking costs and outputs. In the words of a Cabinet Office official:

> Today, a management revolution is already underway in the Civil Service which will greatly increase its effectiveness...This is not just concerned with cost cutting and increased efficiency...It involves targeting investment more closely to identified needs and ensuring that these needs are met in the most effective way. It also means making the best use of people, and so improving personnel management as well as financial management. (Fry et al., 1988, 429-30)

This was not the view of many observers who could not identify any such revolution under way.

> The Thatcher government has had an impoverished concept of management as revealed by several telltale signs: a mechanistic view of control, the disregard for civil servants' morale, and a "costs" mentality. For this government the most basic elements of management – people, dynamic organization, motivation, leadership – often have been left out, replaced by costs and an archaic command and control mystique of leaders and docile followers, coupled uneasily with the belief that recalcitrant civil servants must be brought to heel. (Williams, 1988, 123)

Certainly efforts to change the administrative culture were stalling.

A boost to the cause came with the Efficiency Unit's 1988 proposals for restructuring the civil service wherein public managers would be free to manage and to improve agency performance from a consumer's viewpoint. Short of proposing the privatization of the agencies, this was the closest yet that the business management model had been envisioned as the future for the civil service. Such a sweeping reorganization would require not just a different way of conducting the business of government but "changing the cultural attitudes and behaviour of government" (Efficiency Unit, 1988, 1). This was all very well but F.M.I. had lagged like program analysis and review before that (Gray and Jenkins, 1982). Ministers were still reluctant to assume a managerial role and political considerations overruled managerial findings. Quantitative performance measures overshadowed quality performance measures. The civil service lacked sufficient managerial capacity and skills. Financial cost considerations overrode human resource management considerations.

Little attention had been paid to engineering the attitudes and behaviors of public officials consistent with the desired managerial changes. The government had promised greater decentralization but had in fact increased centralization in managerial systems. Whitehall's "disbelief system" (its refusal to take seriously long-term managerial improvement concepts) was still very much at work (Metcalfe and Richards, 1987, 14-15); its culture of caution remained dominant (Hennessy, 1989, 620). True Mrs. Thatcher had ruled over Whitehall, but she had not transformed it (Ibid, 682). She had encouraged self help and the provision of public services by non-governmental and private voluntary organizations and she had created hybrid forms of organization combining the features of public bureaucracy and private enterprise. But there was "very little evidence of real reduction in scale in public service provision and only some of rivalry and multi-organizational structures as a developing trend in public service provision" (Lane, 1987, 168). Despite the rhetoric, the Thatcher Government was still running the state with much the same bureaucratic instruments and administrative culture of the previous century. As far as it was concerned, managerialism was still insufficiently appreciated.

Nonetheless, no other country in Western Europe came anywhere near close to such sweeping radical reforms of its public sector. Several tried privatization but not to such an extent; they preferred to improve the operational performance of state owned enterprises instead. Others totally revamped their local government systems but did not touch the central machinery of government while a few rearranged their central machinery of government but left intact their local government systems. Almost every country tried decentralization, deregulation, cutback management, and debureaucratization but all were quickly disillusioned as the results were so little for the enormous political price governments paid for their politicization of public service (Leemans, 1987). The Netherlands did embark on a concerted course of reducing the size of the public sector through retrenchment (Stronck and Vaubel, 1988) and privatization, even of the Dutch Post Office. Italy went in for severe salary cuts yet like so many others hoped to humanize public bureaucracy despite demoralization. Sweden preferred simplification, deregulation and debureaucratization, tried freeing local governments from central controls, worked to replace an "authority culture" with a "service culture," and introduced budget reforms as did Belgium and Western Germany (United Nations, 1988). Spain and Portugal advanced democratization of public administration while Denmark and Ireland opted for better public services through managerialism and performance monitoring. France attempted to reduce (deprivilege) the elitism of the Grand Corps (its administrative elite) and resist unpopular or heavyhanded administrative initiatives, and to debureaucratize through managerialism and cost-effectiveness (Rouban, 1989). In Greece, the Papandreou Government attempted to revamp the public bureaucracy, professionalize the public service and modernize administrative operations. Thus, Western European countries continued to be a rich source of administrative modernization and reforms with a variety possibly unmatched elsewhere (Hofmeister, 1988).

But in the 1980s, it had been the Thatcher Government in the United Kingdom that attracted most attention because of its boldness, radicalism and apparent success against an entrenched system that had previously defied all attempts to change the pervasive administrative culture. It was apparent success because, as in all these things, there was more rhetoric than action, more bluster than progress, more continuity than departure, and at best, administrative reform was really marginal or peripheral in reshaping Britain. As for reshaping Western Europe, the 1992 integration of the European Economic Community and the possible disintegration of the East Bloc would probably be more profound. None of the countries, not even the United Kingdom, had rolled back the state to any appreciable extent or indeed at all. While they had tried to contract, public expenditures on defense, welfare services, environmental protection, and education and research had risen faster and local government expenditures had risen faster than central government expenditures. Despite retrenchment, privatization, budget controls, managerialism, revitalized state-owned enterprises and improved public sector performance, the public sector continued to take a greater not lesser portion of G.D.P. What was likely to be more fundamental and more successful was the slow shift of administrative values away from impersonal bureaucracy toward a more personal managerialism particularly in the newly privatized organizations. It seemed as though the message had finally gotten through certainly among O.E.C.D. members that their administrative cultures would have to change if they were to cope with the challenges of the 21st century.

Shaking Up Federal Government Management

Many of the administrative reforms that the Thatcher Government and Western European governments tried in the 1980s had actually been attempted first in North America. Indeed, they had largely been derived from or inspired by academic scholarship there and well-publicized reform campaigns of American presidents. In truth, because of its different constitutional and political circumstances Canada had been the most experimental, adventurous and creative. The Glassco Commission of the 1960s had fired off the managerial ethos in the public sector in a country never ruled by a Whitehall Establishment nor subject to the worst excesses of the spoils system in the United States (Plumptre, 1988). Canada was between the United States and Western Europe, yet ahead of them in many respects in political and administrative innovation. After all, Saskatchewan had had the first socialist government in North America around the same time as Sweden, and Ontario had been the leader in interest group liberalism.

Administratively, the federal government of Canada had led in implementing program budgeting, policy and expenditure management systems, program evaluation, expenditure reviews and affirmative action for women, although it may have been beaten in fact by one or other of the provinces in budgeting practices, privatization, ombudsman, and privacy protection. While others debated, Canadian governments acted and experimented with administrative and financial reforms that were later "discovered" or taken up in other parts of the world (Gow, 1989; Savoie, 1990). As a pacesetter in governmental trends and administrative reforms, Canadians quietly got on with the job – too quietly because they never received the recognition due to them as for instance in *Public*

Service 2000, a process of looking at further demands on the public sector, demographic trends, morale, etc. through nine task forces examining such topics as flexible working hours, day care centers, part-time work, performance pay, decentralized personnel management and expenditure controls to prepare ahead. Instead, their superpower neighbor to the south has always received world attention; what happened in the United States usually travelled around the globe much faster. That had certainly been true of President Carter's civil service reforms and was also for President Reagan's managerial improvements.

President Reagan shared similar world views to Mrs. Thatcher about the legitimacy of the administrative state (Farazmand, 1989) and overturning the liberal mind-set that had dominated public policy for so long. He too wanted to free business from the deadening hand of excessive government regulation, reduce waste in government and dependency on government, cut high taxes that destroyed incentives to work, save and invest, switch resources from the public to private sector to finance new jobs and wealth-producing enterprise, and restore his country's international standing, military preeminence and national confidence. Government was the villain and bureaucrats were so much deadwood, devoid of ideas and obstructive of new policies. Reagan was also going to save the country and reconstruct society. He promised to get the federal government off people's backs, sharply cut federal civilian spending, deregulate hamstrung industries, balance the budget and reduce inflation, reaffirm certain individual values, and improve public sector performance (Kymlicka and Matthews, 1988).

Unlike Mrs. Thatcher who could impose her will on the country, President Reagan could not even get his way with Congress. He had to select his targets carefully and marshall an array of interests to achieve a modicum of success. He knew that administrative reform was perilous; it had defeated the best. Yet the inertia of the system was so great and the times so turbulent, from time to time something radical had to be done. President Nixon had settled on structural reform (reorganization) and President Carter had chosen civil service reform, both having to make the best deal in the circumstances and put the best gloss on it. Reagan decided that his legacy would be management reform, recalling President Franklin Roosevelt's wise words, "A government without good management is a house built on sand". He realized that defective management would let him down as it had let down his predecessors. He could capitalize on their initiatives but he knew that such initiatives had rarely lasted long or amounted to much. Carter's civil service reforms which were supposed to spark the best and brightest and make the senior executives bloom had gotten (or were about to get) caught in the quicksand of budget cuts, policy terminations and personal retrenchments and with them the hopes of motivating career administrators with bonuses and rewarding mid-career executives with merit pay (Ingraham and Ban, 1984, 54). The situation after some sixty years of fitful starts and misses had become intolerable. Government had to be put on a better business footing; it was just too big, too costly, too inefficient, too unwieldy, too poorly managed. The Reagan Administration was determined to reduce government costs and improve public management with the powers allowed the President under the amended Reorganization Act of 1949. Important issues would be the budget and budgetary processes, the proper scope and organization of government, the respective roles of public, private and non profit sectors in delivering public goods and services, and the role of public servants in public policy making (March and Olsen, 1989, 73).

Until 1920, federal government organizations could do what they wanted administratively under Congressional guidance, an archaic and chaotic situation which had led management-minded President Theodore Roosevelt to appoint the first study of federal management (Keep Commission 1905-07) and to request presidential powers to improve federal administrative arrangements, a point strongly endorsed by President Taft's Commission on Economy and Efficiency (Cleveland, 1911-12). Proposals for a manageable executive, an integrated budget and an audit system (validated during World War I) were finally adopted in the Budget and Accounting Act of 1921 which provided for the U.S. General Accounting Office (G.A.O.) and a Bureau of the Budget specifically charged with preparing an executive budget and studying the economy and efficiency of federal management. Placed in the Treasury Department instead of the White House, B.O.B. ignored its management functions. Following President Roosevelt's Committee on Administrative Management (Brownlow 1936-7) to strengthen presidential control of federal government administration and management, B.O.B. was transferred to the new Executive Office of the President in 1939 and its managerial functions were strengthened just in time to enable B.O.B. to exercise some well needed management leadership during World War II.

But by 1949 the first Hoover Commission was again critical of severe managerial shortcomings and lack of administrative leadership and the second Hoover Commission (1955) repeated its calls for a proper managerial president. B.O.B. itself recognized that it had to provide greater managerial leadership but its budget activities swamped its managerial initiatives. Several studies of B.O.B. in the late 1960s recommended its reorganization and in 1970 it was retitled Office of Management and Budget to emphasize its role in management. For a short time, its management side was reinvigorated with a push to adopt management by objectives (M.B.O.) only to deteriorate rapidly after Watergate and the shortlived Presidential Management Initiatives (P.M.I.) of President Ford. By the end of the 1970s, President Carter was relying more on the Federal Personnel Management Project, the new Office of Personnel Management, the Senior Executive Service, and the Inspectors General than on the O.M.B. based Presidential Reorganization Project (P.R.P.). The P.R.P. had begun as an exercise in management improvement but had fallen foul of Congress and internal bureaucratic politics and the ill-fated 1977 O.M.B. Circular A-11 prematurely imposing zero-based budgeting (Z.B.B.). Meantime, Congress had stepped in to create an Office of Federal Procurement Policy (1974) and an Office of Information and Regulatory Affairs (1980) in the Paperwork Reduction Act of 1980, both placed in O.M.B.

Lack of consistent managerial leadership and the veritable eclipse of management concerns in political circles, despite obvious deficiencies revealed daily in the mass media and persistent bureaucrat-bashing by presidential advisors, had brought the National Academy of Public Administration (N.A.P.A.) increasingly into an advocacy role. At first, it had sought to influence O.M.B. to restore and prioritize management concerns, particularly in the neglected areas of intergovernmental management, organization policy and planning, administrative planning, agency management assistance, procurement, information and regulatory affairs, financial management, program evaluation, and interagency relations and coordination. Eventually, N.A.P.A. proposed a separate Office of Federal Management to develop long term government-wide management planning and policy, to lead the drive for major management improvement and the refurbishment of management systems, and to take the lead in management innovation, with sufficient resources to implement badly needed management reforms to unburden managers of rigid, heavy-handed, centrally controlled management systems and free them to be their own management innovators and reformers (N.A.P.A., 1983).

N.A.P.A. believed that the budget process was seriously overburdened and badly needed modernization and simplification. Disconnections between authorizations, reconciliations and appropriations seriously frustrated program planning. Program decisions were deferred; productivity was lost; waste and mismanagement occurred; and potential savings through economies, management efficiency and productivity improvements were discouraged. Procurement had become a nightmare of bureaupathology – so too had personnel management with its 8,800 plus pages of Federal Personnel Manual guidelines that nobody understood and were dysfunctional. The time delays and paper involved were "mind-boggling" (Ibid, 46). Advances in computer technology had largely passed by the federal bureaucracy; public managers were ill-prepared and intimidated by new information systems. Space needs went unmet or were eventually met unsuitably in poorly maintained facilities. Printing was too costly and of inferior quality. This was a litany of complaints that showed a management environment in which managers could not manage and central agencies imposed uniformities on operations that could not be standardized. Moreover, few disputed the diagnosis and the mismanagement that resulted. Would President Reagan grab the tiger by the tail as he promised to do in so many other areas of government?

Right off, it would not be business as usual at O.M.B. Reagan's choice as Director, David Stockman, would not only produce an executive budget but also see that it would reflect Reagan's policies of rolling back the federal government and cutting down government programs. The budget would no longer be a "bottom-up" operation but a "top-down" method. O.M.B. was to be politicized as never before and its staff was to spend more time on Capitol Hill, designing, packaging, justifying and selling the President's budget, advocating and negotiating the President's agenda, than overseeing the bureaucracy, formulating policy options and analyzing long term fiscal trends. There was no other body of people as capable of devising a comprehensive fiscal approach or of monitoring the efficiency of existing programs or of coping with persistent structured deficits or of implementing a novel central budget management system for tracking budget data and legislation. Nor apparently was there any other body as capable of dealing with management initiatives. O.M.B. still had in hand President Carter's reorganization and personnel management programs, paperwork reduction, deregulation, information processing and intergovernmental issues, as well as management improvement and evaluation. So Reagan decided to go with O.M.B. by phasing out the Carter management initiatives that were not going anywhere and to make O.M.B. responsible for his own initiatives.

(a) 1981 The President's Council on Integrity and Efficiency. First of all, in March 1981 he brought the agency Inspectors-General whose job was to prevent fraud, abuse and mismanagement together with the central management control agencies (O.P.M., Treasury, Attorney General, and Federal Bureau of Investigation) under the rubric of O.M.B. in the President's Council on Integrity and Efficiency (P.C.I.E.) and made it the focal point of combatting fraud and abuse and improving overall federal government management. The P.C.I.E., was to initiate projects with government-wide scope and application and undertake special activities to increase professional expertise and to share information on proven tools and techniques. It operated through standing committees representing the major interests of the I.G.s. Among its longer term projects were:

* **Program economy, efficiency and effectiveness**: policy improvements, productivity, savings, streamlining, revised regulations, cash recoveries, loan controls, quality service, accountability, recapturing funds, cost estimation, safety improvements, reduced backlogs, white collar crime detection, reduced documentation, interagency audit and investigation;
* **Financial management**: loan delinquencies and sale of loan assets, grant termination, cash management, debt management and collection, payroll efficiencies, cost avoidance, collections, interest earnings, recovered advances, user fees, civil remedies, prosecutions and sanctions, single audit approach, accounting control (Federal Managers' Financial Integrity Act of 1982), risk management, Prompt Pay Act of 1987;
* **Acquisitions**: contract fraud, mispricing, contract auditing, bid rigging, unnecessary purchases, restitution, cost avoidance, greater competitiveness, excessive payments;

* **Automatic data processing**: system design, contingency planning, data integrity, security and access, information resources management, systems integrity, computer matching, micro computer training.

So successful was P.C.I.E. judged that in 1988 legislation extended the I.G. system to agencies still without it, introduced mini-I.G.s or offices of audit and investigations, and required agencies to provide more detailed follow-up reports. P.C.I.E. maintains a network through its newsletter *Frontline* which summarizes the findings of current investigations of agency I.G.s. and issues two annual reports, one on audit and inspection accomplishments and another on instigative accomplishments. During 1989, the I.G.s recommended recovery or restitution of nearly $5 billion and more efficient use of $37 billion and they reported over 5.600 successful prosecutions, over $700 million in recoveries and 2,851 debarment or suspension actions against people doing business with the federal government. Senate investigators, however, believed that too often the I.G.s covered up governmental wrongdoing and intimidated whistle-blowers. They preferred a single government-wide inspector-general's office limited to a five year term to insulate it's decisions from political considerations.

(b) 1982 The President's Private Sector Survey on Cost Control (Grace Commission). President Reagan did not trust the federal bureaucracy to cure itself. He wanted more than penny ante management changes. To get more dramatic action he would put the fox in the chicken coop. Private business executives would do just that. They would point out what was wrong with government administration and how to put it right. He asked industrialist J. Peter Grace to conduct an extensive inquiry into all aspects of federal government operations. Grace called on the country's leading corporations and some 2,000 business executives altogether took part in a highly publicized investigation that did just what the President expected it to do – to reveal just how wasteful, inefficient and mismanaged the federal administration supposedly was. The Grace Commission produced some 47 reports claiming that over $424 billion could be saved in three years. Its final summary report, released in January 1984, contained over 2,500 specific recommendations for eliminating programs, selling off assets, cutting out waste, eliminating needless red-tape, and generally transforming public management into business management.

Immediately, there were protests of foul play within the public administration community (Goodsell, 1984, 2; Kelman, 1985), some of whom dubbed it the "disgrace commission" for its shoddy work, wrong assumptions, and misconceptions about government operations while the business community accused Grace of being guilty of the same vices of management that he had accused federal managers of (*Business Week*, June 10, 1986, 68). Its findings were submitted to the Cabinet Council on Management and Administration (which had been established in September 1982 to bridge policy and implementation in all managerial initiatives) chaired by the President who had the White House Office of Cabinet Affairs review them. During the 1984 election the Citizens Against Government Waste organized by Grace was set up to push for the adoption of the Grace Commission proposals. After the election, the Grace Commission was studied by the new Domestic Policy Council in the White House. Both houses of Congress also formed caucuses to study the Grace Commission findings. Official consideration was mandated in the Deficit Reduction Act of 1984 which also required a review of their implementation in the president's management report to Congress. The upshot of all this was that the President approved the recommendations of the Domestic Policy Council, which accepted most of the findings, and thereafter worked through O.M.B. with Congress for their implementation. Three years afterwards, the White House claimed that 80 per cent of the Grace Commission savings had been achieved.

(c) 1982 The President's Reform '88 Project. It was not President Reagan's intention to do away with government but to make it work better. First, O.M.B.'s budget process would cap agency spending and then make savings by technologically upgrading management systems and merging operations. Stockman was perturbed by the lack of financial and managerial accountability, the antiquated financial processes and information systems, and the sheer complexity of just tracking the federal government's money, property, and personnel. Resource control needed updated management systems in virtually every area, as G.A.O.'s reports kept indicating. Further there now had to be a response to the Federal Managers' Financial Integrity Act of 1982 which required annual reports on the state of administrative and financial control, which in turn required "an examination of the established structure; assignments of responsibility; directives, plans and schedules; inventories of assessable units; vulnerability assessment and reports...of internal control evaluations; and summaries of actions taken or planned" (Barkley, 1983, 3). A major part of the effort would need to concentrate on long-neglected financial management systems. All this became part of the President's Management Improvement Program, Reform '88, a five year project to encompass all the major government-wide management improvement initiatives, particularly financial management, credit management, personnel management, property management, and information management.

(d) 1983 O.M.B. Management Reviews. Federal government organizations were required to submit management plans along with their annual budget requests and to give special attention to management improvement efforts. As a result, the President was able to issue his first annual *Management of the United States Government Report* in 1985.

(e) 1984 The President's Council on Management Improvement. With these initiatives under way, O.M.B. could again provide a mechanism to monitor management improvement efforts, provide central guidance in implementing the Grace Commission recommendations and the Reform '88 program, and forge a partnership among federal agencies directed at mutual assistance and support in the program to improve, consolidate and streamline management systems. In May 1984 President's Council on Management Improvement (P.C.M.I.) consisting of the Assistant Secretaries for Management and their equivalents in all major agencies, was established to work with O.M.B., Treasury, O.P.M., and the General Services Administration to develop and oversee Reform '88, formulate long range plans to promote management improvements, resolve interagency management issues, and identify specific agency reforms applicable to other agencies.

The P.C.M.I. has met monthly to review projects, identify new opportunities and develop strategies for government-wide implementation. It works through subcommittees (on organization and structure, human resources, information systems, communications and legislation) and a Cooperative Administrative Support Unit Program for joint services in multi-tenanted complexes in regional centers. Among its longer term projects have been the following:

Credit management: comprehensive credit management and debt collection, bankcard program, travelcard program, O.M.B. Circular A-129 for managing credit programs and collecting loans, servicing accounts, collecting delinquent receivables, writing off uncollectible accounts, applicant screening for credit worthiness, user fees, loan asset sales, litigation;

Financial management: grant administration, cash management, controls against fraud and abuse, payment integrity, asset management, financial information and systems, discretionary grants, vulnerability assessments, standard capital expenditure policies for investments, standard general ledger chart of accounts, consolidation of diverse subsidiary systems (accounts receivable, personnel, travel, payroll, property, grants and purchasing), off-the-shelf-software, lockboxes;

Quality and productivity improvement: consumer service, problem solving, quality and productivity achievement rewards, goal setting, measures, productivity investment fund models, shared savings, coproduction, Quality Institute, improving employee morale and image, recruitment and retention, executive development, productivity workshops;

Improved services through technology: automation, paperwork reduction, A.D.P. security guidelines, information technology lease/purchase program, automated directives, public information, standard payroll system, computer standardization and matching;

Procurement management: innovative procurement practices, streamlined acquisition, rights in technical data, value engineering;

Management of government operations: reducing overheads, simplification, supply and property management, real property management, simplified classification, simplified personnel manual, public participation, cross-servicing (warehousing), privatization.

Like the P.C.I.E., the procedures and processes of the P.C.M.I. are self-generating and momentum once started is difficult to restrain.

(f) 1986 Productivity Improvement Program. Once the President was satisfied that government management improvement was well in hand, he moved to improving the delivery of public goods and services. He set a target of improving productivity by 20 per cent by 1992. All agencies were required to establish specific productivity and quality priorities and to draw on the creativity and ingenuity of their employees and to properly reward achievements as was standard practice in the private sector. This "total quality management" approach was to ensure that improvements in service were consistent and incremental rather than ad hoc and ephemeral. As part of implementation, a Federal Quality Institute was established in 1988 to provide quality awareness training.

(g) 1986 Small Agency Council. The smaller federal agencies mostly with fewer than 500 employees formed their own organization to develop management policies and practices on the P.C.M.I. model to deal with their particular concerns and to obtain modifications in central control agency requirements. The S.A.C. was represented on the P.C.M.I.

(h) 1987 Chief Financial Officer. As part of Reform '88, O.M.B.'s chair of P.C.M.I. and head of its management side was appointed in July 1987 Chief Financial Officer of the United States to assure consistency and adherence to sound financial management principles throughout the federal government, to provide leadership for financial plans and systems to assure appropriate compatibility, controls, standards, reliability and effectiveness, and to improve control over accounting, administrative and financial systems and management. Later in the year, agencies designated a chief financial officer to sit on the new Chief Financial Officer Council to deal with improvements in financial management, specifically to implement the Joint Financial Management Improvement Program and "to reduce obsolete systems, eliminate redundant systems, and make systems compatible so that financial information can readily be exchanged, aggregated, and reported to all management levels in a timely manner to support managerial decision-making." (U.S. Executive Office of the President, 1989, 6-26)

(i) 1988 Office of Privatization. Although the federal government has pledged itself since 1955 not to provide any product or service if it could be procured from the private sector, it has moved slowly to divest its commercial activities and public enterprises. Not surprisingly, much pressure was put on President Reagan to privatize and the commission he appointed to look into the matter enthusiastically endorsed privatization when it reported in March 1988. The report had 78 specific recommendations and an Office of Privatization was established in O.M.B. to manage privatization initiatives in coordination with specially designated privatization officers in the agencies.

(j) 1988 Organizational Excellence Project. O.P.M.'s Office of Executive Personnel instigated a project that would identify, document and disseminate examples of excellence in the federal service to provide role models, promote excellence and improve morale and the image of the federal service. In 1989, the first of the profiles in excellence was released as a sample of outstanding managerial leadership.

(k) 1988 Government of the Future Project. As his farewell, President Reagan directed that a forward-looking view be taken of the shape of the federal government in the year 2000 and asked what administrative and management policies should be developed in advance to meet the challenge of the future. The results were put into *Management of the United States Government 1990* where it was implied that a multi-year strategic management plan should be developed.

These eleven management initiatives of the Reagan Administration may not have amounted singularly to much but altogether they started what may turn out to be a quiet revolution in federal government management. It is their cumulative impact that has to be assessed. No doubt much of what was done would have been done without any presidential prompting. No doubt too much reliance had been placed on an overburdened and otherwise preoccupied O.M.B. Probably, too much had been focused on cost cutting and not enough on efficiency, mismanagement and sleaze. Even O.M.B.'s severest critics had to admit progress in standard ledger accounting, payroll standardization, cash and credit management, information technology, and productivity measures. But were these not too narrowly focused? While savings had been made, far greater losses had occurred through gross agency mismanagement and political corruption.

Key federal management problems had not been tackled and while some progress had been made, it had not been fast enough or broad enough. In some cases, the new Presidential arrangements of the 1980s had made hardly any impact at all. A General Accounting Office G.A.O. review in 1988 found mixed results only, with failures in detecting the Federal Savings and Loan Insurance Corporation's insolvency, defective management and safety oversight of weapons complexes, inefficient tax processing, poor contract administration, and other obvious management breakdowns (G.A.O., 1989a). In examining a sample of civilian agency contracts, the G.A.O. reported in September 1989 little improvement in contract management and confirmed that identified weaknesses such as poor planning, poor development of specifications, delays, and inadequate (or no) monitoring, were still widespread. It concluded "that a concerted effort by the Office of Federal Procurement Policy and civilian agency heads is needed to improve contracting and contract administration" and to correct the weaknesses revealed (G.A.O., 1989b). For the G.A.O. generally, management reform extended beyond cost control and efficiency goals, beyond the President's narrow perception of running costs, to embrace the whole machinery of government and the evaluation of public policy, the conduct of intergovernmental and foreign relations, and the national allocation of public sector (not just federal government) resources.

For the federal government employee unions, poor human resource management and bad industrial relations caused them to embrace Congressional invitations to halt or slow down Reagan's managerial reforms and to back Reagan's political opponents. Besides his parsimonious pay policy, they were angered by his politicization of the Senior Executive Service, his verbal support for privatization and contracting out, and his blindness to kleptocracy in the agencies. In short Reagan's reforms

> weakened more than strengthened the more permanent institutions of presidential management, has undermined the morale of the civil service, has taken a narrow auditing approach to improving management in the executive branch, has done little to encourage competent professionals to serve in the federal government, and has overlooked opportunities to strengthen existing partnership arrangements between the federal government and other institutions at the state and local level and in the private sector. (Salamon and Lund, 1984, 23)

They may even have taken federal government management in the wrong direction (Campbell and Peters, 1988, 277). They certainly left "a crippled federal government to his successor" (Kymlicka and Matthews, 1988, 99).

President Bush admitted as much when he promised shortly after taking office to tackle some of the major scandals (defense management and procurement, banking controls, nuclear safety regulation, civil aviation safety provisions) resulting partly from deregulation and a laissez-faire attitude to regulatory enforcement (Swann, 1988). But that he had to dwell in so much detail on management matters was testimony to Reagan's initiatives, the new management control devices in place, and the self-generating reform process that had been institutionalized. O.M.B. would have to monitor management improvements if only for the record. Unless wound up, the P.C.I.E., the P.C.M.I. and the C.F.O.C. would move monthly on their agendas and new business. Without a stronger O.M.B. leadership role, the efforts could well slacken unless a separate Office of Federal Management were created to devise a multi-year strategic management improvement plan, continue agency partnerships to modernize and improve federal government management, and to hold everyone involved to realistic annual performance targets.

Given the reputation of federal government management and the decline of the management side of O.M.B., it seemed that unless some such action were taken, the budget side of O.M.B. would continue to dominate and all the new institutional arrangements would still fail to make much impression on the administrative culture. Congress gave President Bush at the beginning of his term the opportunity of appointing a National Commission on Executive Organization but he passed it up. He did not strengthen the management side of O.M.B. nor did he seem to take much interest in organizational, administrative and managerial arrangements. He appeared satisfied with his predecessor's efforts, apparently leaving initiatives to Congress in a reversion to the mistaken belief that the president could not "and should not try to manage the executive branch" (Moe, 1990, 136), but

> the contemporary President is the manager of the executive branch and cannot escape judgment regarding that stewardship. His choice is not whether to be a manager; but whether to be an effective or ineffective manager. Unfortunately, most recent Presidents have chosen to be ineffective managers and this ineffectiveness has proven cumulative. (Ibid)

In contrast, prime ministers in parliamentary systems have always recognized their managerial responsibilities, and recent experiences in Australasia confirm this.

Introducing New Style Public Managerialism Down Under

Nowhere in the world have the administrative attitudes of a lifetime been so challenged and reordered than in the antipodes, in Australasia, where some of the major radical changes in thinking and institutional design have been taken place, not without throwing everyone concerned into a tizzy. Australia and New Zealand both gained reputations at the turn of the century for their social experiments and their daring innovations in social democracy. Forced by circumstances to develop and rely on the administrative state, they were both pioneers in state enterprise, state welfare, public service reform, economic and industrial arbitration, and administrative fairness. Reformatory zeal took them way beyond the mother country, indeed most of the Old World save Scandinavia. Between the World Wars, they had evolved dedicated, competent and honest public services that were the envy of countries far better placed and they seemed to have discovered the keys to successful administration capable of matching most challenges thrown at them for over half a century.

But success bred complacency and the slavish following of time-honored dogma. Changes and adjustments were made but where once the countries had been administratively radical, they became administratively conservative. Times changed; they did not change or adjust sufficiently. The smaller country, New Zealand, fared better or at least it never wholly forgot its radical tradition in public administration. It was the first non-Scandinavian country to adopt the ombudsman (in 1962) and it did think seriously in the early 1960s about radically altering public sector structure and operations. Later, Australia also adopted the ombudsman and also thought seriously about altering its public sector. Neither did much in the face of official and union resistance, bureaucratic inertia, and public indifference. After all, until the 1970s, both countries, doing quite well, could afford to humor internal critics who tried to point out that they had to think about the morrow too.

When in the 1970s, economic troubles beset them, their previous optimism turned quickly into pessimism. What had happened? What should be done? Who should do it? Governments commissioned inquiry after inquiry (Smith and Weller, 1978). Experts gave contradictory advice. Compromises were fashioned and tried. The electorate would have rejected anything too radical. The public bureaucracy was not at all adept in rapidly changing directions. On the contrary, the public bureaucracy or rather the bureaucratic elites had become accustomed to doing what they had always done and whatever changes had been imposed on them had led to reform backlashes within. They seemed to live in a world of their own. Indeed, their ideas and practices could not cope with the new emerging international order. What should have been their finest hour was muffed. They failed to come up with the necessary bold, imaginative solutions.

Throughout the 1970s when the national predicament first became apparent, inquiry after inquiry into the Australian public bureaucracy revealed that the country lacked an energetic and imaginative administrative leadership capable of generating enthusiasm for change. Fifty years had passed since the bureaucracy had shown such dynamism in public affairs during which there had only been minor tinkering with a system that had obviously failed to keep up with changing times. The managerial philosophies enshrined in the system were quite outdated and inappropriate. In Victoria, the Bland inquiry pointed to the isolation of the public service, major administrative staffing deficiencies, outmoded attitudes and lack of initiative. In South Australia, the Corbett inquiry commented on the discounting of productivity and efficiency. The Coombs inquiry into the federal bureaucracy was critical of its aloofness from the public, its unrepresentative composition, and general lack of managerial accountability in a service that was excessively centralized, hierarchical, and resistant to organizational change. The other inquiries were no less critical and iconoclastic and together they constituted a serious indictment. Together, they advocated a comprehensive reformulation of administrative principles and practices.

The time had passed for piecemeal, incremental reforms. Nothing short of fundamental institutional reorganization and revitalization would suffice. The whole public sector would have to be reconstructed if necessary from the outside simply because too many on the inside seemed unwilling or incapable of providing the necessary leadership and drive and anyway had proven too resistant even to minor alternations and had obstructed change for too long. Reassuring myths would have to give way to scientific assessments. Cherished dogmas would have to be tested by performance. Existing practices would have to be evaluated against possible better alternatives. Public organizations needed to be better managed by their public executives. The public's business needed to be handled in a more businesslike manner. The public sector had to give better value for the public resources invested and altogether the rising costs of government had to be halted. Above all, the condescension of the bureaucratic elites, often bordering on arrogance, that made for hierarchical autocracy, rules application without commonsense, rude, insensitive indifferent performance, self-interest, inefficiency and incompetence, had to be ended. And it was to be ended by a strong dose of managerialism, i.e. the public sector adoption of theories and practices developed in private industry.

At first, there were few signs of the incipient managerial revolution in the public service. The exposure of public maladministration, empire-building (bloated staffing), bureaupathologies (elongated hierarchies, excessive rules, uncommon sense), and more surprisingly, fraud and corruption, by administrative law reforms, ombudsman offices and new efficiency audits, along with the customary public-service bashing of the mass media, was deliberately exploited so that public and political support for reform could be rallied, that a climate receptive to change would be created, and that there could be no further tolerance of abuses (Wilenski, 1986). A new class of young technocrats was advancing into positions of power and influence in all walks of life and was rising to the challenge of turning the public sector around,. Still, the reforms seemed somewhat along conventional lines and quite moderate. In the Hawke (Labor) Government's administration reform policy statement (Commonwealth of Australia, 1983), there was almost no mention of managerialism or managers as such except in a general title (Ibid, 3) and a proposal to produce an annual management improvement plan (Ibid, 7). The intention was to develop an administration that would be more responsive and accountable to elected politicians, that would be more efficient and effective, that would give all citizens equal opportunity to compete for public employment, and that would have a more streamlined and independent system for protecting staff rights, through a new Senior Executive Service (S.E.S.), central resource allocation and review (financial management improvement programs and plans – F.M.I.P.s and program budgeting – P.P.B.S.) and new personnel policies, much on the lines of the American, British and Canadian reforms. Indeed, the state governments in New South Wales (Wran), South Australia (Tonkin), and Victoria (Cain) had already prepared the way.

What was to be the big surprise was that traditionally anti-business Labor governments looked to business, business consultants, business models, and business practices for their inspiration, and took the wind right out of the opposition's sails. Labor's slogan in the 1982 election campaign in Victoria had actually been "To Run the State Like a Business" (Halligan and O'Grady, 1985, 41) and newly elected Premier Cain made plain the businesslike aspirations of his government (Davis et al., 1989). Public administration had not been operating its businesses as if they were businesses and the rest of the state sector lacked the competence, efficiency and vitality of private enterprises. An injection of the business approach would be a desirable stimulant to improving public sector performance and raising the productivity of the public bureaucracy. So governments – Labor and non-Labor – sought the best business advice they could get. They employed reputable business consultants and multinational corporation experts in business and accounting methods to investigate public organizations and produce management plans and strategies, notably David Block who the Prime Minister described as the "toughest, leanest, meanest, most efficient bloke in the private sector" (*Canberra Times*, June 19, 1987). They brought business managers into the higher echelons of the public bureaucracy for policy direction and managerial direction. They insisted that public organizations adopt and adapt business methods (or more businesslike methods) in their operations. They redesigned and restructured the machinery of government more on the lines of the best business practices. They demanded that public administrators be managers skilled in scientific management, speaking management language, practicing management skills, thinking in managerial concepts, and working according to management models (cost cutting, performance measures, management by objectives, computerization, strategic management, efficiency, scrutiny). The aim was to develop a climate in which public managers felt they had control over what they did, that they could assume a "take-charge" mode, and take action on their own initiative, and to build a supporting system that encouraged them and trusted them to act promptly and take personal responsibility for what was done.

Despite practical differences and variations among seven government systems (the federal and six states), the principles of public sector reform were quite similar and very much along managerialistic lines.

* **The Corporate board identity**: the cabinet takes full command of management decisions and policies, in consultation with relevant interests and on the basis of informed analysis and advice; it is supported by cabinet committees, particularly a priorities, planning and strategy committee that determines and uses the budget as a planning instrument, a corporate plan for the whole government; it employs experts and policy advisers independent of the

bureaucracy, and it hires and fires the chief executives of government bodies and agencies; it stresses a purely instrumentalist role of public bureaucracy; it curbs the public's right to know in preference to technical rationality;

* **Streamlining the corporate organization**: amalgamation and consolidation of government bodies and agencies, rationalization of structures, elimination of duplication and overlapping of activities; together with so-called interdepartmental coordinating committees and institutionalized policy differences, to provide opportunities for improved budgetary and corporate management processes and for savings from economies of scale, and speed decision-making; enhance ministerial control; more coherent policy-making and more integrated program delivery mechanisms;
* **Managing or executive directors**: ministers will take charge, run their agencies, direct policy, influence attitudes, style and corporate culture, improve communications, develop teamwork, and generally exercise a leadership role (establish priorities, set directions and goals, make key strategic decisions, assist in assessing performance and achievements); they enter into annual performance contracts with their organizational heads which set out targets and objectives and ensure that these correlate with the government's broader priorities; they set fiscal limits;
* **Service-wide financial and personnel management systems**: central control agencies (e.g. Public Service Boards) are reduced or abolished and replaced by policy advising, monitoring agencies that allow operating agencies to take full control of what they do providing they follow universal, standardized guidelines and procedures, in the case of personnel, the merit system, and in the case of finance, program budgeting, forward planning, performance indicators and efficiency audits; the emphasis is on E.P.E.E. (economy, productivity, efficiency, effectiveness) and redeployment of public resources to where they can be used best; efficiency dividends, asset management, staffing controls, economic forecasting;
* **Managerial elitism**: the S.E.S. is output oriented, proactive performance management, mobile throughout the public sector through job rotation, recruited laterally as necessary, compensated by evaluated performance, rewarded for exceptional performance, management professionals, allowed to manage and expected to manage with flexibility, risk, entrepreneurship and the chance to refine management and policy advice skills, evaluate progress and priorities, measure achievement against objectives;
* **Debureaucratization**: decentralization; flatten hierarchies; eliminate over-regulation; reduce paperwork; institutionalize efficiency scrutinies; employ rational procedures; simplify operations; integrate common services, share locations, effect savings, adopt risk management concepts, delegate more, and generally adopt more businesslike attitudes, reduce borrowing and cut costs; sunset legislation; improved service at counter level;

* **Commercialization**: product definition; cost-effective-ness; user charges; carry over funds; public enterprises are expected to pay their way, make adequate returns on their capital, and reduce non- economic considerations in service delivery; public authorities are expected to operate along accepted commercial principles; greater private sector involvement in non-core activities which are not national monopolies; reduced bureaucratic controls over operations; liability for same taxes as private companies; improve public image; and hold out the threat of privatization, contracting out and deregulation;
* **Managerial culture**: bureaucratic power based on the ability to prove efficiency not political infighting; greater personal freedom of action and accountability; performance incentives and rewards; fostering of more radical/innovative approaches; getting value for money; linking costs and benefits; corporate planning; performance agreements; institutionalized management improvement schemes; continuous reform impacts; fear of calamity if seen as standing still; utilization of human and financial resources; maximizing investments; living within means; regeneration of public infrastructure; devaluation of whistle-blowing, intricate due process, and time-consuming appeals.

The extent to which these principles had impacted public administration was seen in the approach taken by the Purchasing Reforms Group of the federal Department of Administrative Services in reforming the purchase system in 1989. It had been brought about by a lengthy review under the Financial Management Improvement Program (F.M.I.P.) which had found the system too regulatory and prescriptive, too concerned with processes rather than their outcomes, too outdated, too costly, too prolonged, too contributive to a culture of risk avoidance rather than risk management. Purchasing reforms required long-term changes of the rules and the prevailing administrative culture and attitudes. The reform strategy was to

* recognize value for money as the prime objective of purchasing;
* use a professional approach involving better practices and well trained staff to improve purchasing performance;
* adopt the principle of open and effective competition as the guide to purchasing, and avoid unnecessary prescription;
* provide a central framework of policy and ministerial guidelines within which departments should operate;
* leave detailed control of purchasing largely to be determined by management in departments. (*Directions in Government*, Sept. 1989, 28)

While retaining the public service principles of probity, accountability and fair dealing, the new reform program was "aimed at applying a totally new philosophy of sensible business practice and management flexibility to one of the most rule-bound areas in the public sector...too long...relegated to a largely untrained staff who have had to rely on horse and buggy procedures in their dealings in increasingly competitive arenas" (Ibid, 3).

> The approach of the reforms is to instil a confidence in government and industry, the buyer and seller, understanding how each works; how the government can make best use of the what the market can offer, and how the market can equip itself effectively to supply to government. (Ibid)

The reform involved new guidelines for procurement planning, staged procurement, the use of specifications, and post-offer negotiations, changes in legislation, detailing of performance measures, education of departments and business, and professional training of procurement staff with the emphasis "on how to do business well, not on how to avoid doing it badly" (Ibid, 31).

By 1987, the emphasis had been placed so much on managerialism that its critics feared that administrative reform was in danger of being reduced to managerial reform (Yeatman, 1987, 341), that the old Weberian iron cage was being replaced by a new managerial iron cage of modernized red-tapism (Yeatman and Bryson, 1987), that public administration would be retitled public management (Painter, 1988, 1), and that sooner or later government itself would be turned into a business. An intellectual counter-attack backed by public sector professionals and public leaders not enamored with business practices together with some loss of reform momentum prevented managerialism going that far but the writing was clearly on the wall for public service traditionalists who feared the triumph of technique over purpose, style over substance, Theory X over Theory Y, public management over public service, politicization over public accountability, internal priorities of budget management over external impacts of program goals and outcomes, economic rationality over administrative sensitivity. The toning down of some corporate reforms reconciled traditionalists to the assimilation of irreversible changes.

These same points have been made about New Zealand's new style public managerialism which was also adopted as a remedy to economic woes. As in Australia, New Zealand's economy until the 1970s had been able to flourish through favorable balance of payments for its primary products and ability to raise loans to cover public sector expenditures. When the balance of trade reversed, inflation and unemployment increased and public expenditures meant budget deficits and growing indebtedness and a run on the currency just as the new Lange Labour Government took office in 1984. It decided to reduce state regulation of the economy (cut tariffs, float the currency, deregulate finance), increase government control over the public sector, cut public spending, direct public policy, reform the taxation system, reduce non-essential services, and reexamine the role of the state in the economy, including the extent of public ownership and enterprise, the level of public sector productivity and performance, and the lack of incentives in the public sector to improve accountability, efficiency and economic performance. All these issues had been raised in the previous decade in government reports, especially the 1978 Report of the Controller and Auditor General (Shailes) and the 1984 Report of the Public Expenditure Committee (Neilson).

In tackling these issues, the Treasury under the leadership of Roger Douglas, took the initiative. Before the 1984 election, it had prepared a briefing, under the title of *Economic Management*, for the incoming government containing an assessment of the economic situation and outlining steps that ought to be taken. It clearly preferred a market economy and pointed to the need to distinguish between "market" and "non-market" activities of government, pointing out that most departments had no clearly defined goals, management plan, performance measures and controls, managerial freedom, accountability, and incentives. The Lange Government made economic reform one of its major targets. The level of public spending was considered too high at 41 percent of G.D.P. and high taxation was seen as a major drag on economic growth by penalizing innovation, efficiency, hard work and saving, and by diverting people's attention and efforts towards tax avoidance. The priorities were reduced public spending and tax reform. Furthermore, if the government expected business to become more competitive in world markets instead of relying on government patronage, the government must also ensure that its goods and services were provided as competitively and efficiently as possible. This meant putting a stop to continuing to finance public projects that were quite unprofitable and piling up huge debts such as N.Z. Steel Development, Marsden Point Refinery and Synfuels, among the large number of public companies, public corporations and government departments that provided public goods and services. These included "four banks, three transport companies, a hotel chain, a large portion of the country's forests and land surface, and several insurance companies, as well as being involved in broadcasting, construction, mining, manufacturing, telecommunications, energy production and distribution, and research and development" (Boston, 1988, 71-2). It would also end subsidizing inefficiencies in government operations. So the first task was to separate the public from the private sector and then within the public sector, separate the commercial from the policy and regulatory functions. Once that was done, the government then applied commercial principles to the commercial enterprises, in a policy of *corporatization*.

Corporatization was not privatization but the removal of the trading activities of government organizations into state corporate structures with full commercial objectives, rights and responsibilities. Their poor performance in the past had resulted from unclear roles, conflicting objectives, burdensome controls, lack of commercial freedom and inadequate incentive structures. As autonomous financial entities legally separate from the Crown, they were in future to operate as successful businesses, run by boards largely composed of successful business executives, and placed on a sound commercial footing exactly as their private sector counterparts. These new state owned enterprises (S.O.E.s) would no longer enjoy unfair commercial privileges but would have to pay taxes and dividends to the government. After fixing their existing assets and debts, they would be required to fund their activities from commercial returns and private sector loans and would be required to recover their costs from users, including the government, instead of providing them free or below cost at the taxpayers' expense. If the government wanted an S.O.E. to provide non-commercial goods and services, it would have to pay the S.O.E. Among the more important S.O.E.s created have been Electricorp, Telecom, Forestcorp, Landcorp, Post Office Bank, N.Z. Post, Airways Corporation of N.Z. and Coal Corp, none of which have had to be subsidized.

It was not until the second term of the Lange Government in 1987 that corporatization was followed by managerialism similar to that in Australia for the rest of the public (or "core" or "rump") service, namely reorganization of the government, central financial and policy direction, value-for-money (V.F.M.) auditing, introduction of the S.E.S., debureaucratization, decentralization, the radical State Sector Reform Act of 1988 (which replaced public service legislation first enacted in 1912 and overhauled in 1962) aimed "to impart a new spirit into the public service...(and) to bring appropriate private sector practices into the public service...proven in value through a long process of refinement and honing in a competitive environment" (Rodger, 1988, 2), the privatization of public personnel management, the new departmental chief executives (appointed on contract) given responsibility for key managerial functions and judged by their results, retrenchments, increased lateral recruitment, performance incentives, accrual accounting, the complete reform of local government along similar managerial lines, and increased devolution of social services.

> ...the Government is viewed as having two separate interests in all departments:
>
> * the interests of a purchaser of goods and services; and
> * the interests of an owner, or financier.
>
> As an owner the Government seeks a clearer accounting for the management of the capital in a department and, where possible, the return on funds invested. Departments are seen as holders of capital assets, often largely human capital, and are required to account clearly for the investments and divestments which add or reduce this stock. Accounting for depreciation is viewed as generally necessary. As a purchaser of goods and services, the Government seeks to ensure that outputs are clearly identified, are efficiently produced, and have the required effect on outcomes, i.e. are 'effective'. (Chapman, 1989, 46)

Public sector managers would have the same freedom to manage as private sector managers but they would also be held strictly accountable for their performance to the government by strengthened central policy and administrative controls and evaluations. This radical change was made with confidence that public employees would respond well and that the hidden talent in the public sector would more than cope with the transformation of public administration and would quickly adjust and seize the new opportunities presented. Public managers would be held to account not for what they bought but whether they did what they said they would. Public money would be for the costs of producing specific goods and services, not for buying specified inputs with separate budgets for capital purchases and transfer payments. The government would decide what outcomes it wanted and then buy goods and services from departments or non-government suppliers and press departments to rid themselves of assets they did not strictly need (such as the defence forces which owned much underused land and many buildings). The Treasury would issue half yearly and yearly government balance sheets.

The new state service did have a theoretical foundation, not in traditional public administration and management, but in political economy and business, particularly the theory of agency problems in firms (addressing the problems of getting agents such as managers and employees to pursue the interests of their principals), public choice theory's application of economic analysis to bureaucratic behavior, and contract theory (Scott and Gorringe, 1989). Where government activities were difficult or impossible to turn into profit-making corporations (as in the case of the S.O.E.s), they were to be made more efficient and responsive by (i) making chief executives more directly accountable to ministers for the output and efficiency of their departments, (ii) giving chief executives greater managerial discretion shifting emphasis from controls on the inputs used to outputs, (iii) distinguishing between specific outputs and outcomes or success in achieving overall social goals, and (iv) instituting financial accountability based on accrual accounting of inputs and on output measures, thereby moving toward arrangements found in the private sector to help overcome agency problems.

> Under the new system, the performance of bureaucrats can be judged on whether they produce the outputs of services agreed to, and whether they do so efficiently. Politicians can be judged on whether they buy the right services to achieve social goals like wealth, justice and the relief of suffering. The distinction also highlights the fact that politicians need not buy the services they require from the bureaucracy, and that the government need not be the only customer of the bureaucracy. (Ibid, 6-7)

The departments were still expected to be good employers, to treat their employees fairly and properly, to provide good and safe working conditions, to ensure equal employment opportunities, and to recognize the claims of special groups (Maoris, women, handicapped, and other minorities) as well as follow merit principles, protective personal grievance procedures, and labor relations awards and agreements (including compulsory arbitration provisions), under the watchful eye of the State Services Commission. To reinforce these public sector personnel changes, the Public Finance Act was overhauled in 1989 to stress outputs and performance, allow ministers to make performance contracts with their chief executives, and rework financial accounts on a commercial basis with a new format for budgets.

Would the public sector respond to this new system? A former manager in British Telecom operations appointed head of the New Zealand Telecom Corporation, a poorly run state owned enterprise, shrivelled the elongated hierarchy, abolished the head office in favor of five independent network companies with new imported managers to run them, cut down costs by contracting out and staff retrenchment, and developed new products. Despite Treasury opposition, he spent money to earn money and by all accounts improved services at a cost, as people found out in other previously subsidized public goods and services corporatized or privatized in a New Zealand where Mrs. Thatcher had been out-Thatchered by a Labour government. All this was too much for the hard left wing of the government which broke away to form the New Labour Party and the outspoken opposition to the government's market approach to the public sector, also lamented even by official reports that believed social concerns had been sacrificed to economic restructuring.

Public employees with no alternative employment gritted their teeth and went along with the changes, though their unions have not been at all happy with the strange turn of events from their political viewpoint and with their loss of bargaining power as public sector organizations were fragmented and paralyzed. In just five years, the core public service had been more than halved. On the other hand, the Coal Corporation had increased output with only half its previous staff and was making a profit for the first time in twenty years. The Electricity Corporation had tripled its profits with stable prices and New Zealand Post turned its financial position around also with stable prices. Even the core public service had been able to make productivity improvements through better resource allocation without any noticeable effect on the quality of service provided, so the Minister of Finance confidently believed (Caygill, 1989, 10).

Possibly, New Zealand has gone much further into managerialism than other countries. The government realized that it did not have to provide goods and services itself if it could ensure that services were provided equitably. Naturally this raised the question that if the S.O.E.s were wholly commercial, why should they be public? Furthermore, why could not regional and local authority trading activities (L.A.T.A.s) also be converted to S.O.E.s and sold off to reduce public debts? In 1987, the Lange Government did begin to sell parts of public companies (Bank of New Zealand, Petrocorp, New Zealand Steel). With the Minister for State-Owned Enterprises known to favor privatization as was Treasury, it came as no surprise that as from 1988, public assets were being sold off (Boston, 1988) to raise NZ $14 billion by 1992. Furthermore, the philosophy behind the public service reforms spelled out in the 1987 Treasury document *Government Management* was being followed in such a way that the traditional career structure was less important and the new style managerialism was bringing quite a different kind of administrator through, the tough minded rationalist rather than the politically astute public interest servant. Bad medicine had to be administered to New Zealand to relieve some of its economic woes, and it needed willful, skillful, and enterprising practitioners to continue the treatment.

Containing Kasumigaseki

Japan's success in overtaking the U.S.A. as the world's leading economic power sent business executives and managers flocking to Japan to discover the secrets of its success and to examine Japanese management methods. How had Japan done what it did? Could Japanese policies and methods be copied? Westerners certainly discovered a different administrative culture and a different business atmosphere. For a time, Japanese business methods became quite a fad. Theory Z management boomed along with other Japanese practices, such as work quality circles (Ouchi, 1981). Very few looked at the Japanese public sector and how that was being managed. Maybe it was just as well; they may not have liked what they saw. The Japanese administrative elite (Kasumigaseki) was more elitist than Whitehall, probably more "closed, secretive, defensive, over-concerned with tradition and precedent" than its British counterpart (Hennessy, 1989, 687). It was also not as good as it should have been given its talent, and it was a drag on the private sector with its excessive formalism and bureaucratism. No doubt too it suffered from bureaupathologies that ought to be rooted out, so thought Yasuhiro Nakasone who was to rise from the position of the Director General of the Administrative Management Agency into the Cabinet and then in 1982 to become Prime Minister and knew both administrative and political worlds well.

It "was Nakasone's initiative in 1980 which resulted in creation [sic] of the Provisional Commission on Administrative Reform (Rinji Gyosei Chosa Kai or RINCHO) in March 1981" (Wright and Sakurai, 1987, 122) as an advisory council to the Prime Minister. Triggered by the fiscal crisis it was a Hoover style investigation with many committees and subcommittees composed of outsiders. It had its own executive office with a large staff seconded from across the public sector and notably the Administrative Management Agency which was the central management agency responsible for promoting administrative reform in the public sector. It had the highest political backing, broad terms of reference, and strong support from the business community, particularly as it was chaired by the charismatic Toshio Doko, honorary president of the Japanese Federation of Economic Organizations, who was to chair RINCHO's successor, the Administrative Reform Promotion Committee (GYOKAKUSHIN) from 1983 to 1986, when it temporarily went out of existence to be revived in 1987 for another three years.

Unlike administrative reform inquiries usually in the West, RINCHO's examination of the public sector covered both ends as well as means, national goals and policies as well as the machinery of government and public administration. It had distinctly ideological or philosophical overtones that sought to curtail Kasumigaseki or at least contain it, reduce its influence in Japanese society, and make it more directly accountable and responsible (and responsive) to the public. It also had a practical program to lower public expenditures, to balance the budget without tax increases, to reduce public subsidies especially to the railways, rice growers and health service providers, to privatize profitable state owned enterprises, and to devolve and decentralize government activities. Not surprisingly it recommended decrementalism, retrenchment, cutbacks, debureaucratization, devolution, privatization, and structural reorganization not only in the central government but in intergovernmental management too.

RINCHO's proposals were immediately aired and daily they were the focus of extensive public debate. The Nakasone Government which favored RINCHO's recommendations could modify them according to public reactions and it had the machinery in place or was to put the machinery in place to implement them during the 1980s. After RINCHO's first emergency report in March 1981, it issued four others, including its fundamental report in July 1982 and the final report in March 1983. Over the following six or so years, the following reforms were implemented:

* Cabinet Secretariat (Office) reorganized for policy coordination;
* Management and Coordination Agency replaced the Administrative Management Agency to strengthen central management and coordination in July 1984;
* National Government Organization Law amended to allow greater freedom and flexibility in restructuring the machinery of government and reorganizing public bodies; "scrap and build" principle;
* Reorganization of the major central government ministries and agencies; consolidation, streamlining simplification of line organizations; abolition of excessive local offices;
* Personnel reduction plans renewed to achieve 5 percent retrenchment by 1986 and another 5 percent by 1992; reallocation of staff according to workload; compulsory retirement set at age 60;
* Revision of recruitment examination system; training programs; inter-sector mobility; staff rotation;
* Privatization of the three giants – Japanese National Railways, Nippon Telegraph and Telephone, and Japan Tobacco and Salt, and other state owned enterprises and joint ventures; corporatization of public business enterprises;
* Establishment of the Committee on Regulation to deregulate service industries;

* Establishment of large numbers of advisory councils *(shingikais),* conferences, research and study groups; an ombudsman system; greater access to information;
* Reorganization and restructuring central-local government relationships;
* Rationalization of service delivery (social services, postal service, etc.); mechanization of delivery systems;
* Zero-ceiling on budget requests (frozen budgets); retrenchment; economy;
* Computerization of government information systems; protection of personal data and freedom of information; updated technology; coordinated and integrated data collection; office automation. (Ohashi, 1989).

Actually, as impressive as these reforms appear, they may not have been as drastic as the shock treatment administered to the central government administration by an earlier management-oriented RINCHO chaired by Kiichiro Sato in the early 1960s. They had been wider in scope and strongly supported by the business community.

The reforms were aimed at cheaper and simpler government rather than administrative or managerial efficiency which had characterized previous spates of reform and had already resulted in 1982 with less than half the number of public employees per thousand population than in the United Kingdom and one third less than in the U.S.A. (Ku Tashiro, 1986). Their implementation did not immediately halt large government deficits, growing government indebtedness and large interest repayments, imbedded corruption at the highest levels of government, and bureaucratic dominance of public policy-making. In all this, rarely was any mention made of "Japanese management". Probably it was assumed that senior public officials in Japan were (and had always been) expected to devote their lives to government service, to work extremely hard and long hours, to set an example to their juniors of skills, knowledge and maturity, to share decision making with interested and affected parties by signing the *ringi-sho* (proposal sheet), participating in the *teuchishiki* (ritual celebration of reconciliation between disputants) and reallocating surplus staff, and to be accountable personally for group performance (Ouchi, 1986). Apart from the ritual, these managerial norms did not differ much from those being inculcated elsewhere in the West. In contrast with other Western countries, the Japanese did not believe that their administrative values needed that much changing but then again Japanese practices did not seem much different from the West (Thurow, 1985). RINCHO was an attempt to introduce into government the practices Japanese business believe had contributed to Japan's economic sucess and to substitute more of a top-down policy making approach than the consensual bottom-up *ring-sho.*

Changing Cautious Bureaucrats Into Enterprising Managers

While the East Bloc was engrossed in reworking fundamentals, the West had largely settled the shape of the liberal democratic administrative state despite rhetoric to the contrary – a mixed enterprise economy, a welfare society, redistributive taxation, state intervention to minimize social costs and conserve resources, state amelioration of environmental ills, and state promotion of employment, technology, and research and development. A substantial part of the economy would be in public hands and a sizable portion of the labor force would work for public organizations. Despite privatization, deregulation and debureaucratization and emerging cutbacks and retrenchment, the administrative state would not be drastically reduced. Although some functions might be dropped, others would be added. Even if the center were streamlined and slimmed, the periphery would expand and assume greater responsibilities for directly servicing local needs. Baring emergencies there was little beyond administrative reform. After all, the West was not changing the nature of the administrative state or abandoning its entrenched leadership or tackling more complicated things like the East Bloc.

A sticking point in the West was an inherited bureaucratic ethos, a seemingly timeless administrative culture that went back several generations and in the most hardened cases further back into the nineteenth century even to the Napoleonic era when the modern state bureaucracy was being formulated on para-military lines. Weber's ideal model still held up for the contemporary administrative state. His fears about bureaucratization had all been realized and even Kafkaesque shadows fell over Western public administration. Officiousness could be found even in the best of public organizations, especially the self-important bureaucrats who hindered more than helped, who got in the way instead of getting on with the job, who blocked action rather than found ways of removing obstacles to what needed doing. In the late twentieth century, these were now old-fashioned attitudes that belonged in museums of administrative history. A different, more enterprising administrative ethos was required.

To change administrative attitudes, beliefs, norms and values entailed a fundamental change in the prevailing administrative culture. Cautious bureaucrats had to be replaced by enterprising managers. Such was the objective behind much administrative reform in the West in the 1980s. It was pursued by retrenching and retiring the worst of the old guard who set such an antiquated example, by replacing them or placing over or beside them outsiders with the right or better attitudes, by retraining and reeducating the savable, the ambitious and the amenable, by browbeating, threatening and cajoling the unbending, by organizing, restructuring, reequipping and rearranging to give insiders no option than going along with the new, by offering incentives and rewards to those who changed, by breaking up clans, fiefdoms and cliques, by advancing a new generation of upward mobile "with it" opportunists, by spelling out the new order in great detail so that there would be no mistake, by employing shock tactics, by introducing islands of excellence, by insisting on a new style professionalism, and by a whole host of other strategies, old and new. The trouble was that irrespective of the methods used, the objective itself had not been properly thought out. It seemed to have been stumbled onto rather than deliberately planned. To change administrative cultures in less than a generation required a much clearer definition of the objective, a long term, well-thought out strategy, and a great deal of preparation.

Instead, the hazy idea of letting public managers really manage was not properly thought out. Presumably, it meant freeing managers in public organizing to manage as they saw fit. Did it mean granting as much freedom as their private counterparts to hire and fire, make and break contracts, attract or reject new business, write off debts and renege on loans, and abandon unprofitable activities without warning? If not, just how much freedom would be allowed and what controls would be exercised over them? Since most did not operate under market conditions, had no rivals and would not be replaced, what incentives would make them perform better, when they would be subject to strict centralized controls over policy, finance, audits, resource allocation and performance measures? Just where would the line be drawn between central political/policy directives and decentralized managerial discretion? If they failed to exercise discretion properly, how could the damage be confined? How could public organizations operate in contradiction to the government and to one another? To what extent should purely *managerial* values dominate public administration? Who would decide and how were they to be held publicly responsible and accountable?

In this new territory for public administration, there were no ready answers. Each country would have to feel its way and find answers that best fit its peculiar circumstances. But the conditions for such important changes were hardly auspicious. Impatient governments were in a hurry. They could not wait for the cautious bureaucrats. Instead they brought their own people in to hurry things along. Immediately, they were accused of politicization which of course they denied. Nonetheless, fears were raised that they wished to go back to the bad old days of the spoils system and this was their hidden agenda, otherwise why would they have sprung so many surprises, disregarded so many conventions and broken so many time-honored rules? Why had they been so quick to remove this person and appoint that one instead? Once the rumor mill was started, it could not be halted and thereafter every government action was suspected, examined and reexamined, especially after so much public vilification of public employees had been encouraged by the self same governments which had strained relations by depriviligizing the public sector. What kind of incentives were these? On the one hand, government promised a new deal for public managers and on the other, they pushed public employees who had alternatives to shift to the private sector. Worse still, they did not seem to care about the collapse of morale in the public sector, hardly creating an atmosphere receptive to a new administrative ethos. They merely succeeded in putting public employees on the defensive.

And what about all the broken promises? The new administrative ethos was to be accompanied by a whole raft of inducements and provisions. Training and (re-)education facilities were to be available to the new breed of public managers. But what was provided in many countries was inadequate, if not quite pathetic. The new merit pay systems rarely materialized and when they did, they were politically manipulated (or so it was believed) or laughable when compared with the private sector. As to following good (let alone the best) private management practices, that was lost to cost savings and power struggles with public employee unions. When public managers attempted to be ruthless in pursuit of the new managerialism, governments would retreat and give in to the public and to public employee protests. When they attempted to reveal the real costs of government promises and decisions, they were intimidated into silence. What was the point of saving millions managerially when tens of millions were wasted politically? What was the point of doing things better at higher prices when they probably were not worth doing at all? Then what was one to make of the outsiders who brought with them their private business ethics of cutting corners, making deals, skirting the law, and generally acting just this side of criminality?

The new managerialism drove a greater wedge between line and staff and between managers and other public employees. The public managers imposed more and more managerial requirements on those who actually performed the work of government on the line. The line staff had to divert more attention and resources to managerial requests and directions and increasingly they complained with justification about their being unable to do their proper job such as teaching school children, attending to the sick and needy, reducing street crimes, and so forth. They felt themselves being manipulated into grandiose managerial schemes that were not adequately explained to them, in which they had not really shared (or been allowed to share), and that appeared so neat and tidy on paper but were quite impractical out in the field. Whenever the managers tried to exercise their greater freedom to manage, this was seen as diminishing public employees' rights; they just raised internal conflict levels. When the frustrated managerial butterflies flew off, who was left to pick up the pieces of their poor judgment, incompetence and all too often self-exploitation of organizational assets?

Most recognized that public sector performance needed improvement. Most welcomed the assault on obvious bureaupathologies. The old order had few supporters; everyone was glad to see its demise. But few were quite prepared for the upsets, dislocations and wanderings of a hastily imposed new order.

Governments blundered into something that sounded so good and once committed they could not easily back out. They had to go on regardless and hope that somehow solutions would be found for every new difficulty that arose. There was no going back. Governments had gone too far and nobody save the reactionary was prepared to go back. The new order was feeling its way. Mistakes were made but they were also corrected. Governments had not realized the greater ramifications. If public organizations had to behave themselves, and behave much better than private organizations, then political parties and governments also had to behave themselves. If the private sector was unable to absorb excess public employees, then the public sector had to reemploy them or redistribute them to avoid increasing unemployment. If the public sector was not given adequate resources to do what it was supposed to do, then all suffered, sometimes in terrible ways too late to avoid. The task ahead for the West was to fine tune the delicate balance between too little public administration and too much and to raise reform sights once again above purely internal managerial considerations to the much larger underlying obstacles to administrative performance inherent in outmoded institutions and unprincipled politics.

References

Barkley. B., "Management Reform: Back to Basics", *The Bureaucrat*, Vol. 13, No. 3, Fall 1983, pp. 3-5.

Boston, J., "From Corporatisation to Privatisation: Public Sector Reform in New Zealand", *Canberra Bulletin of Public Administration*, No. 57, Dec. 1988, pp. 71-86.

Campbell, C., and Peters, G.B. (eds.), *Organizing Governance, Governing Organizations*, University of Pittsburgh Press, Pittsburgh, 1988.

Caygill, D., Speech to the N.Z./U.K. Conference on Economic and Social Policy Reform, released by Ministry of Finance, Parliament Buildings, Wellington, September 16, 1989.

Chapman, L., *Your Disobedient Servant*, Chatto and Windus, London, 1978.

Chapman, R., "Core Public Sector Reform in New Zealand and the United Kingdom", *Public Money & Management*, Spring 1989, pp. 44-49.

Commonwealth of Australia, *Reforming the Australian Public Service*, Australian Government Publishing Service, Canberra, A.C.T., December 1983.

Davis, G., et al. (eds.), *Corporate Management in Australian Government: Reconciling Accountability and Efficiency*, MacMillan Co. of Australia, Melbourne, 1989.

Directions in Government (Australia), "Purchasing Reform", Vol. 3, No. 8, September 1989, pp. 3, 28-38.

Dunsire, A., and Hood, C., *Cutback Management in Public Bureaucracies*, University of Cambridge Press, Cambridge, 1989.

The Economist Vol. 315, No 7658, June 9, 1990, "Hope after the hop", pp. 57-58

Efficiency Unit, *Improving Management in Government: The Next Steps*, H.M.S.O., London, 1988.

Farazmand, A., "Crisis in the U.S. Administrative State", *Administration and Society*, Vol. 21, No. 2, Aug 1989, pp. 173-199.

Fry, G., "The Thatcher Government, The Financial Management Initiative, and the 'New Civil Service'", *Public Administration*, Vol. 66, No. 1, Spring 1988, pp. 1-20.

Fry, G., et al., "Symposium on Improving Management in Government", *Public Administration*, Vol 66, No. 4, Winter 1988, pp. 429-445.

Fudge, C., and Gustafsson, L., "Administrative Reform and Public Management in Sweden and the United Kingdom," *Public Money & Management*, Summer 1989, pp. 29-34.

Goodsell, C.T., "The Grace Commission: Seeking Efficiency for the Whole People?" *Public Administration Review*, Vol. 44, No. 3, May-June, 1986, pp. 196-204.

Governance, Vol. 3 No. 2, April 1990, Special Issue on Managerial Reform, pp 115-218.

Gow, I., "Diffusion of Administrative Innovations in Canadian Public Administration", paper presented at the Biennial Meeting of the Association for Canadian Studies in the United States, San Francisco, November 20, 1989.

Gray, A., and Jenkins, W., "Policy Analysis in British Central Government: The Experience of PAR", *Public Administration*, Vol. 60, No. 4, Winter 1982, pp. 429-450.

Greenaway, J. R., "Bureaucrats Under Pressure: The Thatcher Government and the Mandarin Elite", *Teaching Politics*, Vol. 13, No. 1, Jun 1984, pp. 66-83.

Halligan, J., and O'Grady, M., "Public Sector Reform: Exploring the Victorian Experience", *Australian Journal of Public Administration*, Vol. 44, No. 1, March 1985, pp. 34-45.

Harrison, A., and Gretton, J. (eds.), *Reshaping Central Government*, Policy Journals/ Transaction Books, New Brunswick, N.J., 1987.

Hennessy, P., *Whitehall*, Secker & Warburg, London, 1989.

Hofmeister, A. (ed.), *Efficiency in the Public Sector – An International Symposium*, Swiss Association of Administrative Sciences, Series 8, Berne, 1988.

Ingraham, P., and Ban, C., *Legislating Bureaucratic Change: The Civil Service Reform Act of 1978*, State University of New York Press, Albany, 1984.

James, M. (ed.), *Restricting Leviathan: Small Government in Practice*, The Centre for Independent Studies, St. Leonards, N.S.W., 1987.

Jeffries, R., "Local Government: Reform and Change", *Public Money and Management*, Summer 1989, pp. 23-28.

Kellner, P. and Crowther-Hunt, N., *The Civil Servants*, MacDonald Futura Publishers, London, 1980.

Kelman, S., "The Grace Commission: How Much Waste?" *The Public Interest*, No. 78, Winter 1985, pp. 62-82.

Ku Tashiro, "Administrative Reform in Contemporary Japan", paper presented to the Symposium on Japanese Management, A.S.P.A. Convention, Anaheim, CA., April 1986.

Kymlicka, B.B. and Matthews, J.R. (eds.), *The Reagan Revolution?*, The Dorsey Press, Chicago, 1988.

Lane, J. (ed.), *Bureaucracy and Public Choice*, Sage Modern Politics Series Vol. 15, London, 1987.

Leemans, A., "Recent Trends: The Career Service in European Countries, *International Review of Administrative Sciences*, Vol. 53, No. 1, 1987, pp. 63-88.

MacAvoy, P.W., et al., *Privatization and State Owned Enterprises: Lessons from the United States, Great Britain and Canada*, Kluwer Academic Publishers, New York, 1989.

March, J.G. and Olsen, J.P., *Rediscovering Institutions: The Organizational Basis of Politics*, Free Press, New York, 1989.

Metcalfe, L., and Richards, S., *Improving Public Management*, European Institute of Public Administration, Sage Publications, 1987.

Moe, R.C., "Traditional Organizational Principles and the Managerial Presidency: From Phoenix to Ashes," *Public Administration Review*, Vol. 50, No. 2, March-April 1990, pp. 129-140.

National Academy of Public Administration, *Revitalizing Federal Management: Managers and their Overburdened Systems*, Washington, D.C., 1983.

Ohashi, T., "Information and Administrative Reform in the Government of Japan," *International Review of Administrative Sciences*, Vol. 55, No. 4, 1989, pp. 587-602.

Ouchi, M., "A Japanese View of Japanese Management", paper presented to the Symposium on Japanese Management, A.S.P.A. Convention, Anaheim, CA., 1986.

Ouchi, W., *Theory Z*, Addison-Wesley Publishing Company, Reading Ma., 1981.

Painter, M., "Editorial:– Public Management: Fad or Fallacy?", *Australian Journal of Public Administration*, Vol. 47, No. 1, March 1988, pp. 1-3.

Parkinson, M. (ed.), *Reshaping Local Government*, Policy Journals/Transaction Books, New Brunswick, N.J., 1987.

Plumptre, T., *Beyond the Bottom Line: Management in Government*, The Institute for Research on Public Policy, South Halifax, Nova Scotia, 1988.

Rayner, D., "A Battle Won in the War on the Paper Bureaucracy", *Harvard Business Review*, Vol. 53 , No. 1, Jan-Feb, 1975, pp. 8, 12-14.

Reich, R., *Tales of a New America*, Times Books, New York, 1987.

Richards, S., "Cultural Change in the British Civil Service", paper presented at the International Political Science Association Congress, Washington, D.C., Aug. 29-Sept. 1, 1988.

Rodger, S., "Public Service No Longer Relevant", *Public Sector*, Vol. 10, No., 4, 1988, pp. 2-4.

Rouban, L., "The Civil Service and the Policy of Administrative Modernization in France", *International Review of Administrative Sciences*, Vol. 55, No. 3, Sept. 1989, pp. 445-465.

Salamon, M., and Lund, M. (eds.), *The Reagan Presidency and the Governing of America*, The Urban Institute, Washington, D.C., 1984.

Savoie, D.J., *The Politics of Public Spending in Canada*, University of Toronto Press, Toronto, 1990.

Scott, G., and Gorringe, P., "Reform of the Core Public Sector: The New Zealand Experience," *Australian Journal of Public Administration*, Vol. 48, No. 1, March 1989, pp. 82-89.

Smith, R., and Weller, P. (eds.), *Public Service Inquiries in Australia*, University of Queensland Press, St. Lucia, 1978.

Stronck, G., and Vaubel, D., *Administrative Reforms in Benelux and Germany*, European Institute of Public Administration, Maastricht, 1988.

Swann, D., *The Retreat of the State: Deregulation and Privatisation in the U.K. and U.S.*, Harvestor-Wheatsheaf, New York, 1988.

Thurow, L. (ed.), *The Management Challenge: Japanese Views*, The M.I.T. Press, Cambridge, MA., 1985.

United Nations, *Selected Studies on Major Administrative Reforms*, Administrative Innovations Series 1, Department of Technical Cooperation for Development, New York, 1988.

U.S. Executive Office of the President, *Management of the United States Government 1990*, U.S. Government Printing Office, Washington, D.C., 1989.

U.S. General Accounting Office (a), *Managing the Government: Revised Approach Could Improve O.M.B.'s Effectiveness*, GAO/GGD-89-65, Washington, D.C., May 1989.

U.S. General Accounting Office (b), *Civilian Agency Procurement: Improvements Needed in Contracting and Contract Administration*, GAO/GGD-89-109, Washington, D.C., September 1989.

Veljanovski, C., *Selling the State: Privatisation in Britain*, Weidenfeld and Nicholson, London, 1987.

Vernon, R. (ed.), *The Promise of Privatization: A Challenge for U.S. Policy*, Council on Foreign Relations, New York, 1988.

Vickers, J. and Yarrow G., *Privatization: An Economic Analysis*, M.I.T.Press, MA, 1988.

White Paper, *Efficiency and Effectiveness in the Civil Service*, Cmd. 8316, H.M.S.O., London, 1982.

Whitehead, C. (ed.), *Reshaping the Nationalised Industries*, Policy Journals/Transaction Books, New Brunswick, N.J., 1988.

Wilenski, P., "Administrative Reform – General Principles and the Australian Experience", *Public Administration*, Vol. 64, No. 3, Autumn 1986, pp. 257-276.

Williams, W., *Washington, Westminster and Whitehall*, Cambridge University Press, Cambridge, 1988.

Wright, D., and Sakurai, Y., "Administrative Reform in Japan: Politics, Policy and Public Administration in a Deliberative Society", *Public Administration Review*, Vol. 47, No. 2, March/April 1987, pp. 121-133.

Yeatman, A., "The Concept of Public Management and the Australian State in the 1980s", *Australian Journal of Public Administration*, Vol. 46, No. 4, Dec. 1987, pp. 339-353.

Yeatman, A., and Bryson, L., "A New Iron Cage? Experiences of Managerial Reform", *Flinders Studies in Policy and Administration*, No. 3, Flinders University of South Australia, Bedford Park, March 1987.

12. Reforms in the Third World: Almost Beyond Realization

During the economic setbacks of the energy crisis and the decline in world trade, the richer countries around the globe were able to embark on ambitious administrative reform programs. Their administrative systems were in reasonable working order and had been for several generations. Their populations had adjusted to the demands of an organizational society and they were attuned to a bureaucratic culture. They had strong governments that could reach all residents. They had residents who respected public authorities and despite their grumbling appreciated public services. They had sufficient resources, technology and expertise to support administrative capacity that could undertake most government tasks, including administrative reform. Even with such favorable conditions, many experienced considerable difficulties not just in transforming their administrative cultures but also in successfully carrying out relatively simple changes in laws, structures, policies and processes.

The poorer countries particularly in the so-called Third World whose need for administrative modernization was the greatest lacked any of these advantages. Their sorry position where lacking energy sources was compounded by adverse terms of trade, a severe drop in earnings of their major exports and a mounting gap between rising expectations and declining ability to satisfy even basic needs. Their development plans were upset and it was all they could do to avoid regressing. Developing countries were forced to borrow. From 1970 to 1985, their debts jumped tenfold from $68.6 billion to $711.2 billion (World Bank, 1986, 44) to have to pay out more in interest than they received in new loans. As much of the aid they had received had been wasted on ill-designed and unproductive projects, corruption and mismanagement, and incompetent and uncaring public employees, their future prospects looked bleak without a revival in world trade and more productive ways of conducting their affairs (Hancock, 1989).

More productive ways of conducting their affairs meant in the spirit of the times freeing people of government restrictions and boosting private sector enterprise and management. International aid switched directions accordingly. Major country donors and international agencies moved to encourage private enterprise and voluntary organizations in poor countries (thereby bypassing government organizations and the public sector), to assist governments to privatize public enterprises (Adamolekun, 1989b), and to strengthen business management education and training. The public sector was not neglected. Efforts continued to improve the planning and implementation of development projects, the reorganization and revitalization of public enterprises, and the modernization of public management processes and training. Administrative modernization still consisted largely of borrowing and transferring Western norms of public administration (Weberian legal-rational bureaucracy, Westminster type civil services, annual budget and financial management systems, decentralization and local government, administrative law, etc.) and building government administrative capacity to deal with development problems.

But administrative modernization was not working out at all as expected. Western administrative technology was being applied to strengthen not transform indigenous administrative cultures with all their bureaupathologies, maladministration and mismanagement, and to entrench bureaucratic elites skillful at manipulating new technologies to self-advantage. Administratively, things often got worse not better. As to building institutional capacity to perform better by creating model islands of excellence that would be able to deliver technical services, internalize innovative ideas, and network, these were largely confined to select government agencies and training and research institutes that were isolated show cases, deprived of adequate resources and unable to impact ineffective, unreformed administrative systems. Instead of their leading the way to transforming administration, they were affected by the prevailing administrative culture and tended to adopt similar bad habits.

Administrative reform remained the hope that somehow things would be improved, that better policies would be formulated, that better arrangements would be devised, that better methods would be adopted, that implementation would actually proceed and succeed, and that the benefits would flow to all and not be confined to a small aristocracy of wealth, position and talent. The facts of administrative deficiency were obvious. Little could be achieved, rarely quickly, rarely well, rarely properly, rarely without a great deal of effort and persistence, rarely without resorting to irregular channels, subterfuges and connections, rarely without being worn down and in the end satisfied with anything better than nothing. No wonder that poverty or lack of development was attributed to administrative incapacity. But the obstacles were overwhelming. The very administrative incapacity meant that things could not be achieved easily or fast or on a grand scale without much effort, persistence and resources, and certainly not administrative reform for which rarely were these available, never mind the support, the risk and the time necessary for effective implementation. The administrative problems went beyond solution by administrative reform alone; they needed fundamental institutional, ideological and societal transformations.

In poor Third World countries (and most were poor), sheer scarcity distorted any distribution system, whether market or public. The lack of effective supply meant that nobody would willingly give up anything they had without a fight and all would compete fiercely for what might be available and pay whatever price was demanded. But the lack of effective demand because of mass poverty confined distribution to the few wealthy and well-connected. Corruption was inevitable, not just a fact of life but a way of life, the usual and expected way of conducting business (any business), very difficult to change and hard to break altogether. Certainly the untaught masses knew no different and did not quite know how to respond to administrative changes. They had to be shown what to do (to obey laws, pay taxes, send their children to school, dress differently, eat differently, follow hygienic rules, respect public agencies, etc.) and this was part of the administrative equation most overlooked in administrative reform. They had little inkling of a civic culture; rather theirs' was an individualistic self-regarding culture entailing a certain blindness to others outside the particularistic groups to which they belonged and with which they were closely bound. Opportunities were exploited to help the group and oneself without too much regard for the general interest. In this, the ingenious found ways for self-advancement and self-enrichment to the detriment of the community; for them, self-service was prized over public service. The formal features of the administrative state appeared modern but the behavior was still pre-state for which administrative reform was ill-prepared.

If these circumstances were not difficult enough, most poor countries were strangers to democracy. They were ruled by unrepresentative elites which exploited office for self-interest. Their whims and fancies governed and had to be met. Fiat ruled. Decision-making was confined to an inner circle that would not share power, delegate authority or trust outsiders. What the few decided had to be followed; defiance was ruthlessly treated. The masses were left out and suppressed. The technocrats were cowed and intimidated. Reform could come only from the top and that was not often. And right or wrong, it would be imposed at least formally. Whether it could really be imposed without coercion was another matter. The fortunate were not going to readily change a system that made them fortunate. They were not going to stick their necks out or draw attention to themselves unnecessarily. On the contrary, they would examine any proposed changes with suspicion and go on doing what they had always done. Privileges would be protected, opportunities exploited, positions entrenched (through seniority and patronage), newcomers kept at bay and the masses kept a good distance away.

> …in the 1980s, the ranks of opposition to reform were full: economic elites supported by existing policies; ethnic, regional, and religious groups favored in allocative decision making; bureaucrats and bureaucratic agencies wielding regulatory power; policy elites sustained through patronage and clientele networks; military organizations accustomed to spending generous budgets with few questions asked. Moreover, decision makers, even those convinced of the economic need for the reforms, could not escape considering the political wisdom of adopting and pursuing them; in the name of efficiency and development, most changes implied a significant decentralization of decision making, a shrinking of the size of the public sector, and an important shift in the strongly

interventionist role of the state in the economy. For policy makers schooled in the importance of state building, practiced in the methods of centralizing power in order to survive politically, familiar with the use of the public sector for patronage and regulation, and imbued with development doctrines emphasizing planning and control, the logic of the new orthodoxy was not always politically or philosophically obvious. (Grindle and Thomas, 1989, 213-4)

The mind-set was to go along, not to buck the system, not to offend, but to be cunning in self-interest and to go through the motions of reform without giving it any real substance or better still to turn reform on its head. Thus, decentralization would result in increased centralization, wider distribution of public goods and services would result in more restricted access, and throwing open public employment would result in narrower selection. The outcomes of administrative reforms would often be the reverse of what had been intended.

Snatching Crumbs of Comfort

If administrative reform had been a total failure, it would have been abandoned. Instead, its many disappointments were discounted in favor of the few really substantive successes for which the reformers could be justly proud, provided one did not expect too much. Given the amount of effort worldwide put into administrative reform in Third World countries, some good had to come out of it. Someone somewhere had to beat the odds and quite a few did. National planning had provided a permanent place for administrative improvement and reform, so too had social engineering approaches to development. Modernizing elites, particularly those coming to power through revolution and military coups, had not been prepared to tolerate traditional ways of doing business and had insisted on new ways. In small countries, a few people had made all the difference and almost singlehandedly had succeeded in reform. In large countries, entrenched elites had been wise enough to change their ways and reform to head off destabilization, violence and revolution. Enlightened bureaucrats had also seen what was in store and had moved on their own initiative, particularly where the bureaucracy had been underemployed and could be made more productive with minimal investment. Institution-building had established successful organizations which had inspired reform and had had the desired ripple effect. Sufficient numbers of overseas educated technocrats had returned to make an impact in public service delivery systems, particularly in health, education, energy, and airlines. International experts had been listened to and their proposals tried out. Those countries which had deliberately ignored international and outside influence had looked into traditional indigenous administrative systems to find extraordinary talent and unusual capacity which were readily mobilized to invigorate public administration and management.

Several such successes were mentioned in the *World Development Report 1983* (World Bank, 1984) clearly as models or show cases for other countries to study, adapt and emulate. In national economic planning, it drew attention to Brazil, Sri Lanka, India (Program Evaluation Organization) and South Korea (Economic Planning Board). In public enterprise management, it highlighted the Kenya Tea Development Authority, and the Ethiopian Telecommunications Authority, while in program and project management it had been impressed by PURSI (an Indonesian fertilizer company) and the National Irrigation Administration of The Philippines, and in public service management training Malaysia's National Institute of Public Administration (INTAN) had caught its eye. When it came to administrative reform, the World Bank generously commended African countries for becoming self-reliant in administration, some Latin American countries (particularly Brazil) for expanding their administrations to cope with urbanization and industrialization, and some East Asia countries for their sophisticated economies.

Otherwise the World Bank had concluded that few developing countries had succeeded in improving public sector efficiency through administrative reform alone. The results had been disappointing, the impact had been limited, and the strategies had "not delivered on their promises" (Ibid, 115). Instead of wholesale reform, it would have been better to have selected a few key targets or priorities (selective radicalism) and built support gradually by showing results. A major oversight had been lack of public accountability, meaning lack of the general public's ownership, as reform had not enjoyed political (leadership) support, had lacked sufficient investment and detailed planning, had been foiled by corruption, rigidity, inertia, and lack of incentives, and had excluded "ordinary people" from the process. What the World Bank did not say was that the ordinary people, the general public, had rarely benefited, if at all, from administrative reform, from improved public sector performance, from development administration, all of which seemed to have been considered as ends in themselves. These had not been considered from the viewpoint of those who really would be benefited and as it had often turned out these had not included the general public or significant groups of impoverished, desperately needy people.

Although the World Bank had mentioned failures which it clearly did not want repeated, it urged studies of successful reform initiatives in the Third World simply because poor countries could not slavishly copy the progress of rich countries in quite different global circumstances and with quite different bases. Countries which claimed success stories paraded them around international seminars and had them written up in professional journals. Truth to tell, almost all were carefully edited versions. Some were almost fiction, recounting what they would like to have achieved rather than telling the real narrative of rejection and failure. Others were disillusioning in their idiosyncracy and virtually unrepeatable circumstances. A few like the debureaucratization program in Brazil had what appeared to be spectacular initial success that rightfully drew world attention only to fade as momentum could not be sustained and circumstances changed against further successful implementation until political change brought their sudden demise.

Time outdated case studies so quickly. Some of the World Bank examples of success even as they were being recorded had already run into trouble and a few years later had to be judged failures. The fact that reform institutions and programs survived did not indicate success; they could be empty shells. On the other hand, the failure of reform plans and proposals did not necessarily indicate that reform had not been achieved. Countless reform commissions on the Indian subcontinent bemoaned bureaucratic inertia and resistance to their initiatives, but administrative reforms had occurred in those countries perhaps not as intended or in the right directions, nevertheless their administrative systems were different one decade compared to another. Some transformations had occurred underneath, out of the public eye, without fanfare, instituted and juggled by their administrative elites. To concentrate on the formalities was to ignore the transformation in the administrative ethos. If the pessimists were to be believed, none of the countries would have survived and adapted in the ways they had. Developing countries were not beyond administrative reform. The task had been underestimated, insufficient attention had been paid to overcoming bureaucratic resistance and inertia, Western models had been inappropriately applied, and Westernized elites together with their Western advisers had failed to understand or appreciate the strengths and weaknesses of prevailing administrative cultures.

That administrative reform could be achieved was illustrated by several country cases that have received world attention and been emulated by other countries in possibly worse straights. The three Third World examples selected have had a global impact because their reforms have gone beyond administration to deal with societal issues and placed the reform instruments right in the thick of politics. They are Hong Kong's attempt to root out systemic corruption in the public sector and the spread of the Scandinavian institution of ombudsman into developing countries as a means of getting aloof bureaucracies to respond directly to public grievances about maladministration and to empower the ordinary people to make direct representations to public administrators. This important point is taken up in the third illustration of people-centered development efforts which is not to be confused with the more popular human resources approach (Haq and Kirdar, 1987).

(a) Combatting corruption. Corruption was a way of life in some areas of the Hong Kong public sector. After all, Hong Kong had long been a notorious harbor for narcotics traffic and this tourist mecca had a thriving underground economy (Lethbridge, 1985). Illegal enterprise was bound to contaminate this outpost of British colonialism. Public officials could make fortunes on the side. Corruption was so institutionalized that it could not be hidden and Hong Kong had that tarnished reputation. In 1973, the new Governor, Sir Murray MacLehose, decided that this intolerable situation would cease. Others had said much the same before and had instituted anti-corruption measures with only temporary, partial impact. Cynics thought that MacLehose's efforts would also come to nothing. But this time they were dead wrong although it looked at first that they would be right.

In 1971, the Hong Kong government enforced a new Prevention of Bribery ordinance by which suspects who lived beyond their means would have to demonstrate their innocence or suffer severe criminal penalties. Several senior officials immediately resigned and in 1973 after the successful prosecution of a Police Superintendent, the suspected Chief Superintendent left the colony (he actually disappeared for a while before reemerging in England) and apparently escaped prosecution. Governor MacLehose ordered an inquiry into the affair which revealed systemic corruption in the police force. He established an Independent Commission Against Corruption (I.C.A.C.) which would not only investigate corruption but also work to prevent corruption. He appointed a distinguished former public official and head of the telephone company, Jack Cater, to head I.C.A.C. which could arrest people on suspicion (but it could not prosecute), search and seize without a warrant, require information, freeze assets and property, and prevent people from leaving the colony. I.C.A.C. reported directly to the Governor alone although to assure some measure of public accountability and confidence, it was assisted by five advisory committees (Corruption, Operations Review, Prevention, Community Relations, and Complaints) drawn from a wide cross-section of residents.

Cater carefully selected I.C.A.C. staff to ensure that I.C.A.C. would not be corrupted and he was given exceptional powers of staff control. He also introduced renewable performance contracts, i.e. short term contracts renewed according to performance. He organized I.C.A.C. into three areas: (a) an operations department to investigate, arrest and help prosecute suspects; (b) a corruption prevention department to restructure government organizations to reduce opportunities ("breakpoints") for corruption, and (c) a community relations department to change people's attitudes toward corruption. The former Police Superintendent was extradited from England and convicted as were many other public officials, so that I.C.A.C. came to be feared by all. After five years (when Cater left I.C.A.C.) I.C.A.C. began to claim that it had reduced the scale of corruption considerably, that it had broken systemic corruption in the police force, and that it had turned the tide against corruption. Such claims attracted global attention and it became "probably the largest and most famous anti-corruption agency in the developing world" (Klitgaard, 1988, 115). Certainly it had driven up the price for engaging in corruption; it had cleansed much public business; it had eliminated unenforceable laws, cumbersome procedures and bottlenecks; it had conducted a mass education campaign reaching even into primary schools; it had instituted public complaints about corruption that would be seriously investigated; and it had shifted public opinion and attitudes about public sector corruption (Clark, 1987), although the colony's uncertain future brought new challanges to law and order from organized crime and the suborning of public officials.

Hong Kong's temporary success was not alone. A dozen or so years before I.C.A.C., Singapore had pursued a similar strategy of enforcing increasingly stringent anti-corruption legislation, establishing an independent anti-corruption body (Corrupt Practices Investigation Board) eventually under the Prime Minister, reorganizing government agencies to minimize the opportunities for corrupt practices, reducing incentives for corruption, and educating the public about the dysfunctional consequences of corruption. It had been "a comprehensive rather than a piecemeal or incremental approach to the problem" (Heidenheimer et al., 1988, 850). But both were small countries or rather city states. Could their experiences be universalized? The I.C.A.C. success has brought anti-corruption units around the world to visit and study its operations. This in turn has been instrumental in organizing regular international conferences on the state of the art in anti-corruption, the most important being its third in Hong Kong in 1987 and its fourth in Sydney in 1989. I.C.A.C. has itself become a model for other countries to break systemic corruption in both public and private sectors, reduce the scale of corruption and turn public opinion strongly against corrupt practices. After all, there are still many countries that do not outlaw corruption and corrupt practices, that have no anti-corruption mechanisms, and that make no attempt to educate public officials about corruption let alone the general public (Caiden and Truelson, 1990).

(b) Investigating public complaints against maladministration. Governments have always had an inspectorate to investigate complaints of misrule and misconduct by their employees. In 1809 Sweden's ombudsman was made independent of the executive and given full powers to receive and investigate complaints of maladministration from the public. This way ordinary people could complain about official actions which grieved them and have their complaints independently investigated. If wrongdoing was discovered, it was expected that it be put right and the victims compensated. Eventually the ombudsman was given additional roles in protecting citizens, ensuring human rights, and generally guaranteeing equitable and good administration. Until 1960, the institution of ombudsman was largely confined to Scandinavia. Thereafter democratic regimes began to adopt it as a fail-safe device to pick up administrative errors that had fallen between cracks in public accountability provisions.

Outside Europe, New Zealand led the way in 1962 followed by Cook Islands, Guyana, and Tanzania in the mid 1960s but once the Commonwealth countries followed the example of the United Kingdom, there was a burst of ombudsmania in the 1970s that carried the ombudsman into the Middle East (Israel), Asia

(India), Papua-New Guinea, the West Indies, and eventually into Latin America (Brazil) in the 1980s. Each country has shaped the institution to suit its own circumstances. Developing countries have used it as an outreach program to incorporate people who otherwise were being neglected by public administration, to bring public pressures to bear on public officials to improve administrative practices, to impress on public sector employees the need to respect and advance human rights, and to reduce the problems of bureaucratization. Several have been employed on other tasks ranging from investigation of corruption to electoral malpractices and racial tension.

Given the perilous state of public administration in unreformed public bureaucracies, the danger was that the ombudsman would be swamped with complaints about which nobody could do anything. This has often been the case initially. Ombudsman offices have been overwhelmed by complaints where their jurisdictions have not been narrow and members of the public have been willing to come forward with complaints, and they have not been able to do much to alter administrative systems although they have helped wronged individuals. Nonetheless, their very presence has had a cautionary effect on the conduct of public officials. They have steadily gained in reputation as the citizen's defender and also as fair, impartial judges of administrative behavior. Their accumulated knowledge on the inside has prompted administrative reform initiatives but their potential in this respect has yet to be realized. They have been handicapped by political instability, bureaucratic intransigence, lack of sufficient resources, restrictive legislation, and public ignorance.

Their growing reputation has attracted more than just curiosity. Wherever an ombudsman office has been established, neighboring countries have sent study missions. The ombudsman offices have joined together into an International Ombudsman Institute which has a permanent secretariat at the University of Alberta in Canada and holds world congresses attended by interested observers, the latest in Canberra, Australia in 1988. The institution has spread into the private sector not just as a public relations gimmick but as a practical device to diffuse public dissatisfaction with administrative performance and as an independent check on managerial wrongdoing and deficiencies. It works best probably where it is least needed, that is, where administrative systems work well and the little wrongdoing that occurs is quickly remedied. Where the reverse situation obtains, the ombudsman is not an effective instrument for administrative reform. Nonetheless, it is difficult to muzzle and it is useful in educating both public and officialdom in administrative norms. The countries that have the ombudsman claim that it has been a welcome addition in their arsenal of reform instruments. Its rapid spread around the world would seem to indicate that more and more countries are coming to this conclusion despite its limitations to realize dreams of responsible, law-abiding citizens who freely and knowledgeably participate in public affairs and expect government to respond speedily, effectively and economically to their demands.

(c) Representing the poor. Ombudsman offices attempt to reach the poor, ill-educated masses who are often dealt with harshly by insolent bureaucrats and have just cause to complain about abuse of official powers detrimental to human dignity and rights. But most Third World countries still have no ombudsman and no anti-corruption measures. In them, the poor are meagerly served if at all by the public sector. Public services are mostly the preserve of the better-off and when the poor flock to enjoy whatever public amenities are available to them, public facilities quickly become overburdened and poorly maintained. Either way, the poor are deprived. Improving public sector management will not help them much since the country is too poor to provide proper and adequate amenities to many more than already enjoy them. Traditional administrative reform is irrelevant to their predicament. Novel strategies have to be devised that go well beyond orthodoxy if development is to be "more equitable, more participative and more effective in reaching the vast majority of the people" excluded in the past (Rondinelli and Ingle, 1981, 25). In fact, several experiments in bureaucracy-free administration have been tried for many years with mixed success in the East Bloc (collectivized, self-help enterprises), Yugoslavia (cooperatives), Israel (collectives and cooperatives), India (the *panchayati raj* system) and Sri Lanka (*Gam Udawa* or village reawakening program), Korea (*Saemaul Undong* or new village movement), and Peru (self-managing communities, CUAVES mothers' clubs), but none of them were really free of government intervention, although self-managing.

A different strategy that evolved in the 1980s was that of people-centered development inspired by David Korten (Korten and Alfonso, 1983; Korten and Klauss, 1984; Korten, 1987) which unlike past strategies did not either totally reject or embrace statism. It envisaged a partnership between local communities and whatever institutional frameworks existed to aid local communities progress, and different from other strategies in several ways. First, most development strategies had been implemented through bureaucracies that never even worked with the poor or the poorest of the poor. They had been imposed and they had not been people-centered. Second, for an effective partnership, the poor had to be empowered. Whereas bureaucracies sought client satisfaction, people-centered development sought to build the capacity of clients to enhance their bargaining power and to get more resources transferred to them, i.e. more power would be conceded to the clients. Third, people-centered development allowed for variety and catered to local circumstances and idiosyncracies in its contingency approach. Grass-root organizations could enlist the energies and inventive capacities of the poorest in a self-reliant, self-sustaining development process aimed at satisfying their interests, meeting their needs, solving their problems, and building their skills, knowledge and capacity to manage by themselves. Bureaucracies would have to be reoriented to permit such flexibility, to reward the strengthening of local community capacity, and to change "job definitions, performance criteria, career incentives, bureaucratic procedure, organizational responsibilities, and the like" (Korten and Uphoff, 1981, 6) accordingly. Fourth, focus switched from the *design* of a given strategy to the *management* of the context that would include "the design of structural relationships, information flows, performance evaluation systems, measurement criteria, and the processes of rewards and sanctions" (Icklis et al., 1986, 1). Administrative reform would concentrate on such strategic management and bureaucratic reorientations (BRO) that transformed inappropriate organizational structures, as had been done in the case of The Philippine National Irrigation Administration (Korten and Siy, 1988).

Such difficult and painstaking efforts at institutional transformation would not be popular among traditionalists and they would be experimental, innovative, challenging, slow. As most traditional strategies had not worked for the poorest, people-oriented development was worth a try given that the plight of the poorest was getting worse with increased numbers unable to maintain even basic needs on marginal farm plots and in mushrooming urban slums. The Inter-American Foundation and the Performance Management Project of the U.S.A.I.D. agreed as did the World Bank development management projects and the World Bank in general in its Sub-Saharan African development strategy (World Bank, 1989, 7). If increased representation of the poor produced results, then in addition to improving private sector management and public sector administration, administrative reform would undertake strategic management designs, bureaucratic reorientations to facilitate participation and entrepreneurship, and a new style debureaucratized public managerialism. Others were not so optimistic.

> While the concepts of decentralization, development from below, freedom from bureaucratic constraints, respect for public opinion and local knowledge, participatory modes of operation, and learning by doing are very attractive, they are also inadequate and misleading…the more impoverished the community, the more it needs outside assistance…development from below requires development from above…The solution…is not less bureaucracy, but better bureaucracy…" (Werlin, 1989, 456-7)

At every turn, improving the performance of the administrative state would be unavoidable.

Back to Basics

Most Third World countries realize that they have been and are likely to remain poorly administered. Administratively, they are backward. Their administrative systems need modernizing. In the meantime, their administrative incapacity severely handicaps their developmental efforts. They continue to place their faith in administrative reform. As much as they would welcome radical transformations of their whole administrative systems and completely different administrative cultures, they are grateful for even minor improvements. They do not have the means to undertake necessary administrative reforms and when they do manage to muster enough resources of their own and receive grateful injections of foreign assistance, they try to invest in reforms that promise the best returns, not show case experiments and innovations but just simple measures improving the basics. Around the world, there are various regional centers that encourage local initiatives and from time to time sponsor seminars and meetings of experts to report progress and publish their proceedings to encourage continuing reform efforts. Among the most active of these are management training institutes and development advisory services such as the European Centre for Development Policy and Management (E.C.D.P.M., Maastricht, The Netherlands), the Center for Latin American Development (C.L.A.D., Caracas, Venezuela), Instituto Centroamericano de Administracion de Empresas (I.N.C.A.E., Alajuela, Costa Rica), the Central American Institute of Public Administration (I.C.A.P., San Jose, Costa Rica), the Arab Organization of Administrative Sciences (A.O.A.S., Amman, Jordan), the Asian Center For Development Administration (A.C.D.A.), the Indian Institute of Public Administration (I.I.P.A., New Delhi, India), and the Eastern Regional Organization for Public Administration (E.R.O.P.A., Manila, The Philippines) and for state owned enterprises, the International Center for Public Enterprises (I.C.P.E., Ljubljana, Yugoslavia). Three regions illustrate why administrative reform has been so painfully unrewarding and slow.

(a) Economic Recovery Programs in Sub-Sahara Africa. Nowhere was hit worse by world economic and trade crises in the 1970s than Sub-Sahara Africa, a situation worsened even more by severe drought and other natural calamities and alas already stagnant economies rapidly running out of cash and credit and largely dominated by post-independence authoritarian, centralized kleptocracies. Nowhere outside of the East Bloc was more statist, more interventionist, more regulatory, more reliant on state-owned enterprises, more monopolized by a bureaucratic bourgeoisie (Nafzinger, 1988). Nowhere was government so bad and administration so incompetent and corrupt, a recipe not just for the nullification of administrative reform, but for the defeat of economic rejuvenation and for global evaluations such as "disastrous", "devastating", and "catastrophic", bringing only more despair to the continent's well-wishers. Nowhere were attempts at relief more frustrated by inappropriate policies, unproductive investments (Mufson, 1986), deteriorating infrastructures, black markets (underground economies), political divisions, violence, tribalism, and public mismanagement. Nowhere were the conditions for administrative reform so daunting and the need so imperative. Nowhere was the task of the premier administrative reform patrons, the African Centre for Administrative Training and Research for Development (C.A.F.R.A.D., Tangiers, Morocco) and the African Association for Public Administration and Management (A.A.P.A.M., Addis Ababa, Ethiopia), so challenging.

The Africanization of public administration had emphasized the institutionalization of public sector education and training and throughout Africa, facilities had been established and expanded at existing and new institutes of higher education or as new quangos, with international assistance and a heavy dose of Western (mostly British, French and American) approaches and techniques to public sector management. Because of the scarcity of resources, they were largely shoe-string operations barely able to survive from one year to another, with English speaking organizations looking to the Commonwealth for help in post entry training and French speaking organizations looking to Western Europe for assistance in pre-entry training to further professionalization. But survive they did and they even managed to branch out into some research and consulting. Survival was also the name of the game for many of their students who went on to occupy key administrative positions in the public sector. They had to cope with invasions, civil wars, purges, crippling inflation, uncertain tenure, poverty, nepotism ("the culture of affection," A.A.P.A.M., 1986, 12), indiscipline, and incredible odds just to keep going. To succeed in improving things in such circumstances was asking too much. It was enough to hold the line against continuing deterioration. The temptation was to capitalize on one's position and to move quickly on to a better prospect.

Administrative reform was not neglected. The international community always included Sub-Sahara Africa in its programs and greatly favored African countries in technical assistance missions. Institutionalization of administrative reform had been recommended as a priority at the Seminar on Urgent Administrative Problems of African Governments in Addis Ababa in 1963 and again in 1968. The latter seminar went so far as to recommend a coordination unit at cabinet office level to give permanent administrative support to the executive and to monitor the drafting and implementation of a master plan for administrative reform (Rweyemamu and Hyden, 1975, 216). Several countries instituted national commissions of inquiry on the British Royal Commission model, such as the Mills-Odoi Commission (1967) in Ghana and the Ndegwa Commission (1970-1) in Kenya, which had "merely led to increased formalism, ritualism and overcentralization" (Ibid, 227). Others like Sudan had preferred management services advisory units in operating agencies but they were "invariably of such a low calibre" and so bereft of real power and influence that they were rarely in a position to bring about fundamental changes (Ibid, 228). A few had tried including administrative reform in national development plans but usually they were more concerned with office space and projected capital expenditure rather than with reform. In any event, administrative reform plans, programs and projects failed because there simply was no capability to see them through. For example, the Sudanese Ministry of Public Service and Administrative Reform failed to follow through properly on public service legislation and long awaited job evaluation and classification and without warning it was dissolved in 1981. Its (overambitious) plans had been based on inadequate research and had been quite poorly designed and in any event they had made "undue demands on the meagre financial, technical and human resources that were available in the country" and the administrative machinery had been just too poor to effect them, particularly in the face of politicization, nepotism, favoritism, corruption and a serious brain drain in a rapidly deteriorating economy (Al-Rahim et al., 1986, 94). The only seemingly successful reforms were those that had strong political backing and were given sufficient resources because they benefited the political power of the regime, as in Zambia (Chikulo, 1985).

The vicious circle was broken during the late 1980s by the structural adjustment programs imposed on Sub-Sahara African countries by the International Monetary Fund and the World Bank. For years, experts from these international agencies had complained about institutional bureaupathologies (particularly bloated public organizations, corruption, mismanagement, low public sector productivity and incompetent state owned enterprises) that had contributed to economic failure and they had recommended structural reforms to improve institutional capacity. The African debt position had grown so serious that the I.M.F. and World Bank stepped in to require fundamental policy reforms and economic restructuring in packages that included:

* boosting self-sustaining economic growth and reduction of macroeconomic imbalances;
* reducing government control over the economy – deregulation, privatization;
* allowing the price of agricultural products to reflect market demands – withdrawal of subsidies, increase productivity;
* reducing budget deficits – retrenchment, freeze on government expenditures, budget reforms, increased efficiency;
* reducing consumer demand for imports and increasing more productive investments;
* keeping interest rates above the inflation rate – market determined real interest rates;
* reducing the rate of growth in the money supply – tighter money and credit;
* floating foreign exchange rates and liberalizing external trade agreements;
* increasing gross domestic product (G.D.P.) and export growth;
* encouraging private sector enterprise and investment and a shift to tradeables;
* reducing surplus public employees and public sector parasitism;
* enlarging the real choice of the public;
* administrative revitalization and re-equipment. (Balogun and Mutahaba, 1989).

To sweeten the pill, African governments were offered new loans or loan forgiveness, increased technical assistance, and help with specific projects such as food production and storage, transportation, tourism, spare parts and medical supplies.

For the public sector, the impact of the economic restructuring programs has been immediate in the reduction of public employment of anywhere between 10 and 50 percent, the freezing of remuneration, maintenance and capital development, the deterioration of the public infrastructure, the divestment and rationalization of state owned enterprises, increased budget controls and reforms, depressed morale, worsening industrial relations, reduced social services, tax reforms and demonopolization. First the Ivory Coast (*The Courier*, 1988, 61) was held up as a model, then Mali (*Highlights*, 1989), and later Ghana (*Insight*, 1988; World Bank, 1989) all of which increased their G.D.P., devalued their currencies, liberalized import restrictions and cut back their public sectors, at the cost of unemployment, inflation, authoritarian rule, and urban impoverishment. Other countries in the world and in Africa had found the internal costs too high and had revoked their I.M.F.-imposed economic recovery programs. Nonetheless, structural adjustment highlighted the need to improve policy analysis as well as management practice, to strengthen coordination mechanisms within government, to streamline public organizations, and, no surprise this, to reinvest in public sector management training and education, this time with the blessing of the World Bank and I.M.F. in principle and the expanded activities of the World Bank's Economic Development Institute and the revitalized Eastern and Southern African Management Institute (E.S.A.M.I., Arusha, Tanzania) in practice. This time, multi-donor efforts were to be formally coordinated under the rubric of the African Capacity Building Initiative to ensure that the foundations on which administrative reforms were implemented were not built on shifting sand thereby guaranteeing their failure. Particular attention was to be given to civil service improvement, capacity building for policy analysis, coordination and implementation of national development policies, and management training (Adamolekun, 1989a). In 1987, some thirty African states embarked on administrative reform programs aided by international organizations (Balogun and Mutahaba, 1989; Mutahaba, 1989).

The economic restructuring and institution building programs included one of the most problematic African states, Nigeria, where administrative reform had struggled against every conceivable obstacle since its establishment as an independent state. The economic crisis coupled with the proposed demilitarization of the regime (by 1992) brought a welcome break through, one that marked the first really significant departure from the inherited British colonial model. Difficulties in implementing the economic recovery program pointed to the dire need to reform and revitalize the public sector, particularly the civil service system, reputedly the most bureaupathologic in the area. The 1988 civil service reforms represented an effort to establish an enduring and stable democratic order based on a solid economic foundation. They were based on previous inquiries, such as the Public Service Review (Udoji) Commission of 1975 and the Phillips Review Committee in the mid 1980s, and were similar to those implemented in the United Kingdom and the U.S.A. Furthermore, they were quite acceptable to the World Bank in their shift away from statism and bureaucratic centralism toward professionalization, productivity, and decentralization in a new presidential system. But they depended on the cooperation and commitment of the notoriously resistant and entrenched senior civil servants and on the availability of resources. In fact, they were slow off the mark. However, they were being monitored by a presidential task force headed by the Minister for Social Duties and all state governments had established implementation committees so perhaps by 1992 with economic recovery this necessary first stage may be followed by others, unless as in the past reform falls victim to the unbeatable combinations of government mismanagement and lawlessness, bureaucratic inefficiency and corruption, and public enterprise exploitation and irresponsibility. Still Nigeria has shown a new willingness to clean up its public sector, to privatize and to reorganize public sector organizations in preparation for civilian government.

(b) The English Speaking Caribbean. Across the Atlantic, the I.M.F. was also active in the Caribbean where it might be expected that the small islands of the area would find reform easier than in impoverished Africa. But the English-speaking countries had the same reluctance to depart from the Westminster-Whitehall system, even worse brain drain, bureaucratic inertia, political indifference, and public mismanagement, and altogether a disappointing public sector record. By the 1980s, they suffered from many problems familiar to Third World countries around the globe:–

- uncontrolled growth of the public sector; poor accounting and auditing; poor value for money;
- declining prestige, image and status of public employment;
- widening gap between public and private sector compensation for talent and performance;
- exodus of experienced officials; declining quality of public employees; scarce management skills;
- overcentralization of decision-making; lack of delegation; secrecy and privatization of information; deficient record keeping;
- lack of coordination among autonomous, competing public organizations;
- insufficient integration of policies, programs and projects;
- chronic misuse and underutilization of skills; underemployment;
- inadequate data, planning and research;
- poor facilities, inadequate accommodation, deficient tools;
- dominance of a clerical mentality; promotion by seniority; narrow vision; slow-moving, "by the book" approach; bureaucratic indifference; slovenly service;
- ignorance of O.&M recommendations; outmoded procedures; antiquated methods;

- low productivity; poor supervision; indiscipline; bad industrial relations;
- poor, ineffectual training;
- corruption; diversion of public funds and resources; patronage; influence peddling; pulling strings;
- inadequate public participation; indifference to the public; insensitivity;
- lack of initiative and enthusiasm; inadequate incentives.

To overcome these problems, governments had exempted more and more public organizations from public service controls and freed them to operate independently as best they could. Not only did this fragment the public sector even more and compound the difficulties in seeking common solutions, but the autonomous agencies acted as if they were private organizations although publicly empowered. The only consoling factor was that nothing in the Caribbean was anywhere near as bad as in Africa.

When things deteriorated beyond the point of tolerance, disturbed governments would follow the Westminster-Whitehall model and appoint public inquiries, investigations by public figures with full powers to probe and diagnose. Their reports would become historic landmarks in modernizing government. In the Caribbean, these inquiries were often conducted by outsiders unacquainted with local conditions, unable to stay long or research deeply, all too ready with their international remedies, and gone before implementation. Since independence, there had been many inquiries, all investigating the same problems, the same annoyances, the same inadequacies, the same faults, all coming up with similar recommendations in virtually the same language. They provided a fund of knowledge about what needed to be done to improve public sector performance. Few seemed to have bothered to explore why so little had been done to implement previous recommendations. Instead, they were emulations of standard Western public management dogma without much reference to local circumstances; they were more like articles of faith than empirical remedies. They gave little indication what might be involved in implementation, where the resources needed for implementation might be found, and what might have to be sacrificed.

Rarely did the inquiries reveal what had been done well. Too often they took corrections, improvements and innovations for granted. They harped on shortcomings and mentioned innovations only in passing. There had been innovations in the public sector – many of then successfully institutionalized, at all levels from intergovernmental and interregional ventures such as the Caribbean Centre for Development Administration (CARICAD, St. Michael, Barbados) to technical assistance for new local government agencies. Most governments, like CARICAD, received technical assistance from international agencies, Commonwealth members, and Western Europe to improve public sector performance. But innovations could not be commanded at will. They were badly needed in the following priority aspects:–

- **Public enterprises**. Something had to be done to turn S.O.E.s around as an alternative to selling them off to private entrepreneurs or abandoning them as beyond redemption.
- **Public service attitudes**. Something had to be done to reduce a clerical mentality among senior officials as an alternative to leaving the where they are or retiring them, to spot managerial talent at junior levels, and to turn indifference into involvement.
- **Political concern**. Something had to be done to educate political leaders about the importance of management performance, to get them interested personally in improving public administration and management, and to get them to provide the necessary leadership, support and resources for public sector improvements.
- **Public accountability**. Something had to be done to revitalize ombudsman-like institutions, to provide greater public participation in public administration, to strengthen inspectorates, to encourage suggestions and to provide incentives for practical ideas.
- **Debureaucratization**. Something had to be done to reduce needless bureaucracy, inconvenient procedures, insensitive and uncaring service, unnecessary red-tape and paperwork, inappropriate regulations, and to tackle self-serving bureaucracies, bureaupathologies, and incompetent bureaucrats.
- **Ignorance**. Something had to be done to collect real information, to conduct empirical work to test data to find out what worked and what did not work, to make actual inventories, compile meaningful guidebooks, and to exchange information.

Jamaica made a valiant effort in the 1980s to do something about administrative reform. In 1978, the Ministry of Public Service established the Administrative Staff College as a central instrument of civil service reform and an agent of administrative change. One of its first projects was to compile a synopsis of all the recommendations of past public sector inquiries, some twenty-one in less than forty years (1942-1980) (Priestley, 1980), which merely illustrated how unsuccessful administrative reform had been. But in the early 1980s, economic crisis had brought World Bank and I.M.F. intervention and with it a structural adjustment program that was handicapped by poor management. In 1983 institutional audits of policy, program, resources, structure and leadership were conducted to determine administrative barriers to increasing productivity and effectiveness. They identified weaknesses in government organizations, including the three core central agencies – the Ministry of Finance and Planning, Ministry of the Public Service, and Office of the Service Commissions. Out of this came the Administrative Reform Programme (A.R.P.) comprising an integrated scheme with three main elements dealing with financial management, human resources management, and line agency restructuring. The Prime Minister (and Minster of Finance) himself headed an Inter-Ministerial Committee on Administrative Reform (I.M.C.A.R.) which directed the work of the A.R.P. Project Office and an operating subcommittee composed of heads of the central agencies, the A.R.P. Project Office and a public administration consultant. In the A.R.P. planning stage, two task forces on financial management and human resources management evaluated proposals put forward by working groups formed to deal with A.R.P. issues. With Jamaica failing I.M.F. tests, naturally the primary focus was on budgeting, financial administration, accounting, public enterprises, revenue and borrowing (Bethune, 1989).

Plans to strengthen the Ministry of Finance and Planning were approved by I.M.C.A.R. but not implemented. Instead, it was restructured to better monitor state owned enterprises and public utilities, to improve the national budget, to establish controllerships in all government organization accounting systems (to see that budgets were adhered to), and to revise financial legislation. A key element in financial reform was the introduction of P.P.B.S. first in the Ministry of Construction. The other two core agencies were also restructured but in the opposite direction, to decentralize human resources management, simplify personnel regulations, and make public service compensation more competitive. They delegated more personnel management functions to line agencies but again fundamental changes in their role were resisted and eventually dropped. Other possible innovations, such as the creation of Management Councils as boards of directors of line agencies, were delayed by drawn out discussions and rarely implemented. The scattered training facilities of the Ministry of the Public Service were supposed to have been combined into a Public Sector Institute but did end up in a College of Public Management, at least on paper. Whether the other A.R.P. proposals, such as the 1986 Human Resources Policy and the revision of the Staff Orders and the Public Service Regulations would ever get beyond discussion remained to be seen at the end of the 1980s. In all probability they would go the way of the much publicized reclassification and pay increases, which really did not amount to much, virtually suffocated by I.M.F. structural adjustment policies.

The one enduring element of the A.R.P. might turn out to be the Performance Improvement Programme (P.I.P.) which was successfully introduced in the Ministry of Education as a model experiment. In preparation, sensitization workshops were conducted with specific objectives in mind, namely the identification of obstacles and facilitators of the ministry's goals and the appointment of teams to develop action plans under the sponsorship of a Ministry Implementation Team (M.I.T.). At least P.I.P. had more of an institutional development framework (Eldridge, 1989), administrative commitment, and some resources allocated to it, which was more than could be said of the A.R.P. generally. Like previous attempts, this one also appeared to have been mishandled, subject to empty promises, bitter infighting, division over objectives and substantive details, and the same bureaucratic inertia, incompetence and incapacity that had impelled the A.R.P. in the first place even though

Jamaica had made sure this time to avoid many of the obstacles that had plagued previous attempts.

Alas Jamaica's experience was different only in the scale of its reform efforts. The smaller Caribbean states had fared little better. In them "the gap between expectations or demands and the public administration system's capacity to deliver continues to widen" (Green and Slyfield, 1982, 10). The obstacles to reform seemed so overwhelming that the Caribbean countries appeared incapable of administrative reform, although their economic recovery depended so much on improved public sector performance. So it did in so many other Third World countries which had opted for a statist model of development that relied so much on good government, as in Latin America.

(c) Latin America. The most important fact about Latin America over the past four decades has been the stubbornness with which it has pursued administrative reform, despite so many failures and disappointments. Possibly nowhere else in the world have so many governments announced bold, imaginative reform plans to achieve so little in practice. Wave after wave of administrative reformers institutionalized near the apex of government or in autonomous research/educational centers and linked through C.L.A.D. and I.C.A.P. have assaulted the seemingly impenetrable fortress of bureaucratic inertia. Public leaders, politicians and generals alike, have stood by helpless as their schemes have just disappeared as if swallowed up in quick sands, gone without trace, or "limped along on skeletal staffing and financing" (Hammergren, 1983, 26). The general public have also stood helplessly by, hoping upon hope that this time something will really happen to ease the bureaucratic burden from them, to release them from so many bureaupathologic nightmares, to get real public service for a change instead of having to put up with so much indignity in dealing with public officials or resorting to middlemen, intermediaries, facilitators, to intercede and do business with the public bureaucracy on one's behalf, at a price of course. Within, so many well-intentioned reformers have banged their heads against a wall of bureaucratic indifference, contempt and corruption. Yet, undismayed, reformers, under both domestic and international pressures, came back and tried again under a different leader, a different banner, a different office; they did not give up. Slowly, then, the bureaucracy did wear down, did give a little, did shift, did respond, and slowly performance did improve. There were few dramatic victories and those who claimed great success were probably deceiving themselves or others. Thus a justifiable skepticism about administrative reform tended to prevail. It prevailed in exaggerated cynicism even about recent reforms that have been achieved in governmental reorganizations, privatization, cutback management, budgeting and financial management, professionalization, public service training and education, public sector legislation, and sectoral outputs and outcomes (Freitas, 1989; Holanda, 1989; Martinez, 1989).

This experience was common from Mexico to Argentina, from Brazil to the Dominican Republic, as if the whole continent were afflicted with common obstacles too difficult to overcome. Every so often as in the case of the Administrative Department of the Public Service (DASP) in Brazil and the National Office of Rationalization and Training for Public Administration (ONRAP) in Peru in the 1960s, the Public Administration Commission (CAP) in Venezuela and the National Institute of Public Administration (INAP) in Peru in the early 1970s, the Administrative Reform Program in Mexico in the late 1970s and the Debureaucratization Program in Brazil in the 1980s, it appeared that at last a significant breakthrough had occurred and great excitement in reform circles was stirred around the continent. Reformers beat a path to the door of the apparently successful who organized conferences to parade their apparent success. But like a lighted match, the flame spluttered and died, and darkness returned. Then it was discovered that the reforms were mostly on paper; they never got implemented much beyond the first enthusiastic phase. And for the usual reasons – they had been too ambitious, too unrealistic, too big, too optimistic, too poorly supported, too inflexible, too underfunded, too starved of resources and time, too short on skilled personnel, too politically insensitive, too poorly planned and executed, too misdirected or wrong-headed, too isolated administratively, too lacking in power, authority and backing, too monopolistic, too outdated, too ill-suited (ICAP, 1971; INAP, 1975; Siegel, 1978; Hammergren, 1983; Flores and Nef, 1984; Groissman et al., 1986). For whatever reason, they never had a chance or they get off to a good start but could get no further or they had raised so much hostility among vested interests that they had to be stopped in their tracks. Consequently, only small gains had been made.

This disappointing record of administrative reform has caused much breast-beating in Latin America. The fault was all theirs. Latin Americans had not slavishly followed foreign models or been forced to implement reforms not of their own making. This may not have been true before the 1960s but certainly thereafter when Latin Americans had been careful to craft their own reforms according to local circumstances. That their rate of success was little different from much of the Third World did not concern them as much as the fact that the record of the poorest Western countries to which at one time they had been administratively superior seemed better, particularly with the democratization of Spain and Portugal with which they were still most closely associated culturally. Explanations were sought in specifically local factors such as tradition, local-style fascism, statism, elitism, kleptocracy, lingering colonial legacy (even after 150 years of independence), formalism, self-interest, the *mañana* syndrome, reductionism, soft government, the peculiarities of military rule and the idiosyncracies of presidents, and political discontinuity (Thurber and Graham, 1973). Possibly, the major conceptual problem had been that reform diagnosis and implementation had taken too much for granted, had not envisaged a changing environment, and had been too institutional, too legalistic, too formal altogether, i.e. insufficiently behavioral (C.L.A.D., 1980).

Reformers had disconnected the fact that the machinery of government contained many competing agencies trying to preserve and promote their own interests and programs and that reforms had to take account of the bargaining and compromises, the alliances and confrontations that took place in society and were reflected in the machinery and operations of the state. They had discounted too much the political nature of administrative reforms (Oszlak, 1980; Hammergren, 1983); they had been too naive and thereby rendered reforms inoperative. They had concentrated on achieving rapid changes by means of basically formal modifications without tackling the underlying causes of maladministration but further complicating them. Such patching up only created more serious problems and preoccupied reformers with incrementalism.

> The effect is aimed at 'doing what is wrong more effectively', instead of revising the very meaning of policies and strategies. Thus procedures and formulas are studied and polished, when the policy that is destined to be implemented should be revised in its entirety. Sophisticated information systems are introduced in processes whose very organizational utility must be examined, or…'how many times have reforms been carried out for institutions which afterwards disappeared, or sectors which do not have priority are reformed?' (Kliksberg, 1983, 18)

Thus the more reforms, the less reform.

Bruce Perlman went further by declaiming that given the tradition of public administration in Latin America was self-service, "reform only makes things worse" (Perlman, 1989, 685). Improving the performance of the public sector in the case of most of Latin America would result not in higher economic development but more public repression, greater diversion of national resources into the hands of the bureaucrats and the elites they serve, more state patrimony and patronage, greater bureaucratization and public dependency, increased social and bureaucratic instability, greater professional frustration and deviance, and more restricted employment opportunities.

> …doing new things may not have the desired result of increased efficiency, effectiveness, and equilibrium, but rather instability, waste and overwhelming complexity…The recreation of a professional public administration may lead to greater technical skill on the part of individual actors, but less skill where needed on the part of bureaucratic institutions. (Ibid, 687)
>
> Stated simply, the problem is attempting to serve a new set of functions with old, ill serving structures, and encouraging altruism when the few incentives that exist are for selfishness. (Ibid, 691)

Nevertheless, Perlman recommended that reform should not be abandoned; if anything, it should be strengthened by taking the paradoxes of administrative modernization into account. First, public agencies should not be given projects such as land reform, where they are unlikely to have commensurate power to implement planned changes. Second, a real merit system, imperative for a proper professional public service, should be top priority, involving strong executive leadership and university participation. Third, home grown management practices should be preferred to foreign imports and initiatives. Fourth, the status of the public service should be improved through positive public relations, competitive compensation, and professionalization. Fifth, a professional ideology of performance should be developed in public administration to reduce legalism and formality. These prescriptions could apply with equal force throughout the Third World. They have been known for several decades but acting on them requires conditions that just don't exist anywhere.

"It's Not a Question of Not Knowing What To Do"

The trouble with the Third World is that there really is no Third World but several different large, diverse worlds neither East or West and none having too much in common administratively and therefore not strictly comparable with another (Elsenhans, 1988). The English-speaking and French-speaking countries of the Caribbean and Sub-Sahara Africa have dissimilar administrative systems and their reform needs differ and have to be approached differently given their contrasting administrative styles. Brazil remains the odd man out in Spanish-speaking Latin America. The Arab countries have been searching in vain for a common Arab or Islamic approach to the administrative state and have their own idiosyncracies (Jreisat, 1988). The common administrative roots of the Indian subcontinent cannot explain their different administrative cultures today (Dwividi, 1989). How can the four Asian dragons of development (Taiwan, Singapore, Hong Kong and South Korea) be placed in the same category as economically backward Nepal, Bhutan, Burma and Afghanistan? Even the A.S.E.A.N. .bloc members differ quite substantially in public sector capacity and performance despite their proximity (Quah, 1989). Perhaps the only thing all these countries share is that they cannot realize administrative reforms at all or only with great difficulty, much more so than in the East and West. They all know what they have to do to improve public sector performance but they cannot follow through sufficiently, not even when everything seems on paper to be right, because they suffer so much from misgovernment and mismanagement.

The frameworks for public administration and even administrative reform folklore may be universal, but the execution of administrative reform certainly is not. Privatization may work in the one country but there is no guarantee that it will work in another or that it will be the same kind of privatization. Budget reforms such as P.P.B.S. may appear to be technical but they are in fact complex social system transformations. People cannot be changed so easily; they are not forms that can be redesigned overnight or new computers that can replace the old. They are temperamental and when set against reform they cannot be budged. In Third World countries, they seem particularly resistant to administrative reforms, usually for very good reasons from their point of view. They are probably going to be losers. They are going to have to work harder or learn new skills or relocate or adopt a different life-style or do something that they don't want to do for whatever reason, rational and irrational. Sure, they can be forced to change and for appearance's sake, they can go along with the changes. But nobody can really make them do exactly what has to be done in the way that others want it done all the time, unless they themselves are willing to do it.

Too often in administrative reform, the erstwhile reformers do not see the world from the perspective of the potentially reformed. They don't know what makes them tick. They don't understand the different perspective. They don't appreciate the reasons why they stick to the way things are. They don't offer sufficient reason let alone incentive to encourage them to shift. They don't strike the right chord. They don't have the resources (political power, skills, time) to make them move. They don't carry enough conviction. They certainly don't have enough weight in the administrative system. This is true everywhere but more especially in Third World countries where:

* resources are scarce or scarcer,
* administrative capabilities are low or lower,
* tradition dies hard or harder,
* divisions run deep or deeper,
* public service ideology is weak or weaker,
* civic culture is poor or poorer,
* choices are narrow or narrower,
* dependence is high or higher,
* administration has low or lower priority,
* enterprise is confined or more confined,
* indiscipline is rife or more rife,
* public ethics are not respected or less respected,
* resentment of strangers is prevalent or more prevalent,
* social costs are not affordable or less affordable.

Peoples are just different and they want different things. They hold different values. They don't want to be Eastern or Western; they want to be themselves if they can ever discover what it is they want to be instead. They just don't like the kind of world that reformers want to impose on them. They won't abide with organizational imperatives or conform to bureaucratic sameness or accept the managerial mind-set. Their resistance to administrative reform is not due to ignorance or cussedness or stupidity but to deep seated concerns that reformers have not properly addressed or refused to acknowledge. Their resistance is manifested through whatever channels exist and however defiance can be expressed in their country. Modern mass communications make all this more obvious today in the Third World than the forgotten history of yesterday's administrative reforms in both East and West bought at the high price extracted by the organizational society. Third World peoples are aware of the price they will have to pay for administrative modernization and they are not that willing or indeed willing at all to pay it, not if they have any say.

The converse is that those who benefit from public maladministration don't yield. Public maladministration damages the public generally but rewards specific groups and individuals including privileged public sector elites like the Indian Civil Service and the Brazilian "maharajahs" who use institutions and rules as "a cover for patronage, favoritism, fraud and sometimes force" (Glickman, 1988, 33).

> Politicians and bureaucrats usually profit from the harm they do, at one extreme by wrecking the economy in return for kickbacks, at the other by merely collecting a salary for doing no useful work. But since they do gain in one way or another, is it not absurd to expect them to show willing restraint? (*The Economist*, 1989, 58)

Corruption certainly benefits the corrupt who get things they otherwise would not get or be entitled to. Pulling strings helps those who can. Fraud pays. Bloated bureaucracies employ people who otherwise would have no other source of income. Paper manufacturers gain from paperasserie. The profits to the minority count for it much more than the losses (often unknown, unfelt, unconnected) to the majority. Therefore, it takes an exceptional kind of public beneficiary to wrest away the profits from the minority to be shared among the general public. That is why pioneer administrative reformers are so often recognized by name and venerated in history. The fact that so few are known or have been recognized in Third World countries indicates that so few have been in a position or have had the abilities or seized the opportunity or had the will to defy convention, battle great odds, take on vested interests, and suffer the personal indignities that usually befall pioneers.

When all is said and done, it *is* the individual that makes the difference and it takes much nerve to persist in pursuing public right when it is so easy to give in to public wrong. Reforms fail in the best of circumstances but reformers succeed even in the worst. Partial successes, as so often recorded in the Third World, are helpful but no substitute for the real thing. Like economic restructuring, administrative reform in much of the Third World will be impossible to do quickly if at all and "without considerable outside help. The best-intentioned efforts will take a long time, and most will be blocked or eviscerated by political opposition and continuing institutional limitations" (Vernon, 1988, 187). Furthermore, the World Bank and the I.M.F. while appearing to favor economic liberalization and stabilization and minimalist government worldwide are still keen for Third World countries to reform rather than roll back their public sectors, to rely more on imperfect markets than imperfect governments, to improve administrative organization and management, and to provide better if not good government.

References

A.A.P.A.M., *The Ecology of Public Administration and Management in Africa*, Vikas Publishing House, New Delhi, 1986.

Adamolekun, L. (a), *Issues in Development Management in Sub-Saharan Africa*, The World Bank, Washington, D.C., October 1989.

Adamolekun, L. (ed.) (b), *Symposium on Privatization in Africa*, Economic Development Institute of the World Bank, Washington, D.C., December 1989.

Al-Rahim, M., et al. (eds.), *Sudan Since Independence*, Gower, Aldershot, 1986.

Balogun, M. J., and Mutahaba, G., (eds.), *Economic Restructuring and African Public Administration,* Kumarian Press, West Hartford, CT, 1989.

Bethune, C., "The Administrative Reform Programme of Jamaica," paper presented to the subregional seminar on "Innovations in the Field of Public Management for C.L.A.D.-member English-Speaking Countries," Georgetown, Guyana, July 1989.

Caiden, G.E., and Truelson, J.A., "Further Light on Combatting Administrative Corruption," in R.M. Arora and L.L. Kanchuk (eds.), *The Universe of Public Administration*, Centre for Administrative Change, Chandigarh, India, 1990.

Centro Latinamericano De Administraction Para El Desarrollo, "La Reforma Del Estado: Aspectos Téoricas y Experiencas", *Seleccion de Documentos Clave,* Vol. 7, No. I, June 1990.

Chikulo, B., "Reorganization for Local Administration in Zambia: An Analysis of the Local Administration Act, 1980," *Public Administration and Development*, Vol. 5, No. 1, 1985, pp. 73-81.

Clark, D., "Dirigisme in an East Asian City: A Community Relations Approach to Corruption in Hong Kong," paper presented to the I.P.S.A. Study Group meeting, Bellagio, May 1987.

The Courier, Special issue on structural adjustment, No. 111, Sept-Oct, 1988.

Dwividi, O., "Editor's Introduction: Administrative Heritage, Morality and Challenges in the Sub-continent Since the British Raj," *Public Administration and Development*, Vol. 9, No. 3 , 1989, pp. 245-252.

The Economist, "A Survey of the Third World: Poor Man's Burden", Sept. 23, 1989, 58 pp.

Eldridge, D., "Toward a More Culturally Compatible Concept of Civil Service Reform in Developing Countries," *International Journal of Public Sector Management*, Vol. 2, No. 1, 1989, pp. 22-34.

Elsenhans, H., "Public Administration in Developing Countries: Specificities of 'Public' and of 'Administration' in Market-Regulated Developing and Capitalistic Societies," paper presented at the Fourteenth World Congress of the International Political Science Association, Washington, D.C., 1988.

Flores, G. and Nef, J. (eds.), *Administracion Publica: Perspectivas Criticas*, I.C.A.P. San Jose, Costa Rica, 1984.

Freitas, R.C., *State Reform: National Office of the Civil Service*, Hans Seidel Foundation, Montevideo, Uruguay, 1989.

Glickman, H. (ed.), *The Crisis and Challenge of African Development*, Greenwood Press, Westport, CT., 1988.

Green, P., and Slyfield, M., "Problems in Strengthening the Administrative Capacity of Small States," Occasional Paper No. 1, Administrative Staff College, Kingston, Jamaica, 1982.

Grindle, M.S., and Thomas, J.W., "Policy Makers, Policy Choices, and Policy Outcomes: The Political Economy of Reform in Developing Countries," *Policy Sciences*, Vol 22, Nos. 3-4, November 1989, pp. 213-248.

Groissman, F., et al., *La Administracion Publica en Tiempo de Crisis*, C.L.A.D., Caracas, Venezuela, 1986.

Haq, K. and Kirdar, U. (eds.), *Managing Human Development*, North-South Roundtable, Islamabad, Pakistan, September 1987.

Hammergren, L., *Development and the Politics of Administrative Reform*, Westview Press, Boulder, CO., 1983.

Hancock, G., *Lords of Poverty: The Power, Prestige and Corruption of the International Aid Business,* The Atlantic Monthly Press, New York, 1989.

Heidenheimer, A.J., et al. (eds.), *Political Corruption: A Handbook*, Transaction Books, New Brunswick, N.J., 1988.

Highlights, "Africans Initiating Economic Reforms," Vol. 6, No. 3, U.S.A.I.D., Washington, D.C., 1989.

Holanda, N., "Administrative Reform and Reform of the State," *Revista Do Servico Publico* (Brasilia), Vol. 117, No. 2, Sept.-Dec. 1989, pp. 117- 132.

Icklis, J.C., et al. (eds.), *Beyond Bureaucracy: Strategic Management of Social Development*, Kumarian Press, West Hartford, CT., 1986.

Insight, September 12, 1988, pp. 8-19.

Instituto Centroamericano de Administracion Publica, *Reforma Administrativa*, San Jose, Costa Rica, 1971.

Instituto Nacional de Administracion Publica, *Reforma Administrativa: Experiencias Latinoamericanas*, Mexico City, 1975.

Jreisat, J., "Administrative Reform in Developing Countries: A Comparative Perspective," *Public Administration and Development*, Vol. 8, No. 1, 1988, pp. 85-97.

Kliksberg, B., "Administrative Reform in Latin America: A Review of the Conceptual Framework," reprinted by C.L.A.D., Caracas, 1983.

Klitgaard, R., *Controlling Corruption*, University of California Press, Berkeley, Ca., 1988.

Korten, D. (ed.), *Community Management: Asian Experience and Perspectives*, Kumarian Press, West Hartford, Ct., 1987.

Korten, D., and Alfonso, F., *Bureaucracy and the Poor: Closing the Gap*, Kumarian Press, West Hartford, Ct., 1983.

Korten, D., and Klauss, R. (eds.), *People-Centered Development: Contributions Toward Theory and Planning Frameworks*, Kumarian Press, West Hartford, Ct., 1984.

Korten, D., and Uphoff, N., "Bureaucratic Reorganization for Participatory Rural Development," N.A.S.P.A.A. Working Paper No. 1, National Association of Schools of Public Administration and Affairs, Washington,D.C., 1981.

Korten, F., and Siy, R., *Transforming Bureaucracy*, Kumarian Press, West Hartford, Ct., 1988.

Lethbridge, J.J., *Hard Graft in Hong Kong: Scandal, Corruption, and the I.C.A.C.*, Oxford University Press, Hong Kong, 1985.

Martinez, R.R., "Reforms of the Basic Law of State Public Administration," *Revista Del Instituto Do Administracion Publica Del Estado De Mexico*, No. 4, Oct.-Dec. 1989. pp. 23-26.

Mutahaba, G.R., *Reforming Public Administration for Development: Experiences From Eastern Africa,* Kumarian Press, West Hartford, CT., 1989.

Mufson, S., "White Elephants in Black Africa," *The New Republic*, December 29, 1986, pp. 18-20.

Nafzinger, F.W., *Inequality in Africa: Political Elites, Proletariat, Peasants and the Poor*, Cambridge University Press, New York, 1988.

Oszlak, O., "Politicas publicas y regimenes politicos: reflexiones a partir de algunas experiencias latinoamericanas," Centro de Estudios y Sociedad (C.E.D.E.S.), Buenos Aires, 1980.

Perlman, B., "Modernizing the Pubic Service in Latin America: Paradoxes of Latin American Public Administration," *International Journal of Public Administration*, Vol 12, No. 6, 1989, pp. 671-704.

Priestley, M., *Administrative Reform Enquiries in Jamaica 1942-1980*, Administrative Staff College, Kingston, Jamaica, 2 vols., 1980.

Quah, J., "Bureaucracy and Administrative Reform in ASEAN Countries: A Comparative Analysis," in R.B. Jain (ed.), *Bureaucratic Politics in the Third World*, Gritanjali Publishing House, New Delhi, 1989.

Rondinelli, D., and Ingle, M., "Improving the Implementation of Development Programs: Beyond Administrative Reform," S.I.C.A. Occasional Paper Series, No. 10, American Society for Public Administration, Washington, D.C., April 1981.

Rweyemamu, A., and Hyden, G. (eds.), *A Decade of Public Administration in Africa*, East African Literature Bureau, Nairobi, 1975.

Siegel, G., *The Vicissitudes of Governmental Reform in Brazil: A Study of DASP*, University Press of America, Washington, D.C., 1978.

Thurber, C., and Graham, L. (eds.), *Development Administration in Latin America*, Duke University Press, Durham, N.C., 1973.

Vernon, R. (ed.), *The Promise of Privatization: A Challenge for U.S. Policy*, Council on Foreign Relations, New York, 1988.

Werlin, H., "The Community: Master or Client? – A New Review of the Literature," *Public Administration and Development*, Vol. 9, No. 4, 1989, pp. 447-457.

World Bank, *Sub-Sahara Africa: From Crisis to Sustainable Growth*, Washington, D.C., 1989.

World Bank, *World Development Report, 1983*, Washington, D.C., 1984.

World Bank, *World Development Report, 1985*, Washington, D.C., 1986.

13. Unfinished Business

Administrative reformers around the globe certainly have their work cut out over the next decade. In the East Bloc, they will be grappling with the complex problems of shifting from bureaucratic centralism to various experiments in market socialism and mixed economies, reducing institutionalized corruption and tackling imbedded bureaupathologies. In the West, they will be fine-tuning the administrative state, restoring the status and attractiveness of public employment, and grappling with the issues of the accountability and discretion of public sector managers. In the so-called Third World, they will be modernizing their administrative systems, searching to debureaucratize, and identifying administrative norms in keeping with their preferred administrative cultures. In the international agencies, they will be assisting all these global activities, boosting management education and training, aiding self-help grassroots organizations and strengthening institutional development (Israel, 1987). All of them will be coping with the changing impacts of technological innovation, the further internationalization of their administrative systems in the global society, and the redefinition of what is or should be public. All of them will be trying to humanize and sensitize bureaucracy and to make public administration more truly public. All of them will be seeking to advance the state-of-the-art of administrative reform.

Opinions among their target audiences about the worth and necessity for administrative reform range from those who anticipate large returns from a relatively small investment to those who believe that administrative reform does not work and is largely a waste of time and resources. As usual, the truth is somewhere between. In some circumstances, where public maladministration and mismanagement predominate, administrative reform can indeed turn things around such that large economies can be made, productivity increased and ineffective organizations and services can be reversed. In other circumstances, the resources necessary to implement administrative reform do not exist, and even if they did they would be used on higher priority items such as feeding starving people, repairing run-down facilities and employing jobless persons; when actually assigned to administrative reform the improvements are barely noticed.

Administrative reform is still mostly process-oriented. Better processes may result in better outcomes, better substantive performance, even better policy directions. Although administrative reform is intended to make the administrative state perform better, it will not of itself solve political crises, economic problems and social dissent, as unfortunately reformers sometimes promise. It rarely provides solutions to these societal problems; it merely helps implement solutions. If the policies are wrong or the objectives undesirable, administrative reform compounds the errors. In this sense, it is morally neutral, a tool in the hands of the user and its benefits depend on what it is used. If it is employed to make the administrative state more economic and efficient, the resources saved can be redirected to provide greater returns to society. Similarly, if the emphasis is on effective service delivery, more people can obtain access to public services and amenities and enjoy higher quality services. But in and of itself, administrative reform cannot transform society. It can, however, bring the Good Society that much nearer. Administration of resources is increasingly important in contemporary society. Therefore good or better administration is also increasingly important, and since administrative reform promises better or improved performance, it can only be ignored at risk.

But administrative reform, if done well, is greatly demanding and ill-afforded. Something cannot be achieved with nothing. Administrative reform requires an investment of resources, energy and time. Successful reform requires strong political backing, new institutions, legal amendments and personal incentives (Wilenski, 1986). It demands the unfreezing of a situation, alterations and a refreezing. It eventuates in a realignment of political power, a redistribution of resources, a reallocation of assignments and responsibilities, and a redirection of efforts. It culminates in a change of administrative attitudes, behavior and values, i.e. in a different administrative ethos or culture. None of these things occurs easily. Some countries, governments, organizations, and administrators are much more amenable to reform than others. In any event, the relatively deprived are handicapped, doubly handicapped in that their performance is already inferior and they lack the ability or capacity to improve it. Those most in need can least afford. Conversely, administrative systems already performing well can better undertake reform and can better afford to innovate, experiment and even lose their investment altogether. The poorest systems cannot risk any losses; they cannot afford to experiment and innovate; they cannot indulge too much in administrative reform as such. On the other hand, too much administrative reform so unsettles administrative systems that they may cease to function at all (Campbell and Peters, 1988, 202). This is the worst of all worlds, as both the investments made in reform and the anticipated outcomes (in reduced maladministration, revitalization, better services, higher productivity, fewer bureaupathologies, etc.) are lost.

Too much administrative reform also illustrates the dilemma, frequently experienced, in exchanging one set of problems for another. Tackling administrative deficiencies and shortcomings is a ceaseless activity. Improvements can always be made somewhere. But in settling one set of administrative problems, such as centralization, so another set of problems to do with decentralization immediately presents itself. Similarly, better financial management procedures will reveal outdated legislation, poor operating methods and deficiencies in employee qualifications and training. Administration is an integrated activity and one part cannot be touched without affecting all the other parts. Accordingly, administrative reform resembles a treadmill. Failure to keep going means the whole process slows down and the lost momentum sooner or later leads to disappointments and omissions, and may well result in purely cosmetic changes that do not amount to much. Far from enhancing performance, it may actually diminish effectiveness. On the other hand, persistent administrative reform pressure keeps administrative systems in trim and administrators on their toes. It certainly diminishes the prospects of bureaucratic inertia. Above all, since administrative reform concerns the performance of the administrative state and the effectiveness of government, it does make a difference, perhaps a crucial difference in governability, stability, capacity, accessibility, credibility and action, as long as it is understood that instantaneous returns are rare except in the case of selling public assets.

Although administration and management are recognized as being of increasing importance in governance, that what governments can achieve depends increasingly on their administrative and managerial capacity and competence, that politicians and bureaucrats, elected and non-elected officials, are inseparable in the modern administrative state, that public and private sectors are becoming increasingly integrated and fused, administrative reform still concentrates on traditional concerns or folklore, leaving large and significant gaps that need to be explored in the next decade. Administrative reform itself has failed to keep up with the times, leaving out some of the key administrative issues and problems of the day.

Reforming The International Public Sector

Administrative reform almost entirely concentrates on state or country level of analysis. It fails to recognize the emergence of a global economy, an intricate network of international organizations and a superstructure of world authorities possessing real power and influence. It acknowledges that administrative reforms flow across state borders and that what happens in one country affects reforms campaigns in other countries. It has little to say about the performance of international bodies and the need for administrative reform at international level. Yet, in recent years the United Nations Organization has come under increasing criticism for being sluggish, top heavy, and overly bureaucratic. The United States temporarily left U.N.E.S.C.O. in protest at its policies and at its mismanagement, and demanded administrative reforms before it would rejoin. The World Bank has undergone several reorganizations in order to streamline its operations and prevent organizational dry-rot. An international civil service has existed for nearly half a century but still the same problems with it persist. Even international agencies that promote administrative and managerial reforms at state level have not taken their own medicine. Indeed, there is good reason to believe that internal critics and possible whistleblowers in international organizations as elsewhere are intimidated into silence and have few outlets through which they can push for long overdue administrative reforms.

Members of international organizations have the right to question how well or badly international organizations are run, whether their contributions are being put to the best use, and what could be done to improve performance, increase efficiency, and reduce waste. In the case of the U.N.O., several countries have exercised that right but have been frustrated in the responses they have received. The U.N.O. family of organizations undertakes a variety of activities crucial to the peace, security, health, diet, and development of all peoples in the world and employs staff to serve in over 120 countries around the globe. It is an immense administrative undertaking overseen by the U. N. Secretariat and subject to the vagaries of the General Assembly within the broad objectives of the Charter and other international agreements and declarations. Although an intricate system of program planning, budgeting, monitoring and evaluation has been evolved in a six-year fixed horizon plan (Mathiason, 1986, 5), it has been difficult to determine exactly how its resources have been allocated and where administrative expenses have occurred or how much the whole edifice costs world citizenry, let alone whether value for money is being received by member states.

The administrative problems of the U.N.O. are particularly serious and deep-seated. Although its own boards of inquiry have found administrative irregularities, unfair discrimination and professional misconduct, it has rarely admitted error or made any atonement for its failures, acting as if it were accountable to no one but itself. It has not lived up to the norms of a true international civil service, succumbing to self-gratification, self-aggrandizement and self-importance and failing to adopt long-recognized public personnel principles and practices (Hazzard, 1990). Instead it has been dominated by nationality and geographical considerations in a world wide spoils system characterized by grade creep, particularism, fragmentation, politicization (in the sense of "the progressive replacement of rationality norms by narrow partisan considerations"), diffraction and dispersion, causing its perceptible marginalization in activities it might have played a leading role.

> In an organizational climate which seldom proves conducive to nondefensive problem-solving, decisions are quite often the outcomes of bureaucratic infighting, mutual accommodation or at best an arduous process of consensus-building. Predictably, the causalities are principally merit, professional integrity and rationality norms. Morale and motivation are also hard to foster and to sustain. But more than that, the system severely circumscribes the scope and possibilities for administrative discretion and managerial initiative. It also sets strict limits on organizational change. (Argyriades, 1988, 488)

Left to itself, the prospects of reform are low, although threatened withdrawal of contributions and resource scarcity may provoke reforms. Eventually something will have to give, as has been the case in private sector international organizations and some regional organizations like the Organization of American States which started with overhauling budgetary processes. Threats to survival usually stimulate innovation and reform.

Some of the U.N.'s larger contributors have objected to footing an ever increasing bill for activities that they do not agree with or for programs over which they have, so they claim, no control. Thus the U.S.A. and the East Bloc have always opposed the U.N. technical co-operation program, not because they disagree with the substance of the program but as a protest about the size and administration of the U.N. itself. Recent attempts to grapple with the financial and administrative problems of the U.N. reveal how little traditional approaches to administrative reform can contribute. As the U.N. family and other international organizations are likely permanent fixtures, this neglected area of administrative reform presents quite a challenge. To quote Brian Urquhart:

> The present U.N. "system" cannot respond readily to the great emergencies – war, famines, floods, earthquakes or other disasters – that require humanitarian aid; nor can it yet effectively organize international and national responses to the vast complex of interconnected social and economic problems we now face – the polluted environment, poverty and migration, or drugs, for example. This is not so much an indictment of the system devised in 1945 as a recognition of the vast changes that have taken place since. To bring the international system up to date will demand a major effort of imagination and reorganization. The problem is to convert an intergovernmental system, in which national sovereignty and interests are paramount, to an international system in which an increasing number of activities beyond the control of individual governments can be carried out by international, or even supranational institutions. The particular interests involved and the extreme sensitivity of governments in matters touching on their sovereignty will inevitably make this evolution laborious and frustrating. (Urquhart, 1990, 12)

And obviously worthwhile. An expert committee reviewed the administration and finances of the U.N. and reported to the forty-first General Assembly in 1986. It made 71 recommendations covering the intergovernmental machinery, secretariat structure, personnel, superintendence and finance but by 1990 there had been little action.

Reforming Military Administration

While the role of the international public sector is relatively new, the presence of military administration is not. Yet administrative reform has concentrated almost entirely on civil administration, despite the fact that most governments in the world are military regimes or are led by persons drawn from the military and influenced by their training and experience in military organizations and that the highest single activity expenditure by many governments is on the military. Since the mid 1980s, the governments of the world have been spending annually over 1 trillion U.S. dollars on armed forces and their weapons and a substantial part of the global labor force is employed directly by the military. What belongs to the military is obviously denied to the civil side of government, unless the military is deployed delivering civil services. Public resources wasted or mismanaged by the military are lost to other parts of the public sector and to the private sector. Thus everyone has a stake in the administrative performance of the military.

Historically, the military has not been particularly management-minded. True, it has perfected organizations capable of conducting wars and fighting battles. Indeed, the bureaucratic model owes much to military inspiration and experimentation. But stories are legion everywhere how the military has been unable to sustain levels of readiness, how it has stuck to outmoded tradition long after the need has disappeared, how it has discounted and wasted human resources for nothing, how it has recklessly destroyed its own property, capital and equipment, how it has virtually institutionalized every conceivable bureaupathology and been afflicted with bureaucratic inertia to extreme, how, in fact, it has been unable to perform militarily because it has been so badly disorganized administratively. The military has an insatiable appetite. It believes in excess, abundance, overkill, overcapacity, for it fears scarcity, undercapacity, inadequacy, insufficiency and cares little for the cost.

The enlightened professional military of today understands all this and has taken steps to improve administratively and managerially. It boasts that so well prepared managerially are its officers that they can readily obtain civil employment in executive positions and they are actually sought out by both public and private employers. If, indeed, this is true, administrative reform has overlooked it because virtually nothing exists on the administrative performance of ex-military officers. The military profession still seems to have a monopoly of administrative reform in military organizations. Much the same could be said about para-military organizations and intelligence services. But in recent years administrative reformers have discovered police forces and police organizations have discovered administrative reform so that this is no longer so true of the police profession. It is even less true of other notoriously non-management minded public professions, such as diplomacy or foreign service, public health, public education, and tax administration which have been integrated more and more with general administration and are rapidly losing their autonomy and self-management, unlike the courts which have steadfastly held to their independence not with the best administrative results either. All, but particularly the military, have to adjust to a turbulent world in which their rationale may not be so credible any more.

Para-statal Organizations

Governments have spawned many different varieties of independent or semi-autonomous or self-contained units outside their direct lines of control through departments and public corporations. Often there are so many that nobody even has an up-to-date list as they are being created, reorganized and abandoned all the time. They include advisory and consultative bodies, accreditation boards, statutory authorities, non-governmental organizations (N.G.O.s), quasi-autonomous non-governmental organizations (quangos), public companies, educational and training institutes, joint enterprises, regulatory commissions, government-assisted private voluntary organizations (P.V.O.s), conciliation and arbitration councils, commercial outlets and marketing boards, sports complexes, cultural patrons, state-supported religions, and so on, combined here under the title of para-statals. Governments seem to know what they want done and they seem to believe that what needs doing is feasible and economical. They are prepared to foot the bill but they leave the details to outside experts and people who claim to know how to do what needs doing. They don't exercise the same detailed controls as in the case of governmental organizations nor do they seem to evaluate their performance so carefully or interfere in their administration.

Obviously para-statals are important in government and to government, and generally to the public. They are considered necessary and indispensable, at least at the time of their creation. Yet there is no consistency among them. Administratively, chaos reigns. Nobody knows just where they fit into government, how they should be treated, and what administratively and managerially should be expected of them. Outside the stateowned enterprises, administrative reform is largely silent as if they did not exist or were of little consequence, although they serve community purposes, produce public goods and services, use public resources, and are ultimately backed by government sanctions. The quality of their administrative and managerial performance should concern all but apparently does not because many of them fall into that shady area between public and private sectors where nobody seems sure what administrative norms should apply.

Yet, the number of such fringe bodies has been increasing and will continue to increase as governments privatize their state-owned enterprises without totally freeing them of public controls and accountability. Australia and New Zealand have probably gone farthest in attempting to establish performance guidelines and bringing them under at least government audit supervision to ensure that they do not abuse whatever special governmental privileges they may enjoy and that they do further the public interest. Undoubtedly, they facilitate desirable variations in the style and method of public administration and management and they do allow for greater direct public participation in the conduct of public affairs. On the other hand, they tend to run themselves as if they were totally private bodies responsible only to themselves, their links to government are tenuous, often indirect and undefined and therefore personalized and impenetrable, their legal situation is ambiguous, and while their fundamental administrative performance can be assessed, judging their effectiveness in terms of outputs and outcomes is probably more difficult than any other area of public administration (Taylor, 1980).

Freeing public agencies to manage themselves does not free them from public scrutiny and the need to conduct themselves in a publicly responsible manner. There are many questions that administrative reformers will eventually have to tackle, particularly as more and more state-owned enterprises and public activities are freed from traditional government arrangements and encouraged to operate as private businesses. How do governments ensure that all these fringe organizations, some of which are quite important in the life of the community like the broadcasting services, banking services, multi-purpose river valley development agencies, and trade promotion commissions (Curnow and Saunders, 1983), are responsible, representative and responsive and follow public service norms? What additions to the conventional notions of accountability are needed for mixed or joint enterprises and publicly assisted private bodies and voluntary associations besides just funnelling public money into private hands? What legal immunities, if any, should they enjoy? How open should the conduct of their business be? To whom does a frustrated client or member of the public complain when policy or administration goes awry? What rules should be standardized for the notion of public trusteeship? What limitations on the notion of independence should be formalized? What should be the policy guidelines governing N.G.O.s, especially those operating in the international arena through which public development and disaster relief funds are distributed (Moharir, 1989)? In short, what is to be done about the growing privatization of the public sector and government?

Monitoring The Privatization of Government

The private production and distribution of public goods and services has become more popular as an administrative reform policy to roll back the state, reduce the public sector and take advantage of private management practices. The advocates of privatization take as axiomatic that private sector performance is superior to public sector performance, although this has yet to be proved conclusively. Probably more important than ownership are the presence of competition and consumer choice, the amount of public subsidization (particularly hidden subsidies) and the quality of decision-making and management, neither sector having a decided let alone exclusive advantage. Freed from public sector operating norms (controls, accountability, central direction, openness, due process, public ethics), private contractors should be able to perform administratively better. In practice, they have been giving cause for alarm, to which little reference has been made in administrative reform. Since sizeable portions of the public sector are being contracted out, the warning signals should no longer be ignored.

An area which best illustrates the problems in the privatization of government is the manufacture of weapons and other high technology research and development items specifically for the government that cannot be purchased on the open market. First, the government really does not know what it wants and when it does define specifications, nobody knows in advance whether they can be met. Second, the anticipated or estimated or projected costs can only be guesses and when costs escalate there is no choice but to pay them or abandon sunk costs altogether without any return. Third, once committed, the government cannot readily abandon the contractor and find another at all or not without incurring heavy legal penalties and political costs. In such cases, contractors can make the government dance to their tune and give them what amounts to a blank check. Administrative reform has been somewhat silent about how to avoid profiteering, fraud, waste, deceit and private mismanagement under these circumstances. It also has had little to say about costly overruns, interminable delays, non-performance or totally inadequate performance, massive write-offs, unreliability, low productivity, over-charging, conflicts of interest, scams and corruption, as if all these were beyond administrative or managerial control. In fact many have resulted from faulty administration and gross mismanagement not only within private contracting organizations but also within the government contracting agency often appearing as if in deliberate collusion to cheat the public which pays the bills.

Is the fault undermanagement (Fitzgerald, 1989) or overmanagement (Gregory, 1989) or just poor management? In the case of U.S. defense procurement, probably the largest contracting area in the world, even with abundant information, it is difficult to decide. Between 1946 and 1986, there were scores of studies conducted by the President, the Department of Defense, the U.S. General Accounting Office, the Congressional Research Service, blue-ribbon committees, the Grace Commission, research institutes, professional societies and the armed forces themselves. Many of these inquiries resulted in different policies, reorganizations, new laws and procedures, and changes in personnel. Probably the most important was the Commission on Government Procurement (1969-1972) which went beyond procurement to make recommendations on budget reforms, agency organization, personnel management and even Congressional oversight. It blamed premature program commitment, over optimism of system advocates, uncertain and delayed funding, and unstable program requirements. It recommended the use of phased or incremental development, natural rather than forced competition and Congressional commitment to orderly systems planning and approval. In short, the fault was with management and funding not procurement, with political decision-making not with administrative procedures. Unless the politicians reformed themselves, the problems would continue. And they did, far worse than before because the scale was so much enlarged.

When the scandals grew to such proportions that the public or rather the mass media got into the act on their behalf, President Reagan appointed a Blue Ribbon Commission on Defense Management (Packard) 1985-1986 which did not go much beyond previous recommendations except to propose "centers of excellence" (then much in vogue in business management) which were not pursued and contractor "self-governance" that had not worked previously. Nonetheless, the major thrust was consistent with standard wisdom in government contracting, namely that the practice of having the Pentagon set defense objectives, figure out the costs and send the package to the White House should be reversed. The President should decide national security goals and their fair share of public income, set policy by choosing among alternative military structures, figure out how America's allies might help, compare the costs of different ways of putting defense forces together, reduce incentives for cheating, waste, goldplating (pushing performance and costs beyond reason), and cut out excessive bureaucratization, regulation and hierarchy. Three years later President Bush still had not acted. So much for administrative reform against vested interests, political self-interest and bureaucratic inertia. In the meantime, contracting abuses continue, not just in defense procurement, but wherever contractors feel they can get away with extra money undetected and when exposed, merely slapped on the wrist without apparently being excluded from follow-up contracts, new bidding and new projects. The problem is not confined to the United States: it is universal.

Ensuring Accountability

Private contractors are accountable only to themselves, to the public in so far as they follow public laws guiding their business practices, and to the contracting agency in meeting the terms of the contract. If through public maladministration, the law and the terms of the contract are not enforced, then they can run wild. This is not supposed to happen to public agencies institutionally encaged. Administrative reform has assumed this and sought only to strengthen traditional political, budgetary and management controls, even though annual reports of government bodies reveal little, governments exempt themselves from safety and health, environmental, labor relations and securities laws, and public organizations frequently act as if they were privately owned. Worse still, governments have done things in the name of national security, the public interest and science that horrified when they finally came to light, demonstrating the breakdown of administrative/organizational, legal, political, professional and moral accountability (Jabbra and Dwividi, 1989).

Most breakdowns in public accountability can be attributed to incompetent political overseers, corrupt officials, an authoritarian administrative ethos, bureaucratic inertia, and anonymity when dealing directly with the public. None of these is insurmountable and administrative reforms can take care of many of them. But the size and complexity of big government, the scope and indeterminate reach of the administrative state, and the novel forms of public and private sector partnership have given rise to some intractable problems of ensuring public accountability. The public does not have effective means of assessing performance and of exercising control in the following cases:

* **unconstitutional government** where constitutional limitations are ignored and no public officials have to answer to any external authority;
* **secret government** where activities are hidden and those involved are prohibited from revealing them;
* **special interest government** where single-issue demands dominate over considerations of the general interest and block changes in the status quo;
* **bureaucratic government** where bureaucratic self- interest predominates;
* **collaborative government** where inter-governmental arrangements confuse jurisdictions and jumble powers and responsibilities;
* **discretionary government** where officials legally exercise absolute power;
* **independent government** where whole agencies are allowed absolute discretion;
* **contracted government** where contractors are independent and given wide latitude in public service delivery;
* **professional government** where practitioners determine what should be done and govern themselves;
* **privileged government** where the public has no legal redress against wrongdoing.

In the worst cases, public accountability is a farce, amounting to very little, protecting very few and meaningful only to the privileged. Although something much stronger than administrative reform is required to restore full and proper public accountability, just enforcing existing laws and strengthening the legal system, law enforcement and government tracking abilities would certainly help. Indeed, administrative reformers need to turn their attention to the whole area of law enforcement, white collar crime, and organizational liabilities.

Answering The Question of Bureaucracy

Administrative reform is ambivalent about bureaucratic organization. On one side can be found those who detest bureaucracy and want no part of it. They seek to abolish or abandon bureaucracy altogether and replace it with alternative forms of organization. They are joined by others who just about tolerate bureaucracy but believe that it is far from the optimal arrangements for human beings or that it is a historical phenomenon likely to be outmoded by changes in technology and culture. They too seek alternatives to bureaucracy better suited to individual needs or more adaptable to turbulent environments. Although many of these radical reformers do not distinguish between public and private sectors or between public and private organizations, their main target is government bureaucracies which they see as being particularly dehumanizing, uninventive, rigid, and insufficiently adaptive.

On the other side can be found those who accept bureaucracy, recognize that despite its imperfections it seems a reliable, dependable and effective form of organization for carrying out activities on a large scale, and prefer to patch it up rather than replace it. They believe that bureaucracy is here to stay. It has been around for thousands of years and it is likely to be around for some time yet. It has become the preferred form of organization, irrespective of culture, environment, ownership, objectives, and technology, so much so that organization theory or the bulk of organization theory assumes no other form of organization. Most people have become bureaucratized or they are currently being bureaucratized. Rather than seeking alternatives to bureaucracy, a worthwhile activity if it does come up with something better or points to better ways of structuring bureaucracies, this more conservative wing of administrative reformers concentrates on improving bureaucracy and reducing its dysfunctions.

Inevitably, the pro-bureaucracy wing clashes with the anti-bureaucracy wing not only over the strategy of administrative reform but also over the substantive details. The libertarian and anarchical factions want minimal organization and no government bureaucracy at all and wage constant war against those they identify as bureaucratic aggrandizers, empire-builders, collectivists, public interferers, organizers and general busybodies. Their determined resistance makes up for their lack of numbers and they are invariably a nuisance factor in any administrative reform, no matter how petty an issue, and a force to be reckoned with especially when it comes to diversion, disruption, and sabotage. Likewise, the pro-bureaucracy forces can be equally bloody-minded when confronted with proposals that seem to them too far-fetched, too experimental, too off-beat, too disruptive (of traditional bureaucratic modes of thinking or operating procedures), too discomforting. Of course, such internecine warfare between rival reform factions plays straight into the hands of those opposed to reform. Since there is usually dissent among reformers, differences and splits are easy to exploit if not in the advocacy stage, certainly in the implementation process, particularly when reformers have few ideas how to implement their reforms or are dependent on their adversaries to implement them.

Even if these factional differences could be discounted, there still remains the unresolved and possibly unresolvable question of "How much bureaucracy?" The academic world is much divided over this central question, disputing what Max Weber really meant, arguing over different ideal models of bureaucracy, disagreeing over such fundamental concepts as "power", "authority", "efficiency", "effectiveness", "control", "competence", "leadership", "management", "self-regulation", and "merit" and splintering when it comes to such concrete issues as whether bureaucratization has gone too far, whether government bureaucracy has grown too big, whether public bureaucrats exercise too much power, whether multinational corporations are beyond public accountability, whether the public sector promotes or obstructs development, and whether community self-help organizations and charitable non-governmental organizations really deliver cost effectively and meet societal goals. To add to the confusion is the absence of sufficient definitive or conclusive evidence and the paucity of empirical research backing most claims. All that may be said is that the world has become increasingly bureaucratized (Jacoby, 1973; Presthus, 1978) and that organizations have more pronounced bureaucratic characteristics (Grunow, 1988), both at substantial social cost but compensated by societal benefit. The current issue is whether such trends should be continued or halted or reversed. Administrative reform is divided and academic research provides no clear answers and "few workable solutions to the bureaucracy 'problem', if it is a problem" (Meyer et al., 1985).

What administrative reform and academic research have done recently is to look closer into the possibilities and desirability of debureaucratization, that is, making the world less bureaucratized and organizations less bureaucratic, or, more concretely, reducing the role of the state in modern society and diminishing government activities and the public sector and making public bureaucracies less intrusive in the private lives of people and more client-oriented. Politically, bureaucracy-bashing is popular sport and is welcomed by the populace suffering daily from bureaupathologies and maladministration. It is also popular among ideologues of all political persuasions. Debureaucratization is one area where substantial agreement may be reached in principle even to the point of bureaucide or the desire to kill bureaucracies (O'Leary, 1988). In practice, it has not worked out that way at all because while all may agree on symptoms, they are divided on causes and solutions. Moreover, there are definite non-ideological, non-political limitations to debureaucratization. Indeed, contrary to what futurologists may have been predicting (Bennis, 1973; Schumacher, 1973, 1977; Toffler, 1971, 1984), bureaucratization may still be on the increase and technology may strengthen rather than undermine bureaucracy, creating the prospect of "bureaucratization without bureaucrats". This is reason enough why administrative reform will have to be even more concerned with the whole bureaucracy question, which is not going away and not likely to be resolved.

A start could be made by examining the two opposite faces of public bureaucracy, one dominated by administrative entrepreneurs whose missionary zeal in the public interest spurs the whole organization into ever better performance, and the other dominated by the administratively handicapped whose unfitness makes for a parasitic, rapacious organization. Both extremes work within the same framework but produce quite different results. Sometimes they can be found in the same government, side by side, physically next to each other in the same building even. One looks in vain in administrative reform for such direct comparisons and what brought them to such different levels of performance. Again this is where organization theory has let administrative reform down. Even a comparison between trouble-makers and trouble-shooters, between people who supposedly disrupt organizations and people who supposedly settle them down when disrupted has never been drawn.

Perhaps it all boils down to concentrating on the basics and ensuring that the simple, routine things get down quickly and properly, that people know what needs to be done and do it right, that staff are adequately distributed according to the work load to be done, that employees do actually work together and not as if they were at war with one another, that individuals actually do want to work and do work, that everyone involved actually talks with one another and helps each other out, and that they all appreciate and respect one another and cooperate together to improve performance (Rosenbaum, 1982). Or is the problem much more fundamental – an inherent contradiction between outputs and inputs, bureaucratization and participation, administration and democracy? Are public bureaucracies to be service institutions accountable to society or control institutions that increasingly rule society (Denhardt and Jennings, 1987, 14)?

Democratizing Public Administration

Immediately after World War II, interest was shown in the possibilities of democratizing not just government but also public administration and even private administration to avoid the reemergence of tyrannic fascism and nazism and to make organizations less authoritarian, imperious and bureaucratic, and more humane, human, responsible, responsive, sensitive, representative, participative, and generally more likeable. Max Weber had struggled to reconcile bureaucracy as an organization with democracy as an political ideal and his solution was to have bureaucracies ruled or regulated by popularly elected governments. Clearly, this had not been sufficient to prevent the bureaucratization of political activities from becoming non-democratic. From time to time, there had been attempts to reconcile the hierarchical, elitist tendencies of organizations with popular grass roots participation and control, but the issue had never been resolved to satisfaction and the postwar efforts proved no more rewarding. Democratic administration, like democratic management, seemed oxymoronic, except perhaps on a small scale, as in a party cell or cooperative enterprise.

Administrative reform has tended to downplay the contradictions in democratic societies between democratic political institutions and non-democratic administrative institutions. Occasionally, there has been a flurry of concern. Workers' participation in management or in privately managed organizations has been broached for publicly managed enterprises. It received sympathetic hearing and token representation in the British nationalized industries. It was adopted en bloc in workers self-management in Yugoslavia (Pateman, 1970). The Great Society anti-poverty programs had provision for "maximum feasible participation". Participation rarely amounted to control or even to a predominant say in key decision-making. Nor did other reforms intended to make public administrators more representative of their clients. Greater success was achieved through indirect representation and complaint mechanisms but still minor when compared with the empowerment of clients, decentralization of government operations, and sensitivity training of public officials, backed by the extension of individual rights to include social and economic benefits (Glassman et al., 1987).

In the 1970s, a serious effort was made by Vincent Ostrom to switch the predominant paradigm in the study of American public administration from a top-down Weberian bureaucratic approach to a "democratic administration" bottom-up approach based on (a) decentralized, fragmented authority, (b) diverse, overlapping jurisdictions with veto power, and (c) public choice among competing delivery systems (Ostrom, 1973). Clearly, Ostrom was applying public choice theory as formulated in political economy to government and public administration and opened himself to the opponents of that theory. Nevertheless, Ostrom was also echoing the concerns of the New Public Administration movement that (American) public organizations should better reflect the values and composition of the whole society not just those of the power elite, that they should promote social justice and equity, and that relations between them and their clients should be closer and softer. When he failed to convince his peers, it was difficult to rescue the idea of democratic administration from his particular version that decentralized government would be better, more democratic, more moral and that smaller organizations would be more efficient and responsive (Golembiewski, 1977). Nonetheless, his was a genuine attempt to challenge bureaucratic administration. Few others even raise the issue, an issue that demands attention from administrative reform, especially if bureaucracy is here to stay, if public officials are gaining in power, and if bureaucrats maximize their self-interests as the public choice theorists presume (Niskanen, 1971, 36). Just who does the administrative state serve – the state, the public, or itself. If all of them, then which comes first and which last? Is it to be elitist or populist? Is it to govern or be governed?

To offset the specter of bureaucratic or imperial government (Peters, 1981), administrative reform might be expected to come up with a revived version of citizenship and civic culture administration. Presumably if all citizens know their duties and obligations, their responsibilities and rightful conduct, then when they become administrators, public administrators, they will be responsible administrators as befits a democracy. But virtually nowhere has administrative reform included citizenship. Instead, the focus has been on how customers, consumers and clients (significantly not citizens) can better influence public service delivery. The citizens are seen as no more than users, not as owners of public goods and services. They are merely recipients, presumably passive recipients, which fits well with public choice theory and management theory but hardly with democratic theory, and not at all with social theory that seeks enhanced citizenship rights rather than enhanced administrative discretion in the welfare state and that would join "social citizenship" to civil and political citizenship (Marshall, 1964; Waxman, 1983).

A hopeful exception in the 1980s appeared to be a recovery of civicism in American public administration (Denhardt and Jennings, 1987, 25). Government cutbacks had seen some "public" instead of government provision of community services where high technical expertise was not required through new forms of citizen involvement such as coproduction, neighborhood organization delivery, self-help and public/private partnerships. By reducing the gap between the role of citizens and public employees, they had the potential for a more communitarian arrangement of civic life, a revitalization of a communitarian spirit, and a restoration of citizen trust and support for public institutions. But

> Those who believe that citizenship, civic virtue, and "public service" should be an important part of our national culture, should be distressed that these features of democracy have come to be regarded as a mere myth in a polity that increasingly rewards narrow self-interest. (Levine, 1984, 85-6)

and that was well on the way to destroying an indispensable element of idealism in the public service. Citizenship should mean more than passively doing what public authorities want done and voting at elections or serving on juries. The public has to be brought more actively into public administration and citizens and public officials brought closer together to apply the "consent of the governed" principle to both employee and citizen interactions in more significant ways (Gardner, 1974).

Restoring The Appeal of Public Service

The 1980s saw a general trend throughout the world to revive economic fortunes through private enterprise rather than public initiatives. At the same time, privatization became more popular and business management was boosted while public sector employment conditions fell behind those obtaining in the private sector and governments cut back on public service education and training. Not surprising, the appeal of public sector employment in general and public service professions in particular declined. In some countries where public service had traditionally been well respected and honorable such as the United Kingdom, higher executive jobs went begging even at a time of high unemployment. In the United States where federal government salaries fell over 25 percent below private sector counterparts, the new Bush Administration had considerable difficulty filling higher executive positions. While prospective public servants were turned off by bureaucrat-bashing in the mass media and voiced by political leaders, the uncertainty about career prospects in public organizations, and the relative (and in some cases the absolute) decline of living standards of public employees, long-serving, experienced, highly competent and resourceful public executives were leaving public employment for greener pastures elsewhere (where they received much higher compensation) or taking early retirement.

The short run effects were serious enough. The longer term implications were ominous. Even if public employment managed to recover within a decade, the damage had already been done. The loss of morale alone had brought sullen resentment, a sense of (justifiable) grievance, a general souring reflected in work performance and interpersonal relations. But administrative reform relies on a cooperative if not enthusiastic reception, and generally on competent, experienced executives to smooth the way and ease the transition. Administrative reform requires exceptional talent and a motivated public service. Maintaining the appeal and attraction of public service should always be high on the agenda of administrative reform. Yet in the 1980s, administrative reform had very little to say on the subject and whatever it said was drowned out by reformers eager to seize the opportunity presented by economic difficulties to cut down the public sector, reduce public employment, rid public bureaucracy of any excess, reserves and fat, and generally criticize the public sector to which the major share of economic difficulties were attributed.

That the pendulum had swung too far was only recognized belatedly. Even without the constant bombardment from outside, enough turmoil had been generated within public sectors to cause much confusion about goals and objectives, guidelines and regulations, operating procedures, communications, inter-organizational relations, public relations, and client rights. Now had been added the fear that nobody really cared about the fate of public employees, not even their own organizations which had once not so long ago been so understanding, respectful, protective, and supportive. With the downturn in public sector fortunes, public organizations were proving to be heartless, disloyal (to their employees) and even vindictive, particularly for lower echelon staff and lower and middle level managers from whose ranks the future leadership of the public service would be largely drawn and on whom the fate of administrative reforms largely depended. Devoted public servants were becoming disillusioned and no longer recommending that others follow in their footsteps.

What has come to be at stake is no less than the heritage of public service, of commitment to public life, of looking after the public's business, so carefully nurtured for two centuries (Perry and Wise, 1990). This "quiet crisis" in government was recognized in Canada in *Public Service 2000* and in the United States by the Brookings Institution and the American Enterprise Institute in a symposium held in 1987 which led to the creation of the National Commission on the Public Service (Volker), a non-governmental inquiry into the erosion of the quality of America's public service and government's inability to recruit and retain a talented workforce. Although the Volker Commission's report, *Leadership for America: Rebuilding the Public Service* (N.C.P.S., 1989) was specifically addressed to the President and Congress, it did emphasize the need for political leadership generally to uphold the reputation of public service, strengthen the career concept, improve civic education and volunteerism, and increase public sector compensation and terms of employment, and for public servants to commit themselves to efficiency, responsiveness and integrity. In the chairman's words,

> ...keeping America strong and maintaining our leadership will rest on restoring a sense of high ethics and professionalism and challenge in public service itself. It needs to be attractive to the most talented and energetic among us, able to compete with professions which will pay a lot more. (Volker, 1989)

The immediate impact of the Volker Report was to curb or tone down bureaucrat-bashing and to set in motion machinery to improve public confidence in government and self-pride in public employment. The Volker Commission continued to put pressure on the federal government to implement its recommendations and issued a regular newsletter on progress. It was a step in reversing the trend against public service, and it may have been a turning point. Elsewhere around the globe, similar concerns were being expressed and action taken to restore the appeal of public service and the confidence of public officials, such as improving administrative leadership, reorganizing structures to provide more collaboration, redefining jobs to make work more interesting and less boring, permitting more flexible working hours and conditions of employment, undertaking job satisfaction studies, and generally beefing up research into public employee dissatisfaction and discontent (Davies, 1988).

Undertaking Research

That a privately sponsored inquiry into the deterioration of the appeal of public service in the United States should have been found necessary points to the paucity of public funding for research on administrative reform. Private organizations readily understand the need for research and investigation into their performance, into finding out how wisely they are using their resources and whether they are achieving the results they expect, and into the possibilities of doing things differently to improve their market position, investment returns, profitability and output. But public organizations do little and spend little above and beyond obligatory accounting and auditing requirements finding these things out in regard to their own operations. Yet administrative reform inquiries pay off handsomely when their recommendations are acted on. It would not seem too much to ask of governments to spend 1 percent of their resources finding out exactly what happens to the other 99 percent but few governments ever approach even one-hundredth of 1 percent. When they do the outcomes are unimpressive.

> ...evaluation is difficult, takes a lot of time to carry out, and can be very expensive...the information generated...is often incomplete, suspect, and unrelated to the problem at hand. We have found bureaucratic and organizational constraints so formidable that today, after investment of significant resources and effort, *not one* [U.S] federal agency has an overall evaluation system and few programs are able to make any use of the evaluations produced. (Wholey, 1972, 361-2)

The state-of-the-art has improved in the meantime but its application has barely improved (Wholey, 1989). How in such circumstances can administrative reform be institutionalized as governments profess?

This lack of evaluation applies throughout government, from judging the quality of life and standards of living to national planning and administrative reform. Much that is written about administrative reform is about what people propose to do or are in the process of doing. Thereafter, little is said about what was done or what was achieved. Most reforms that are not aborted fall below the expectations of their sponsors and rarely achieve what was promised at the outset. This does not mean that they failed. On the contrary, they may have been quite successful. One would have to know what would have happened in their absence and what happened just because they were threatened. The methodological problems are difficult but not insurmountable. As long as too little investment is made in evaluation, the rest of the world has to rely on the prejudiced opinions of reformers and their critics.

Without adequate research and evaluation, theory-building in administrative reform cannot advance much. Patient researchers collect what evidence they can and formulate common-sense generalizations which is about the best that can be done. Subsequent evidence may or may not confirm them. As more evidence accumulates and more generalizations are made, so they can be refined and modified into plausible hypotheses and general guidelines or pointers for would-be reformers. Every decade, the situation improves but it will probably take a few decades yet before a really solid theoretical foundation can be laid, although there is no telling when this process might be speeded up. It cannot be near as long as the gap in research and evaluation remains.

Researchers in administrative reform are fortunate in that there seems no ready alternative. To abandon administrative systems wholesale would result in the collapse of civilization and in anarchy. Doing nothing about them means regression given that governments the world over already cannot cope and largely blame their defective administrative systems for failing to anticipate crises, devise appropriate, workable policies, mobilize resources in time and seize opportunities. All leaders can seemingly do is to make encouraging noises and spare token funds while people seethe at "big talk and small deeds" (*Time*, October 23, 1989, 31). Intervention is unavoidable to prevent further deterioration, and action has to be taken despite "the extraordinary overload of supervisory and managing agencies and the impotence of overworked officials, all of whom are incapable of getting anything done" (Crozier, 1982, 15-16). The fact that so many people are involved and so many views have to be taken into account means that often the original point is lost and "nobody really knows how the initial decision was made, who is responsible, and why the big decisions were made the way they were" (Ibid, 17). Michel Crozier instances poor public decisions about the Concorde airplane, the Narita airport, and the San Francisco Bay Area Rapid Transit (B.A.R.T.) system and warns about the risks in "following the easy way of what seems to be the general agreement" when the facts point otherwise. "Beyond a certain level of complexity nobody can control results" (Ibid, 20). Research may well reveal this is exactly what happens in administrative reform and may explain why reform actions often produce perverse effects.

Research into B.A.R.T., one of Crozier's examples, has produced other sobering reflections on administrative reform. Crozier summed up B.A.R.T. as follows:

> The experts advised against the project on two occasions and it was rejected by a referendum, but it was finally approved after twelve years bitter controversy, thanks to an unholy alliance of environmentalists and businessmen who waged a tremendous advertising campaign. The job of managing it was given to the man who had run this campaign and who was the only person who could cope with its consequences. But it created a financial bottomless pit and turned out to be technically disastrous. For more than a year, the B.A.R.T. was not able to function more than a few hours per day. At present its operating costs are so high that they are a heavy burden on the municipal budgets involved. And the nearby towns, which had been counted on to enlarge the system, have refused to join it. (Ibid, 17-18).

In short, "it was undertaken on the basis of grossly mistaken estimates of the actual costs, of the social benefits, and even of the traffic and revenue". What went wrong? B.A.R.T. had had time and money to undertake proper feasibility studies but the methods and theories employed were inadequate and not "scientific". Each feasibility study consisted of partisan analysis, overstated benefits and understated capital costs.

Indeed, the researchers went on to generalize that most attempts at governmental efficiency and effectiveness had failed, citing P.P.B.S., M.B.O., Z.B.B. reorganizations, personnel reforms, fiscal reforms, cost-benefit analysis, cost-effectiveness, decision analysis, commissions of inquiry (in this study, the Grace Commission) and productivity (Downs and Larkey, 1986). They had been flawed by poor base information, the short-term political horizon, the wrong-problem problem, misallocation of political attention, and misrepresentation of the value of efficiency. The researchers concluded that chances for dramatic breakthroughs in administrative reform were slim, that there was an inverse relationship between the amount of fanfare associated with any given reform and its positive effects on government efficiency, and that the limits on government efficiency were real and operative duc to the nature of problems, constraints, scale and adversarial processes. In short, administrative reform did not come up to scientific standards and until it did, consumers should be warned that the product was highly suspect. Was its product real medicine or snake oil or a mixture of both? Only further research could tell.

References

Argyriades, D., "The Administrative Problems of International Organizations", in P. Pararas (ed.), *Melanges en L'Honneur Phedon Vegleris: La Crise des Institutions de l'Etat*, Editions Ant. N. Sakkoukis, Athens, 1988, Vol. 2, pp. 477-490.

Bennis, W., *Beyond Bureaucracy*, McGraw Hill, New York, 1973.

Campbell, C., and Peters, B. (eds.), *Organizing Governance, Governing Organizations*, University of Pittsburgh Press, Pittsburgh, PA., 1988.

Crozier, M., *Strategies For Change: The Future of French Society*, The M.I.T. Press, Cambridge, Ma., 1982.

Curnow, R. and Saunders, C., *QUANGOS: The Australian Experience*, Hale and Iremonger, Sydney, 1983.

Davies, C., "Motivating Public Officers: Participative Mechanisms," paper presented to the Budapest Round Table, International Institute of Administrative Sciences, 1988.

Denhardt, R., and Jennings, E. (eds.), *The Revitalization of the Public Service*, Dept. of Public Administration, University of Missouri- Columbia, Columbia, MO., 1987.

Downs, G., and Larkey, P., *The Search for Government Efficiency: From Hubris to Helplessness*, Random House, New York, 1986.

Fitzgerald, A., *The Pentagonists*, Houghton Mifflin, Boston, 1989.

Gardner, N., "Power Diffusion in the Public Sector: Collaboration for Democracy," *The Journal of Applied Behavioral Science*, Vol. 10, No. 3, 1974, pp. 367-372.

Glassman, R., et al. (eds.), *Bureaucracy Against Democracy and Socialism*, Greenwood Press, Westport, CT., 1987.

Golembiewski, R., "A Critique of 'Democratic Administration' and Its Supporting Idealism", *American Political Science Review*, Vol. 71, No. 4, Dec. 1977, pp. 1488-1507.

Gregory, W., *The Defense Procurement Mess*, Lexington Books, Lexington, MA., 1989.

Grunow, D., "From Bureaucratization to De-Bureaucratization? Theoretical Issues of a New Field of Research," paper presented to the Budapest Round Table, International Institute of Administrative Sciences, 1988.

Hazzard, S., *Countenance of Truth*, Viking Press, New York, 1990.

Israel, A., *Institutional Development: Incentives to Performance*, World Bank/The Johns Hopkins University Press, Baltimore, MD., 1987.

Jabbra, J. and Dwividi, O. (eds.), *Public Service Accountability: A Comparative Perspective*, Kumarian Press, West Hartford, CT., 1989.

Jacoby, H., *The Bureaucratization of the World*, University of California Press, Berkeley, 1974.

Levine, C., "Citizenship and Service Delivery: The Promise of Coproduction", *Public Administration Review*, Vol. 44, March 1984 Special Issue, pp. 178-187.

Marshall, T., *Class, Citizenship and Social Development*, Doubleday & Co, Inc., Garden City, N.Y., 1964.

Mathiason, J., "Evolution of Tasks and Functions in the United Nations and Its Implications For Reform", paper presented at the 47th annual A.S.P.A. conference, Anaheim, CA., April 1986.

Meyer, M. et al., *Limits to Bureaucratic Growth*, Walter de Gruyter, New York, 1985.

Moharir, V., "Administration Without Bureaucratization: What Alternatives?" *International Review of Administrative Sciences*, Vol. 55, No. 2, 198, pp. 165-181.

National Commission on the Public Service, *Leadership for America: Rebuilding the Public Service*, Lexington Books, Lexington, MA, 1989.

Niskanen, W., *Bureaucracy and Representative Government*, Aldine, Chicago, 1971.

O'Leary, B. "The Limits to Bureaucide: A Critical Analysis of Three Visions of Debureaucratization," paper presented to the Budapest Round Table, International Institute of Administrative Science, 1988.

Ostrom, V., *The Intellectual Crisis in American Public Administration*, University of Alabama Press, University, Ala., 1973.

Pateman, C., *Participation and Democratic Theory*, Cambridge University Press, Cambridge, 1970.

Perry, J.L., and Wise, L.R., "The Motivational Bases of Public Service," *Public Administration Review*, Vol. 50, No. 3, May/June 1990, pp. 367- 373.

Peters, B. G., "The Problem of Bureaucratic Government", *Journal of Politics*, Vol. 43, No. 1, 1981, pp.56-82.

Presthus, R., *The Organizational Society*, St. Martin's Press, New York, 1978.

Rosenbaum, A., "Federal Management: Pathologic Problems and Simple Cures", *P.S.*, Spring 1982, pp. 187-193.

Schumacher, E., *A Guide for the Perplexed*, Harper and Row, 1977.

Schumacher, E., *Small is Beautiful*, Harper and Row, New York, 1973.

Taylor, M., "Quangos," *Public Sector*, No. 3, 1980, pp. 5-7.Toffler, A., *Future Shock*, Bantham Books, New York, 1971.

Toffler, A., *The Third Wave*, Bantham Books, New York, 1984.

Urquhart, B., "The United Nations & Its Discontents," *New York Review of Books*, March 15, 1990, pp. 11-16.

Volker, P.A., "Who Says We Can't Pay the Costs of Leadership?" *Washington Post*, December 17, 1989.

Waxman, C., *The Stigma of Poverty*, Pergamon Press, New York, 1983.

Wholey, J., et al., *Improving Government Performance*, Jossey-Bass, San Francisco, 1989.

Wholey, J., "What Can We Actually Get from Program Evaluation?," *Policy Sciences*, Vol. 3, No. 3, September 1972, pp. 361-369.

Wilenski, P., "Administrative Reform – General Principles and the Australian Experience," *Public Administration*, Vol. 64, No. 3, Autumn 1986, pp. 257-276.

14. Necessary Preventive Medicine

Administrative reform is difficult and fraught with problems. It rarely succeeds as expected and usually fails through faulty implementation. Its success rate is rather disappointing and there are few "definitive evaluation studies showing that they produced the effects they were designed to produce" (Dunsire, 1982, 4). It is somewhat like nasty medicine that has to be taken. People try to get out of taking it if they can or rid themselves of it at the first opportunity. Deep down they do not really believe that it will end their troubles which they know are not so easily cured. Should they feel better after taking the medicine they do not attribute their recovery to it but to something else and wished they had just waited instead for nature to take its course. In any event, in the case of administrative reform the cure usually takes too long and works too slowly. No wonder that it is fairly low on any political agenda. To raise it higher, some terrible calamity has to occur or it has to be oversold. Even then political leaders are prone to select only those aspects likely to strengthen not change the political status quo and to opt for quick fixes and emergency repairs that patch up rather than transform. Furthermore, reformers do not help their own cause by exaggerating the defects of the present and the promises of a much better future without offering substantive proof that what they propose will actually work. At least, existing arrangements do work after a style, however faulty, frustrating, mistake-prone. The altered arrangements may not work at all or they may slow the machinery of state down so much that everyone would have been better off if nothing had been done, no reforms adopted, no reformers heeded.

There is good reason, then, why political leaders are hesitant about administrative reform, even when the administrative machinery of state is obviously defective. To launch a reform initiative is risky business. It is to put faith in optimists and dreamers, idealists and visionaries, and to rouse the ire of powerful conservative elements and the bitter opposition of all those who feel threatened by change or who believe they will lose by change. It wins few new friends and makes many enemies, all too keen to see reform fail and to glow in the satisfaction that comes with the phrase "we told you so". The public at large rarely shows any enthusiasm for administrative reform; few know about such technical things; most rely on political leaders and experts to deal with such matters for them.

If anything, administrative improvements are suspect. For ordinary folk, in the past administrative reform often meant and may still entail strengthening bureaucracy, empowering officials even more, making intrusive regulations more effective, imposing more rigidity and inflexibility in their lives, reducing their feeling of independence, control, choice, and hope while intensifying their fear of manipulation or rather of being manipulated by unseen and unknown power brokers. They worry about what for them as recipients (or victims) of reform is mischief-making, insufficiently sensitive or caring about individuals in the pursuit of administrative modernization, higher productivity, greater efficiency, simplification and organizational rationality, and the further edification of the administrative state which seems to forget about the ordinary folk in the engineered, organized, managed society. They have been stung too often by reforms which promise to benefit them "ultimately" but end up costing them plenty. They have had to pick up the pieces while those responsible for miscalculation, mistiming, and misapplication advanced on their reputation for innovation, firmness and ability to get things done, unfortunately not always things that should have been done or were worth doing.

Much administrative reform has been purely cosmetic, i.e. spurious medicine, a placebo. Publicly announced reforms were not intended to take effect and nobody on the inside took them seriously. They were a sop to pubic opinion. There had been a problem. There had been a demand for a solution, any solution. Reform had been an appropriate answer. It had been formally adopted and thereafter it had dropped out of sight. It had never been given sufficient resources and backing. There had been no meaningful participation. The formalities had been correctly observed. People had gone through the proper motions. But nothing had really changed. Quality circles had been formed but nothing came out of them or nothing considered important enough to bother with. Complaint offices had been established but little notice had been taken of complaints or not enough to change things from giving rise to identical complaints. Suggestion schemes had been introduced but no suggestions had been adopted or sufficiently acknowledged to encourage anyone to make further suggestions. Budgeting procedures had been changed but the same practices had continued. The best strategy to defeat administrative reform is to adopt the reforms formally and ensure they are not implemented or implemented in such a way that they cannot possibly succeed or that they achieve the exact opposite of what was intended. No doubt, many reforms meet such a fate. The cures were not meant to cure. Unfortunately, continued neglect of the diseases, like unprofessional and wrong treatment, may be far worse.

Diagnostic Science

Administrative reformers could well model themselves on diagnostic procedures followed by the medical profession. First, physicians take a general history of their patients and try to acquire the detailed notes on past illnesses and treatment.

Unless their patients' illnesses are critical, in which case they dispense with further details and concentrate on immediate treatment, they check on the general state of their patients' health before concentrating on their particular complaints. Based on past studies and an acquired feel, they prescribe general remedies and ask their patients to let them know whether they have worked. If not they prescribe something else until the patients recover or seek a second opinion. They combine focused trial and error ("knowing where to start the search for an effective intervention, and checking outcomes at intervals to adjust and modify the interventions") with tentativeness ("a commitment to revise one's course as necessary").

> A good doctor does not invest prestige and ego in the treatment prescribed. On the contrary, what distinguishes good physicians from poor ones is precisely their sensitivity to changing conditions, their pronounced willingness to change directions on the basis of results, their humility in the face of reality. (Etzioni, 1989, 125)

Most public organizations need to consult such administrative diagnosticians every so often and most governments need to have them somewhere on their premises even if they cannot stomach the preventive medicines that may be prescribed.

The medical analogy is not misplaced. Managed organizational change, i.e. administrative reform, involves much the same skills and techniques as in preventive medicine. Both are conscious, deliberate and collaborative efforts to improve the well being and performance of their clients through the application of scientific knowledge and technology. Their clients are constantly being bombarded by potentially destructive diseases, both communicable and chronic, and though they successfully ward off such diseases, there are times when the balance turns against them and they become ill and need professional help (Jones, 1965). Unfortunately, there are phony doctors and phony cures – that is why medical practice had to be professionalized. Medical procedures have become more difficult, more complicated, more intricate, less personalized; they are always risky, problematical, even dangerous, and sometimes self-defeating. Postmortems have been institutionalized to discover why things went wrong and whether something could be learnt to prevent or minimize the risk of possible recurrence. Since there is always an element of doubt, of discomfort, of pain, and people shirk their responsibilities (from patients who refuse to take prescribed medicines to less than perfect diagnosticians who mistake symptoms and try to put the blame elsewhere on defective instruments and incompetent staff) discipline is so important in medicine. As even the most careful and scrupulous health fanatics grow old, get ill, and meet with unknown health risks, people support the field of medicine, invest much in it, and appreciate its returns to mankind even if it cannot delay the aging process, find cures for every sickness, or prevent death. The failures of medicine, and there have been many, do not detract from its quest and its benefits. Prevention is better than cure, and human beings could do without cures altogether if only they knew how to avoid illnesses. "In preventive medicine, a goal is never quite realized because disease itself cannot be eradicated. Disease can only be controlled to some extent" (Ibid, 254).

So it is in the organization society. The maladies of everyday living are caused not only by physical and mental sickness but also by organizational diseases – bureaupathologies – which still remain unavoidable and unpreventable and are responsible for much suffering in society and among individuals. There are clear links between organizational ill-health and individual ill-health in such areas as work-related injuries, occupational hazards and diseases, job strain and stress, burn-out, fatigue, victimization, alienation and so forth. Medical practitioners and organization psychologists have been growing more concerned about ill-health generated by work places, work conditions and organizational pressures. But whereas medicine is highly organized, well-funded, research oriented, professional in every sense, administrative reform, its closest parallel in the administrative sciences, is none of these things and is unlikely to reach such heights until bureaupathology is seen in the same light as human sickness. Administrative reform today is well behind where medicine used to be even a hundred years ago. Until organizations learn how to avoid bureaupathologies altogether, there will always be need of cures and a science of administrative health with a branch devoted to organizational diagnosis, containing purgatives and antidotes (Argyris, 1970; Levinson, 1972; Galbraith, 1977).

As in medicine, once the causes of illness are known, it is possible to work on providing an environment in which diseases cannot flourish, preventative measures akin to isolation, vaccination, balanced diet, personal hygiene, and regular check-ups, proper diagnostic instruments, an identification text equivalent to *Gray's Anatomy*, pharmaceutical equivalents, and possibly operating theatres where drastic surgery has to be performed on particularly malignant bureaupathologies. In the past one hundred years, such embryonic devices have been developed. The profession of management has been devoting itself to the improvement of organization performance and the determinants of organization health. So too in the public sector has the profession of government and the study of public administration. Together, they are fortifying instruments that will eventually reduce the need for administrative reform or so institutionalize administrative reform that its prescriptions will not be so feared, they will be more palatable and they will become part of normal operations instead of isolated events in the life cycle of administrative systems.

Institutionalization

Once it is recognized that administrations invariably go wrong, develop all kinds of bureaupathologies and need to constantly take self-correcting measures, so the functions of diagnosis and prognosis will need to be institutionalized. That cannot be left to chance, accident, disaster, political maneuvering, entrepreneurship and fear as has so often been the case in administrative reform in the past. Somewhere within the machinery of government formal responsibility has to be placed on some body to superintend or monitor administrative operations, to evaluate managerial performance, to detect serious shortcomings and failures, and to devise suitable remedial measures together with back-up devices throughout should that body itself fail to perform properly. The affairs of state are so important, the impact of the administrative state on everyday living so intrusive, the proper functioning of public services so crucial to the welfare, security and progress of society that redundancy is required as an imperative fail-safe device. Here is one area in administrative systems where overlapping and duplication are indispensable. Compared with the total costs of government, they are still only incidental expenses but their potential returns make them a good investment and an indispensable safety valve.

While one of several bodies could be designated as the chief or leading source of administrative reform, a combination is more appropriate to assure adequate performance.

Publicly sponsored

* **Chief executive office**: a unit under the immediate responsibility of the leader of the government or cabinet office or equivalent or deputy C.E.O.
* **Separate ministry**, solely devoted to administrative matters or combining the function with planning or productivity or finance or personnel or general services administration or inspection
* **Separate ministry for public enterprises and government commercial activities**
* **Independent audit agency**, with access to all organizations conducting public business or using public funds
* **Legislative and judicial research, investigatory and advisory bodies**
* **Independent legal agency**, with responsibility for all public organizations established by public law, exercising public powers, and issuing delegated legislation or exercising administrative discretion
* **Independent rights agency**, with responsibility for enforcing human rights, protecting privacy (including information), and ensuring equal opportunity and non-discrimination
* **Independent anti-corruption agency**
* **Independent education, training and research agency**

Voluntarily sponsored
* **Independent mass media**
* **Independent higher education**
* **Independent professional societies, employee associations, and trade unions**
* **Independent think-tanks and equivalent** (for military, police and intelligence activities as well as civil)
* **Citizens' research bodies**
* **Political party research bodies**.

What is implied in this network of administrative reform is that no one body has a monopoly of knowledge or expertise or invention, that some aspects of maladministration require special investigation and handling and that operating agencies are remiss if internally they do not have counterparts that have links to all relevant channels. Of course, rich countries with a long tradition of administrative reform already have elaborate networks that include all or nearly all of these elements. They also belong to international associations that bring individual elements together for regular exchanges of ideas and experiences and that are used to bring external pressure on their own governments when facing domestic difficulties. Poor countries are much less fortunate and their very poverty prevents their active participation in international circles. Nevertheless, the potential exists for a more dynamic institutional presence in administrative reform in the future. Several of these bodies, both nationally and internationally, are of relative recent origins, inexperienced, underfunded and powerless, but their very existence is more than just symbolic. As they gain momentum, they should be a force to be reckoned with and quicken the global pace of administrative reform.

Value for Money

The 1980s was a decade of budgeting and financial management reforms as the budget surpluses of the previous decade became budget deficits, serious budget deficits in many countries. Economic turbulence made financial forecasting difficult if not impossible. Tax revolts produced tax relief as government reduced rates, and tax avoidance as potential taxpayers tried to escape the burden. Meantime, governments continued to spend, to meet ongoing obligations and to generate economic activity. Increasingly complex and centralized budgetary and financial systems were developed to take advantage of new computer technology and "to account for transactions, maintain financial controls and report on operation outcomes" (St. Hilaire, 1988, 1). Governments embarked on the simplification of taxation systems and budgetary procedures, centralized budgetary and financial systems and decentralized financial management, and experimentations in finance controls and performance measures and accountability. The emphasis was on expenditure restraint, structural adjustments to improve economic performance, increased quality and effectiveness of government spending, and enhanced responsiveness and flexibility of the public sector.

In the O.E.C.D. countries, for instance, three main budgetary strategies adopted were (a) imposing "top-down" limits whereby governments set goals for total spending within which reallocations, cost increases, program changes, etc. had to be accommodated, (b) ensuring that spending outcomes adhered to plans and unanticipated developments did not force overruns, and (c) increasing value for money.

> One of the key concerns…is the development of adequate performance measures, and of effective accounting and reporting systems for monitoring spending and results. Budget officials seek effective means to allow increased flexibility and freedom of choice for individual departments and managers, within the framework of the collective priorities of government while ensuring that the desired level of overall expenditure control is maintained and that sufficient knowledge is available at the centre of government to provide informed and effective budget advice to Ministers and the Cabinet. (O.E.C.D., 1987, 12)

The issue is not so much about surpluses or deficits, inflation or deflation, favored projects and multi-year budget cycles, but on what exactly happens to expenditures, how much seepage occurs (through corruption, fraud, deceit, mismanagement), what governments obtain in return, and whether they could do much better both for themselves (and the public) and the economy. "Balancing the budget is not the name of the game. The name of the game is making good use of the national output" (Stein, 1989, 2), i.e. budgeting the G.N.P., improving government decision-making to achieve a better allocation of national output, and getting "more bang for the buck". What offends the public most about governments is that they do not seem to know what they get for their money, that they waste money, and they cannot account for the money they spend.

High on the future agenda of administrative reform will be ensuring that governments do get better value for their money, do spend well and wisely, and do safeguard public money as a true guardian should. As a sign of things to come, the Auditor General of the Canadian Province of British Columbia emphasizes the "heavy responsibility on those charged with disbursing public funds if they are to ensure that value will be received for the money spent". In the 1989 report, written comments received from the government on internal control reviews were published along with responses to value-for-money (comprehensive) audit observations of various government programs, including the government's privatization initiative and health services (hospitals, medical services, continuing care and public health). These audits were based on two principles – that public business should be conducted in a way that makes the best possible use of public funds and that people who conduct public business should be held accountable for the prudent and effective management of the resources entrusted to them (Auditor General's Annual Report 1988-9, 67). They were concerned with assessing whether programs were implemented in an economical and efficient manner and whether legislators and the public were provided with appropriate accountability information. They did not demand theoretical perfection from public managers but whether they were meeting reasonable expectations and whether management processes ensured value for money. They went well beyond financial audits to challenge government policy, administrative valuations and assessments and managerial qualities, and made harsh judgments that grated the government and the bureaucracy and gave grist to mass media ridicule. Clearly, new ground was being explored and the eventual outcome can only enhance government performance.

Value-for-money indicators of government performance should eventually go beyond accounting and auditing principles and link up with several other indicators that have been or are being developed:

* **Net national product indicators** such as the stock of natural resources, the efficient and effective use of national resources, investment and savings, extent of unused or underused capacity, quality of life, social relations, standard of living, ownership, purchasing power, congestion and travel time, sustainable income and development, pollution costs;
* **National security indicators** such as external threats, incidence of terrorism, espionage, treason, readiness of armed forces, quality of weaponry, quality of trained personnel;
* **Economic indicators of public sector performance** such as investment returns, capital utilization, viability of public enterprises, cost- reduction, cost recovery, work stoppages, absenteeism, distribution and accessibility of public sector goods and services, monopoly/ competitiveness;
* **Social (justice) indicators** such as reduction of poverty, freedom from discrimination, social and political participation, civil liberties, social errors, alienation, family relations, leisure opportunities, housing/accommodation standards;
* **Health (and welfare) indicators** such as demography, incidence of epidemics, outbreaks of preventable diseases, work loss attributable to sickness, hospitalization, quarantine, rates of illness, physically handicapped, mental illness, suicides, nutrition, addictions and addictives, welfare recipients, institutionalization, social insurance coverage, quality of working life;
* **Crime (and safety) indicators** such as victimization, reported crime statistics, nature and incidence of crimes, prison statistics, court statistics, arrest rates, accidents, violent demonstrations;
* **Education (and research) indicators** such as literary, language skills, school attendance, higher education opportunities, research funding, patents and

inventions, R & D investments, adult education and retraining, dropout rates, quality of instruction, library facilities, information technology, broadcasting reception;

* **Environmental indicators** such as renewable resources, depreciation of natural capital, conservation and reforestation, energy saving, smog control, water and air quality, wilderness and wildlife preservation, accessibility to national parks, park space, recreational facilities;
* **International/global treasures indicators** such as irreplaceable natural, biological, cultural, archeological, literary, artistic sources and masterpieces.

P.P.B.S. has ensured that such indicators have not become an end in themselves or mere statistical exercises. Much of the difficulty implementing P.P.B.S. has been attributable to problems in devising meaningful performance indicators, especially where public administrators clung to the myth that government was different (from business) because its outputs could not be measured. In the past two decades, considerable progress has been made in devising appropriate measures (Schick, 1990). Once applied, they should have a momentum of their own propelling improved performance and administrative reform as they are important tools for goal setting, planning, monitoring and feedback.

Productivity

Value-for-money advocates have pushed for three objectives, namely the elimination of unnecessary government activities, the reduction of public spending and costs, and the increase of public sector productivity. Even where public organizations meet public expectations and perform satisfactorily by any reasonable measures, there is almost universal belief that they are not as productive as they ought to be. In short, there is great room for improvement: more could be done with fewer employees ("more for less"). For too long, public employees have been overly sheltered by paternal governments unwilling to provoke their employees, by benign managements unchallenged from the outside, by institutionalized tenure in law and practice, by powerful employee unions and associations, by embedded patronage systems, by tolerant work norms, and by indifference to public costs. Saved from private exploitation, they have been over indulged under public protection. There has been no hiding of grossly bloated staffing in poor countries and the public everywhere has been treated to many examples of laziness, non-performance and indifference, ranging from the closing of shutters for breaks despite long lines of people awaiting service to groups of public employees just standing around apparently doing nothing for hours. Though people may get the same treatment from private employees it does not rankle as much as from public employees and any indictment reconfirms the common impression that public employees are underworked.

Until studies of public sector productivity were undertaken, nobody really knew whether or not public employees were underemployed. What was suspected and then confirmed in the 1960s was that productivity in the private sector in the United States had begun to decline: it seemed to have peaked and other countries were about to outperform American enterprise. With the encouragement of National Productivity Councils and the like, it was only natural for researchers to turn their attention to the public sector too and to apply similar techniques they had developed to measure and increase private sector productivity. Not that scientific management had previously neglected the measurement of public sector productivity. Output measures had been devised in public industrial employment and among certain white-collar occupations but they just had not received the publicity that later studies were to enjoy. Merit systems had matched competent people with the jobs they had to perform and ensured that the best available candidates had been selected. Public employees had seemed motivated enough and provided with proper working conditions to enable them to work well enough. Public management systems should have provided sufficient work to do and weeded out the unfit except maybe they did not. That was the flaw. Public managers did not have sufficient control over workflow, establishment (number of employees allowed to be employed) and discipline. They did not determine how much work had to be done, how many employees would be available to do it, and what should be done with non-performers. And the simple management answer was to empower public managers more in these respects. If public managers were allowed to manage like their counterparts in the private sector, productivity should improve.

Improving productivity of organizations, especially public organizations, is not so simple. Taking the management solution alone, it appears that few public "managers" have any management background and education, have received adequate management training and are management-minded. Even if they were management-minded, there are insufficient incentives to improve productivity. Most public budgeting systems give no incentives for saving public money; on the contrary, they encourage spendthrifts. Most public personnel systems give no incentives for exceptional performance or even good performance; they encourage mediocre performance. Most public purchasing systems emphasize quantity over quality or economy over value. It is not enough to change the managers: the systems have to be changed too. The whole top-down managerial ethos has to be overhauled to allow greater participation in decision-making from below and more involvement by those actually doing the work as to how it should be done and what changes are needed to increase output. Quick fixes such as self-managing teams and quality circles and other decentralized approaches clash with the dominant centralized control mechanisms that both political leaders and senior administrators are reluctant to relinquish. In any event, labor productivity is a diminishing component of public sector productivity as governments move into automation and computers, although it would be most beneficial if public organizations could find ways of capturing and applying the enterprise and expertise that probably exists in all work groups and remains untapped by gainsharing schemes (Campbell et al., 1988).

A different strategy was initiated by the National Center for Public Productivity (not to be confused with the defunct National Center for Productivity and the Quality of Working Life) in the United States when it decided to concentrate on lowering "a thousand organizational barriers to productivity" in the realization that

> In the long run public administrators often lack the political support to invest in technology (computers, vehicles, maintenance facilities, energy-saving devices, buildings), human capital (training, education, medical and psychological support services, labor-management cooperation), and even information (data bases, clearinghouses, publications, objective studies, case lessons). (Holzer and Halachmi, 1986, 2)

It has provided a forum since 1976 through *Public Productivity Review* and since 1989 through an international network to facilitate the development and application of innovative techniques, stimulate research, present integrated analyses, explore elements of productivity improvement strategies, and provide an impetus for a productivity ethic among public sector organizations. Its concerns have been eclectic, ranging from motivation and job design to measurement and productivity bargaining, and skewed to American practitioners, but it invariably provides something of universal interest. Likewise specific barriers to increased productivity are dealt with in other international forums, such as *Corruption and Reform* and *Public Enterprise*, with a similar philosophy of improvement, careful analysis of inhibiting processes, and encouragement and support to practitioners to improve the state of the art.

What has emerged from all these activities around the globe is the realization that despite difficulties of definition, measurement and evaluation, the productivity of public sector goods and services has been higher than commonly realized and that efforts to raise productivity have pushed up rates in the public sector even surpassing the private sector (*The Economist*, 1986; Fisk, 1985). Although costs may have risen higher over the same period, i.e. output may have doubled but costs increased even more (Lane, 1987, 189), the difference was attributable to improved quality of public services, heavy initial investment in mechanization, and inflation. Several countries have developed quite sophisticated measures of public sector productivity although some areas of government activity such as international relations, defense and social welfare services are still proving somewhat elusive. Nevertheless, the state-of-the-art should continue to improve in the near future such that by the turn of the century there should be few gaps left. The outputs if not the outcomes of public sector activities should be better known and more accurately calculated.

A different approach to finding out why some public organizations achieved higher productivity and generally got better results was taken by the Auditor General of Canada. Superior performers in terms of quality, responsiveness, and timeliness of services provided, operational cost-effectiveness and employee satisfaction were studied to find out what consistent attributes they might share. Five such characteristics were identified as being keys to their success:

(1) emphasis on people – people in them were challenged, encouraged and developed; they were given power to act and to use their own judgment;
(2) participatory leadership – high standards were articulated and enforced by leaders who communicated easily and consulted often;
(3) innovative work styles – largely self-reliant staff maintained strong monitoring feedback and control systems to improve performance; they sought to solve problems creatively;
(4) strong client orientation – everyone involved focused on serving clients not bureaucracy;
(5) optimum performance mindset – people sought improved performance and adjusted with changing conditions (A.G.C., 1989).

In short, high performance was a product of people who cared not systems that constrained, and of organizations where collaboration in achieving goals was not inhibited. These findings prompted the Auditor General to instigate further research on why some public managers initiated reforms and improvements. Was their mind-set inborn or could it be developed? Could such a mind-set be derived from academic learning or was it best developed by observation or imitation of role models?

Whether it is formal performance measures or a special mind-set, the fact remains that there is a vast array of workable approaches and techniques (Miller, 1984) which can boost public sector productivity. Barriers to employing them can be overcome, providing governments and public organizations drop their obsession with sheer economy, cutback management and incrementalism (Mushkat, 1987). Public providers can look at public markets the same way as their counterparts in the private sector, that is, they can market themselves as well as their products, they can create market images and impressions, they can research clients' needs and satisfaction, and they can be as entrepreneurial in enlarging their internal markets and seeking access to possible international, or at least regional, markets, providing issues of national sovereignty can be resolved. This is more likely to happen in the case of tangible products such as energy supply, transportation, public utilities and armaments than in social services where the products tend to disappear immediately. Even in this area, the superior quality factor makes for enlargement of market or clients even when not desired, such as the provision of superior benefits for welfare recipients and the homeless which acts as a magnet for the socially underprivileged. (Hence, the demand for nationalized, uniform social services.) On the other hand, superior tax collection may scare away wealthy people. Higher public sector productivity is not always considered a virtue among certain sections of the community, not when it leads to stricter enforcement of the law and less social freedom. Nonetheless, boosting public sector productivity is a reality that should promote administrative reforms in the immediate future although it may reduce the pressures for them thereafter when the public perceive that public organizations really are in healthier shape.

The Healthy Public Organization

Healthier organizations are not necessarily healthy organizations which is the ultimate objective of administrative reform. The best that can happen to any organization is not to get ill in the first place. But even healthy public organizations will always be subject to illnesses, even terminal illnesses. At least, they will be in better shape to prevent minor ailments from becoming serious through lack of care. They should be able to function at a higher level and to do things that previously may have been out of their reach. Keeping fit should be easier too. Healthy public organizations should resemble other healthy organizations in searching for excellence, maintaining the highest attainable levels of service and quality of product, satisfying clients and customers, providing an enjoyable work place for employees and a supportive atmosphere in which they can develop their full potential, encouraging innovation and creativity, and enhancing the quality of life of everyone, all of which is the stuff of organizational dreamers.

A more realistic description can be derived from advertisements of companies dedicated to organizational health maintenance. Their recipes include the following elements:

* a clear sense of identity and purpose based on community values
* an awareness of the world, "the here and now," and the resources available to achieve potential;
* a capacity and capability to make a significant impact on operational performance;
* skill and capability to solve problems, set and achieve realistic goals, and to continue to grow by setting and achieving new goals;
* an organizational climate that enables members to relate honestly and openly;
* an awareness of its power and how to use it to influence its environment;
* members that feel important because they are effective as persons and believe they find fulfillment;
* ongoing performance improvement programs.

But there are certain obligations that apply particularly to public organizations beyond such generalizations.

* **Maintaining capacity and capability of performing effectively necessary public activities on demand**. Not only should public organizations meet felt social needs (not otherwise being met satisfactorily), they should perform effectively in normal conditions and be capable of operating even under abnormal conditions. Their services should be available when needed and ideally never break down. The public should be able to expect them to function reasonably well at all times, i.e. to do the job they are expected to do and do it well. Furthermore, they should demonstrate and prove their effectiveness and show that they are intent on increasing their capacity and capability by advancing the state of the art through research and experimentation, that they go from strength to strength.
* **Obeying the rule of law, both the spirit of the the law and its substantive requirements**. Public organizations should not seek to evade the law or interpret its provisions contrary to what was intended. Should the law be cumbersome or obstructive or otherwise deficient in enabling them to perform effectively, then they should seek to have the law changed. Until it is changed, they should not take the law into their own hands, except when continuing to obey the law results in crimes against humanity and similar grave offenses against universal human rights. Whatever they do should be sanctioned by law and subject to legal approval, and they should never be placed above or beyond the law or act as if they were. Their role is to enhance the legitimacy of the administrative state and advance administrative justice.
* **Remaining publicly accountable at all times for all actions taken in the name of the public**. Being public agencies, public organizations should as far as possible operate in the open, reveal all their doings or at least be prepared to reveal all to the proper authorities, and report periodically on what they do, explaining all details as required. They should not attempt to hide or deceive or evade responsibility for any item of public business. They should maintain as complete records as possible and produce them on demand and they should be prepared to give reasons for actions taken. They should act as public guardians, safeguard all resources put into their hands, and promote the public's interests always.
* **Treating all persons alike without fear or favoritism or discrimination**. Public organizations should follow the principle of social equity, being fair and just to all alike, and giving dignity to every person. Their services should be accessible to all and should be available to all on demand; and no person should be deprived without proper justification. Special consideration and treatment to individuals should be extended to all individuals in like circumstances. Public organizations should apply the principles of natural justice or

administrative due process and be human and humane even in the most trying situations.

* **Adhering to the highest standards of honesty and integrity**. Public organizations should set the example of public morality and ethics, in a sense, acting righteously. They should not only do good but act good. They should enforce professional codes of public ethics and be jealous of their reputation, allowing no defaulters, no compromisers, no exemptions. They should root out all forms of corruption and be constantly on their guard against non-feasance, mal-feasance and mis-feasance, providing a full and sufficient range of institutional supports for the conscientious.
* **Being identified with progress**. Public organizations should be seen as progressive organizations, advancing the interests of all concerned – the public at large, their specific clients, their employees, and the public professions. They should be looking all the time to be better and to push everything else to be better, never relaxing on their achievements but striving to make each higher level the minimum for the future. They should be among the leaders in organizational, administrative and managerial research, particularly, in debureaucratization, deregulation, decentralization, self-correction, paperwork reduction, safety, cleanliness, marketing, counselling, civic activities, and adult education.

By and large, these obligations on public organizations are reasonable demands. They are within everyone's reach. And many countries can boast that they are the norm in the public sector and obviate the need for much administrative reform. While they may even meet with ideas of excellence such as "managing public service organizations for improved performance, humanely and responsively, while creating organizations capable of adroitly and continuously responding to changes taking place in their environments" (Denhardt and Jennings, 1988, 22), they still do not come up to the idealistic expectations of Guerreiro Ramos that all organizations, public and private, provide conditions for self-actualization (Ramos, 1981).

The problem in many countries is not so much attaining healthy public organizations (that battle has been successfully fought over many generations) as maintaining them in vastly different circumstances and altered conditions. One solution has been to plump for "islands of excellence," "enclaves of innovation," "selective radicalism" (Dror, 1983; Lee, 1983; O.E.C.D., 1979) whereby reform energies are put into models of excellence or the healthiest possible public organizations where they most count to ensure the highest attainable performance in those areas, to eliminate bottlenecks in the whole system, and to induce surrounding organizations to come up to their level. Poor performers cannot be reversed instantaneously, if at all, because when threatened by reform they tend to close up and cut off their most flexible, reform-minded elements. It is better to bypass them altogether and create new organizations and new programs from scratch that will eventually supplant and replace the old, or attach brand new units staffed with outsiders as invigorating forces within. The more progressive elements will gravitate to the new where they will find a more receptive atmosphere and in time their better performance will present few political difficulties in eventually abandoning the old. This way, the administrative culture will eventually become readier to innovate, take risks, assume responsibility, and be more accommodating to the public (O.E.C.D., 1979, 11) particularly if jollied along with occasional shocks administered by determined, tough, firm leaders that bulldoze through resistance and inertia.

Realistic Expectations

The ultimate aim in administrative reform paradoxically is to eliminate the need for radical surgery. Some bureaupathologies are so serious that nothing short of shock treatment, drastic operations and intensive care will do. But the remedies may prove too severe for the weaker patients who cannot be revived, and the good in them expires along with the bad. Alternatively, the patient just freezes into a catatonic state in which nothing seems to help or so many doctors try so many different cures, that they all cancel out one another and the poor patient is bemuddled and befused by the different advice. Fortunately, administrative systems and public organizations are made tough and they can withstand a great deal of abuse and mistreatment; they seem to weather most reform blitzes fairly well. Nonetheless, practitioner folk wisdom does not recommend across-the-board assaults as being the optimum strategy. The preference is for gradualism or continuous adaptation. Don't treat everything that is wrong all at once; be selective. Don't expect that the patients will recover immediately; give the healing process time; allow the patients to recuperate at their own pace according to their individual circumstances. Otherwise, reforms prove too ambitious an effort for organizations to digest and implement. When this happens, as all too frequently it does, the following is a typical lament.

> ...Far too much was attempted, we did not have the time to oversee them all. We did not have the energy to nurture them all. We did not have the power to push them all. We did not have the insight to involve all the people who should have been made a part of them. (Mirvis and Berg, 1978, 143)

Gradualism or piecemeal, selective reform on a continuous cycle, has much to commend it. Administrative systems progress at their own pace, some faster than others, with the more progressive leading the way and pulling others along with them while the laggards dragging behind sooner or later will receive the necessary shock treatment to quicken their pace so they catch up to everyone else. This way, the enlightened are not handicapped by the reactionary and proven experiments will be generally adopted in across-the-board measures and the outmoded will be abandoned. All reforms are experiments. There is no guarantee that they will succeed or be worth the trouble and it is wise to wait honest evaluation, in short, to justify reform "on the basis of the importance of the problem, not the certainty of [the] answer" (Campbell, 1969). In the case of pervasive bureaupathologies, there are no easy cures, and there may still be no sure cures, and the threatened malignancies are such that even when cured once, there is no guarantee they will not immediately reattack and reinfect. Administrative reformers have to avoid being committed to one "complete" cure but open and flexible to try anything that promises to work.

In any event, all cures take time, particularly administrative cures when the time between their first conceptualization and their actual implementation is added on. In the case of fundamental reforms in public budgeting and personnel administration, it has taken generations before they could be said to have been assimilated. Reorganizations and structural changes take up to a decade to be consolidated. Even relatively simple and straightforward changes in policy guidelines take a few years to take full effect. Hurrying the process merely panics and delays. And piling reform upon reform in too quick succession sows much confusion that few can be absorbed properly. All that is produced is saturation psychosis (Laframboise, 1979) and an inbred cynicism that one just has to wait to see that all will be changed back again. Just because reforms worked on a small scale or in an experimental situation does not mean that they will work on a large scale under normal operating conditions, and the time factor involved is much longer.

Working systems cannot stop to take time out for reorganization and reform. Auto plants stop production while they adjust equipment for new models. Premises close down for refurbishing and structural remodelling. But administrative systems cannot be halted. They have a job to do and any reforms have to be incorporated as they continue their daily operations. Fortunate is the public organization that gets a breathing space coincident with reform implementation. Often, the opposite occurs, that just when reforms are readied, so pressures build up, crises crop up and whatever resources were available for reform have to be diverted to meet work overload. This is not a question of poor timing but of unanticipated and unforeseen events that occur frequently in the public sector without warning. Organizations cannot just stop for reform no more than they can shift gears suddenly. As in all future-oriented programs, there has to be a lead-in, a gradual run up, an easing in of the new with the old. The aim of administrative reform is improvement, not perfection.

Resources for administrative reform are scarce. International transfers can provide temporary injections and public sector resources can be boosted by borrowing from the private sector, but neither source is exactly abundant. Theoretically, the number of experts experienced or capable of carrying through administrative reforms should be sufficient for most purposes but in reality few are available and fewer still can be spared. They have to be used selectively and resources applied sparingly. For at least twenty years, social science literature has pleaded for more resources to be devoted to change and reform, for more effort to be put into training change agents, and for more investment to be made in the preparation of reform instruments. Whatever has been done in the meantime has been insufficient to meet growing demands worldwide. They cannot be manufactured overnight. So even if countries were to embark on elaborate administrative reform campaigns, they would be stymied by lack of expertise.

Even if the expertise were suddenly made available, there remains the imposing problems of resistance to reform and administrative inertia. Much has been written about overcoming the cultural, social, organizational, and psychological barriers to change (Zaltman and Duncan, 1977) and implementing organization change (Oman and Masters, 1987). Few underestimate the task. Almost all emphasize that getting reforms accepted is a long arduous process, winning people over against their instincts and convictions. Compelling reforms is self-defeating. Uncommitted participants will go through the motions but they will not really change. Going along is rarely sufficient for success. Indeed, it is a bad recipe for outward appearances may well hide deliberate sabotage. A much better recipe is involvement that brings identification, responsibility and ownership, active cooperation rather than passive non-commitment. But there are no magic formulas; techniques for overcoming resistance, reversing attitudes and gaining confidence are still largely of the trial and error variety. Reform can be an agonizing experience and it can tear the fabric of the organization (Mirvis and Berg, 1978, 112). Caution is obviously warranted.

The objective of administrative reform is not temporary success but a permanent improvement in administrative performance. It is no less than a permanent transformation of administrative culture. Changes in ethos and attitudes cannot be forced: they must come from within, from a genuine change of heart. When dealing with the sheer size and complexity of government organization as a whole, and the diversity and variations among so many government professions, there are no miracles, no instant successes. Changing any characteristic of an administrative culture is a long, hard slog, an uphill battle all the way. To persist, one really has to be truly committed. Far from being utopian, it is necessary preventive medicine. Those who indulge believe it worthwhile and claim excitement, fun, enthusiasm, and an unparalleled sense of freedom, energy, commitment, and accomplishment that even without any final victories, was meaningful, rewarding and beneficial, and above all brought good government and the Good Society a little nearer (Feldman, 1981). In any event, the reform clock, driven by ideology, example, fear, breakdown, dissatisfaction and innovation, ticks on relentlessly.

Keeping Perspective

At the beginning of the 1990s, administrative reform was only part of much wider and more sweeping institutional reforms around the world in response to attempts by governments to regain national purpose and direction, strike out in new directions, rise above political stalemates and bureaucratic inertia, reshape state and society to meet the challenges of the 21st century, and generally reinvigorate sluggish governmental systems to respond better to political initiatives. Clearly, current institutional arrangements were not coping at all well with longstanding problems. They had not been adjusted to changing circumstances. They were in fact exacerbating societal problems. Things were amiss; they could not be repaired by just tinkering with the system; they demanded structural and cultural changes; they revealed that whole systems had lost their ability to respond to issues of public significance; they showed that public affairs were not being managed properly and that the public had soured and lost confidence in public institutions. People looked to public leaders to take bold initiatives to end *immobilisme* in government, to overrule vested interests that perpetuated the status quo and prevented any departures, to restore dynamism in the body politic, and to raise societal aspirations by improving current performance.

The boldest and most risky steps were being taken in Eastern Europe where economic and political systems were being overturned literally overnight. But that was not the only region in institutional turmoil. Whatever happened there would have immediate and possibly devastating impact on the whole of the Communist/Marxist world including socialist regimes in Latin America and Africa. Western Europe was preparing for greater economic and possibly political integration and that too would cause ripples around the world but especially in bordering areas of the Mediterranean and the Middle East. In Africa, the I.M.F. policies were still being imposed relentlessly while the Republic of South Africa had abandoned apartheid. In Asia, as elsewhere, nationalist, racial and religious pressures were promoting instability and making several spots flashpoints for regional war. In South America, Brazil and Argentina were going through particularly hard times and much of the Andes region was being destabilized by international narcotics developments. Even North America was not spared as Canada faced constitutional problems still over the French Canadians while the checks and balances of the American system of government were suffocating policy initiatives and making for an ineffective bureaucracy. All of these events revolved around government and the inability of their administrative systems to cope with the most pressing problems of society (March and Olsen, 1989, 97). Thus, for the United States,

> Perhaps the essence of the problem of governance today is that current administrative structures, erected mostly during the Progressive era and the New Deal, are so entrenched

> that their adaptations to new conditions contribute little to overall government effectiveness. Established structures no longer can contain political tensions between Congress, the president, and the bureaucracy, and riven by conflict, they often do not permit successful management of the nation's problems. (Chubb and Peterson, 1989, 5)

This lament could have been echoed almost anywhere in the world and similar comments were being made in countries as diverse as Grenada, Israel, The Gambia, Sri Lanka, Papua New Guinea and Fiji where public policies crucial for the future were being mangled by defective institutional, particularly administrative, arrangements.

Administrative reform was only a minor part of global institutional initiatives but the larger transformations could not take place without fundamental overhauls of the machinery of government and long needed changes in administrative systems had to be linked to wider political initiatives. There was no mistaking the linkages between institutional, governmental and administrative reforms. In this, the general lessons that had been learned from past experiences in administrative reform were all the more relevant:-

* reform reflects and reaffirms optimism in bettering the human condition
* reform requires full commitment, not half hearted measures readily compromised
* reform politics are complicated and unpredictable and the outcomes are uncertain
* reform politics generate excessive rhetoric at the cost of effective action
* reforms rarely work as intended, sometimes do not work at all, and often have mixed results and unintended consequences that make matters worse not better
* reforms come in cycles and are quickly imitated
* reforms have to be selective for not everything wrong can be righted at once
* reformers have to move quickly while they have attention and resources, before opponents have time to consolidate and sabotage and other events crowd in and shift focus
* reforms must appeal in terms of values as well as substance, values that are shared and around which there is considerable consensus and are not considered too out of line
* reforms must be tailored to specific circumstances and not considered too out of place
* reforms are invariably altered during implementation
* reformers have to persist as reforms rarely live up to original expectations and often are frustrated in the short run by the strength of resistance and inertia
* reformers have to understand that affirmation of values, getting a place on the public agenda, and civic education may be as important if not more important than substantive changes

* reformers have to accept that half a loaf is better than none and that whatever gains are made have to be consolidated into a springboard for further gains
* reformers have to realize that participation eases acceptance given that at any point of time capacity for reform is restricted and capability poor
* reformers have to institutionalize their reforms, change the prevailing culture and provide ongoing machinery for continuous reform
* reform is endless, oscillating and repetitive for there is always need for improvement.

When people tire of reform, they tire of life.

References

Argyris, C., *Intervention Theory and Method*, Addison-Wesley, Reading, MA., 1970.

Auditor General of Canada, *Attributes of Well-Performing Organizations*, Office of the Auditor General, Ottawa, 1989.

Campbell, D., "Reforms and Experiments," *American Psychologist*, Vol. 24, No. 4, April 1969, pp. 409-429.

Campbell, J. et al., *Productivity in Organizations*, Jossey-Bass, San Francisco, 1988.

Chubb, J.E., and Peterson, P.E. (eds.), *Can the Government Govern?*, The Brookings Institution, Washington, D.C., 1989.

Denhardt, R., and Jennings, I. (eds.), *The Revitalization of the Public Service*, Department of Public Administration, University of Missouri- Columbus, MO, 1987.

Dror, Y., "Prescriptions for Administrative Reform: Lessons from a Historic- Comparative Study," paper presented at the A.S.P.A. National Conference, New York, April 1983.

The Economist, Vol. 298, No 7435 March 1, 1986, p. 53. "Making mandarins manage".

Dunsire, A., "Organization and Management of State and Administration," S.I.C.A. Second Occasional Paper Series, No. 1, American Society for Public Administration, Washington, D.C., 1982.

Etzioni, A., "Humble Decision Making", *Harvard Business Review*, Vol. 67, No. 4, July-August 1989, pp. 122-126.

Feldman, D., *Reforming Government*, Morrow, New York, 1981.

Fisk, D., "Productivity Trends in the Federal Government", *Monthly Labor Review*, Vol. 108, No. 10, October 1985, pp. 3-8.

Galbraith, J., *Diagnosing Complex Organizations*, Addison-Wesley, Reading, MA., 1973.

Holzer, M., and Halachmi, A. (eds.), *Strategic Issues in Public Sector Productivity*, Jossey-Bass, San Francisco, 1986.

Jones, G., "Preventive Medicine at Work: A Hypothetical Case of Managed Organizational Change," *Philippine Journal of Public Administration*, Vol. 9, No. 3, July 1965, pp. 241-255.

Laframboise, H. L., "Administrative Reform in the Federal Public Service: Signs of a Saturation Psychosis," *Canadian Public Administration*, Vol. 14, No. 3, 1979, pp. 303-325.

Lee, H., "Two Critical Combinations for Successful Administrative Reform", paper presented at the Tenth E.R.O.P.A. General Assembly and Conference, Seoul, Korea, October 1983.

Levinson, H., *Organizational Diagnosis*, Harvard University Press, Cambridge, MA., 1972.

March, J.G., and Olsen, J.R. (eds.), *Rediscovering Institutions: The Organizational Basis of Politics*, The Free Press, New York, 1989.

Miller, T., *Public Sector Performance: A Conceptual Turning Point*, The Johns Hopkins University Press, Baltimore, 1984.

Mirvis, P. and Berg, D., *Failures in Organization Development and Change*, John Wiley & Sons, New York, 1978.

Mushkat, M., "Towards Non-Incremental Strategies in Developing Public Products and Services", *European Journal of Marketing*, Vol. 21, No. 1, 1987, pp. 66-73.

Oman, R., and Masters, B., *Implementing Change in Organizations, Based on Analysis and Evaluation Studies: A Bibliography*, Vance Bibliographies P2112, Monticello, IL., 1987.

Organization for Economic Cooperation and Development, *The Control and Management of Government Expenditure*, Paris, 1987.

Organization for Economic Cooperation and Development, *Strategies for Change and Reform in Public Management*, Paris, 1979.

Ramos, A. G., *The New Science of Organizations: A Reconceptualization of the Wealthy*, University of Toronto Press, 1981.

St. Hilaire, G., Introductory Report of the Research Committee on Public Finance and Financial Administration, International Institute of Administrative Sciences, Budapest Round Table, 1988.

Stein, H., *Governing the 5 Trillion Economy*, Oxford University Press, New York, 1989.

Zaltman, G., and Duncan, R., *Strategies for Planned Change*, John Wiley & Sons, New York, 1977.

Bibliography

A.A.P.A.M., *The Ecology of Public Administration and Management in Africa*, Vikas Publishing House, New Delhi, 1986.

Adamolekun, L. (a), *Issues in Development Management in Sub-Saharan Africa*, The World Bank, Washington, D.C., October 1989.

Adamolekun, L. (ed.) (b), *Symposium on Privatization in Africa*, Economic Development Institute of the World Bank, Washington, D.C., December 1989.

Aganbegyan, A., *Inside Perestroika: The Future of the Soviet Economy*, Harper and Row, New York, 1989.

Agarwala, R., *Planning in Developing Countries: Lessons of Experience*, World Bank Staff Working Papers, No. 576, Washington, D.C., 1983.

Agarwala, R., *Price Distortions and Growth in Developing Countries*, World Bank Staff Working Paper no. 575, Washington D.C., 1984.

Aguirre, C. A., Griffith, P. S., and Yucelik, M. Z., *Taxation in Sub-Saharan Africa, Part I: Tax Policy and Administration in Sub-Saharan Africa*, International Monetary Fund, Washington, D.C., 1981.

Al-Rahim, M., et al. (eds.), *Sudan Since Independence*, Gower, Aldershot, 1986.

Al-Saigh, N. M. (ed.), *Administrative Reform in the Arab World: Readings*, Arab Organization of Administrative Sciences, Amman, 1986.

Anthony, R., "Closing the Loop Between Planning and Performance", *Public Administration Review*, Vol. 31, No.3, May-June 1971, 388-398.

Argyriades, D., "The Administrative Problems of International Organizations", in P. Pararas (ed.), *Melanges en L'Honneur Phedon Vegleris: La Crise des Institutions de l'Etat*, Editions Ant. N. Sakkoukis, Athens, 1988, Vol. 2, pp. 477-490.

Argyris, C., *Intervention Theory and Method*, Addison-Wesley, Reading, MA., 1970.

Auditor General of Canada, *Attributes of Well-Performing Organizations*, Office of the Auditor General, Ottawa, 1989.

Backoff, R., "Optimizing Administrative Reform for Improved Governmental Performance", *Administration and Society*, Vol. 6, No.1, 1974, pp. 73-106.

Balogun, M. J., and Mutahaba, G., (eds.), *Economic Restructuring and African Public Administration,* Kumarian Press, West Hartford, CT. 1989.

Barkley. B., "Management Reform: Back to Basics", *The Bureaucrat*, Vol. 13, No. 3, Fall 1983, pp. 3-5.

Bayley, L. G., *Local Government: Is It Manageable?,* Pergamon Press, New York, 1979.

Belmiro, V., Castor, J. and Franca, C., "Administracao Publica no Brasil: Exaustao e Revigorameto do Modelo," *Revista de Administracao Publica*, Vol. 20, No. 3, 1986, pp. 3-26.

Bennis, W., *Beyond Bureaucracy*, McGraw Hill, New York, 1973.

Bennis, W., *Changing Organizations*, McGraw-Hill, New York, 1966.

Bennis, W, Benne, K., & Chin, R. (eds.), *The Planning of Change*, Holt, Rinehart and Winston, New York, 1961.

Bergson, A., *Planning and Performance in Socialist Economies: The U.S.S.R. and Eastern Europe*, Unwin Hyman, Boston, 1988.

Berkowitz, M. (ed.), *Measuring the Efficiency of Public Programs: Costs and Benefits in Vocational Rehabilitation*, Temple University Press, Philadelphia, PA, 1988.

Bethune, C., "The Administrative Reform Programme of Jamaica," paper presented to the subregional seminar on "Innovations in the Field of Public Management for C.L.A.D.-member English-Speaking Countries," Georgetown, Guyana, July 1989.

Bjur, W.E., and Caiden, G.E., "Administrative Reform and Institutional Bureaucracies", in S.K. Sharma, ed., *Dynamics of Development: An International Perspective*, Vol. 1, Concept Publishing, New Delhi, 1978, pp. 365-378.

Boisot, M., and Child, J., "The Iron Law of Fiefs: Bureaucratic Failure and the Problem of Governance in the Chinese Economic Reforms", *Administrative Science Quarterly*, Vol. 33, No. 4, December 1988, pp. 507-527.

Bonwit, B., "Reform of Public Administration: From Tasks to Goals," *International Review of Administrative Sciences*, Vol. 55, No. 2, 1989, pp. 211-228.

Boren, J. *Have Your Way With Bureaucrats*,, Chilton Book Co., Radnor, PA., 1975.

Boston, J., "From Corporatisation to Privatisation: Public Sector Reform in New Zealand", *Canberra Bulletin of Public Administration*, No. 57, Dec. 1988, pp. 71-86.

Bowden, E., "Maladministration: A Thematic Analysis of Nigerian Case Studies in the Context of Administrative Initiative", *Human Organization*, Vol. 35, No. 4, Winter 1976, pp. 391-394.

Bowman, J. (ed.), "Civil Service Reform", *Review of Public Personnel Administration*, Vol. 2, No. 2, Spring 1982, pp. 1-4.

Boyle, J. M., "Reorganization Reconsidered: An Empirical Approach to the Decentralization Problem," *Public Administration Review*, Vol. 39, No. 5, September/October 1979, pp. 458-465.

Braibanti, R. (ed.), *Political and Administrative Development*, Duke University Press, Durham, N.C., 1969.

Brodkin, E., *The False Promise of Administrative Reform: Implementing Quality Control in Welfare*, Temple University Press, Philadelphia, 1986.

Brown, R.E. (ed.), *Accounting and Accountability in Public Administration*, American Society for Public Administration, Washington, D.C., 1988.

Brown, R.G., *Reorganizing the National Health Service: A Case Study in Administrative Change*, Blackwell/Robertson, Oxford, 1979.

Brumberg, A., "Moscow: The Struggle for Reform", *The New York Review*, March 30, 1989, pp. 37-42.

Bulmer, M., *Social Research and Royal Commissions*, Allen and Unwin, London, 1980.

Burnheim, J., *Is Democracy Possible?*, Polity Press, Cambridge, 1985.

Burns, J.P., "Chinese Civil Service Reform; the 13th Party Congress Proposals," *The Chinese Quarterly*, No. 120, December 1989, pp. 739-770.

Burns, J.P., "Reforming China's Bureaucracy, 1979-82", *Asian Survey*, Vol. 23, No. 6, June 1983, pp. 692-722.

Caiden, G.E., *Administrative Reform*, Aldine, Chicago, 1969.

Caiden, G.E., and Truelson, J.A., "Further Light on Combatting Administrative Corruption," in R.M. Arora and L.L. Kaushik (eds.), *The Universe of Public Administration*, Centre for Administrative Change, Chandigarh, India, 1990.

Caiden, N. and Wildavsky, A., *Planning and Budgeting in Poor Countries*, John Wiley & Sons, New York, 1974.

Calista, D. (ed.), *Bureaucratic and Governmental Reform*, JAI Press, Greenwich, CT., 1986.

Cameron, K.S., Sutton, R.I., and Whetten, D.A. (eds.), *Readings in Organizational Decline*, Ballinger Publishing Co., Cambridge, MA, 1988.

Campbell, A., "Running Out of Steam," *Civil Service Journal*, Vol. 18, No. 3, Jan/Mar 1978, pp. 4-10.

Campbell, C., and Peters, G.B. (eds.), *Organizing Governance, Governing Organizations*, University of Pittsburgh Press, Pittsburgh, PA., 1988.

Campbell, D., "Reforms as Experiments," *American Psychologist*, Vol. 24, No. 4, April 1969, pp. 409-429.

Campbell, J. et al., *Productivity in Organizations*, Jossey-Bass, San Francisco, 1988.

Caporaso, J.A. (ed.), *The Elusive State: International and Comparative Perspectives*, Sage Publications, Newbury Park, CA, 1989.

Carneiro, J. P., *National Bebureaucratization Program: three Years of Debureaucratization*, National Debureaucratization Program, Brazil, 1982.

Caygill, D., Speech to the N.Z./U.K. Conference on Economic and Social Policy Reform, released by Ministry of Finance, Parliament Buildings, Wellington, September 16, 1989.

Centro Latinamericano De Administracion Para El Desarrollo, "La Reforma Del Estado: Aspectos Téoricas y Experiencas", *Seleccion de Documentos Clave,* Vol. 7, No. 1, June 1990.

Champion, H., "State and Local Government: Where the Action Is," Second Annual Bollens Memorial Lecture, University of California, Los Angeles, 1987.

Chapman, L., *Your Disobedient Servant*, Chatto and Windus, London, 1978.

Chapman, R., "Core Public Sector Reform in New Zealand and the United Kingdom", *Public Money & Management*, Spring 1989, pp. 44-49.

Chapman, R.A. (ed.), *The Role of Commissions in Policy-Making*, Allen and Unwin, London, 1973.

Chen Wen-tsung, "Testing for Talent", *Free China Review*, Vol. 39, No. 12, Dec 1989, pp. 4-14.

Chevallier, J., Introductory Report of the Research Committee on Law and Science of Administration, Budapest Round Table, International Institute of Administrative Sciences, 1988.

Chikulo, B., "Reorganization for Local Administration in Zambia: An Analysis of the Local Administration Act, 1980," *Public Administration and Development*, Vol. 5, No. 1, 1985, pp. 73-81.

Chikulo, B. C., "The Zambian Administrative Reforms: An Alternative View," *Public Administration and Development*, Vol. 1, No. 1, January-March 1981, pp. 55-65.

China News Analysis, (Hong Kong), No. 1383, April 15, 1989.

Chow, K., "Public Administration as a Discipline in the People's Republic of China: Development, Issues and Projects," paper presented at the National Conference of the American Society for Public Administration, Portland, Oregon, April 1988.

Chubb, J.E., and Peterson, P.E. (eds.), *Can the Government Govern?*, The Brookings Institution, Washington, D.C., 1989.

Chunmei, Y., "Current Administrative Reform in China", *International Review of Administrative Sciences*, Vol. 52, No. 2, June 1986, pp. 123-144.

Chu-Yuan, C., "A Troubled Economy", *Free China Review*, November 1989, pp. 49-52.

Chu Yun-Han, "The Search for Common Ground", *Free China Review*, Vol. 39, No. 11, Nov. 1989, pp. 12-19.

Clark, D., "Dirigisme in an East Asian City: A Community Relations Approach to Corruption in Hong Kong," paper presented to the I.P.S.A. Study Group Meeting, Bellagio, May 1987.

Cochrane, G., *Policies for Strengthening Local Government in Developing Countries*, World Bank Staff Working Paper no. 582, Washington, D.C., 1983.

Cohen, S., and Heuvel, K. (eds.), *Voices of Glasnost: Interviews with Gorbachev's Reformers*, W.W. Norton, New York, 1989.

Commonwealth of Australia, *Reforming the Australian Public Service*, Australian Government Publishing Service, Canberra, A.C.T., December 1983.

Conyers, D., "Decentralization: The Latest Fashion in Development Administration," *Public Administration and Development Vol.* 3, No. 2, April-June 1983, pp. 97-109.

The Courier, Special issue on structural adjustment, No. 111, Sept-Oct, 1988.

Crozier, M., *The Bureaucratic Phenomenon*, Phoenix Books, The University of Chicago Press, 1964.

Crozier, M., *Etat Modeste, Etat Modern: Strategie pour un Autre Changement*, Paris, 1987.

Crozier, M., *How to Reform the State?: Three Countries, Three Strategies: Sweden, Japan, United States*, La Documentation Francaise, Paris, 1988.

Crozier, M., *Strategies For Change: The Future of French Society*, The M.I.T. Press, Cambridge, MA., 1982.

Davies, D., "Motivating Public Officers: Participative Mechanisms," paper presented to the Budapest Round Table, International Institute of Administrative Sciences, 1988.

Davis, G. et al. (eds.), *Corporate Management in Australian Government: Reconciling Accountability and Efficiency*, Macmillan Co. of Australia, Melbourne, 1989.

DeGuzman, R., Pacho, A., and Legada, R. T., *Institutional Organizational Arrangements for Planning and Implementation of Administrative Reform.* College of Public Administration, University of the Philippines/EROPA, Manila, 1982.

Denhardt, R., and Jennings, E. (eds.), *The Revitalization of the Public Service*, Department of Public Administration, University of Missouri- Columbia, Columbia, MO., 1987.

Desai, P., *Perestroika in Perspective: The Design and Dilemmas of Soviet Reform*, Princeton University Press, Princeton, N.J., 1989.

Dillman, D. L., "Personnel Management and Productivity Reform: Taming the Civil Service in Great Britain and the United States," *International Journal of Public Administration*, Vol. 8, No. 4, 1986, pp. 345-367.

Directions in Government (Australia), "Purchasing Reform", Vol. 3, No. 8, September 1989, pp. 28-38.

Douglas, J., *The Myth of the Welfare State*, Transaction Publishers, New Brunswick, N.J., 1989.

Downs, G., and Larkey, P., *The Search for Government Efficiency: From Hubris to Helplessness*, Random House, New York, 1986.

Dror, Y., "Prescriptions for Administrative Reform: Lessons from a Historic-Comparative Study," paper presented at the A.S.P.A. National Conference, New York, April 1983.

Drucker, P., "The Deadly Sins in Public Administration", *Public Administration Review*, Vol. 40, No. 2, March/April, 1980, pp. 103-106.

Drucker, P., "Management and the World's Work', *Harvard Business Review*, Sept-Oct 1988, pp. 65-76.

Dunsire, A., "Organization and Management of State and Administration," S.I.C.A. Second Occasional Paper Series, No. 1, American Society for Public Administration, Washington, D.C., 1982.

Dunsire, A., and Hood, C., *Cutback Management in Public Bureaucracies*, University of Cambridge Press, Cambridge, 1989.

Dwividi, O. "Editor's Introduction: Administrative Heritage, Morality and Challenges in the Sub-continent Since the British Raj," *Public Administration and Development*, Vol. 9, No. 3, 1989, pp. 245-252.

Eaton, J., and Lvov, Y., "Soviet Business: A Micro Analysis," a draft monograph of the U.S.-U.S.S.R. Joint Research Project, University of Pittsburgh, Pittsburgh, PA., 1990.

The Economist, Vol. 298, No. 7435, March 1, 1986, "Making mandarins manage," p.53.

The Economist, Vol. 315, No. 7658, June 9, 1990, "Hope after the hop", pp. 57-58.

The Economist, Vol. 315, No. 7652, April 28, 1990, "Perestroika: Ready to Fly? A Survey," 22 pp.

The Economist, Vol. 315, No. 7656, May 26, 1990, "A Survey of Italy: Awaiting an Alternative," 30 pp.

The Economist, Vol. 315, No. 7621, September 23, 1989, "A Survey of the Third World", 58 pp.

Efficiency Unit, *Improving Management in Government: The Next Steps*, H.M.S.O., London, 1988.

Eisenstadt, S.N., *The Political Systems of Empires*, Free Press, New York, 1963.

Eldridge, D., "Toward a More Culturally Compatible Concept of Civil Service Reform in Developing Countries," *International Journal of Public Sector Management*, Vol. 2, No. 1, 1989, pp. 22-34.

Elsenhans, H., "Public Administration in Developing Countries: Specificities of 'Public' and of 'Administration' in Market-Regulated Developing and Capitalistic Societies," paper presented at the Fourteenth World Congress of the International Political Science Association, Washington, D.C., 1988.

Ericson, R.E., "What Is To Be Done?" *The New Republic*, March 5, 1990, pp. 34-38.

Etzioni, A., "Humble Decision Making", *Harvard Business Review*, Vol. 67, No. 4, July-August 1989, pp. 122-126.

Falkenheim, V.C., "Administrative Reform and Modernization in PostMao China", *Pacific Affairs*, Vol. 53, No. 1, Spring 1980, pp. 5-28.

Farazmand, A., "Crisis in the U.S. Administrative State", *Administration and Society*, Vol. 21, No. 2, Aug 1989, pp. 173-199.

Feldman, D., *Reforming Government*, Morrow, New York, 1981.

Fisk, D., "Productivity Trends in the Federal Government", *Monthly Labor Review*, Vol. 108, No. 10, October 1985, pp. 3-8.

Fitzgerald, A., *The Pentagonists*, Houghton Mifflin, Boston, 1989.

Floate, N., *Management Services in the Sudan Public Services*, Directorate of Organisation and Administrative Reform, Ministry of Public Service and Administrative Reform, Khartoum, 1976.

Flores, G. and Nef, J. (eds.), *Administracion Publica: Perspectivas Criticas*, I.C.A.P., San Jose, Costa Rica, 1984.

Frank, B., "The Ombudsman and Human Rights Revisited," *Israel Yearbook on Human Rights*, Vol. 6, 1976, Tel Aviv University, pp. 122-156.

Freitas, R.C., *State Reform: National Office of the Civil Service*, Hans Seidel Foundation, Montevideo, Uruguay, 1989.

Friedmann, J., *The Good Society, 1979*, The M.I.T. Press, Cambridge, MA., 1979.

Fry, G., "The Thatcher Government, The Financial Management Initiative, and the 'New Civil Service'", *Public Administration*, Vol. 66, No. 1, Spring 1988, pp. 1-20.

Fry, G., et al., "Symposium on Improving Management in Government", *Public Administration*, Vol 66, No. 4, Winter 1988, pp. 429-445.

Fudge, C., and Gustafsson, L., "Administrative Reform and Public Management in Sweden and the United Kingdom," *Public Money & Management*, Summer 1989, pp. 29-34.

Galbraith, J., *Diagnosing Complex Organizations*, Addison-Wesley, Reading, MA., 1973.

Galbraith, J.K., "Can the Russians Reform?", *Harper's Magazine*, June 1987, pp. 52-55.

Gardner, J.W., *No Easy Victories*, Harper Colophon Books, Harper & Row, New York, 1968.

Gardner, N. "Power Diffusion in the Public Sector: Collaboration for Democracy," *The Journal of Applied Behavioral Science*, Vol. 10, No.3, 1974, pp. 367-432.

Garson, D., and Overman, S., *Public Management Research in the United States*, Praeger Publishers, New York, 1983.

Geist, B., *State Audit*, Macmillan, London, 1981.

Gilbert, C. E. (ed.), "Implementing Governmental Change," *The Annals of the American Academy of Political and Social Science*, Vol. 466, March 1983, pp. 9-205.

Glassman, R., et al. (eds.), *Bureaucracy Against Democracy and Socialism*, Greenwood Press, Westport, CT., 1987.

Glickman, H. (ed.), *The Crisis and Challenge of African Development*, Greenwood Press, Westport, CT., 1988.

Global Network, "Frey Briefs A.E.I.P.A. on Beijing Session," Vol. 10, No. 4, Fall 1989.

Godwin, P., and Needham, J., "Reforming Reform – Challenging the Assumptions for Improving Public Employee's Performance," *Public Personnel Management*, Vol. 10, No. 2, Summer 1981, pp. 233-243.

Goldman, M.I., "Gorbachev the Economist," *Foreign Affairs*, Vol. 69, No. 2, Spring 1990, pp. 28-44.

Golembiewski, R., "A Critique of 'Democratic Administration' and Its Supporting Idealism", *American Political Science Review*, Vol. 71, No. 4, Dec. 1977, pp. 1488-1507.

Golembiewski, R. "The Demotion Design: An Option for Forward Looking Organizations," *National Productivity Review*, Vol. 2, No. 1, Winter 1982-1983, pp. 63-70.

Goodsell, C.T., "The Grace Commission: Seeking Efficiency for the Whole People?" *Public Administration Review*, Vol. 44, No. 3, May-June, 1986, pp. 196-204.

Gorbachev, M., *Perestroika*, Collins, London, 1987.

Gould, D. J., and Amaro-Reyes, J. A., *The Effects of Corruption on Administrative Performance: Illustrations from Developing Countries*, World Bank Staff Working Paper no. 580, Washington, D.C., 1983.

Gouldner, A.W. *Patterns of Industrial Bureaucracy*, Free Press, Glencoe, IL., 1954.

Governance, Vol. 3, No. 2, April 1990, Spcial Issue on Managerial Reform, pp. 115-218.

Gow, I., "Diffusion of Administrative Innovations in Canadian Public Administration", paper presented at the Biennial Meeting of the Association for Canadian Studies in the United States, San Francisco, November 20, 1989.

Graham, L. S., "Centralization versus Decentralization in the Administration of Public Service," *International Review of Administrative Sciences*, Vol. 46, No. 3, 1980, pp. 219-232.

Gray, A., and Jenkins, W., "Policy Analysis in British Central Government: The Experience of PAR", *Public Administration*, Vol. 60, No. 4, Winter 1982, pp. 429-450.

Green, P., and Slyfield, M., "Problems in Strengthening the Administrative Capacity of Small States," Occasional Paper No. 1, Administrative Staff College, Kingston, Jamaica, 1982.

Greenaway, J. R., "Bureaucrats Under Pressure: The Thatcher Government and the Mandarin Elite", *Teaching Politics*, Vol. 13, No. 1, Jun 1984, pp. 66-83.

Gregory, W., *The Defense Procurement Mess*, Lexington Books, Lexington, MA., 1989.

Grindle, M.S., and Thomas, J.W., "Policy Makers, Policy Choices and Policy Outcomes: The Political Economy of Reform in Developing Countries," *Policy Sciences*, Vol. 22, No. 3,4, November 1989, pp. 213-218.

Groissman, F., et al., *La Administracion Publica en Tiempo de Crisis*, C.L.A.D., Caracas, Venezuela, 1986.

Grunow, D., "From Bureaucratization to De-Bureaucratization? Theoretical Issues of a New Field of Research," paper presented to the Budapest Round Table, International Institute of Administrative Sciences, 1988.

Guy, M.E., *Organizational Decline to Organizational Renewal*, Quorum Books, New York, 1989.

Hallett, L.A., *Royal Commissions and Boards of Inquiry*, The Law Book Company, Ltd., Sydney, 1983.

Halligan, J., and O'Grady, M., "Public Sector Reform: Exploring the Victorian Experience", *Australian Journal of Public Administration*, Vol. 44, No. 1, March 1985, pp. 34-45.

Hammergren, L., *Development and the Politics of Administrative Reform*, Westview Press, Boulder, CO, 1983.

Hancock, G., *Lords of Poverty: The Power, Prestige and Corruption of the International Aid Business,* The Atlantic Monthly Press, New York, 1989.

Hankiss, E., "In Search of a Paradigm," *Daedelus*, Vol. 119, No. 1, Winter 1990, pp. 183-214.

Hanser, C.J., *Guide to Decision: The Royal Commission*, The Bedminister Press, Totowa, N.J., 1965.

Haq, K. and Kirdar, U. (eds.), *Managing Human Development*, North-South Roundtable, Islamabad, Pakistan, September 1987.

Harding, H., Address to S.I.D.-D.C. Chapter Luncheon, October 17, 1989, reported by S. Von Oehsen, "Harding Presents Dilemmas Reforming Socialist States Face", *Develop-*

ment Connections, Newsletter of the Washington Chapter of the Society for International Development, Vol. 10, No. 3, Dec. 1989, pp. 1-2.

Harding, H., *Organizing China: The Problem of Chinese Bureaucracy: 1949-1976*, Stanford University Press, Stanford, 1981.

Harrison, A., and Gretton, J. (eds.), *Reshaping Central Government*, Policy Journals/ Transaction Books, New Brunswick, N.J., 1987.

Hawker, G., *Who's Master, Who's Servant? Reforming Bureaucracy*, Allen and Unwin, Sydney, 1981.

Hayward, F.H., *Professionalism and Originality*, Allen and Unwin, London, 1917.

Hazzard, S., *The Countenance of Truth*, Viking Press, New York, 1990.

Heidenheimer, A.J., et al. (eds.), *Political Corruption: A Handbook*, Transaction Books, New Brunswick, N.J., 1988.

Heller, P. S., and Tait, A. A., *Government Employment and Pay: Some International Comparisons*, International Monetary Fund, Washington, D.C., 1983.

Hennessy, P., *Whitehall*, Secker & Warburg, London, 1989.

Henriques, D., *The Machinery of Greed: Public Authority Abuse and What to Do about It*, D.C. Heath & Co., Lexington, MA., 1980.

Hewett, E.A., "Economic Reform in the U.S.S.R., Eastern Europe, and China: The Politics of Economics", *A.E.A. Papers and Proceedings*, Vol. 79, No. 2, May 1989, pp. 16-20.

Highlights, "Africans Initiating Economic Reforms," Vol. 6, No. 3, U.S.A.I.D., Washington, D.C., 1989.

Hofmeister, A. (ed.), *Efficiency in the Public Sector – An International Symposium*, Swiss Association of Administrative Sciences, Berne, Series 8, 1988.

Holanda, N., "Administrative Reform and Reform of the State," *Revista Do Servico Publico* (Brasilia), Vol. 117, No. 2, Sept.-Dec. 1989, pp. 117-132.

Holland, S, (ed.), *The State as Entrepreneur*, International Arts and Sciences Press, Inc., White Plains, N.Y., 1973.

Holzer, M., and Halachmi, A. (eds.), *Strategic Issues in Public Sector Productivity*, Jossey-Bass, San Francisco, 1986.

Hood, C., "Administrative Diseases: Some Types of Dysfunctionality in Administration," *Public Administration*, Vol. 52, No. 4, Autumn 1974, pp. 439-434.

Hood, C., and Dunsire, A., *Bureaumetrics*, Gower, Farnborough, 1981.

Icklis, J.C., et al. (eds.), *Beyond Bureaucracy: Strategic Management of Social Development*, Kumarian Press, West Hartford, CT., 1986.

The Indian Journal of Public Administration, Vol. 31, No. 3, July-Sept 1985, Special Number on Administrative Reforms – Revisited, T. Chaturvedi, (ed.), pp. 459-1189.

Ingraham, P. W., and Ban, C., *Legislating Bureaucratic Change: The Civil Service Reform Act of 1978*, State University of New York Press, Albany, 1984.

Insight, September 12, 1988, pp. 8-19.

Instituto Centroamericano de Administracion Publica, *Reforma Administrativa*, San Jose, Costa Rica, 1971.

Instituto Nacional de Administracion Publica, *Reforma Administrativa: Experiencias Latinoamericanas*, Mexico City, 1975.

Israel, A., *Institutional Development: Incentives to Performance*, World Bank/The Johns Hopkins University Press, Baltimore, MD., 1987.

Jabbra, J. and Dwividi, O. (eds.), *Public Service Accountability: A Comparative Perspective*, Kumarian Press, West Hartford, CT, 1989.

Jacoby, H., *The Bureaucratization of the World*, University of California Press, Berkeley, 1974.

James, M. (ed.), *Restricting Leviathan: Small Government in Practice*, The Centre for Independent Studies, St. Leonards, N.S.W., 1987.

Jeffries, R., "Local Government: Reform and Change", *Public Money and Management*, Summer 1989, pp. 23-28.

Joao, B. O., *Desburocratizacao e Democracia*, Papirus, Sao Paulo, 1984.

Jones, G., "Preventive Medicine at Work: A Hypothetical Case of Managed Organizational Change," *Philippine Journal of Public Administration*, Vol. 9, No. 3, July 1965, pp. 241-255.

Jos, P.H., Thompkins, M.E., and Hays, S., "In Praise of Difficult People: A Portrait of the Committed Whistleblower", *Public Administration Review*, Vol. 49, No. 6, Nov./Dec. 1989, pp. 552-561.

Jriesat, J., "Administrative Reform in Developing Countries: A Comparative Perspective," *Public Administration and Development*, Vol. 8, No. 1, 1988, pp. 85-97.

Jun, J., and Storm, B. (eds.), *Tomorrow's Organizations*, Scott, Foresman & Co., Glenview, IL., 1973.

Kagarlitsky, B., *The Dialectic of Change*, Verso, New York, 1990.

Kagarlitsky, B., *The Thinking Reed*, Verso, New York, 1988.

Kaufman, H., "Reflections on Administrative Reorganization," In *Setting National Priorities: The 1978 Budget*, edited by J.A. Pechman, The Brookings Institution, Washington, D.C., 1977.

Kearney, R.C., "Sunset: A Survey and Analysis of the State Experience," *Public Administration Review*, Vol. 50, No. 1, Jan-Feb, 1990, pp. 49-57.

Keating M., and Hainsworth, P., *Decentralization and Change in Contemporary France*, Gower, Aldershot, 1986.

Kellner, P. and Crowther-Hunt, N., *The Civil Servants*, MacDonald Futura Publishers, London, 1980.

Kelman, S., "The Grace Commission: How Much Waste?" *The Public Interest*, No. 78, Winter 1985, pp. 62-82.

Kets de Vries, F.R., and Miller, D., *The Neurotic Organization*, Jossey-Bass Publishers, San Francisco, 1985.

Khan, M. M., "Administrative Reform," *Indian Journal of Public Administration*, Vol. 24, No. 2, April-June 1979, pp. 170-180.

Khan, M. M., "Ruling Elites and Major Administrative Reforms: The Case of the Pakistan Civil Service," *Indian Journal of Political Science*, Vol 41, No. 4, December 1980, pp. 729-760.

Kharasch, R.N., *The Institutional Imperative*, Charterhouse Books, New York, 1973.

Kimmel, W., Dougan, W., and Hall, J., *Municipal Management and Budget Methods: An Evaluation of Policy Related Research*, The Urban Institute, Washington, D.C., 1974.

Kliksberg, B., "Administrative Reform in Latin America: A Review of the Conceptual Framework," reprinted by C.L.A.D., Caracas, 1983.

Klitgaard, R., *Controlling Corruption*, University of California Press, Berkeley, CA., 1988.

Korten, D. (ed.), *Community Management: Asian Experience and Perspectives*, Kumarian Press, West Hartford, CT., 1987.

Korten, D., and Alfonso, F., *Bureaucracy and the Poor: Closing the Gap*, Kumarian Press, West Hartford, CT., 1983.

Korten, D., and Klauss, R. (eds.), *People-Centered Development: Contributions Toward Theory and Planning Frameworks*, Kumarian Press, West Hartford, CT., 1984.

Korten, D., and Uphoff, N., "Bureaucratic Reorganization for Participatory Rural Development," N.A.S.P.A.A. Working Paper No. 1, National Association of Schools of Public Administration and Affairs, Washington,D.C., 1981.

Korten, F., and Siy, R., *Transforming Bureaucracy*, Kumarian Press, West Hartford, CT., 1988.

Kovacs, J.M., "Reform Economics: The Classification Gap," *Daedalus*, Vol. 119, No. 1, Winter 1990, pp. 215-247.

Krannich, R. L., "Administrative Reform and Role Responses in Thailand," *International Journal of Public Administration*, Vol. 2, No. 3, 1980, pp. 263-296.

Krishnamachari, V., Forward to Special Number on Administrative Reforms Since Independence, *Indian Journal of Public Administration*, Vol. 9, No. 3, July-Sept 1963, vi.

Ku Tashiro, "Administrative Reform in Contemporary Japan", paper presented to the Symposium on Japanese Management, A.S.P.A. Convention, Anaheim, CA., April 1986.

Kubr, M., and Wallace, J., *Successes and Failures in Meeting the Management Challenges: Strategies and Their Implementation*, World Bank Staff Working Paper no. 585, Washington, D.C., 1983.

Kymlicka, B.B. and Matthews, J.R. (eds.), *The Reagan Revolution?*, The Dorsey Press, Chicago, 1988.

Lambramboise, H. L., "Administrative Reform in the Federal Public Service: Signs of a Saturation Psychosis," *Canadian Public Administration*, Vol. 14, No. 3, pp. 303-325.

Lane, J. (ed.), *Bureaucracy and Public Choice*, Sage Modern Politics Series Vol. 15, London, 1987.

LaPalombara, J. (ed.), *Bureaucracy and Political Development*, Princeton University Press, Princeton, N.J., 1963.

Lee, H. B., "An Application of Innovation Theory to the Strategy of Administrative Reform in Developing Countries," *Policy Sciences,* Vol. I., No. 2, Summer 1970, pp. 177-189.

Lee, H. B., "Two Critical Combinations for Successful Administrative Reform", paper presented at the Tenth E.R.O.P.A. General Assembly and Conference, Seoul, Korea, October 1983.

Lee, H. B. and Samonte, A. (eds.), *Administrative Reforms in Asia*, E.R.O.P.A., Manila, 1970.

Leemans, A. (ed.), *The Management of Change in Government*, Institute of Social Studies, Martinus Nijhoff, The Hague, 1976.

Leemans, A., "Recent Trends: The Career Service in European Countries, *International Review of Administrative Sciences*, Vol. 53, No. 1, 1987, pp. 63-88.

Lethbridge, J.J., *Hard Graft in Hong Kong: Scandal, Corruption, and the I.C.A.C.*, Oxford University Press, Hong Kong, 1985.

Levin, A. *The Satisficers*, The McCall Publishing Company, New York, 1970.

Levine, C., "Citizenship and Service Delivery: The Promise of Coproduction", *Public Administration Review*, Vol. 44, March 1984 Special Issue, pp. 178-187.

Levine, C., *Managing Fiscal Stress: The Crisis in the Public Sector*, Chatham House, Chatham, N.J., 1980.

Levinson, H., *Organizational Diagnosis*, Harvard University Press, Cambridge, MA., 1972.

Li, C., and White, L., "The Thirtieth Central Committee of the C.C.P.: From Mobilizers to Managers", *Asian Survey*, Vol. 28, No. 4, April 1988, pp. 371-399.

Lippitt, G., *Organization Renewal*, Appleton-Century-Crofts, New York, 1969.

MacAvoy, P.W., et al., *Privatization and State Owned Enterprises: Lessons from the United States, Great Britain and Canada*, Kluwer Academic Publishers, Norwell, MA., 1989.

Maheshwari, S., *Administrative Reform in India*, MacMillan, New Delhi, 1981.

March, J. G., and Olsen, J. P., "Organizing Political Life: What Administrative Reorganization Tells Us about Governing," *American Political Science Review*, Vol. 77, No. 2, June 1983, pp. 281-296.

March, J.G., and Olsen, J.R. (eds.), *Rediscovering Institutions: The Organizational Basis of Politics*, The Free Press, New York, 1989.

Marshall, G., "Technique of Maladministration", *Political Studies*, Vol. 23, Nos. 2-3, 1975, pp. 305-310.

Marshall, T., *Class, Citizenship and Social Development*, Doubleday & Co, Inc., Garden City, N.Y., 1964.

Martin, T., *Malice in Blunderland*, McGraw-Hill, New York, 1973.

Martinez, R.R., "Reforms of the Basic Law of State Public Administration," *Revista Del Instituto Do Administracion Publica Del Estado De Mexico*, No. 4, Oct.-Dec. 1989. pp. 23-26.

Mathiason, J., "Evolution of Tasks and Functions in the United Nations and Its Implications For Reform", paper presented at the 47th annual A.S.P.A. conference, Anaheim, CA., April 1986.

Mayo-Smith, I., and Ruther, N. L., *Achieving Improved Performance in Public Organizations: A Guide for Managers*, Kumarian Press, West Hartford, CT., 1986.

Merton, R. "Bureaucratic Structure and Personality", *Social Forces*, Vol. 18, 1940, pp. 560-568.

Merton, R. "The Unanticipated Consequences of Purposive Social Action", *American Sociological Review*, Vol. 1, 1936, pp. 894-904.

Metcalfe, L., and Richards, S., *Improving Public Management*, European Institute of Public Administration, Sage Publications, 1987.

Meyer, M. et al., *Limits to Bureaucratic Growth*, Walter de Gruyter, New York, 1985.

Meynaud, J. (ed.), *Social Change and Economic Development*, U.N.E.S.C.O., Paris, 1963.

Miller, T., *Public Sector Performance: A Conceptual Turning Point*, The Johns Hopkins University Press, Baltimore, 1984.

Mirvis, P. and Berg, D., *Failures in Organization Development and Change*, John Wiley & Sons, New York, 1978.

Mitroff, I., *Break-Away Thinking: How To Challenge Your Business Assumptions (and Why You Should)*, John Wiley & Sons, New York, 1988.

Moe, R.C., "Traditional Organizational Principles and the Managerial Presidency: From Phoenix to Ashes," *Public Administration Review*, Vol. 50, No. 2, March-April 1990, pp. 129-140.

Moharir, V., "Administration Without Bureaucratization: What Alternatives?" *International Review of Administrative Sciences*, Vol. 55, No. 2, 1989, pp. 165-181.

Montgomery, J., and Siffen, W.J. (eds.), *Approaches to Development: Politics, Administration and Change*, McGraw-Hill, New York, 1966.

Mosher, F.C., *Governmental Reorganizations*, Bobbs-Merrill Co., Indianapolis, IN., 1967.

Mosher, F.C., *The G.A.O.*, Westview Press, Boulder, CO., 1979.

Mufson, S., "White Elephants in Black Africa," *The New Republic*, December 29, 1986, pp. 18-20.

Mushkat, M., "Towards Non-Incremental Strategies in Developing Public Products and Services", *European Journal of Marketing*, Vol. 21, No. 1, 1987, pp. 66-73.

Mutahaba, G. R., *Reforming Public Administration for Development: Experiences From Eastern Africa,* Kumarian Press, West Hartford, CT, 1989.

Nafzinger, F.W., *Inequality in Africa: Politial Elites, Proletariat, Peasants and the Poor*, Cambridge University Press, New York, 1988.

National Academy of Public Administration, *Revitalizing Federal Management: Managers and their Overburdened Systems*, Washington, D.C., 1983.

National Commission on the Public Service, *Leadership for America: Rebuilding the Public Service*, Lexington Books, Lexington, MA., 1989.

Nellis, J., *Public Enterprises in Sub-Saharan Africa*, The World Bank, Washington, D.C., Discussion Paper 1, 1986.

Nellis, J. and Kikeri, S., "Public Enterprise Reform: Privatization and the World Bank", *World Development*, Vol. 17. No. 5, 1989, pp. 659-672.

Niskanen, W., *Bureaucracy and Representative Government*, Aldine, Chicago, 1971.

Ohashi, T., "Information and Administrative Reform in the Government of Japan," *International Review of Administrative Sciences*, Vol. 55, No. 4, 1989, pp. 587-602.

Oi, J.C., "Market Reforms and Corruption in Rural China," *Studies in Comparative Communism*, Vol. 22, No. 2/3, Summer/Autumn 1989, pp. 221-233.

O'Leary, B., "The Limits to Bureaucide: A Critical Analysis of Three Visions of Debureaucratization", Paper presented to the Round Table on Administration Without Bureaucracy, International Institute of Administrative Sciences, Budapest, 1988.

Oliver, D., "'Perestroika' and Public Administration in the U.S.S.R.", *Public Administration*, Vol. 66, No. 4, Winter 1988, pp. 411-428.

Oman, R., and Masters, B., *Implementing Change in Organizations, Based on Analysis and Evaluation Studies: A Bibliography*, Vance Bibliographies P2112, Monticello, IL., 1987.

Organization for Economic Cooperation and Development, *The Control and Management of Government Expenditure*, Paris, 1987.

Organization for Economic Cooperation and Development, *Strategies for Change and Reform in Public Management*, Public Management Series 1, Paris, 1980.

Ostrom, V., *The Intellectual Crisis in American Public Administration*, University of Alabama Press, University, AL., 1973.

Oszlak, O., "Politicas publicas y regimenes politicos: reflexiones a partir de algunas experiencias latinoamericanas," Centro de Estudios y Socieda (C.E.D.E.S.), Buenos Aires, 1980.

Ouchi, M., "A Japanese View of Japanese Management", paper presented to the Symposium on Japanese Management, A.S.P.A. Convention, Anaheim, CA., 1986.

Ouchi, W., *Theory Z*, Addison-Wesley Publishing Company, Reading MA., 1981.

Ozgediz, S., *Managing the Public Service in Developing Countries: Issues and Prospects*, World Bank Staff Working Paper no. 583, Washington, D.C., 1983.

Painter, M., "Editorial:– Public Management: Fad or Fallacy?", *Australian Journal of Public Administration*, Vol. 47, No. 1, March 1988, pp. 1-3.

Parkinson, C. Northcote, *Parkinson's Law*, Houghton Mifflin, New York, 1957.

Parkinson, M. (ed.), *Reshaping Local Government*, Policy Journals/Transaction Books, New Brunswick, N.J., 1987.

Pateman, C., *Participation and Democratic Theory*, Cambridge University Press, Cambridge, 1970.

Paul, S., *Training for Public Administration and Management in Developing Countries: A Review*, World Bank Staff Working Paper no. 584, Washington, D.C., 1983.

Perlman, B., "Modernizing the Public Service in Latin America: Paradoxes of Latin American Public Administration," *International Journal of Public Administration*, Vol. 12, No. 6, 1989, pp. 671-704.

Perry, J.L., and Wise, L.R., "The Motivational Bases of Public Service," *Public Administration Review*, Vol. 50, No. 3, May/June 1990, pp. 367-373.

Peter, L., and Hull, R., *The Peter Principle*, William Morrow & Co., New York, 1969.

Peters, B.G., "The Problems of Bureaucratic Government", *Journal of Politics*, Vol. 43, No. 1, February 1981, pp. 56-82.

Pierce, W.S., *Bureaucratic Failure and Public Expenditure*, Academic Press, Harcourt Brace Jovanovich Publishers, New York, 1981.

Pious, R., "Prospects for Reform," in R. M. Pious (ed.), *The Power to Govern: Assessing Reform in the United States*, Proceedings of the Academy of Political Science, Vol. 34, No. 2, The Academy of Political Science, 1981, pp. 1-4.

Plowden, W., et al., "New Directions in Administrative Reform," *International Review of Administrative Sciences*, Vol. 49, No. 1, 1983, pp. 96-109.

Plumptre, T., *Beyond the Bottom Line: Management in Government*, The Institute for Research on Public Policy, South Halifax, Nova Scotia, 1988.

Poister, J., and Larson, T., "The Revitalization of PennDOT: Strategies for Effective Public Management", Paper presented to 48th National A.S.P.A. Conference, Boston, MA, 1987.

Premchand, A. (ed.), *Government Financial Management: Issues and Country Studies,* International Monetary Fund, Washington, D.C., 1990.

Presthus, R., *The Organizational Society*, St. Martin's Press, New York, 1978.

Preston, M., *The Politics of Bureaucratic Reform: The Case of the California State Employment Service*, University of Illinois Press, Urbana, 1984.

Priestley, M., *Administrative Reform Enquiries in Jamaica 1942-1980*, Administrative Staff College, Kingston, Jamaica, 2 vols., 1980.

Prybyla, J.S. (ed.), "Privatizing and Marketing Socialism," *The Annals of the American Academy of Political and Social Science*, Vol. 507, January 1990, pp. 9-141.

Public Administration and Development, Vol. 9, No. 3, June-August 1989, Special Issue: South Asia: Policy Developments and Administrative Changes Since Independence, O. Dwivedi (ed.), pp. 245-330.

Pye, L.W., "Political Science and the Crisis of Authoritarianism," *American Political Science Review*, Vol. 81, No., 1, March 1990, pp. 3-19.

Quah, J., "Administrative Reform: A Conceptual Analysis", *Philippine Journal of Public Administration*, Vol. 20, No.1, Jan. 1976, pp. 50-67.

Quah, J., "Bureaucracy and Administrative Reform in ASEAN Countries: A Comparative Analysis," in R.B. Jain (ed.), *Bureaucratic Politics in the Third World*, Gritanjali Publishing House, New Delhi, 1989.

Ramos, A.G., *The New Science of Organizations: A Reconceptualization of the Wealthy*, University of Toronto Press, Toronto, 1981.

Rayner, D., "A Battle Won in the War on the Paper Bureaucracy", *Harvard Business Review*, Vol. 53 , No. 1, Jan-Feb, 1975, pp. 8, 12-14.

Reddaway, P., "Gorbachev the Bold", *The New York Review*, May 28, 1987, pp.21-25.

Reich, R., *Tales of New America*, Times Books, New York, 1987.

Rhodes, G., *Committees of Inquiry*, Allen and Unwin, London, 1975.

Richards, S., "Cultural Change in the British Civil Service", paper presented at the International Political Science Association Congress, Washington, D.C., Aug. 29-Sept. 1, 1988.

Ro, C., and Reforma, M., *Social Change and Administrative Reform Towards the Year 2000*, E.R.O.P.A., Manila, 1985.

Robson, W., *The Governors and the Governed*, Allen and Unwin, London, 1964.

Rodger, S., "Public Service No Longer Relevant", *Public Sector*, Vol. 10, No., 4, 1988, pp. 2-4.

Rondinelli, D., and Ingle, M., "Improving the Implementation of Development Programs: Beyond Administrative Reform," S.I.C.A. Occasional Paper Series, No. 10, American Society for Public Administration, Washington, D.C., April 1981.

Rondinelli, D. A., Nellis, J. R., and Cheema, G. S., *Decentralization in Developing Countries: A Review of Recent Experience*, World Bank Staff Working Paper no. 581, Washington, D.C., 1983.

Rose, R., "Ungovernability: Is There Fire Behind the Smoke,?" *Political Studies*, Vol. 27, No. 3, September 1979, pp. 351-370.

Rosen, B., *Holding Government Bureaucracies Accountable*, Praeger, New York, 1989.

Rosenbaum, A., "Federal Management: Pathologic Problems and Simple Cures", *P.S.*, Spring 1982, pp. 187-193.

Rouban, L., "The Civil Service and the Policy of Administrative Modernization in France", *International Review of Administrative Sciences*, Vol. 55, No. 3, Sept. 1989, pp. 445-465.

Rowat, D. C. (ed.), *International Handbook on Local Government Reorganization*, Greenwood Press, Westport, CT., 1980.

Rweyemamu, A., and Hyden, G. (eds.), *A Decade of Public Administration in Africa*, East African Literature Bureau, Nairobi, 1975.

St. Hilaire, G., Introductory Report of the Research Committee on Public Finance and Financial Administration, International Institute of Administrative Sciences, Budapest Round Table, 1988.

Salamon, M., and Lund, M. (eds.), *The Reagan Presidency and the Governing of America*, The Urban Institute, Washington, D.C., 1984.

Savoie, D.J., *The Politics of Public Spending in Canada*, University of Toronto Press, Toronto, 1990.

Saxena, A. P. (ed.), *Administrative Reforms for Decentralized Development*, Asian and Pacific Development Administration Centre, Kuala Lumpur, 1980.

Schick, A., "Budgeting for Results: Recent Developments in Five Industrialized Countries," *Public Administration Review*, Vol. 50, No. 1, Jan/Feb 1990, pp. 26-34.

Schick, A. (ed.), *Perspectives on Budgeting*, American Society for Public Administration, Washington, D.C., 1986.

Schultz, D.S., and Rafferty, M.P., "Soviet Health Care and Perestroika," *American Journal of Public Health*, Vol. 80, No. 2, Feb. 1990, pp. 193- 6.

Schumacher, E., *A Guide for the Perplexed*, Harper and Row, 1977.

Schumacher, E., *Small is Beautiful*, Harper and Row, New York, 1973.

Scott, G., and Gorringe, P., "Reform of the Core Public Sector: The New Zealand Experience," *Australian Journal of Public Administration*, Vol. 48, No. 1, March 1989, pp. 82-89.

Selznick, P. *T.V.A. and the Grass Roots*, University of California Press, Berkeley, 1949.

Shirley, M. M., *Managing State-Owned Enterprises*, World Bank Staff Working Paper no. 577, Washington, D.C., 1983.

Siegel G. *The Vicissitudes of Governmental Reform in Brazil: A Study of DASP*, University Press of America, Washington, D.C., 1978.

Smigel, E.O., and Ross, H.L. (eds.), *Crimes Against Bureaucracy*, Van Nostrand Reinhold Co., New York, 1970.

Smith, R., and Weller, P. (eds.), *Public Service Inquiries in Australia*, University of Queensland Press, St. Lucia, 1978.

Spiegel, A., "How Outsiders Overhauled a Public Agency," *Harvard Business Review*, Vol. 53, No. 1, Jan-Feb 1975, pp. 116-124.

Stahl, G., and Foster, G., *Improving Public Services: A Report on The International Conference on Improving Public Management and Performance*, U.S. Agency for International Development, Washington, D.C., 1979.

Stein, H., *Governing the 5 Trillion Economy*, Oxford University Press, New York, 1989.

Stojanovic, S., *Perestroika*, Prometheus Books, Buffalo, N.Y., 1988.

Stronck, G., and Vaubel, D., *Administrative Reforms in Benelux and Germany*, European Institute of Public Administration, Maastricht, 1988.

Swann, D., *The Retreat of the State: Deregulation and Privatisation in the U.K. and U.S.*, Harvestor-Wheatsheaf, New York, 1988.

Szanton, P. (ed.), *Federal Reorganization: What Have We Learned?*, Chatham House, Chatham, N.J., 1981.

Tait, A. A., and Heller, P. S., *International Comparisons of Government Expenditure*, International Monetary Fund, Washington, D.C., 1982.

Taylor, M., "Quangos," *Public Sector*, No. 3, 1980, pp. 5-7.

Thompson, V. *Modern Organization*, Knopf, New York, 1961.

Thurber, C., and Graham, L. (eds.) *Development Administration in Latin America*, Duke University Press, Durham, N.C., 1973.

Thurow, L. (ed.), *The Management Challenge: Japanese Views*, The M.I.T. Press, Cambridge, MA., 1985.

Tierney, J. T., *Postal Reorganization: Managing the Public's Business*, Auburn House Pub. Co., Boston, 1981.

Toffler, A., *Future Shock*, Bantham Books, New York, 1971.

Toffler, A., *The Third Wave*, Bantham Books, New York, 1984.

Torpey, W.G., *Federal Productivity: A Management Challenge*, Byrd, Richmond, VA., 1988.

Truelson, J.A., *Blowing the Whistle on Systemic Corruption*, Ph.D. dissertation, University of Southern California, School of Public Administration, 1986.

Truelson, J.A., "Blowing the Whistle on Systemic Corruption: On Maximizing Reform and Minimizing Retaliation," *Corruption and Reform*, Vol. 2, Spring 1987, pp.55-74.

Tsou, T., *The Cultural Revolution and Post-Mao Reforms: A Historical Perspective*, The University of Chicago Press, Chicago, 1986.

Tummala, K. K., *The Ambiguity of Ideology and Administrative Reform*, Allied Publishers, Bombay, 1979.

Twentieth Century Fund, *The Government's Managers*, Priority Press Publishers, New York, 1987.

Ukeles, J., *Doing More With Less; Turning Public Management Around*, AMACOM, New York, 1982.

United Nations, *Enhancing Capabilities for Administrative Reform in Developing Countries*, ST/ESA/SER. E/31, New York, 1983.

United Nations, *Handbook on the Improvement of Administrative Management in Public Administration*, ST/ESA/SER. E/19, New York, 1979.

United Nations, *Interregional Seminar on Major Administrative Reforms in Developing Countries*, ST/TAO/M/62, New York, 1973.

United Nations, *Reforming Civil Service Systems for Development*, TCD/SEM. 85/7-INT-85-R61, New York, 1985.

United Nations, *Selected Studies on Major Administrative Reforms*, Administrative Innovations Series 1, Department of Technical Cooperation for Development, New York, 1988.

U.S. Agency for International Development, *International Development*, Washington, D.C., March 1983.

U.S. Executive Office of the President, *Management of the United States Government 1990*, U.S. Government Printing Office, Washington, D.C., 1989.

U.S. General Accounting Office, *Civilian Agency Procurement: Improvements Needed in Contracting and Contract Administration*, GAO/GGD-89-109, Washington, D.C., September 1989.

U.S. General Accounting Office, *Managing the Cost of Government Proposals for Reforming Federal Budgeting Practices*, GAO/AFMD-90-1, October 1989.

U.S. General Accounting Office, *Managing the Government: Revised Approach Could Improve O.M.B.'s Effectiveness*, GAO/GGD-89-65, Washington, D.C., May 1989.

U.S. General Accounting Office, *Paperwork Reduction: Mixed Effects on Agency Decision Processes and Data Availability*, GAO/PEMD-89-20, Washington, D.C., 1989.

U.S. News & World Report, Sept. 3, 1979, "Where Bureaucracy Really Runs Riot," pp. 31-2.

U.S. Office of Management and Budget, Statistical Policy Division, *Social Indicators, 1973*, U.S. Government Printing Office, Washington, D.C., 1974.

Urquhart, B., "The United Nations & Its Discontents," *New York Review of Books*, March 15, 1990, pp. 11-16.

Veljanovski, C., *Selling the State: Privatisation in Britain*, Weidenfeld and Nicholson, London, 1987.

Vernon, R. (ed.), *The Promise of Privatization: A Challenge for U.S. Policy*, Council on Foreign Relations, New York, 1988.

Vickers, J. and Yarrow G., *Privatization: An Economic Analysis*, M.I.T. Press, Cambridge, MA., 1988.

Volker, P.A., "Who Says We Can't Pay the Costs of Leadership?" *Washington Post*, December 17, 1989.

Warner, R., *The Principles of Public Administration*, Pitman, London, 1947.

Warwick, D.P., *A Theory of Public Bureaucracy*, Harvard University Press, Cambridge, MA., 1975.

Waxman, C., *The Stigma of Poverty*, Pergamon Press, New York, 1983.

Weiss, J., "The Powers of Problem Definitions: The Case of Government Paperwork", *Policy Sciences*, Vol. 22, No. 1, 1988, pp. 97-121.

Weitzel, W., and Jonsson, E., "Decline in Organizations: A Literature Integration and Extension", *Administrative Science Quarterly*, Vol. 34, No. 1, 1989, pp. 91-109.

Werlin, H., "The Community: Master or Client? – A New Review of the Literature," *Public Administration and Development*, Vol. 9, No. 4, 1989, pp. 447-457.

Wheare, K., *Maladministration and Its Remedies*, Stevens & Sons, London, 1973.

White Paper, *Efficiency and Effectiveness in the Civil Service*, Cmd. 8316, H.M.S.O., London, 1982.

Whitehead, C. (ed.), *Reshaping the Nationalised Industries*, Policy Journals/Transaction Books, New Brunswick, N.J., 1988.

Wholey, J., "What Can We Actually Get from Program Evaluation?," *Policy Sciences*, Vol. 3, No. 3, September 1972, pp. 361-369.

Wholey, J. et al. (eds.), *Improving Government Performance*, Jossey-Bass Publishers, San Francisco, 1989.

Wilenski, P., "Administrative Reform – General Principles and the Australian Experience", *Public Administration*, Vol. 64, No. 3, Autumn 1986, pp. 257-276.

Williams, R., *Political Corruption in Africa*, Gower, Aldershot, 1987.

Williams, W., *Washington, Westminster and Whitehall*, Cambridge University Press, Cambridge, 1988.

Wingo, L., "Introduction: The Ideal and the Real in the Reform of Metropolitan Governance," in *Reform as Reorganization*, Resources for the Future, Inc., Washington, D.C., 1974.

Wolf, T.A., "Reform, Inflation and Adjustment in Planned Economies," *Finance & Development*, Vol. 27, No. 1, March 1990, pp. 2-5.

Woodham-Smith, C., *Florence Nightingale*, Penguin Books, Harmondsworth, 1955.

World Bank, *Sub-Sahara Africa: From Crisis to Sustainable Growth*, Washington, D.C., 1989.

World Bank, *World Development Report, 1983*, Washington, D.C., 1984.

World Bank, *World Development Report, 1985*, Washington, D.C., 1986.

Wraith, R. and Lamb, G., *Public Inquiries as an Instrument of Government*, Allen and Unwin, London, 1971.

Wright, D., and Sakurai, Y., "Administrative Reform in Japan: Politics, Policy and Public Administration in a Deliberative Society", *Public Administration Review*, Vol. 47, No. 2, March/April 1987, pp. 121-133.

Yackle, L., *Reform and Regret*, Oxford University Press, New York, 1989.

Yan, G., "Corruption and Clean Government Drive in China." paper presented to the Thirteenth E.R.O.P.A. Conference, Kathmandu, Nepal, December 1989.

Yeatman, A., "The Concept of Public Management and the Australian State in the 1980s", *Australian Journal of Public Administration*, Vol. 46, No. 4, Dec. 1987, pp. 339-353.

Yeatman, A., and Bryson, L., "A New Iron Cage? Experiences of Managerial Reform", *Flinders Studies in Policy and Administration*, No. 3, Flinders University of South Australia, Bedford Park, March 1987.

Zaltman, G., and Duncan, R., *Strategies for Planned Change*, John Wiley & Sons, New York, 1977.

Index

Name Index

Subject Index